The Open Society Playbook

THE OPEN SOCIETY PLAYBOOK

—SCOTT HOWARD—

Author of *The Transgender-Industrial Complex*

ANTELOPE HILL PUBLISHING

Copyright © 2021 Scott Howard

Second printing 2021.

All rights reserved.

Cover art by sswifty.
Edited and formatted by Margaret Bauer.

The author can be contacted at:
Scott2hotthoward@protonmail.com

Antelope Hill Publishing
www.antelopehillpublishing.com

Papaerback ISBN-13: 978-1-953730-99-2
Hardcover ISBN-13: 978-1-956887-00-6
EPUB ISBN-13: 978-1-956887-01-3

"Nations are the wealth of mankind, its collective personalities; the very least of them wears its own special colors and bears within itself a special facet of divine intention."

- Alexander Solzhenitsyn

Contents

Introduction 1
1: The Open Society Foundations and the Soros Network 5
2: The American Foreign Policy Battering Ram 21
3: The Color Revolutions 55
4: Demographic Warfare 101
5: The Hand that Feeds and the Church of Clientology 143
6: The Zionist-Occupied Government 191
7: The New Normal 225
8: The Dark Underbelly 249
Conclusion 279

Appendices

A: World Bank and IMF Meeting 284
B: Chatham House Funders 287
C: ICIJ Media Partners 295
D: ECRE Member List 297
E: ODI Major Funders 302
F: MPI Major Funders 303
G: New American Century 305
H: Partnership for NYC 307
Bibliography 313

Introduction

Noticing that the world seems to be falling apart around you? This is largely by design, and this book will chart exactly how that has happened through the embrace by the ruling class of the so-called "open society." The concept of the open society is not some off-the-wall idea thrown around by conspiracy theorists looking to defame George Soros at every turn—although as we will see he is, in fact, central to the maintenance and expansion of the current globalist system which superficially espouses liberal democracy and in practice adheres closely to neoliberalism, a system defined largely by the unrestricted movement of people, goods, and capital. The open society as an explicitly-articulated idea and ideal owes its origin to the Jewish philosopher Henri-Louis Bergson and especially the ethnically-Jewish Karl Popper, who published *The Open Society and Its Enemies* in 1945, appropriately enough coinciding with the ushering-in of its global hegemony as an operating model for the next seventy-five years.

According to Council on Foreign Relations President Richard Haass, "The globe's traditional operating system—call it World Order 1.0 — has been built around the protection and prerogatives of states. It is increasingly inadequate in today's globalized world." It is "inadequate" because of the conditions created by his co-beneficiaries, the kinds of conditions that are creating a de-industrialized and hollowed-out West with its gutted and soon-to-be-non-existent middle class, throngs of alien peoples, and a bloated, parasitic "elite" class of the decadent and depraved. From Brazil to the UK, the poorest 10 percent are now paying a higher proportion of their incomes in tax than the richest 10 percent as citizens become subjects, gigantic corporations like Amazon pay nothing or next-to-nothing in corporate tax rates, central banks make money out of thin air, and high finance treats entire countries like distressed assets. Indeed, it would seem that on the whole it is globalization that is inadequate from the citizen's perspective, but the ruling class views us with contempt, as an obstacle to be dismantled and shoved aside, or else crushed totally underfoot.

We did not just stumble into this sad state of affairs, on the cusp of a soul-crushing globalist Panopticon, as we are. No, this has been in the works for some time now, and though within the "elites" there are competing factions, the intended end result is the same: the subjugation of humanity under a One World totalitarian state with corporate and financial oligarchs living in unfathomable opulence while the rest of humanity is blended into nondescript nothingness. From the World Economic Forum to the Open Society Foundations, the so-called "conspiracy" is out in the open. They'll tell you exactly what they're doing if you're willing to listen, but woe to the individual who should repeat it. Censorship, opprobrium, and worse await you. I can attest to the first two points, certainly: my first book, *The Transgender-Industrial Complex*, was promptly banned by World Economic Forum partner Amazon in the blink of an eye for the thoroughly postmodern crime of telling the truth *using the words of the actors committing the acts themselves as evidence.*

I shall be committing that crime again.

The purpose of this book is not to be a postmortem of the West, as this has been done extensively elsewhere, and if you are reading this, you very likely understand that the previous era—neoliberalism—is now rapidly transitioning into a transhumanist-informed, bio-digital age, which lies beyond the purview of this book. My purpose here is, rather, to investigate the means by which so-called "open societies" are created, why, and to what ends. Through various intersecting ideologies and their applications, the individual nations of this planet have been and are continuing to be directed toward a singular all-controlling global entity, with the individuals comprising said nations directed into a bio-digital hive. If this all sounds rather conspiratorial, well—it is. But not all conspiracies are "theories" or wild fiction.

The neoliberal system (Haass's World Order 1.0 coming out of World War II) is characterized by more outside private investment as vital for economic development (read: profit) and so-called "social development" (i.e. the Pride-Woke variety pumping sex hormones into five-year-olds, a tradgedy now well-familiar to most readers), as then-Secretary of State Hillary Clinton stated in 2011 referring to Central Asia, a region prized for its tremendous natural resources especially in a coming time of scarcity, such as natural gas, oil, and "rare earths," to say nothing of the geo-strategic buffer between Russia, China, and the Gulf States. The goal of Clinton and company has been for decades to knock down "bureaucratic barriers and other impediments to the flow of goods and people" to create the vaunted Open Society of "liberal democracy"—the kind that features marginalization of dissidents, censorship, and veneration of the defective while ruthlessly exploiting the population with an ersatz smile. Such a society is open, but not in the way that it's presented.

The rhetorical tropes of "democracy," "inclusion," and the like are designed specifically in the West to disarm the native population's objections to the flooding of their nation with often hostile aliens, facilitated by the vast machinery of the globalist Establishment, which encompasses NGOs, national governments, international governing bodies, corporations, financial institutions, various ideological and religious and ethnic interest groups, and a host of others. Though not entirely uniform, in that there are subsets within the Establishment jockeying for position as ultimate hegemons with sometimes competing visions, the general thrust remains uniform in its support for the noxious policies that have been so central to neoliberalism, from open borders to the erosion of civil liberties to vast amounts of wealth accruing in increasingly-few hands. For the post-humans/post-humanists, as globalism becomes lockdowns, social credit scores, and mandatory "vaccines" for COVID-19, the reader would do well to remember that those hands are the architects of this system, and the obvious beneficiaries; the only real disagreements are how they will allocate power to themselves and in what manner, who will occupy the very top, and what form humanity itself will take. It has been a long and step-by-step process, and the role of creating an "open society" with fertile ground for what comes next is the essential step in the agenda.

Whether it is demographic warfare masked as compassion or more humans-as-widgets for consumption in the neoliberal model, there is a vast matrix of organizations that is part of this globalist infrastructure from the highest point down to the most local, which this book will explore. Thus we see the role of government agencies, proxies, and supra- and intra-governmental organizations melding with that of the "private sector" and various NGOs and grievance groups in not just weaponizing philanthropy, but in creating this vast infrastructure to enable social engineering and demographic transformation, a process that has been rapidly accelerating from the nineteenth century and industrialization onward, although the seeds and the core struggles are millennia-old—really as old as humanity itself.

This goes all the way to the top, public and private sector, Republican and Democrat, Left and Right. Whether immigration or the LGBTQ agenda, the primary actors are more or less the same or analogous and they have the same or similar goals; indeed, as Mister Open Society himself George Soros said in a 2005 *NPR* interview, "The Open Society Foundation has the same objectives as the [US] State Department." The reader would do well to see past the kabuki theater of politics (which is just showbiz for the unattractive at this stage) and propaganda-spewing media; this book will greatly aid you in your endeavors.

With this in mind, let us consider first the archetypal figure of Soros and his Open Society Foundations, and then the US State Department's objectives and methods, since as Soros himself says, they're essentially one and the same.

1

THE OPEN SOCIETY FOUNDATIONS AND THE SOROS NETWORK

The transformation of a closed society into an open one is a systematic transformation. Practically everything has to change... What the foundations have done is to change the way the transformation is brought about.

– George Soros

Since its inception, the Open Society Foundations have officially dispensed nearly $17 billion over tens of thousands of grants. But to what purpose? Is this charity and good works for their own sake? Of course not. George Soros admits in his 1997 piece for *The Atlantic* entitled "The Capitalist Threat" that the function of his foundation network active in countries under communism was designed to be "subversive," and that, "For five or six years following the fall of the Berlin Wall, I devoted practically all of my energies to the transformation of the formerly Communist world." He hasn't stopped, and neither was this the beginning of his endeavors.

Soros' "philanthropic work" began in the late 1970s by funding scholarships for black university students in South Africa during apartheid to ultimately weaponize them against whites, particularly the Boer and the system of self-preservation they had in place. In 1979, according to the Open Society Foundations' website, Soros said, "[South Africa] was a closed society with all the institutions of a first world country, but they were off-limits to the majority of the population on racial grounds. Where could I find a better opportunity for opening up a closed society?" Indeed, and the sad fate of the Rainbow Nation reminds us precisely what the future holds.

The Open Society Foundations have, as highlighted, been particularly active in the former Eastern Bloc countries, owing in no small part to the Jewish Soros' upbringing in Hungary.

In 1986, at the same time Mikhail Gorbachev launched new policies of *glasnost* (openness) and *perestroika* (restructuring) in the USSR, George Soros was allowed to open a private foundation in Poland, which was followed the year after by one in Moscow. On June 17th, 1991, George Soros and Ante Marković, the Prime Minister of Yugoslavia, signed an agreement founding the Soros Yugoslavia Foundation, which would undertake projects in all six of the country's republics. In 1992, Soros and the Open Society Foundations established separate foundations in Croatia and Slovenia, followed by Macedonia and Bosnia and Herzegovina, with the Soros Yugoslavia Foundation operating in Serbia (including its provinces Vojvodina and Kosovo) and Montenegro. Also in 1992, Soros launched Central European University, which has "offered young people across the region a new, international, and pluralist perspective" (read: that of open borders activism and neoliberalism). Over 14,000 students have graduated from Central European University, including Giorgi Margvelashvili (president of Georgia from 2013-18), two former justice ministers (one from Croatia and one from Romania), a Hungarian Member of Parliament, and a number of other prominent figures, including many functionaries in the Open Society Foundations itself.

In a glowing Soros feature from *The New Yorker* in 1995, titled "The World According to Geroge Soros," his influence over the political process in several Eastern European countries is framed as a positive for democracy, but in what way is the following democratic, other than that "liberal" and "democratic" have been taken to be synonymous:

> Ljupčo Georgievski, the right-wing head of the opposition V.M.R.O. (International Macedonian Revolutionary Organization) Party, charges that the Soros foundation is "a support machine to the government." Virtually all foundation grants, he says, go to those associated in some way with the ruling party. Referring to a television station, A1, that receives Soros support, Georgievski said, "It is truly an alternative in its cultural programming; however, in politics…you see ministers of the present Macedonian government more often than on state TV…" Contrasting the Soros foundation in Ukraine with its counterparts in other countries, [Bohdan Krawchenko, a Ukrainian-Canadian historian who returned to Ukraine in 1991 and was recruited by Dr. Bohdan Hawrylyshyn and Soros to work for the foundation] told me, "There is no other place where the Soros foundation is so plugged in at the top…The deputy minister of finance sat with George and me in a basement almost four years ago and we tried to figure out what to do about monetary reform." That deputy minister of finance, Olech Havrylyshyn (a nephew of Bohdan), was on the payroll of the Soros foundation—as was the deputy governor of the National Bank (George Yurchyshyn,

a Ukrainian-American who had previously been a vice-president at the Bank of Boston)...Soros had placed his own agents in key positions... What Soros undoubtedly did do was enable the successful Kuchma to win for Ukraine a commitment for a crucial, I.M.F.-administered loan program of nearly four billion dollars. The loan had been strongly recommended by the United States at a Group of Seven economics meeting just before Kuchma's victory, but it was contingent on Ukraine's instituting economic reforms... Soros was galvanized. He got in touch with Anders Åslund, of the Carnegie Institute, who has worked on economic reform in Russia, and asked him to come with him and John Fox to Ukraine...After meeting with President Kuchma, Soros directed Åslund to organize a team to work with the Ukrainians on their negotiations with the I.M.F. And he fired off a memo, distributed to the White House, the Treasury, the State Department, the I.M.F., and the World Bank, in which he argued that this *was* the moment, and this *was* the group....The day the agreement was announced, Soros was attending a conference in Kiev sponsored by the American-Ukrainian Advisory Committee, a group organized by Zbigniew Brzezinski; Henry Kissinger was there as well....Roman Shpek, the Minister of the Economy, who is leading the reforms, is a graduate of Soros' Management Training Institute. The Institute for Public Administration, which Krawchenko heads, has also produced significant players...During Soros' late-September visit a task force—including people from the World Bank, the Ukrainian government, and the Soros foundation— was created to wage a media campaign for the reforms.

"Reform" here is yet another shining example of newspeak.

Also of crucial importance, the 1995 feature ominously foreshadows the fate of Slobodan Milošević and resistance to the "open society," as "the Belgrade foundation...is repeatedly threatened with being closed down by the government of Slobodan Milošević." We all know how that turned out. Be it NATO bombs or subversive propaganda—in the case of Yugoslavia, both—all resistance must be dealt with. Though Soros claims that "We are not running McDonald's. Open Society is a different story," it does seem like the Open Society Foundations are intent on knocking down every barrier and every unique structure to make way for a McDonald's instead.

While remaining fixed in a capitalist-communist binary remains advantageous to the ruling class, the reality is that neoliberalism is in its own right a fusion of the two, though with communism mutating into the social sphere in the form of Cultural Marxism. It is mutating, however, with the fusion of superficially-separate entities into one Leviathan. In effect, it does not matter if it's Microsoft or the state that's imposing social reengineering and demographic transformation on the terrestrial square it lays claim to, irrespective of ethnic and generational ties to it. Whether ostensibly Blue or Red, they're all on the same team. Governments are more accountable to the shareholders than the voters in the much-vaunted "democracy" of the modern world, one where outside forces shape elections all the time, but only fictitious Russian scandals are blared over virtually every corporate media channel in America. Tellingly, as the article continues:

> The broadcast stations of Radio Free Europe / Radio Liberty continue to be funded by the United States government,[1] but in early 1994 Soros entered a joint venture to acquire the organization's research institute and, under a fifty-year lease, its archives. Both operations are now subsumed under a new entity, the Open Media Research Institute (OMRI). Based in Prague, it has a seven-member board: Soros and two others from his staff; two people from the Board for International Broadcasting (the government agency that oversees Radio Free Europe); and two "independents" (one chosen by Soros and one by the B.I.B.). It should be noted that if the independents were to side with their selectors, the lineup would, predictably, be 4–3, Soros.

Today, RFE/RL remains very active, funded by a grant from the US Congress through the United States Agency for Global Media (USAGM) as a private grantee; its budget for fiscal year 2021 was $637.3 million, according to their website and the Fiscal Year 2021 Budget. The USAGM provides "oversight" and according to their website:

> ...serves as a firewall to protect the professional independence and integrity of all U.S. international public service media, including Voice of America, Radio and TV Marti, and the non-profit corporations that are BBG grantees: Radio Free Asia, RFE/RL, and

---

[1] From the Hearings before the Committee on Foreign Relations of the US Senate (92nd Congress) running June 6th and 7th, 1972, we learn that from 1949 to the hearings, $553 million in US government funding went to these projects in addition to $46 million from private sources. The West European Advisory Committee to Radio Free Europe at that time included: a pair of Danish Parliamentarians; Paul van Zeeland (NATO, Bilderberg Group, former Belgian Prime Minister); numerous prominent figures within NATO; several German Federal Parliamentarians; Samuel Schweizer (Chairman of the Board, Swiss Bank Corporation); Karl Birnbaum (Director of the Swedish Institute of International Affairs); and the list goes on.

the Middle East Broadcasting Networks (MBN). USAGM also provides oversight of the work of the Open Technology Fund, which finances the development and distribution of cutting edge technologies and techniques to counter efforts by repressive regimes and closed societies to block access to objective news and information.

According to their 2018 Annual Report, they signed an agreement with Plex, a multi-platform video streaming company, to place USAGM content on its Plex News app, which has fourteen million users. USAGM programming will now slot alongside other propaganda outlets like CNN and the BBC. A recent project saw the establishment of a 24/7 Russian-language TV and digital channel with a "specialized web and social media team that counters Kremlin disinformation." No propaganda campaign for "open societies" would be complete without the incessant promotion of the LGBTQ agenda, either: in 2018, RFE/RL's Radio Mashaal publicized a "sports festival for transgender individuals" in Pakistan and Radio Martí launched Arcoiris (Rainbow), to "explore LGBTQ life in Cuba, the United States and around the world, including the social and cultural status of that community as well as their civil and human rights." Speaking of Cuba, in late 2014 it emerged that USAID was employing the "urban youths" strategy the US State Department prefers in France by using rappers in Cuba "to break the information blockade" and foment unrest through "activism," agitating for "social change."

The nine-member USAGM Broadcasting Board of Governors includes: the Jewish Leon Rabinovich Aron, who immigrated to the United States from Moscow in 1978 as a refugee and is a resident scholar and the director of Russian studies at the American Enterprise Institute (AEI)[2]; the Jewish Michael Kempner, Hillary Clinton mega-donor and Barack Obama "bundler," Obama-appointee to the White House Council for Community Solutions (a council that works to "reengage disenfranchised youth"), and whose PR firm was hired by Israel's Ministry of Tourism ("the firm will also seek to reach out to the LGBT community")[3]; the Jewish Karen Kornbluh, Senior Fellow and

---

[2] From Aron, "Russian Revolution": "Russian Jews…were among the first to profit from the arrival of economic liberty in their country. Among the no more than twelve Russian 'oligarchs'—the owners or majority stockholders of the largest industrial and financial groups—five are Jews, and the top managerial level of the Russian oil industry is heavily Jewish as well."

[3] From Palmer, "Stronger than the Storm": "The first significant Jewish leaders to support him were Morton and Marian Steinberg, the founders of UJA in Bergen County [and his wife's parents]… Mr. Kempner is a member of Temple Emanu-El of Closter, and although he is not particularly observant, he feels deeply Jewish, he said. 'I don't think that you can be a Jew without having a worldview. Religion has a lot to do with my progressive politics.'"

Director of German Marshall Fund's Technology Policy program "which works to help shape a future in which technology strengthens rather than undermines democratic values," former Senior Fellow for Digital Policy at the Council on Foreign Relations, former Executive Vice President of External Affairs for Nielsen, former US Ambassador in Paris to the Organization for Economic Co-operation and Development (OECD), former Policy Director for then-Senator Barack Obama as well as serving as deputy chief of staff at the US Treasury Department, and former Director of the Office of Legislative and Intergovernmental Affairs at the Federal Communications Commission in the Clinton administration; the Jewish Jeff Shell, CEO of NBCUniversal; and the Jewish Kenneth Weinstein, Chairman of the Board and President and CEO of the Hudson Institute.

From sustained effort financing projects that actively undermined the regime of Slobodan Milošević in Serbia, after the neoliberal Establishment toppled Milošević and held him captive, as Mirko Klarin writes in the Open Society Foundations' *Building Open Society in the Western Balkans* report:

> The fact that these protribunal [sic] media and NGOs were supported by the Open Society Foundations did not go unnoticed by Slobodan Milošević and Vojislav Šešelj, a Serbian nationalist politician also indicted for war crimes by the tribunal. They both, on more than one occasion, described the ICTY as "Soros' Court."

For Milena Dragićević-Šešić, from the same report:

> Open Society–backed activism in the arts and other cultural institutions in Serbia began with a radio station: Belgrade's B92. Its music and information programs challenged the state media's nationalistic worldview…The idea was not to underwrite art for art's sake. The aim was to use targeted funding…B92 blazed a path for other artists ready to challenge xenophobia, patriarchal values, hate speech, and ethnic stereotypes…In September 1994, Radio B92's cultural center, Rex, opened in an abandoned building of Belgrade's Jewish community center… "Worried September! Wilhelm Reich in Belgrade—Lust for Life" was a project devoted to the common individual—of Belgrade and the world— who, in despair, withdraws from life and cedes responsibility for his or her being and future. "Lust for Life" had multiple dimensions, including publication of a translation of *Listen, Little Man!*, a book by Wilhelm Reich, a highly controversial psychoanalyst who studied under Freud…In Zagreb, Croatia, ZCCE3000 undertook conferences, art festivals, exhibitions,

workshops, lectures, presentations, publications, and media productions. A crucial component of the project was to reform the institutional settings of independent culture, increasing its influence and strengthening its resources. One of its collaborators, What, How and For Whom, organized a complex exhibition on the 152nd anniversary of the *Communist Manifesto*'s publication, returning Marx to the public sphere in Belgrade for the first time since 1989.

Returning to the January 1995 profile of Soros from *The New Yorker*:

> Soros funds are involved as co-investors in certain projects in developing countries with the International Finance Corporation, the private-sector arm of the World Bank Group...With the Clinton Administration, Soros, a newly turned Democrat, has made the kind of inroads that he was unable to make before...He has cultivated excellent relationships with high-ranking officials in the State Department and at Treasury. He has opened a Washington office, which, as one Soros associate told me, will function as "his State Department." While intense lobbying efforts he has made on behalf of Macedonia over the past year or so have not really succeeded, in the last several months he has thrown the weight of his influence and his resources behind achieving Western aid for Ukraine, and there he has won at least a preliminary victory. Recently, too, he said that he intends to focus increasingly on the West, concentrating on finding ways of making "our own open society more viable..." Morton Abramowitz, the former United States Ambassador to Turkey, who is now the president of the Carnegie Endowment for International Peace, and has participated in a Soros-funded advocacy group on the Balkans, [said,] "He's now become a player..." György Jaksity, an analyst at Concorde Securities, in Budapest, told me, "The first book on business that I read that was written not from a Marxist but from a free-market standpoint said, 'Sponsored by the Soros Foundation.'... People like me know that the book they are reading, the teacher who teaches them, were sponsored by Soros."

Abramowitz and Michele Dunne are both Carnegie Endowment for International Peace alumni as well as former Board members of the National Endowment for Democracy. Other names you might recognize as former NED Board members include Madeleine Albright, Zbigniew Brzezinski, Wesley Clark, Paula Dobriansky, Kenneth Duberstein, Francis Fukuyama, Orrin Hatch, Richard Holbrooke, Walter Mondale, Henry Kissinger, Robert

Zoellick, Paul Wolfowitz, and Anne-Marie Slaughter, plus other figures such as Instagram CEO Marne Levine and Princeton Lyman (ambassador, USAID, Aspen Institute, Harvard, Council on Foreign Relations, Johns Hopkins School for Advanced International Studies). This is how these things go.

Joining with the economic "impetus" has increasingly been the "humanitarian" angle, with Soros but one figure, albeit a central one. Looking once to the January 1995 profile of Soros from *The New Yorker*:

> In philanthropy…which Soros began in earnest about ten years ago—when he started a foundation in Budapest which aimed to foster the democratic values of an "open society" as defined by the philosopher Sir Karl Popper, and which supported dissidents living under the Communist regime—he kept a relatively low profile. After the fall of the Berlin Wall, in 1989, however, he began to reposition himself. He turned over the day-to-day management of the fund to an exemplary trader, Stanley Druckenmiller, and he immersed himself in the world of his foundations—by then, there were four—multiplying their number in Central and Eastern Europe and the former Soviet Union and dramatically accelerating the level of his giving. At the same time, he began to advocate that the West follow his lead, providing aid, in what he often referred to as an updated Marshall Plan, to the countries of the former Communist bloc.

We see here the fusion of ideology, economics, and extreme in-group favoritism that defines neoliberalism almost perfectly reflected in the figure of Soros, and as the Fourth Industrial Revolution and the COVID-19 lockdowns usher in the Great Reset, the next mutation will be completely fused.

According to Žarko Papić, the Open Society Foundations endeavored to use the ethnic conflicts in the Balkans as proof that their "liberalizing" projects had not gone far enough, much like the neoliberals do with the failure of diversity (or success from their perspective, though they won't let that out):

> Published under the title *Developing New International Support Policies – Lessons (Not) Learned in Bosnia-Herzegovina*, the analysis was widely distributed to international organizations, including departments of the United Nations and bilateral donors, as well as government bodies and other stakeholders in Bosnia and Herzegovina.

As always, the "lessons" are at odds with the reality and excuse the culpability of the worst actors in fomenting crisis in the first place, such as the neoliberal Establishment's backing of the Kosovo Liberation Army, which was basically a collection of criminals, traffickers, drug dealers, and jihadi terrorists responsible for the ethnic cleansing of Serbs; and yet, like the Crusades, it is the defensive response to the provocation that is misrepresented as evidence of "unprovoked hostility," totally divorced from context in the narrative that has been constructed to always paint one side—white, Christian—as the villains and the other as the perpetual victims, regardless of the truth of the matter.

Additionally, for the Yugoslavian conflicts of the 1990s particularly as regards Kosovo, there was a large Albanian-Muslim population to weaponize, as NATO and the globalist Establishment did against Serbia. The United States has been waging a war against its ostensible allies in Europe for generations; within the last few decades this has ranged from working with George Soros to destabilize and undermine the conservative government in North Macedonia to NATO's plans for Greater Albania, where drug-runners and Islamist terrorists trained by the CIA in Afghanistan were a key part of the astroturfed "insurgency" in the break-down of Yugoslavia during the 1990s, a Yugoslavia which had actually developed a successfully managed economic counterpoint to neoliberalism. That was, as the college professors say, "problematic."

The Balkans have long been a target of Soros—the Open Society Foundation in Croatia supported the establishment of the Croatian Law Center and ZAMIR, Croatia's first independent internet service provider, and the Open Society Index was developed to "measure the level of openness of Croatian society through criteria in education, media, entrepreneurship and economic freedom, transparency of political processes, rule of law, and marginalized groups and minorities." In North Macedonia, the Open Society Foundation expanded the Step by Step preschool program to 60 schools and "sponsored seminars to improve school curricula, teaching methods, and management" (read: neoliberal indoctrination). In the province of Kosovo, the Open Society Foundation in Serbia provided a $2 million grant to support a "parallel education system."

Next door, the Open Society Foundations have spent nearly $100 million (that we know about) in North Macedonia since 1992, and have partnered with the US government, Switzerland, France, and the European Union for "development work" in the Balkan country. Between February 27th, 2012, and August 31st, 2016, nearly $5 million in US taxpayer money went to the Open Society Foundation – Macedonia (FOSM), in partnership with four local "civil society" organizations. USAID says on their website the project trained hundreds of young Macedonians "on topics such as freedom of association,[4] youth policies, citizen initiatives, persuasive argumentation and use of new media." USAID has earmarked at least $9.5 million to intervene in North Macedonia's governmental affairs for 2016-2021; as Tom Fitton writes for *Judicial Watch*:

> Here's how the clandestine operation functions, according to high-level sources in Macedonia and the U.S. that have provided Judicial Watch with records as part of an ongoing investigation. The Open Society Foundation has established and funded dozens of leftwing, nongovernmental organizations (NGOs) in Macedonia to overthrow the conservative government. One Macedonian government official interviewed by Judicial Watch in Washington D.C. recently, calls it the "Soros infantry." The groups organize youth movements, create influential media outlets and organize violent protests to undermine the institutions and policies implemented by the government. One of the Soros' groups funded the translation and publication of Saul Alinsky's "Rules for Radicals" into Macedonian. The book is a tactical manual of subversion, provides direct advice for radical street protests and proclaims Lucifer to be the first radical.

In case you had any illusions that this was just a political struggle.

Naturally *Foreign Policy* jumped to the rescue, publishing a piece by Goran Buldioski calling these allegations—what else?—"conspiracy theories," despite the fact that much of this information is readily available from the sources themselves. Sure, they'll whitewash what their activities are to cast them in the best light possible, and why wouldn't they? It's the tried-and-true tactic of the neoliberal regime: frame subversion as "democratizing," fostering "inclusion," focusing on "human rights," and the like. We know what that actually looks like.

Buldioski, by the way, is the director of the Open Society Foundations' Berlin office and the Open Society Initiative for Europe. No conflict of interest there. The push-back was in response to the January 2017 formation of the Stop Soros Movement—SOS—in North Macedonia. It was founded by editor-in-chief of the state-run news agency MIA, Cvetin Cilimanov; editor-in-chief of the *Republika* news portal, Nenad Mircevski; and Nikola Srbov, a columnist for news portal, *Kurir*. As *Balkan Insights* reports:

---

[4] This is a sick joke if you know anything about the way "civil rights" have been weaponized in the United States.

NGOs backed by the Soros Foundation have long been a target of nationalist governments in Russia, Hungary, Macedonia and elsewhere, where authorities are deeply suspicious of their politically and socially liberal agenda...Russia more or less outlawed Soros-affiliated organisations in 2015. This January, authorities in Hungary said they would use "all the tools at its disposal" to "sweep out" NGOs funded by the Hungarian-born financier, which "serve global capitalists and back political correctness over national governments." Hungarian Leader Viktor Orban last year accused Soros of destabilizing Europe by encouraging mass immigration to Europe from Middle Eastern war zones.

Those are very legitimate accusations.

Metamorphosis is one such group that receives funding from the Open Society Foundations, as well as the US Embassy, USAID, and the National Endowment for Democracy; despite claiming to stand for "liberal values," they and other Soros/US government projects have worked to foment unrest under the guise of "democratic" protests. From *The American Spectator*:

Last March [2016], the Macedonian government boldly closed its border to prevent the tsunami of economic migrants and refugees surging from Greece toward Western Europe, allowing restricted numbers to enter. Open borders is one of George Soros' most keenly felt priorities. How did his Team respond? Activism! With an admixture of violence and vandalism. The fertilized grassroots...broke into the president's office, vandalized property, and burned office furniture. Three policemen were injured. Filip Stojanovski, Metamorphosis' program director and main man, maintains a Twitter profile pic (@razvigor) obscured by bright paint splats — an overt reference to his glory days during last summer's "Colorful Revolution," as it is known. "I heard Soros and SDSM activists chanting, 'No Justice, No Peace,' which isn't even a meaningful slogan in Skopje," recalled Cvetin Chilimanov. "The transfer of tactics from U.S. Left-wing groups funded by Soros to Macedonia is striking." Simultaneously, the government had to defend its southern border with Greece, while diverting security forces 100 miles away from Skopje, to defend property against political agitators. The traveling MP remembers, "It was a nightmare. The Soros army threw rocks at police guarding VMRO headquarters. Meanwhile, they were handing scissors out on the border to help people cut fences. Chaos." Information Service editor Chilimanov considers last summer's melee to signal George Soros' deepest objectives: "By controlling Macedonia, he can open or close the flow of migrants. The far Left Greek government has accepted no end of migrants. [Soros is close to the Greek Prime Minister, Alexis Tsipras.] It was our government that stopped the flow so his grand objective is to control this situation."

In the same article, Jason Miko stated that with North Macedonia:

> Low-level State Department bureaucrats are calling the shots because the President hasn't been able to fill key jobs on the seventh floor...This directly contradicts what President Trump said in his Inaugural address, that we want to let other nations put their own interests first. Instead, in Macedonia, we have an activist ambassador, Jess Baily, working with and funding the Soros organizations saying that no, you don't have a right to put your own interests first.

Naturally Baily is an alumnus of Columbia University, which readers of *The Transgender-Industrial Complex* will recognize for the cancerous tumor that it is. For Chris Deliso: "[North Macedonia] is a simple, conservative society of people who know who they are." For Soros and company, this is intolerable. Instead, they should be getting sex changes and welcoming thousands of unassimilable people from parts unknown to demographically swamp, displace, and eventually replace them. *This* is liberalism!

According to the Open Society Foundations' *Building Open Society in the Western Balkans* report, in Slovenia:

> Approximately 100 journalists received grants to visit media organizations abroad, to carry out projects abroad, or to participate in conferences and seminars. The foundation also funded more than 500 civil society projects concerned with ecology, human rights, volunteer work, ethnic minorities, women's rights, lesbian, gay, bisexual, and transgender rights.

One of the major priorities in Montenegro in the Open Society Foundations' own words is to "promote diversity." Further, the Open Society Foundations have indeed been working with the United Nations since at least 1992, when under the guidance of a five-member committee of individuals connected to the Open Society Foundations, $36 million was given to the United Nations High Commission for Refugees (UNHCR). The activist-ambassador to North

Macedonia, Jess Baily, coordinated US policy on political issues before the UN Security Council and UN General Assembly as Director of the Office of UN Political Affairs from 2008 to 2010.

The National Endowment for Democracy (NDI) is involved in dozens of countries, including Soros pet project North Macedonia where, in the NDI's own words from their website, they are focused on:

> Reconfiguring political discourse to be more inclusive...NDI's programming in the country reflects those needs. With technical support from the U.S. Congress' House Democracy Partnership...NDI also works with political parties, supporting pluralism and the promotion of women and youth leadership; with civil society organizations, conducting public opinion research, voter education and election observation; and with the country's historically marginalized groups, including Roma and LGBTI citizens.

To the south, Greece is targeted and even its attempts to quarantine corona-positive migrants were decried as "xenophobic" and the like by *Balkan Insight*, in an article sponsored by the Resonant Voices Initiative in the EU, funded by the European Union's Internal Security Fund. Interesting. Really, the Establishment has used COVID-19 as a justification for the most draconian totalitarianism most Westerners have ever experienced, and it is positioned to get a whole lot worse. Notice, as well, that it's always "far-right," as though preventing the spread of what appeared to be at the time a serious pandemic is some kind of extreme position. We do know Soros has dialogued with the EU and at his behest has increased the funding for "refugees" significantly in the last decade, especially since the onset of the "migrant crisis."

The Open Society's International Migration Initiative "has worked with governments [in Ireland, Spain, and the UK] on the development of refugee resettlement schemes based on a successful Canadian model for helping newly arrived families adjust to their new homes." Its Advisory Committee includes former Ford Foundation fellow Arturo Sarukhan and Imelda Nicolas, IOM Migration Advisory Board member and consultant for the UN's Institute of Training and Research focusing on international migration, gender, and development. Staff members include Colleen Thouez (Chair to the capacity-building portfolio of the World Bank's knowledge partnership on migration); Maria Teresa Rojas (member of the Advisory Committee of the Andrew and Renata Kaldor Center for International Refugee Law at the University of New South Wales); and Elizabeth Frantz ("a researcher for one of the UK's leading charities giving legal advice and representation to immigrants and asylum seekers").

The Open Society European Policy Institute, based out of Brussels, "works to place human rights and open society values at the heart of what the European Union does." Not that the EU needs any prompting: its motto is the Orwellian "United in Diversity." The Open Society European Policy Institute's staff includes Natacha Kazatchkine (former senior executive officer at the European Office of Amnesty International) and Marta Martinelli ("responsible for work on gender, democratization, security governance, and development issues in Africa").

The Open Society Initiative for Europe works to "support groups that combat discrimination and xenophobia, and ensure the protection and well-being of refugees and migrants." Its staff includes: Brandee Butler ("specialized in international justice as a program officer at the John D. and Catherine T. MacArthur Foundation…Earlier in her career, Butler received the Yale Law School Bernstein Fellowship for International Human Rights"); Goran Buldioski ("Before joining the Open Society Foundations, he worked for the Council of Europe, the Macedonian Center for International Cooperation, and the National Youth Council of Macedonia"); Magdalena Majkowska-Tomkin ("Prior to joining the Open Society Foundations in 2016, Majkowska-Tomkin served as the chief of mission for the International Organization for Migration offices in Hungary and Slovenia"); and Beka Vučo ("joined the Open Society Foundations in 1991, working as a regional director in the New York office where she helped establish Open Society foundations in the Western Balkans").

In 2007, the Open Society Foundations spent $440 million on its various initiatives. Among its targeted areas included Albania ($1.791 million), Bosnia ($3.11 million), Estonia ($1.769 million), Czech Republic ($1.739 million), Hungary ($289,000), Bulgaria ($2.142 million), Kosovo ($2.438 million), Lithuania ($1.546 million), Moldova ($4.149 million), Montenegro ($1.657 million), Macedonia ($7.229 million), Latvia ($1.853 million), South Africa ($7.452 million), Slovakia ($1.985 million), Poland ($5.699 million through the Stefan Batory Foundation), Romania ($3.555 million), Russia ($6.472 million), Serbia ($4.212 million), Belarus ($1.377 million through OSI-Paris Belarus support), and the Ukraine ($7.809 million through the International Renaissance Foundation). Targeting Central and Eastern Europe as well as the Caucasus and Central Asia have been long-standing priorities for Soros, although his activities have been by no means confined to these regions, with 2007 grants ranging from $4.282 million to the Baltimore, Maryland-based Open Society Institute to $4.287 million to Fundación Soros in Guatemala to the $13.991 million to the Open Society Initiative for West Africa.

In 2006, the Open Society Foundations spent over $415 million on its various initiatives. Disbursals were similar to the year following, although in Europe, $395,000-worth of efforts in Croatia were underwritten by the Soros Network. Soros' Central European University, which also has its own press established in 1992, has been an instrumental hub for these subversive activities and ideas at the meeting-point of Central and Eastern Europe. As the 2002 Open Society Foundations report brags:

> Evidence of CEU's influence in the world can be found in graduates who have gone on to serve as ministers for education, minorities, and energy, and to represent their countries as senior officials in the UN, EU, Council of Europe, International Monetary Fund, and World Bank.

The Open Society Foundations were represented at the World Bank and IMF's annual meeting in 2019 along with the Council on Foreign Relations, the UN, Freedom House, USAID, Goldman Sachs, Rothschild & Co., and a slew of other major organizations and institutions that essentially define the neoliberal Establishment (see Appendix A for a more complete list).

For reference, observing organizations at the World Bank's annual meeting in 2019 included: The World Trade Organization (WTO); United Nations Development Program (UNDP); European Commission; OPEC; United Nations Populations Fund; Organization for Economic Cooperation and Development (OECD); European Central Bank; Office of the UN High Commissioner for Human Rights; Food and Agriculture Organization of the United Nations (FAO); United Nations Capital Development Fund; European Bank for Reconstruction and Development; Green Climate Fund; European Investment Bank Group; ASEAN+3 Macroeconomic Research Office; Council of Europe Development Bank; World Health Organization; Joint United Nations Program on HIV/AIDS. There are essentially no limits to the subversive and destructive reach of Soros and the Establishment.

2

THE AMERICAN FOREIGN POLICY BATTERING RAM

American foreign policy in large part had, and has, less to do with anything pertaining to national security, and more to do with the advancement of ideologically-motivated business and financial interests (and that of its "greatest ally"). It is vital to understand this. The coopted American leadership is not alone in its endeavors, though it is more often than not the spearhead of, as A.S. Brychkov and G.A. Nikonorov put it, "the task of weakening or destroying sovereign nations and placing their national resources under control of transnational corporations." With that work largely complete, the US is being targeted for Balkanization while China will form the far more hardline state backbone of the system over the coming decades. In order to best understand how we got here and where we are going, however, we must first investigate the central and transformational role the US government and intelligence agencies, as well as their proxies, have played abroad.

The general thrust of American foreign policy can best be summed up in one image, that of the US Embassy in Seoul, South Korea, which until mid-June 2020 featured a massive Black Lives Matter banner and an LGBTQ rainbow flag on its exterior. This is not an outlier, and although they were removed due to senior State Department pressure, it is the removal, not the banner and flag and the agendas they represent, that is the outlier. As Michael K. Lavers reported in June 2019:

> The State Department in recent months has publicly criticized the anti-LGBTI crackdown in Chechnya and a provision of Brunei's new penal code that sought to impose the death penalty upon anyone convicted of engaging in consensual same-sex sexual relations. The White House in March announced openly gay U.S. Ambassador to Germany Richard Grenell will lead an initiative that encourages countries to decriminalize homosexuality. Tremenda Nota, the Blade's media partner in Cuba, reported the U.S. Embassy in Havana on its Twitter page acknowledged IDAHOBiT, which took place less

than a week after police in the Cuban capital arrested several people who participated in an unauthorized LGBTI march. A State Department spokesperson told the Blade last week in response to a request for comment about the postponement of the Tbilisi Pride parade in Georgia that "senior U.S. officials have and will continue to urge the government of Georgia to protect and defend human rights and fundamental freedoms for all—including LGBTI individuals." The U.S. Embassy in Kyiv on Twitter said "dozens of U.S. Embassy Kyiv members participated" in Sunday's Pride march in the Ukrainian capital.

A leaked US embassy document from 2006 on WikiLeaks shows the push to open up the small Eastern European nation of Estonia to the same "diversity" bomb lobbed into so many other parts of the West, enabled in no small part by the United States government through various methods ranging from external pressure to subversion to outright military intervention to some combination thereof. In this instance, we see the push for cultural transformation targeting both the top and bottom, from prominent officials to schoolchildren, through active intervention by the United States government in pushing neoliberal ideologies, with the goal of making Estonians more amenable to the importation of alien, and often hostile peoples, thereby bringing about their ethnic and racial replacement:

> Discussion in Estonia about tolerance and integration has focused mainly on the cultural and linguistic divide between the Estonian and Russian communities. Looking forward, the GOE intends to broaden its Integration Action Plan to include initiatives designed to address integration of new, and non-European, arrivals....
>
> On Feb 21, the European Commission against Racism and Intolerance (ECRI) report on Estonia made a number of recommendations to improve the atmosphere for tolerance. The report has been criticized in some quarters for having been poorly sourced and based on incomplete information. However, ECRI made a number of recommendations and observations with which we agree: Estonia has no hate crime specific legislation, and Estonian prosecution of hate crimes has not been aggressive. Punishment for first-time offenders is particularly lax....
>
> Estonian authorities ought to add the teaching of the benefits of diversity and living in a multicultural society in school programs....
>
> Estonian authorities need to provide support for the Press Council of Estonia and the Estonian Newspaper Association for

training journalists on issues related to racism and racial discrimination.... More training is needed for law enforcement on issues related to racism and racial discrimination....

To date the Embassy has organized the following series of events and activities, specifically targeting GOE officials, local government officials, educators, NGOs, law enforcement, students, and young people in order to raise the level of awareness, sensitivity, and understanding of tolerance issues....

On April 18 Post hosted a DVC between the Southern Poverty Law Center (SPLC) and Estonian working-level government officials (national and local) and NGOs to discuss promoting tolerance in education and sharing best practices. The Estonian participants found the SPLC's relationship with local government and law enforcement very informative, and the SPLC has promised to share its latest tolerance material for use and adaptation by Estonian officials....

A recently-returned ILVP recipient (February/March), Ken Koort, Advisor to Minister of Population and Migration Paul Eerik-Rummo, wrote an article on May 20 based on his experience in the U.S. for one of Estonia's leading Russian dailies. Koort praised U.S. multiculturalism and reflected on what Estonia could learn from U.S. diversity....

Supervisor Special Agent (SSA) Stan Strauss, FBI Civil Rights Unit (CRU), offered a presentation on U.S. hate- crime legislation, enforcement, and investigation to Estonia's Public Service Academy on May 30. SSA Strauss spoke to an audience of MFA officials, law enforcement, and Public Service Academy instructors....

The Ambassador spoke on the U.S. perspective and experience in promoting racial tolerance and diversity, and a diverse group of Embassy staff provided views on the theme....

During a six-week exchange program in April and May, visiting Fulbright School Administrator Gale Frazier helped to increase racial sensitivity and awareness among Estonian youth. Frazier, an African-American Director of Education at a private school in Chicago, spoke to at least 500 students at more than ten schools....

With special funding secured from State/EUR, the Embassy is providing $4,000 for the Tartu Black Nights Film Festival to screen U.S. films on the theme of cultural and racial tolerance....

Embassy has requested DS/IP (reftel) to provide for Estonian audiences the "Racial Intolerance" seminar presented by Chuck Hunter in Riga in January 2006.

Should Estonians find themselves convinced that constant civil unrest, crime, and declining quality of life constitute "social progress" as many other Western nations have, they might want to pause and re-consider.

It is unlikely to be coincidental that also in 2006, Toomas Hendrik Ilves was elected President of Estonia. Ilves grew up in New Jersey and attended Columbia University and the University of Pennsylvania. Ilves was a journalist with Radio Free Europe from 1984-1993, was the Estonian Ambassador to the US, Canada, and Mexico, was the Estonian Minister of Foreign Affairs from 1996-1998, and has also been involved with the World Economic Forum and the World Bank; he has received awards from the National Democratic Institute, the Atlantic Council, Bertelsmann Stiftung, the Aspen Institute, and the Casimir Pulaski Foundation in Warsaw, which also gave the same award to Georgian President Mikheil Saakashvili. Ilves was given an honorary degree by Tblisi State University in Georgia in 2007.

Ilves is on the Advisory Council of the Alliance for Securing Democracy, an American NGO that is housed at the German Marshall Fund of the United States and features members such as Zack Cooper (American Enterprise Institute), the Jewish Laura Rosenberger (its director, a former Bush and Obama State Department official, and senior fellow at the German Marshall Fund of the United States), Jake Sullivan, Jewish neocon Bill Kristol (co-founder of the Project for the New American Century and its successor the Foreign Policy Initiative), the Jewish Michael Chertoff (co-author of the PATRIOT Act), John Podesta (Center for American Progress), and Michael McFaul. It will likely not surprise the reader to learn that Ilves's successor, Kersti Kaljulaid (who become president of Estonia in 2016), holds pro-LGBTQ and pro-immigration views, and in 2014, the Open Estonia Foundation awarded her the Award of Unity. The Open Estonia Foundation is part of George Soros's Open Society Foundations, which not only funds huge numbers of subversive NGOs, but also serves as a veritable training academy and incubator for "activists."

Toomas Hendrik Ilves's first wife is the senior director of the American Psychological Association's (APA) Office of International Affairs and coordinates the APA's representation at the United Nations; his brother Andres has worked extensively for the BBC, for Radio Free Europe/Radio Liberty, and worked on an "election monitoring and political party capacity building project" in Serbia for the National Democratic Institute (NDI). He was a Coro Fellow, where fellows "learn by experience...Each Fellow participates in a series of full-time projects across a variety of sectors in public affairs," according to their website. Participating organizations listed on the Foundation's website have included: the Open Society Institute, Bloomberg for Mayor, JP Morgan Chase, the Tides Foundation, the San Francisco Mayor's

Office of Criminal Justice, Edelman, Goldman Sachs, the United Federation of Teachers, Advantage Capital, and more. Andres Ilves was the director of Radio Free Afghanistan (now Radio Azadi), director of Radio Farda (Iran), and Chair of the Board of Trustees of NGO Peace Direct (which has contracts with USAID and the London School of Economics and has received grants from the UK's DFID: Department for International Development, SIDA: Swedish International Development Cooperation Agency, the EU, and more).

On the state side of things, we know that many of the "activists" involved in the Arab Spring were trained by the United States, as Kerry Bolton has written,[5] and the US has even trained the mostly-Muslim "activists" fomenting unrest within the borders of their ostensible allies such as we will see in Chapter Six. Interestingly but unsurprisingly, one of the few genuine color revolutions in the twenty-first century, France's Yellow Vests, has been actively suppressed because it runs contrary to the aims of undercutting extant native populations for the benefit of global capital. Unfortunately for Americans, this has been the orientation of their government for over a century.

The strong tendency to isolationism in the US almost held the day around World War I before President Woodrow Wilson's desire to insert America into global geopolitics finally won out, though his Fourteen Points and the League of Nations (which Congress outright rejected) reflected a sort of proto-neoliberalism and were an outgrowth of Wilson's academic beliefs in universal egalitarianism. These principles and ideals have never been shared by Americans at large; they are very much self-serving ideals held by a small elite, generally of Puritan stock, which are foisted on the general populace and twisted by the "new elite" that first began intermarrying with and then mostly replacing the old one in the late nineteenth and early twentieth centuries. England in particular was subverted in similar fashion earlier, with the United States and its Anglospheric cousins at a slight delay. That said, some of the old ruling families of Europe formed part of what is otherwise a neo-aristocracy (see: Otto von Habsburg and the World Economic Forum), but with industrialization and the explosion of the power of capital, the bedrock has nevertheless shifted considerably, perhaps no more so than after the seismic shifts first of World War II and then of the onset and acceleration of the Internet Age and the digitized Fourth Industrial Revolution.

The era of mercantilism drew to a close with the double-blows to traditional empires in the form of the World Wars. A privatized "plausible deniability" by the state can be witnessed in the corporate-driven betrayal of the colonial populations in Africa by the United States in order to access and

---

[5] Bolton, "Are American Interests."

exploit the rich reserves of that continent. As a result of their "special relationship," Israel has been a major beneficiary as well. This is not the sole cause of Africa's dysfunction, but it has contributed to it, and it violates the fundamental principles of national self-determination for all peoples. This is categorically unacceptable.

The need for the ruling class to condition, rather than simply dictate—soft versus hard power if you like—is particularly pronounced with Westerners for the aforementioned reasons as well as our relative tendency to individualism. The Second Amendment in the United States is one such testament to the particular heroic vision of Western Man as exemplified in our mythos (from Hercules and Odysseus to the characters played by John Wayne and Clint Eastwood). We are generally much more difficult to manage, in some ways, but uniquely susceptible to particular kinds of subversion. To quote Lothrop Stoddard in *The Revolt Against Civilization: The Menace of the Under-Man*, "Before the revolutionary onslaught can have any chance of success, the social order must first have been undermined and morally discredited. This is accomplished primarily by the process of destructive criticism." Detonate the foundation and the body of the population becomes plastic in the hands of the ruling class, ready to be made into whatever shapes they so choose.

After the negation, the sprawling synthetic neoliberal empire can flourish and continue to expand. By canceling-out that which is substantive, that which gives people real meaning and binds them together, it may then metastasize. But if a population is not sufficiently indoctrinated, it cannot. A healthy, conscious people would never embrace the self-negating contradictions of hyper-individualism-meets-suicidal-universalism, nor would they worship at the altar of an economic system where consumption is not just considered a substitute for meaning, but a *source* of meaning. That distinction makes all the difference.

To that end, US- and privately-backed organizations ranging from Freedom House to the National Endowment for Democracy (NED) have used the "end of history" to push the "inevitability" of their version of "liberal democracy." From the NED's 1992 Strategy Document, there are three major functional areas to be funded for transforming attitudes and values: pluralism; democratic governance; and education, culture, and communications. For them, pluralism:

> ...involves the development of strong, independent private-sector institutions, especially trade unions and business associations, as well as civic and women's organizations, youth groups and cooperatives. Endowment programs in the areas of labor and business are carried

out, respectively, through the Free Trade Union Institute (FTUI) and the Center for International Private Enterprise.

"Free trade" has been an essential element of the functioning of the neoliberal system, and the NED is but one organization pushing the idea that unfettered "free trade" and the movement of peoples is somehow a democratic value. Economics for too many people, especially libertarians, has become an ideology in and of itself, where the system in question places human beings as subservient to "the market," as opposed to an economic structure that best benefits the people. It is not an accident that the ideology of "equality" is so incessantly pushed, as it serves numerous functions, not least of which is the human-as-widget market function.

National Security Action is a prime example, which, via their "Our Focus" page on their website, opposes "nationalism, isolationism, unilateralism, and xenophobia" and declares that "we [must] fully fund our State Department and development agencies" such as USAID. National Security Action believes "that instead of embracing isolationism, we should forge economic partnerships to open markets." It is Co-Chaired by the Jewish Ben Rhodes[6] (former Obama speechwriter and a central figure in the Arab Spring, the removal of Muammar al-Gaddafi of Libya, and the Syrian conflict) and Jake Sullivan (former Deputy Chief of Staff and Director of Policy Planning for Secretary of State Hillary Clinton and key advisor to Vice President Joe Biden, another central figure regarding US involvement in the Middle East and North Africa).

Members of National Security Action's Advisory Council include (with current or former positions of note): Rosa Brooks (Board member for the Open Society Foundations' US Programs); Dan Feldman (Senior Fellow at the Center for American Progress and represented the United States at

---

[6] From Landler, "Worldly at 35": "Two years ago, when protesters thronged Tahrir Square in Cairo, Mr. Rhodes urged Mr. Obama to withdraw three decades of American support for President Hosni Mubarak of Egypt. A few months later, Mr. Rhodes was among those agitating for the president to back a NATO military intervention in Libya to head off a slaughter by Col. Muammar el-Qaddafi. 'He became, first in the speechwriting process, and later, in the heat of the Arab Spring, a central figure,' said Michael A. McFaul, who worked with Mr. Rhodes in the National Security Council and is now the American ambassador to Russia… Mr. Rhodes has exerted influence outside the Middle East as well. In 2011, he worked with Jacob J. Sullivan, a top aide to Mrs. Clinton, to persuade Mr. Obama to engage with the military rulers of Myanmar, formerly Burma, after gaining the endorsement of the pro-democracy leader, Aung San Suu Kyi…[Rhodes] favors equipping the rebels [in Syria] with more robust nonlethal gear and training that would help them in their fight against Mr. Assad's government, a position shared by Britain and other allies."

multilateral forums regarding Afghanistan and Pakistan arranged by the United Nations, the World Bank, the International Monetary Fund, and the World Food Program); Valerie Jarrett (Senior Advisor to President Barack Obama); Jenna Ben-Yehuda (President and CEO of the Truman Center for National Policy and Truman National Security Project); Ron Klain (Obama "Ebola Czar"); Penny Pritzker (Obama Secretary of Commerce); Dan Shapiro (US Ambassador to Israel); Jim Steinberg (Deputy Secretary of State); Ben Wikler (Washington Director of MoveOn.org); Susan Rice (National Security Advisor); and Rand Beers (counter-terrorism expert, senior national/homeland security government official, National Security Network founder). The reader may note that many of those figures are Jewish.

Returning to the NED, its website database features a record of over $21 million for financing of "Developing Market Economies" abroad, which range from "women's entrepreneurship" in Turkmenistan to grants for the Center for International Private Enterprise (CIPE).[7] Allen Weinstein, son of Russian-Jewish immigrants and then-NED President, stated in a 1991 interview with David Ignatius that, "A lot of what we do today was done covertly 25 years ago by the CIA." The NED has been very active in Hong Kong, Venezuela, and Egypt in recent years. Its current president, Carl Gershman, has worked in the research department of the Anti-Defamation League (ADL), was on the Governing Council of the American Jewish Committee, and was Ronald Reagan's first-term ambassador to the United Nations Human Rights Council.

The NED received a US State Department grant of $170 million in 2017 in addition to over $16 million from various other government grants. As an extension but "unofficially" representative of the US government, the NED has more latitude, though this is not to say that the US government is shy

---

[7] From CIPE website, "What We Do: Trade": "The Global Alliance for Trade Facilitation is a unique public-private platform dedicated to international trade facilitation. Launched in 2016, the Global Alliance for Trade Facilitation (the Alliance) helps developing countries implement the World Trade Organization (WTO) Trade Facilitation Agreement (TFA). Jointly led by the Center for International Private Enterprise (CIPE), International Chamber of Commerce (ICC) and World Economic Forum (WEF), in cooperation with Deutsche Gesellschaft für Internationale Zusammenarbeit (GIZ) as an implementing partner, the Alliance works to leverage private sector expertise and leadership to accelerate ambitious and commercially meaningful trade policy reforms to create broad-based opportunity, economic growth, and development. The Alliance is funded by the United States, Germany, the United Kingdom, Canada, and Australia. CIPE is currently leading programs in Vietnam, Colombia, and Sri Lanka that will help those countries ultimately expedite the movement of goods across borders in accordance with the TFA. Globally, CIPE and the Alliance are developing projects that emphasize private-sector driven measurable solutions to trade issues."

about putting its name on these subversive projects. As we are living in the "end of history," it is only natural that Francis Fukuyama would be on the NED's Board of Directors, along with figures such as Anne Applebaum, Elliott Abrams, Ben Sasse, Tim Kaine, Mel Martinez, and Ileana Ros-Lehinten.

The NED's 1992 Strategy Document lists USAID, the British Know-How Fund, and the Canadian Center for Human Rights and Democratic Development as key allies. The document states that, "democracy promotion, which only a few years ago seemed like a pioneering venture, has become an established form of international assistance"—assistance with plenty of strings attached. The goal of organizations like the NED is to totally transform the targeted culture(s) to prime their "opening up" to free trade, mass migration starting first with "migrant workers," liberalizing tendencies, and the subsequent dominoes of advanced societal decay we can readily witness across the Western world.

Regarding these "migrant workers," after the threat to the neoliberal order had been destroyed in central Europe with the removal of the Axis regimes, which subsequently froze the binary of capitalism/liberalism versus communism in place for the next half-century, the September 1996 report entitled "Migration from the developing countries to the European industrialised countries" from the Council of Europe provides useful context:

> The first phase of migration from Third World countries after the Second World War derived from colonial relationships. The major colonial countries (Belgium, France, the Netherlands, the United Kingdom) defined their dependent territories as part of their national territory. Even as early as the nineteenth century, former colonial officers as well as people of other trades, such as seamen and soldiers, who had served the colonial power were accepted as immigrants. Collaborators were also admitted. As a rule, no racial differentiation was made. Immigration flows thus developed at an early stage from West Africa and the Maghreb to France, from the Indian colonies and other parts of the later Commonwealth to the United Kingdom and from Indonesia and the South American possessions to the Netherlands. The first immigrant populations came into being that would later further the admission of other immigrants as chain migrants. These migration processes continued into the sixties. They intensified even later in Portugal in the wake of the 1974 democratic revolution...[8]

---

[8] From Bolton, "Last Empire": "While the Portuguese armed forces were engaged in fighting Black guerrillas in Angola and Mozambique, to their rear they were being 'stabbed in the back'

The events of the second [sic] World War intensified the colonial and post-colonial migration flows to Europe and gave rise to the movement of what were called displaced persons and diaspora refugees from the eastern and central European war theatres to Western Europe, where they received support through settlement programmes....

Immigration from the British colonies was promoted by the State and adapted to industrial development in the British Isles; the Benelux countries, too, recruited labour first of all from their former colonies, though some was recruited from Mediterranean countries. France intensified migration from the Maghreb on a planned basis; it was later reinforced by the Algerian civil war. But on the whole this recruitment basis was insufficient, so migrants from Turkey, Morocco and Tunisia were also recruited in the individual European countries. These migration waves very quickly led to the formation of migration focal points in Europe's traditional industrial regions. The interest shown at that time in limiting the duration of stay of such workers was later put aside because of the cost that would be involved in training new workers, so that the rotation systems collapsed and the duration

---

by a much more lethal enemy based in the U.S.A. The Portuguese territories in Southern Africa were the last vestiges of European colonial power that had not long previously spanned the world. The old empires had created self-contained trading systems, buttressed by an ethos that saw the European as having a world civilising mission. The Congress of Berlin of 1884-1885 sought an agreement among the European powers for the colonisation and development of Africa, indicating the potential for a collective European arrangement. The U.S.A. on the other hand, represented an entity quite different, and still does.... With the increasing internationalisation of capital, or what we today call 'globalisation,' the European empires had become anachronisms. Rather than facilitating trade they had become restrictive to the increasing world scope of a merchant class that steadily displaced the old aristocracies as the ruling elite.... The remnants of the European empires were finished off by another devastating intra-European war that saw the U.S.A. and the U.S.S.R., emerge as rivals in entering the power vacuum created by the scuttling of the empires. Like the 'Fourteen Points,' the 'Atlantic Charter' was intended to eliminate the imperial trading blocs and impose international free trade under the auspices of the United Nations Organisation.... The [Africa-America Institute] A.A.I.'s initial programme for 'refugees' (fleeing terrorists) from Portuguese Africa was for the training of personnel 'in anticipation of independence.' After Portugal's departure from Africa the program was directed towards 'Namibia, South Africa and Zimbabwe, for employment in their countries of asylum with a later focus on the repatriation of trainees.' This programme was continued through 1976-1981, with funds from USAID. In 1975, soon after the Portuguese departure from Africa, the A.A.I. established the Development Training Program for Portuguese-Speaking Africa (DTPSA) to establish the post-colonial leadership for the former colonies of Angola, Mozambique, Guinea-Bissau, Cape Verde and Sao Tome and Principe. This programme was also funded by USAID, which serves as a means by which U.S. influence is extended world-wide via foreign aid."

of stay of the immigrant workers constantly grew. This created one of the preconditions for the family reunification phase of immigration, which continued on into the nineties after direct recruiting ended with the 1973 oil price shock....

The costs of international mobility fell and communication routes were modernized, so that growing international mobility was observed from the sixties onwards....

The intensified use of the European asylum laws since the end of the seventies has led to repeated asylum legislation reforms. In the eighties, and then in the wake of the opening of the Iron Curtain, the number of asylum-seekers increased. The western European countries reacted with mutually reinforced restrictions on the right of asylum and with a frontier policy to be framed in common. Since then those migrating to Western Europe tend rather to be civil war refugees and persons classified as illegal immigrants. In the nineties, there has been a revival of «guest worker» and service contract programmes....

The metropolises known as «global cities» have novel characteristics connected with the internal migration outlined above. They have a large manpower potential that is supplemented from abroad to fill special niches, and their economies are oriented towards the world market. Corporations from the First and Third Worlds have their business offices there, and the working conditions and conditions of production are virtually indistinguishable from those in the First World....

Since the mid-eighties it has been possible to speak of a fundamental transformation in migration flows within the Third World. These migration flows are generally conditioned by short-term labour migrations or mass flight. Moreover, since the seventies the industrialised countries of Europe, North America and East Asia have been more intensively integrated in new, world-wide migration systems.

With Western Europe sufficiently "liberalized"/subverted, the focus for the Establishment remains on "opening up" the former USSR and other former communist countries, as per the National Endowment for Democracy's website:

In Russia, Georgia, Belarus, Ukraine, and Central Asia, NED will continue to support independent organizations that are the foundation of civil society, including pro-democratic political parties, trade unions, NGOs, think tanks, business associations and media, which are working to promote peaceful, democratic change.

In Europe, NED will concentrate its activities in Serbia, Kosovo, and Bosnia and Herzegovina, and will remain active in Albania and Macedonia. NED has been a leader in assisting democracy-building groups from more advanced countries to share their experiences, skills and program models with their counterparts in less developed states, and will expand its cross border programs from Central Europe to the Balkans, as well as regional programs within the Balkans and Eastern Europe.

The NED acknowledges in its 1992 document that this transformation must be all-encompassing, and to that end:

> The fact that the Endowment is a non-governmental institution suggests that it should position itself at the "cutting edge" of democratic advance.... The Endowment's multi-sectoral structure enables it to provide a "full package" response to the complex needs of emerging democracies—especially important in light of the close relationship between political and economic reform—as well as targeted assistance to movements struggling to defend democratic values in closed societies.

Democratic values, of course, being a euphemism for the pre-determined package of changes that will take sequential effect in the "liberalizing" process, and as we've seen, "trans" and "migrant workers" are by design on the same continuum, and with increasing globalization and interconnectedness, to say nothing of the immense pressure put on the remaining nationalist/"closed" societies, the timeline is condensed.

Alongside the NED are many other similar organizations, such as Freedom House and the National Democratic Institute (NDI); both are active in "opening up" the societies in which they operate. Freedom House, the NED, and the NDI, along with USAID and the Soros network, among a few others, are principally responsible for the various astroturfed "Color Revolutions" of the late twentieth and into the twenty-first centuries, but we will return to this later. Like the NED, CIPE, and what is now the International Republican Institute, the NDI was founded in 1983 during the first term of Ronald Reagan. It is chaired by Council on Foreign Relations member Madeleine Albright, born Marie Jana Korbelová, whose parents converted to Catholicism from Judaism.

While the extent of its role appears inconclusive, the NDI may well have been a party to the unrest that gripped Armenia in 2018 (the Velvet

Revolution),[9] where since 1994 they have been "supporting political parties to develop youth wings, improve campaign and outreach skills, build cross-party alliances and launch local initiative projects," according to the "Armenia" page on their website. The NDI is active in a number of former communist countries such as those of the former USSR, where they have certain "pet projects" that align with the raft of "liberalizing" policies that accompany the open society project. In Bulgaria, in the NDI's description of activities for the regions they're active in on their website:

> In 1990, NDI supported students and other democracy activists from the Bulgarian Association for Fair Elections and Civil Rights (BAFECR)—a citizen election monitoring group that observed the country's first post-communist election—which helped to pioneer domestic, nonpartisan election observation in Central and Eastern Europe. Recently, Bulgarian security has been strained by the influx of refugees and migrants from the greater Middle East, and hate speech targeting refugees, migrants, and the country's sizable, indigenous Roma minority has been on the rise. NDI supported Roma political leaders as they competed for elected office and encouraged Romani youth to engage in civic and political processes by joining political parties, volunteering for campaigns, and educating their communities about their rights as citizens. The Institute trained young Roma political activists in an effort to strengthen their capacities to formulate and communicate opinions on key national policy issues, and supported the mainstream

---

[9] From Jennings, "Upgrading US Support": "For U.S. and other Western business interests, one of the new Armenian government's strongest signals of its intent to create a friendly climate for foreign investment will emerge from how it resolves the Lydian mine crisis. Lydian Armenia, a subsidiary of the U.S.-based firm Lydian International, began constructing its Amulsar mine near the Armenian resort area of Jermuk in 2016.... Assisting the new government in its attempts to mediate this dilemma should remain a high priority for Washington. At the moment, no other issue may be as pivotal in moving Armenia from 'aid to trade.'... A range of sectors including energy, tourism, and information technology require investment and foreign partnerships to be competitive. The United States should leverage the 2015 TIFA, the U.S.-Armenia Joint Economic Taskforce, and the 1992 Armenia Bilateral Investment Treaty to identify promising partnerships, secure much-needed capital, and identify opportunities for technical assistance.... The United States should work with other Western counterparts to mitigate the constraints placed on Armenia by its accession to the Eurasian Economic Union (EAEU). The union's questionable benefits, constraints on trading with other countries, and low trade volumes are a strategic setback for the country. Moscow threatened to withdraw security guarantees for Armenia if it signed a negotiated Association Agreement with the EU, pressuring Yerevan to join the EEU instead in 2013.... The United States should encourage its EU counterparts to expedite Armenia's access to EU technical assistance and material support.... Armenia stands to gain much from deepening its relationship with the EU."

integration of Roma through informal forums that connected politically-active Roma and non-Roma youth.

In the Czech Republic:

As part of a regional program focused on combating religious-based discrimination and xenophobia that started in 2016, NDI has engaged Czech civic groups that champion ethnic, religious, and racial tolerance to build coalitions and raise public awareness on religious and ethnic tolerance. This included a coalition of Jewish, Roma, and Muslim groups that worked with university students from the three minority groups on building interethnic bonds and promoting youth civic engagement. NDI is presently supporting political actors to engage young people through modernized communication strategies and leadership skills, as part of NDI's Central Europe Democracy Initiative (CEDI), which enables young politicians to engage each other and experts from outside of the region on efforts to reinvigorate mainstream, democratic politics. Starting in 2009, NDI has partnered with the Czech parliament in sharing its institutional expertise with legislatures in the Balkans, primarily developing the research and lawmaking capacities, improving committee operations, legislative transparency and civic engagement.

In Poland:

Throughout the 1990s, NDI supported the development of a multiparty political system, helping center-right and center-left parties build local branches across the country, attract youth and women to party ranks, and develop and augment communication links between headquarters and members. Many NDI training participants have gone on to serve in elected office. NDI currently supports leaders in the Jewish, Christian Orthodox, and Islamic communities to deepen their collaboration with each other and with mainstream religious and cultural bodies to construct effective responses to xenophobia and nativism.

All of this is because according to the NDI, "democracy in Central and Eastern Europe is at a crossroads" as the European Union wants to force multiculturalism on its member states and as ethnic self-preservation comes increasingly under fire.

Freedom House, founded in 1941 with Eleanor Roosevelt and Wendell Willkie as honorary chairpersons, has been undermining Europeans' right to their own homelands even longer; it was instrumental in the establishment and implementation of NATO and the Marshall Plan, and in the US, the Civil Rights Movement, as well as Lyndon B. Johnson's efforts in Vietnam and "post-communist" efforts of "liberalization." Board alumni include Donald Rumsfeld and Paul Wolfowitz of the Project for the New American Century (PNAC). Freedom House is today helmed by Michael J. Abramowitz, a member of the Council on Foreign Relations and former US Holocaust Memorial Museum's Levine Institute for Holocaust Education Director and German Marshall Fund fellow. Other Board members include Francis Fukuyama (another signatory of the PNAC's June 1997 Statement of Principles), Ellen Blackler (Vice President, Global Public Policy at The Walt Disney Company; prior to joining Disney, she was Executive Director, Public Policy at AT&T), Jim Kolbe (Senior Transatlantic Fellow at the German Marshall Fund), and Jørgen Ejbøl (Chairman of the Jyllands-Posten Foundation and Jyllands-Posten Holding, former member of UNESCO's World Press Freedom Prize).

They are very active in Europe, especially in the Ukraine and Moldova. In the region, Freedom House works with the Organization for Security and Cooperation in Europe (OSCE), the Parliamentary Assembly of the Council of Europe (PACE), the European Parliament, the UN bodies, and the US Congress to "seek international accountability for impunity for rights violations across the Eurasia region," per their website's "Eurasia Programs" page. In the Ukraine, Freedom House's initiatives are prioritized as (with each linking to a more specific description):

- Expanding Allies for LGBT+ Rights in Ukraine
- Strengthening Champions for Free Expression in Ukraine in a Time of Conflict
- Security Services Under Civic Oversight in Ukraine
- Defending and Expanding Civic Space in Ukraine
- United to Confront Hate-Motivated Violence in Ukraine

Some of their local partners include the Ukrainian Helsinki Human Rights Union, the Congress of Ethnic Communities of Ukraine, the Center for Civil Liberties, and the Ukrainian Institute for Human Rights. In Moldova, their local partners include a number of astroturfed NGOs including the Press Council of Moldova, the Center for Investigative Journalism in Moldova, Lawyers for Human Rights, and the Center for the Analysis and Prevention of Corruption. You'll notice the policy proposals, the types of organization names, the nomenclature, and the like are all essentially the same since the actors are as well—and speaking of corruption, it may be gratuitous to point out the hypocrisy of the ubiquitous "Russian collusion" red herring the Establishment media pushed for years in the US, but it is worth mentioning for the fact that the double standard is the only standard.

Unfortunately, this kind of crime and corruption won't be viewed as worth reporting on by the Organized Crime and Corruption Reporting Project, which does indeed cover crime and corruption, but in a selective manner akin to lies by omission, although there are also plenty of straight lies as well. You can read hit pieces on Nicolás Maduro and on certain aspects of organized crime and corruption, some real and some invented, but you will not get an accurate picture of the state of play, in no small part because the ruling class itself is criminal despite its claims to legitimacy. Secondarily, the ruling class itself finances this project, a self-styled "last word" on hard-boiled, shoe-leather journalism. Hardly. With funding from the very same organizations financing mass immigration, "social justice," transgenderism, the color revolutions, and the rest of the noxious package of neoliberalism, the OCCRP is just another globalist Pravda; their primary financiers are the Open Society Foundations, the Omidyar Network, the National Endowment for Democracy, the Sigrid Rausing Trust, Google News Initiative, USAID, the Rockefeller Brothers Fund, the European Instrument for Democracy and Human Rights, arms of the Danish, Swedish, and British governments, and more.

Should the *obvious* benefits of "Westernizing" such as hormone blockers for children, civil unrest, rampant criminality, non-existent social capital, and the whole rotten package prove unappealing through the various covert and "soft" methods of conversion, there is always the American military juggernaut. This is the method preferred by the overwhelmingly Jewish neocons (see: people like Max Boot and much of the George W. Bush administration). The sheer volume of failed states as a consequence of US foreign policy through means direct and indirect has in turn created thousands if not millions of genuine refugees and millions more economic opportunists, who are then pumped into the West for reasons "humanitarian" or economic, or as penance for the Original Sin of Whiteness. This serves the globalist Establishment just fine.

When American military might is bandied about the globe in the service of internationalist projects (including those of Israel which do paradoxically fit into the internationalizing puzzle) that do not help but rather harm not just Americans but basically every non-Israeli sovereign nation on earth sans China, then we are right to question the status quo. As just one example, the US-driven NATO as an extension of the Zionist Occupied Government, per

Gearóid Ó Colmáin for *Dissident Voice*, is now intensifying its attentions on Azerbaijan:

> The important oil-rich country has been moving closer to Russia and is facing conflict from both an Armenia moving closer to the United States who are also backing Karabakh independence and colour revolutionary activity inside Azerbaijan. The destabilization of Azerbaijan would have enormous consequences for the security of Russia and Iran. Northern Iran has an ethnic minority of 22 million Azeris. A colour revolution in Azerbaijan could bring ultra-nationalists to power, who are advocating an annexation of "Southern Azerbaijan." Meanwhile tensions inside Iran between Kurds and Azeris are running high over the Iranian government's attempts to create a new Kurdistan province that would include part of Iran's Western Azerbaijan province. Given the incessant media war currently being waged against Azerbaijan, a colour revolution attempt by NATO against that country is not unlikely. This would mean that the entire region from the Baltic Sea to the Black Sea and from the Eastern Mediterranean to the Caspian Sea would be engulfed in internecine warfare. Furthermore, the constant influx of migrants towards Western Europe from these war zones will be managed by Zionist Coercive Engineered Migration with a view to maximizing ethnic and inter-religious tension in Europe, thereby reinforcing the ideology of the "war on terror" and the "clash of civilisations…" George Friedman of Stratfor argued that US geopolitics in Europe is based on the objective of keeping Russia divided from the European peninsula by creating a US occupied corridor or "intermarium" (a term coined by Pilsudski) from the Baltic to the Black Sea.

Military geostrategist Thomas Barnett has stated that Europe has to "move beyond guest workers and into American-style encouragement of immigration flows. The right-wing anti-immigrant politicians need to be shouted off the political stage and pronto."[10] Barnett, one of the leading figures in his field, worked as a chief analyst at Wikistrat, a geostrategic analysis and business consultancy firm co-founded by Australian-Israeli "social media expert" Joel Zamel and headquartered in Washington, DC. Zamel had also owned Psy-Group, now closed, an Israeli "private intelligence company" described thusly in a 2018 *Calcalist* article:

---

[10] Barnett, *The Pentagon's New Map*. 385.

Incorporated as Invop Ltd. in Israel in 2014, Psy-Group has ties to Israel's intelligence arms through its employees and managers. [CEO Royi] Burstien, a former lieutenant colonel in the Israeli army, headed an intelligence unit under Israel's government before the company was founded.

As *The New Yorker* reported in February 2019:

> Psy-Group's slogan was "Shape Reality," and its techniques included the use of elaborate false identities to manipulate its targets. Psy-Group was part of a new wave of private intelligence firms that recruited from the ranks of Israel's secret services—self-described "private Mossads…"
>
> In Gabon, Psy-Group pitched "Operation Bentley"—an effort to "preserve" President Ali Bongo Ondimba's hold on power by collecting and disseminating intelligence about his main political rival….
>
> In New York, Psy-Group mounted a campaign on behalf of wealthy Jewish-American donors to embarrass and intimidate activists on American college campuses who support a movement to put economic pressure on Israel because of its treatment of the Palestinians….
>
> Terrogence, which became the first major Israeli company to demonstrate the effectiveness of avatars in counterterrorism work… spawned imitators, and other former intelligence officers began to open their own firms, many of them less risk-averse than Terrogence. One of the boldest, Black Cube, openly advertised its ties to Israeli spy agencies, including Mossad and Unit 8200, the military's signals-intelligence corps. Black Cube got its start with the help of Vincent Tchenguiz, an Iranian-born English real-estate tycoon who had invested in Terrogence. In March, 2011, Tchenguiz was arrested by a British anti-fraud unit investigating his business dealings….
>
> He asked Meir Dagan, who had just stepped down as the director of Mossad, how he could draw on the expertise of former intelligence officers to look into the business rivals he believed had alerted authorities. Dagan's message to Tchenguiz, a former colleague of Dagan's said, was: I can find a personal Mossad for you…Tchenguiz became Black Cube's first significant client….
>
> In 2016, Romanian police arrested two Black Cube operatives for illegal hacking and harassment of the country's leading

anticorruption officer...Psy-Group...like Black Cube, used avatars to conduct intelligence-collection operations. But Burstien also offered his avatars for another purpose: influence campaigns....

In one meeting, Burstien said that, before a parliamentary election in a European country, his operatives had created a sham think tank. Using avatars, the operatives hired local analysts to work for the think tank, which then disseminated reports to bolster the political campaign of the company's client and to undermine the reputations of his rivals. In another meeting, Psy-Group officials said that they had created an avatar to help a corporate client win regulatory approval in Europe. Over time, the avatar became so well established in the industry that he was quoted in mainstream press reports and even by European parliamentarians....

Zamel was a skilled networker. He cultivated relationships with high-profile Republicans in the U.S., including Newt Gingrich and Elliott Abrams,[11] who served in foreign-policy positions under Ronald Reagan and George W. Bush, and whom Psy-Group listed as a member of its advisory board. (The Trump Administration recently named Abrams its special envoy to oversee U.S. policy toward Venezuela.)

Nothing suspicious there, right?

Today, Anne-Marie Slaughter, former Advisory Board member of the National Security Network, is a featured expert for Zamel's Wikistrat. Current clients include various branches of the US armed forces and intelligence community, as well as Lockheed Martin, Deloitte, Ernst & Young, Grant Thornton, the Royal Air Force, and the French Air and Space Force. Joel Zamel's biography from his company Joel Zamel Investment Group reads:

> Joel Zamel is a founder and investor in a series of private firms whose services span: crowdsourced intelligence analysis, expert wargaming, forecasting simulations, influence operations, social media campaigns, private investment brokering and election campaign strategy and management. Zamel's group of companies currently includes a number of private intelligence firms including Wikistrat—a geostrategic consultancy firm, White Knight Group—specializing in counter-extremism campaigns, and several other firms in the information technology space. The Group is also an

---

[11] Another Jewish neocon and signatory of the Project for the New American Century's Statement of Principles.

active investor in transnational infrastructure projects, property development and disruptive technologies across various sectors—including artificial intelligence and blockchain platforms.

As Ariel Ben Solomon wrote in a 2019 piece for the *Daily Caller*:

> [Zamel] is reported to have established various other social media influence companies based in Eastern Europe and Asia, and is known to have cultivated a close advisory team of 30 renowned former senior government officials that served at the highest levels of government in the U.S., UK and the Middle-East. Some sources have said he serves as a trusted power-broker, and facilitates special intelligence services and private media campaigns for tycoons and governments."

For Joe Liebkind in a 2019 article in *International Policy Digest:*

> Erik Prince…The ex-U.S. Navy SEAL and founder of the private security contractor formerly known as Blackwater was an important adviser to the UAE as it developed what is probably the Persian Gulf region's best-equipped and trained military… Prince, the brother of U.S. Education Secretary Betsy DeVos, was one of two businesspeople recruited by Trump's advisers to develop alternatives to the Pentagon's plan to send thousands of additional troops to Afghanistan. He and Stephen Feinberg,[12] a billionaire financier who owns military contractor DynCorp International, devised proposals to rely on contractors instead of American troops…Another colleague of Prince, Australian-Israeli businessman Joel Zamel, first received public attention in 2018 with a number of media reports on the Mueller investigation… Having cultivated a wide network of former government officials and politically active billionaires, Zamel is an active investor in cybersecurity companies that can bring technological capabilities to such CVE efforts. Zamel's focus revolves around private sector counter-extremism campaigns — designed to supplement government CVE (countering violent extremism) programs…Wealthy executives are not the only powerbrokers shaping private diplomacy. The likes of former U.S. Secretary of State Henry Kissinger and World Economic Forum founder Klaus Schwab have also had an impact…Despite a controversial foreign policy track record that includes accusations of war crimes, Kissinger

---

[12] Yes, Jewish.

has met with Trump several times in the last few years, showing that he still has political clout.

A.B. Krongard may well have been the connection between Erik Prince of Blackwater Security Consulting and the CIA, and in 2007 there was controversy over whether Krongard had joined Blackwater as a member of its Advisory Board; he was also mentioned in the 9/11 Commission Report in connection to possible insider trading through trades made by Alex. Brown & Sons, where he was at one time Chief Executive Officer and Chairman of the Board:

> A single U.S.-based institutional investor with no conceivable ties to al Qaeda purchased 95 percent of the UAL puts on September 6 (2001) as part of a strategy that also included buying 115,000 shares of American on September 10. Similarly, much of the seemingly suspicious trading on September 10 was traced to a specific U.S.-based options trading newsletter...which recommended these trades.

Krongard was named Executive Director of the CIA in March 2001, having joined the agency in 1998.

Krongard is on Apollo Global Management's Board of Directors with wealthy and powerful Jews Leon Black (co-founder, Chairman, and CEO of Apollo) and New England Patriots football franchise owner Robert Kraft. Black, *The New York Times* reported, paid Jeffrey Epstein at least $50 million between 2012 and 2017. Krongard's wife was a senior partner of Apollo Global Management from January 2002 to December 2004. From 1994 to 2000, she served as the Chief Executive Officer of Rothschild Asset Management and as Senior Managing Director for Rothschild North America. Additionally, she served as a director of Rothschild North America, Rothschild Asset Management, Rothschild Asset Management BV, and Rothschild Realty Inc. and as Managing Member of Rothschild Recovery Fund. She served as a director of US Airways Group Inc. from 2003 until its merger with American Airlines.

A.B. Krongard is also an Emeritus Trustee of Johns Hopkins Medicine, as is Sharon Percy Rockefeller. Johns Hopkins Medicine Deputy Director Anita Cicero's expertise areas according to Johns Hopkins Medicine's website are: Public health law; epidemic and pandemic preparedness policy; global catastrophic biological risk issues; biosecurity; bio surveillance; and international disease surveillance. Her professional profile informs that "Cicero has also launched a number of initiatives to improve mutual understanding and collaboration with countries including the People's Republic of China," and that Cicero's work as an attorney "required constructive engagement with members of Congress; the World Health Organization; the European Commission; the US Food and Drug Administration; the US Departments of State, Defense, and Health and Human Services; and the Environmental Protection Agency." The CEO of Johns Hopkins Medicine, Paul Rothman, attended MIT, accepted a postdoctoral fellowship at Columbia University prior to joining its medical school faculty, and is on the Board of Merck. In a July 2020 interview with *The Jerusalem Post*, Rothman stated that "big data sets assisted by artificial intelligence technologies could help doctors personalize treatments for coronavirus patients." That same month, the Johns Hopkins Center for Health Security published a report entitled *Resetting Our Response: Changes Needed in the US Approach to COVID-19*. "Unlike many countries in the world, the United States is not currently on course to get control of this epidemic. It's time to reset." Huh, reset you say? That sounds awfully familiar…

Returning to Zamel, according to a 2013 article from *Fast Company*:

> Other simulations [Wikistrat] has recently worked on that Zamel was able to discuss include the future of Al Qaeda, a thought exercise on "White House initiatives designed to recast America's relationship with Latin America"; "Countering Conventional Wisdom: The Coming Resource Wars"; and a forecasting exercise on relations between Turkey, Iran, and Saudi Arabia.

Intersecting with the aims of Israel, Gearóid Ó Colmáin makes the vital observation that:

> One only has to observe the clenched fist of the US colour revolutions and the constant appeal to youthful rebellion to understand how capitalism is now deepening its grip on humanity through the appropriation of leftist, revolutionary symbology. Indeed, contemporary US capitalism is, to employ a phrase of Trotsky's, "permanent revolution." Or, in the words of…Thomas Barnett (Barnett was a strategic advisor to former US Secretary of Defense Donald Rumsfeld), "US-style globalisation is pure socio-economic revolution." But it is a revolution which wages war on the working class. One of the results of the 'Arab Spring' in Egypt was the abrogation of labour laws requiring companies to pay workers during periods of factory closure due to lack of product demand… Colour revolutions often involve the transportation of thousands of

foreigners to the place of protest by US intelligence agencies operating through NGOS. This happened in Belarus in 2010. Many of the youths (read: "migrants") attempting to get into Hungary could be used as a battering ram to destablize the Hungarian nation-state...Since the fomentation of the 'Arab Spring' by the CIA and its numerous NGOS in 2011, NATO's total destruction of Libya and its proxy war against Syria, millions of people have been turned into refugees. That is why they are fleeing to Europe. But it is not the principal reason for the 'current crisis', or rather the current phase of an ongoing and deepening crisis...This new geostrategic initiative involves using desperate refugees as weapons for the purposes of US/Zionist divide and rule of the European continent. France's *Radio Internationale* has revealed that over 95 percent of migrants in the current flow into Europe are young males between 20 and 35 years old.

The free movement of people and goods is absolutely central to the neoliberal system, and it does not matter if the people in question are genuine refugees or economic migrants for the purposes of the ruling class. Within the confines of their new "open societies," these mostly fighting-age males serve a variety of functions, first realized by the United States in the fracture of European societies and as economic units, but not to be out-done, many countries such as the Netherlands (and the US within its own borders) have adopted similar tactics against themselves! Well, against their own people in any case, and sometimes, as with the Netherlands and the US, hand-in-glove, as Giles Scott-Smith writes of:

> Efforts by the Dutch government itself to promote a positive understanding of citizenship in alliance with civil organizations. One important partner in this venture was the Islam and Citizenship Foundation, founded in 2000 to stimulate "dual-citizenship" awareness by highlighting the compatibility of Islamic values with a multicultural Dutch society. As part of its function, the Foundation compiled a comprehensive database of all Muslims active in Dutch society and evolved into the main mouthpiece for this diverse and disconnected community. In the wake of 9/11 the Foundation, led by Islamic convert Yassin Hartog, became a key ally in the U.S. Embassy's public diplomacy outreach effort, providing contacts on "the future Muslim leadership of tomorrow." Hartog was a member of a predominantly Muslim multi-regional group that toured the U.S. in 2003, and he has described how, despite the evident suspicion

amongst the participants, the program's openness and ability to provide access to a genuine cross-section of opinion in the U.S. had the desired effect. At some point everyone "was cured of their paranoia," generating a real awareness of what the U.S. could offer. Hartog himself was most struck by the ability of U.S. citizens to accommodate dual identities (e.g. Japanese-American), in contrast to the situation in the Netherlands. From Hartog's unique position in facilitating the program, he remains convinced that it "touched" in some way all the Dutch Muslims who participated, from removing "insensitive judgements" to being "inspired that things can happen in a different way." By 2005, in the wake of the murder of film-maker Theo van Gogh by Mohammed Bouyeri, the U.S. embassy in The Hague was running an all-mission Integration Issues Working Group to prioritise and coordinate these efforts. The IVLP was said to be an "especially effective tool."

According to the US State Department's website under the Bureau of Educational and Cultural Affairs, the International Visitor Leadership Program (IVLP) is their:

> ...premier professional exchange program. Through short-term visits to the United States, current and emerging foreign leaders in a variety of fields experience this country firsthand and cultivate lasting relationships with their American counterparts. Professional meetings reflect the participants' professional interests and support the foreign policy goals of the United States...Participants are selected by Foreign Service Officers at U.S. Embassies around the world... Alumni who are Current and Former Heads of State: 350+.

As with many of the organizations founded around or just after the conclusion of the First World War with the world ripe for a remodeling on the back of global capitalism, the Foreign Policy Association was founded in 1918 to support Woodrow Wilson's internationalist proposals, including the League of Nations, as the League of Free Nations Association. In 1923 it was reconstituted as the Foreign Policy Association with "a commitment to the careful study of all sides of international questions affecting the U.S. John Foster Dulles and Eleanor Roosevelt were among the incorporators." Its current President and CEO Noel V. Lateef worked for the US State Department and Daisy Soros, widow of George Soros's brother Paul, sits on the Foreign Policy Association's Board.

Daisy Soros is also an Honorary Trustee of the International House of

New York—opened in 1924 primarily on the back of funding from John D. Rockefeller, Jr., and it has maintained heavy Rockefeller involvement to this day—as is Henry Kissinger. Past Board of Trustees Chairmen include David Rockefeller, John McCloy (former Chairman of both the Council on Foreign Relations and the Ford Foundation), Gerald Ford, Dwight D. Eisenhower, George Marshall (as Secretary of State oversaw the implementation of the Marshall Plan), and Paul Volcker (Twelfth Chairman of the Federal Reserve). I-House's current Board of Trustees Chairman is Frank G. Wisner (US State Department "negotiator" with Egypt during the Arab Spring color revolutions, Refugees International, AIG, the Arab Gulf States Institute, the National Security Network; his father was a major CIA figure and is covered in *The Transgender-Industrial Complex*) and recent President Calvin Sims was formerly with *The New York Times* and the Ford Foundation. Its current Board members include connections to major globalist names like JP Morgan Chase, Columbia University, Harvard, and the Council on Foreign Relations, among a litany of others ranging from high finance to biotechnology and pharmaceuticals; the Board also includes CFR member Fareed Zakaria, who is like a bad penny.

Wisner is also a member of the Advisory Council of Ergo alongside David Cohen, who spent decades at the CIA before serving as the NYPD's Deputy Commissioner for Intelligence from 2002-2013. Another member of the council, Chairman and CEO of Relationship Science (described by Ergo as, "an innovative networking tool that the *New York Times* says 'could radically change the way Wall Street does business'") Neal Goldman, was an investment banker at Lehman Brothers and a term member at the Council on Foreign Relations, as well as a Young Global Leader with the World Economic Forum. Other Advisory Board members include ties to MI6, the International Rescue Committee, Kissinger Associates, NATO, the Atlantic Council, and more intelligence-gathering, high finance, and senior governmental connections.

Jeffrey Epstein associate and globalist functionary Bill Richardson is a former member of the Advisory Council of Ergo, which describes itself as an intelligence and advisory firm specializing in dynamic markets and geopolitical analysis. Bill Richardson, former Governor of New Mexico and Chairman of Freedom House, alleged rapist of an underage girl trafficked to him by Jeffrey Epstein and Ghislaine Maxwell, with both Epstein and Richardson also Council on Foreign Relations members, is also connected to Genie Energy, joining its Strategic Advisory Board in September 2015. Richardson taught courses at Columbia University, partnered with Virgin Galactic to build a commercial spaceport as governor, has made some very bizarre and covert "diplomatic missions" to North Korea, and in 2001, joined "geopolitical consulting firm" Kissinger Associates, Inc., founded by Henry Kissinger. In 1999, Mack McLarty joined to create a specific branch in Washington, DC called Kissinger McLarty Associates, which became a corporate member of David Rockefeller's Council of the Americas, which was central to the conception of what became NAFTA; Kissinger McLarty Associates is now a separate entity.

Kissinger Associates has worked closely with the Blackstone Group as part of a "strategic alliance," and the firm's staff and Board include prominent former senior officials in the US government as well as alums of NATO, the CIA, the Federal Reserve, and more. One representative would be Jami Miscik, CEO and Vice Chairman of Kissinger Associates, Inc., a member of the Council on Foreign Relations, former Deputy Director for Intelligence of the CIA, one-time Global Head of Sovereign Risk for Lehman Brothers, former director for intelligence programs on the National Security Council, and Board member of Morgan Stanley, General Motors, and In-Q-Tel (alongside Krongard and former CIA Director George Tenet; In-Q-Tel is for all intents and purposes the CIA's venture capital firm and forms a clear alliance with Silicon Valley), as well as Co-Vice Chairman of the American Ditchley Foundation, described on their own website as:

> ...established in 1958 to advance US-UK understanding following World War II. Over time, that transatlantic purpose has expanded to a broader mission—promoting global understanding and dialogue among nations around the globe. Today, the American Ditchley Foundation works with The Ditchley Foundation in the UK and the Canadian Ditchley Foundation to bring together experts and leaders from a variety of fields to foster a better understanding of, and solutions to, issues of global concern.

The American Ditchley Foundation's Chairman is former Ambassador R. Nicholas Burns, Professor at the Kennedy School at Harvard University, former US Under Secretary of State for Political Affairs, and yes, Council on Foreign Relations member. Prominent members of the American Ditchley Foundation's Board include representatives from the RAND Corporation, Carnegie Endowment for International Peace, *The Washington Post*, the Council on Foreign Relations, Human Rights Watch, the London Stock Exchange Group, numerous former senior officials and diplomats in the US government, the Brookings Institution, Goldman Sachs, the German Marshall Fund of the United States, the International Rescue Committee UK, and Rockefeller & Co. The Ditchley Foundation's UK Board looks much the same: Huawei Technologies UK, Google, Microsoft, Santander, Goldman Sachs,

Ridge Clean Energy, Bloomberg, the Council on Foreign Relations, and numerous government officials. The Canadian Ditchley, more of the same: Alberta's Climate Change and Emissions Management Corporation, Deloitte, Power Corporation of Canada, Montreal Stock Exchange, et cetera.

Returning to Bill Richardson, he was also the US Ambassador to the United Nations (1997-1998) and Energy Secretary in the Clinton Administration (1998-2001), and engineered a sweetheart deal for Israel while governor with the 2008 New Mexico-Israel Business exchange, "signed together with Israeli Minister of Industry Eli Yishai, spells out a process to create strategic partnerships to cooperate on the advancement of joint water and energy technologies," according to *Jewish Virtual Library*. Grant recipients in New Mexico from US-Israel binational foundations include: the New Mexico Institute of Mining and Technology, the University of New Mexico, New Mexico State University, Aguila Technologies Group, Los Alamos National Lab, and Loveplace Respiratory Research Institute. Epstein held a major estate in New Mexico called the Zorro Ranch. John Q. Publius, in his book *The Way Life Should Be?* connects insiders and former Maine Senators George Mitchell—another Epstein associate—and William Cohen. He writes:

> Cohen is also on the Advisory Board of the Partnership for a Secure America, which, like Mitchell's American Security Project, considers "climate change" to be a "threat multiplier." Other organizations of which Cohen is currently or has been involved with include ViacomCBS, the Council on Foreign Relations, AIG, MIC Industries, the Brookings Institution, the Atlantic Partnership, Thayer Capital, and the Trilateral Commission.[13]

Additionally, the Cohen Group and globalist firm DLA Piper, where Mitchell (who "earned high praise from former ADL National Director Abe Foxman while serving as Special Envoy for Middle East Peace under Barack Obama," is in the Bilderberg Group, and according to his DLA Piper biography "In 2000 and 2001, at the request of President Clinton, Prime Minister Ehud Barak, and Chairman Yasser Arafat, Senator Mitchell served as Chairman of an International Fact-Finding Committee on violence in the Middle East...The Committee's recommendation, widely known as The Mitchell Report, was endorsed by the Bush Administration, the European Union and by many other governments") was Chairman of the Global Board and remains a consultant, have a very cozy long-standing relationship. This relationship also

---

[13] Publius, *The Way Life Should Be?*, 345.

includes the Council of Foreign Relations (CFR) as Laurence Shoup illustrates:

> The Cohen Group was founded by former Defense Secretary and CFR director William S. Cohen when he left the Clinton administration in early 2001. The objectives of the firm are: "helping multinational clients explore opportunities overseas as well as solve problems that may develop. The Cohen Group has the unique ability to provide our clients with truly comprehensive tools for understanding and shaping their business, political, legal, regulatory, and media environments." The Cohen Group has a strategic alliance with the international law firm DLA Piper, one of the largest law firms in the world. Both the Cohen Group and DLA Piper have multiple connections to the CFR. Besides Cohen himself, Marc Grossman, a vice chair at the Cohen Group, is a Council member, and former ambassador and undersecretary of state Nicholas Burns is both a CFR member and a senior counselor at Cohen. Former Senator George J. Mitchell, DLA Piper's former chairman, was a Council director, and former U.S. senator and CFR member Tom Daschle is a policy adviser at this law firm.[14]

How the West was won and reality spun. John Q. Publius expands:

> The Cohen Group—which was among the organizations represented at the World Bank Group's 2019 annual meeting that also included the CFR—and DLA Piper each feature both current and former members within or affiliated with the CFR, as well as other major geo-political players; these connections are anything but incidental. Major DLA Piper alumni include: A.B. Krongard, former Executive Director of the CIA; Mel Martinez, former Senator, member of the Bipartisan Policy Center, and JP Morgan Chase's Chairman of the Southeast US and Latin America; and Harry Cummings McPherson, Jr., who served as counsel and special counsel to Lyndon B. Johnson from 1965 to 1969 and was Johnson's chief speechwriter from 1966 to 1969. DLA Piper has a "global pro bono initiative" called New Perimeter, where the President of the NGO the Public Welfare Foundation (PWF)—endowed by the Tides Center, the ACLU, and Van Jones's Color of Change, among others—Mary McClymont serves on the Advisory Board; McClymont was previously Chairwoman of the Board for the Migration Policy

---

[14] Shoup, *Wall Street's Think Tank*, 124.

Center, National Director for Legalization at the Migration and Refugee Services of the US Catholic Conference of Catholic Bishops, President and CEO of InterAction (an alliance of US-based "international development" and "humanitarian" NGOs that subscribe to the UN's Sustainable Development agenda), a trial attorney for the US Department of Justice's Civil Rights Division, and she performed various functions for the Ford Foundation and Amnesty International. She is the also the co-founder of Grantmakers Concerned with Immigrants and Refugees... Additionally, DLA Piper represents over 150 Israeli companies and investors. From the firm's website: The firm has also assisted over 75+ of its foreign clients who require legal assistance in Israel...Our Israel Country Group delivers all the benefits of a global elite law firm through a team of lawyers dedicated to the Israel market. Our broad knowledge and access to local advice has led to us becoming a key address for advising Israeli clients as they do business across the globe. Recent involvement has included advising on M&A transactions in Japan, Norway, Spain and South Africa; HR matters in Brazil, Singapore and Italy; real estate deals in the US, Germany and the UK; IP and tax in Turkey, Dubai, Australia and Czech Republic; fund formation in Poland and the US; commercial and mining advice in Africa; and litigation advice in the UK, Africa and the US.[15]

Returning to Ergo, according to their website, "across the globe Ergo taps into a range of intelligence streams—human sources, government records, company data, local press, and social media—to provide customized solutions and subscription products for our clients." Ergo's CEO is RP Eddy, described in his website biography thusly:

Previously, he served at the White House National Security Council and as a senior US diplomat. He was Chief of Staff to US Ambassador to the UN Richard Holbrooke, Senior Adviser to Secretary of Energy Bill Richardson, and Senior Policy Officer to UN Secretary-General Kofi Annan, where he served as an architect of the Global Fund to Prevent AIDS, TB, and Malaria. R.P. was a Managing Director at the Gerson Lehrman Group and a Team Leader at the Monitor Group. The World Economic Forum honored him as a "Global Leader for Tomorrow." He is a life member of the Council on Foreign Relations,

---

[15] Publius, *The Way Life Should Be?*, 348-351.

50 | THE OPEN SOCIETY PLAYBOOK

and was an associate at Harvard University's Belfer Center. R.P. is co-author, with Richard Clarke, of the best-selling and award winning, "Warnings: Finding Cassandras to Stop Catastrophes."

Speaking of the World Economic Forum, the half-Jewish Isabel Maxwell (Epstein co-trafficker Ghislaine's sister; Isabel's first husband was the son of the Jewish Carl Djerassi, nicknamed "the father of the birth control pill," a leading figure with the Jewish George Rosenkranz on the team that created progestin norethisterone to be used as an oral contraceptive) is a Technology Pioneer of the World Economic Forum; her WEF biography states Maxwell has:

> Over fifteen years' experience in Silicon Valley, Israel and Los Angeles. Formerly: Senior Adviser, Grameen America, which makes microloans to poor women; co-founded Magellan, the earliest online search engine, acquired by Excite in 1996; experience in television and feature film documentary production, UK and US. Technology Pioneer, World Economic Forum. President Emerita, Commtouch. Director, Israel Venture Network including, since 2004, built up its social entrepreneur programme in Israel. Governor of the Board, since 1999, Peres Center for Peace; since 2003, American Friends of Rabin.

From Isabel Maxwell's Wikipedia page, "mother stated that while all of her children were brought up Anglican, Isabel was 'very taken by the Jewish faith and the politics in Israel.'"

Continuing with Ergo, their website declares that:

> In 2017, Richard Clarke [MIT alumnus, US State Department, US National Security Council] and R.P. Eddy in their best-selling and award winning book, *Warnings: Finding Cassandras to Stop Catastrophes*, stated that an infectious disease pandemic, much like the one we're suffering through today, was on its way.

Ergo's COVID-19 Intelligence Forum, a sub-set of its Flashpoints Forum (both chaired by General HR McMaster), according to their website:

> ...focuses exclusively on the outbreak and its impact and consists of: intelligence seeking to predict global government actions (or inaction), including economic stimulus predictions and implications, ongoing disease progression and epidemiological curve tracking,

intelligence on leading vaccines and other medical interventions, potential for social unrest, and access to other key indicators and warnings to navigate COVID-19.

Clarke is a Contributing Expert, as is former Food and Drug Administration (FDA) Commissioner Mark McClellan, and many other experts feature ties to the transgender agenda and medical-industrial complex, itself a key part of the intended global overhaul and transhumanist global laboratory in the works which will, if successful, see complete consolidation of power in these people's hands from a digital-social currency to the food supply. The gravity of people quite literally trying to modify/experiment on everything from anthrax-spliced "vaccines" and other highly experimental vaccines, which have the potential to literally alter your DNA, to your food, water, and "gender" having total control cannot be understated.

With Ergo, similar connections proliferate and often overlap such as Managing Partner Evan Pressman (CNN, Council on Foreign Relations term member), Senior Advisor Rachel Bitecofer ("Her innovative election forecasting model accurately predicted the 2018 midterms five months before Election Day, far ahead of other forecasting methods"), Partner Kate Crumrine ("previously worked at the CIA and for Booz Allen Hamilton, where she was responsible for monitoring open-source reporting on counterterrorism threats across South Asia"), and all sorts of military (Senior Advisor HR McMaster)-media-intelligence-academia-governmental overlap, the kind so pervasive in and central to the maintenance and expansion of this system's grip.

Frank G. Wisner is also the Chairman of the Board of the Arab Gulf States Institute; its President is Douglas A. Silliman of the US State Department, the Bilateral US-Arab Chamber of Commerce, and the Council on Foreign Relations. Corporate Members include Raytheon, Lockheed Martin, General Atomics, Chevron, and EOG Resources (named Enron Oil & Gas Company before its separation from Enron in 1999, Wisner is on its Board of Directors). Wisner was also on the Advisory Board of the now-defunct National Security Network along with the half-Jewish Wesley Clark who stated, according to *The National Interest*, "There is no place in modern Europe for ethnically pure states. That's a 19th-century idea and we are trying to transition it into the 21st century, and we are going to do it with multi-ethnic states" and was responsible for the deaths of hundreds of civilians during NATO's "peacekeeping" bombing operations in Yugoslavia as NATO's Supreme Allied Commander Europe (SACEUR).

Other Advisory Board members included Anne-Marie Slaughter (University of Chicago, Harvard, US State Department) and the Jewish Sandy

Berger (National Security Advisor, long-time friend of Bill Clinton, Harvard and Cornell alum—while at Cornell he was in the Quill and Dagger society with Jewish neocon, former President of the World Bank, US Deputy Secretary of Defense, US Ambassador to Indonesia, dean of Johns Hopkins School of Advanced International Studies, and currently a visiting scholar at the American Enterprise Institute, Paul Wolfowitz). According to Nancy Pelosi, quoted in a January 1997 *Washington Post* piece, Berger was also "the point person at the Hogan & Hartson law firm for the trade office of the Chinese government. He was a lawyer-lobbyist," and per his Wikipedia entry, "Key achievements during Berger's NSC tenure included the 1995 peso recovery package in Mexico, NATO enlargement, Operation Desert Fox...[and] the NATO bombing campaign against Yugoslavia."

Chairman of the National Security Network's Advisory Board was the Jewish Leslie Gelb, who cut his teeth in the mid-1960s as an Executive Assistant for Jewish Senator Jacob Javits, one of the key figures in the passing of the Hart-Celler Act of 1965 that would subsequently flood the United States with mass migration from the Third World. According to his *New York Times* obituary, "he was discovered at Harvard by Prof. Henry A. Kissinger." Gelb held key posts with the US government such as Assistant Secretary of State and Director of the Bureau of Politico-Military Affairs during the Carter administration from 1977 to 1979, as well as with the Brookings Institution, *The New York Times*, the International Institute for Strategic Studies (IISS), Columbia University, and the Carnegie Endowment for International Peace,[16] among many more. He was also the President of the Council on Foreign Relations from 1993-2003.

Despite the calls for democracy, the state itself is ultimately subservient to unaccountable figures who have used it to further their own aims, endeavoring to render everywhere exactly the same. The purpose of this book is to hold those figures accountable, with the reader gaining insight into not only who they are and how the globalist system works in their favor, but the various mechanisms employed to ensure that all of the impediments to their project are destroyed. The general thrust in the late-twentieth and now twenty-first century with regards to non-compliant and -integrated states has increasingly taken the "color revolution" form, a new kind of hybrid that has been concurrent with forcible regime changes by military might such as in Iraq and less-direct but still Establishment-sponsored coups such as in Bolivia and Libya, respectively. Typically coinciding with an election a disfavored

---

[16] Its current Chair is none other than the Jewish Penny Pritzker of the Pritzker family so central to the transgender agenda and thoroughly documented in my book *The Transgender-Industrial Complex*.

candidate is likely to win (such as Alexander Lukashenko in Belarus), the color revolution's rough format is, as A.S. Brychkov and G.A. Nikonorov write:

> International "independent observers" are usually hooked up with this whole "industry" and perform the function of "objective" external assessment of how legitimate the election was carried out. This assessment usually coincides with the data provided by NGOs and that is the goal. The purpose is to bring the people to conclusion that authorities are deceiving them and draw them out onto the streets to protest. Social networks, the Internet, and cell phones are commonly used to organize such protests. It is possible that rallies will be staged with slogans like "they stole our victory" with Western liberal media at hand. It is also possible that during these rallies and marches provocations may take place initiated by trained individuals who have no real stake in these protests...On the whole, it can be stated that the principal goals of defeating a geopolitical adversary by provoking an internal overthrow are the following: Weakening the opponent; Change the political course from "Our nation comes first" to pro-Western; Gaining control over the country's resources using "controlled chaos" technologies. Authors of the "controlled chaos" conception are specialists from a number of US research institutes, such as Rand Corporation, etc. and main clients are the Roman Club which later on became the Three Party Commission, Bilderberg Club. The general concepts they developed in the 1970's were placed in motion by IMF, World Bank, and WTO. The United States is the principal instigator and financier of "reformatting" the global geopolitical map, which is consistent with the role this country has been playing as the world policeman and fundraiser for...transnational capital.[17]

The US as a cohesive entity, as its 2020 Presidential Election evidenced, is ceding ground amid its own color revolution to the globalist Establishment's next iteration; nevertheless, the massive infrastructure of the military-industrial complex and the vast matrix of NGOs, think tanks, and the like will continue serving the interests of those at the top of the pyramid while the country is engulfed in conflict. With over two decades of practice, the color revolution model is now being imported; with these color revolutions:

---

[17] Brychkov, "Color Revolutions in Russia," 6.

We can see the connection between street protests and grants/fellowships offered by such US funds as Open Society, a George Soros Fund, Harvard University, Albert Einstein Institute, International Republican Institute, National Democratic Institute, International Center for Nonviolent Conflicts, International Institute for Strategic Studies in London, and many others. Considerable funding for "color revolutions" was provided through SEED (Support of East European Democracy), which is fiscally supported by the US State Department. Finally, we should acknowledge that international bodies, such as UN, OSCE, International Tribunal, and international alliances that US has joined are nothing but tools for transnational financial institutions, having gained control over the US, to achieve their objectives and serve their interests. The main historic mission of the United States is believed to be in establishing world order under American management...According to this law [of Spreading Democracy] the US has to create conditions for promoting human rights and democracy as fundamental and inextricable part of the project for toppling "dictators." The US Congress and the Federal Government declare and legally establish their right to decide what government and in what country are subject to removal.[18]

The color revolutions model requires a closer inspection, to which we will now turn.

---

[18] Ibid., 5.

3

THE COLOR REVOLUTIONS

The name color revolution is derived from the fact that the names of these "revolutions" were based on the colors of what were often flowers used as symbols. In order for these "revolutions" to be successful, with the exception of the uses of Islam as a medium-term ideological wedge and long-term economic investment, they must not be ideological and instead focus on vagaries such as "freedom," "democracy," and "reform." The Armenian Velvet Revolution of 2018 was warmly-received by the globalist Establishment; immediately following the installation of the new government, the International Monetary Fund (IMF) approved a $248.2 million standby facility to support Armenia. Outgoing EU ambassador Piotr Świtalski praised the new government's efforts to grow the economy and "maintain a balanced foreign policy." USAID has had its hooks in Armenia since 1992 and has been working tirelessly since to peel it away from the Russian axis and bring it into the neoliberal globalist fold. Following this dubious color revolution, as Justin Keay writes for *Global Finance*:

> In mid-February [2019], the government launched a five-year plan it calls an "economic revolution..." The government plan also prioritizes solar energy...The government has already taken steps to make the economy more attractive for investors. Sectors including IT and tourism have been earmarked for development and as targets for foreign direct investment (FDI). Infrastructure is another priority, especially the key transport corridor to Georgia.... "The authorities have moved to root out corruption, have initiated a major tax-reform program and have tackled monopolies in what were essentially uncompetitive, closed areas of the economy," says Dimitar Bogov, the European Bank for Reconstruction and Development's regional lead economist for Eastern Europe and the Caucasus.... One of the largest FDI projects in Armenia [is] headed by Anglo-American firm Lydian International, [a] mine...expected

to yield some 225,000 ounces of gold a year.... Bank reform is another priority, even though nonperforming loans are only around 5%, capital levels are strong and the sector is well regulated by the Central Bank of Armenia.... Olga Ignatieva, senior director in the banks team at Fitch Ratings [says] "Consolidation is needed if banks are to realize economies of scale and play a bigger role in the economy."

Certainly this raft of "reforms" and opening-up to global capital should be familiar to the reader, and affirming that Armenia is headed in the "right" direction from the perspective of the ruling class, "Pashinian's revolution is a predominately positive one; because it has swept away an authoritarian, patronage-based system that the country couldn't afford and is being led by people with a genuine commitment to change," says Laurence Broers, a Caucasus specialist at Chatham House in London, quoted in the same article.

Chatham House, one of the central cogs in this network and a British analog to Freedom House and the National Endowment for Democracy, is a perfect encapsulation of globalist interests: the Queen of England herself is a patron, and its Council includes people like Mark Spelman (Future of the Internet Initiative, World Economic Forum; member, American Chamber of Commerce Executive Council); Jim O'Neill (Commercial Secretary to the Treasury 2015–16; Chairman, Goldman Sachs Asset Management 2010–13); Simon Fraser (Managing Partner, Flint Global Ltd; Permanent Under-Secretary, Foreign & Commonwealth Office and Head of the Diplomatic Service 2010–15); Ann Cormack (Executive Head of Human Resources, DeBeers Group; Non-Executive Director, Foreign & Commonwealth Office Audit and Risk Assurance Committee; council member, British Institute of Energy Economics 2005–16); and Jawad Iqbal (Visiting Senior Fellow, Institute of Global Affairs, London School of Economics and Political Science; previously senior executive roles at the BBC). Corporate members include Barclays, Bloomberg, the British Army, the City of London, the UK Defense Solutions Center, Apple, the European Investment Bank, Google, the Saudi Center for International and Strategic Partnerships, the European Bank for Reconstruction and Development, GlaxoSmithKline, Morgan Stanley, and Goldman Sachs International.

Already in 1939, Chatham House was exploring post-war possibilities for this new world order through the Committee on Reconstruction, and alumni would go on to join the United Nations and the International Monetary Fund (IMF). In the 1950s, Chatham House increasingly became "concerned" with "racial equality" and "de-colonization." Chatham House would eventually spawn the Institute of Race Relations, which would receive funding from the

Ford Foundation and the Africa Private Enterprise Group (including Unilever and Barclays). It was an early prototype for the kinds of ideologically-driven "social justice" organizations we see today, but as is the case with the vast majority of these initiatives, it was undertaken with the expectation that it would produce a significant financial windfall. The connections between "social justice," governmental and supra-governmental entities, big business, and high finance are not incidental. They all mutually reinforce each other and work synergistically to amplify profit and accelerate what is framed as "progress," but is really a world-wrecking endeavor.

Chatham House functions the same way as the NED, NDI, CIPE, Freedom House, et cetera and actually receives funding from the NED and the US State Department, in addition to the European Commission, the UN High Commissioner for Refugees (UNHCR), NATO, Bloomberg, the Rothschilds, the Rockefeller Foundation, the British Army, the European Bank for Reconstruction and Development, Fitch Ratings, Alexander Soros, the European Endowment for Democracy, Google, BlackRock UK, and the World Health Organization (see Appendix B for a full list of Chatham House funders—this is well worth referring to as it shows just how uniform and wide-ranging support for these seismic and destructive projects is). Bear in mind that these individuals, organizations, and institutions don't just support the current state of affairs, *they actively fund it.*

Chatham House is to be distinguished from the Chatham House Foundation, a 501(c)(3) tax-exempt "charity" registered in the United States in 1982. The Foundation is a separate legal entity from Chatham House and has its own Board of Trustees. It makes grants to Chatham House under its objectives. The Foundation's primary donors include the Jewish Jacob Safra, described by Katharina Bart as "the most likely representative of the Safra family to inherit the patriarch's role" of the Safra banking dynasty, and Edward M. Siskind, formerly of Goldman Sachs and founder of Cale Street Partners European real estate finance firm.

Chatham House is squarely in support of oligarchic "one world-ism." As indicative of their position, they refer to a "descent towards populist authoritarianism," which is obviously an oxymoron. They simply object to Europeans—and all people for that matter—having a say in their own governance. Again evidencing their clear bias toward the ruling class and the status quo, Chatham House's European Program is supported by the likes of the City of London, the US government, HSBC, and the Carnegie Corporation of New York.

The European Partnership for Democracy was also very supportive of Armenia's Velvet Revolution; a July 2019 paper written by Hasmik Grigoryan with contributions from Stepan Grigoryan notes that because it is in the "EU neighborhood," it remains of strategic interest (also consider the geo-strategic positioning particularly as regards the United States discussed earlier). The EU-Armenia Comprehensive and Enhanced Partnership Agreement (CEPA) is cited as an "important opportunity to further European cooperation with Armenia and must be a major focus of political and economic relations."

The Office for Democratic Institutions and Human Rights of the OSCE (OSCE/ODIHR), the Parliamentary Assembly of the Council of Europe, and the European Parliament have in the past sent "observers" to Armenia to oversee the "democratic process," and in 2009, Armenia joined the EU's Eastern Partnership (EaP) initiative and began negotiations with the EU over a potential Association Agreement and a Deep and Comprehensive Free Trade Agreement, but in 2013 they reversed course and began exploring membership in the Russia-dominated Eurasian Economic Union (EAEU). Unsurprisingly, in the months preceding this decision, a number of NGOs began fomenting unrest against the government. Tellingly, during the Velvet Revolution five years later, major neoliberal Establishment press vehicles such as Radio Free Europe gave the protestors positive coverage, as always framing the protests as "against corruption" and "for democracy," rather than as engineered protests to serve the Establishment. What is of supremely vital importance beyond geography and potentially-lucrative trade and foreign investment is that the main strategic assets in Armenia are along the Russian axis.

The Open Society Foundations has been active in Armenia since 1997; the Open Society Foundations-Armenia's current Board Chair Artak Kyurumyan, per their website, "As an independent consultant...worked in the World Bank, European Union, USAID, DFID funded projects on implementation of medium term expenditure framework, programme budgeting, public debt management, etc." The Establishment at large began pouring much more money and external support into Armenia beginning in the mid-2000s, surely as a response to a resurgent Russia that was breaking away from its "Wild West" heyday that had proven so lucrative to global capital and its disproportionately-Jewish oligarchs. George Soros was quoted in the 1990s again from the *New Yorker* about his foundation functionaries in Russia:

> "I invited people, took them on the trip, and it turned out that they were all too old and too Jewish!" He chuckled. "And not acceptable. I mean, you can't be that Jewish in Russia. So I told them, 'You can't have more than one-third Jews on the board.'"

Too obvious, especially in light of the fact that in 2014 from *Y Net News*, a report by Russian banking website lanta.ru, revealed 48 of the 200 richest people in Russia were Jews, with a combined net worth of $132.9 billion. Alex Tenzer, "a prominent activist in the Russian Jewish community," was unhappy with the publication of the list as "dangerous" because it "could fan the flames of xenophobia." Tenzer said, "If you sum up the Russian elite, you can say that most of the funds and most of the wealth in Russia belongs to a population of people who are not Russian, and this is a real danger, especially now." Ashkenazim represent 21% of all the billionaires in Russia, even though they comprise only 0.12% of the population.[19] The Ashkenazi billionaires include Viktor Vekselberg (net worth of $17.2 billion), Leonid Michelson (net worth of $15.6 billion), German Khan (net worth of $11.3 billion), Mikhail Prokhorov (net worth of $10.9 billion), and Roman Abramovich (net worth of $9.1 billion). Additionally, and proving once again that reality is no obstacle, a 2018 *Haaretz* article noted that:

> The special prosecutor's probe into Russian meddling in the 2016 election offers an unsettling journey for anyone steeped in Russian Jewry.... Of ten billionaires with Kremlin ties who funneled political contributions to Donald Trump and a number of top Republican leaders, at least five are Jewish.

Interesting that CNN never got around to mentioning this fact.

Returning to the ample support of the European "liberal democracies" in Armenia:

> During the last ten years the EU, EUMS, Switzerland and Norway provided assistance to independent observers so that they could monitor the electoral process and issue recommendations. In total, the EU provided approximately €7 million in electoral assistance, including support to electoral reform and election observation. Through a UN Basket Fund to Support Electoral Processes in Armenia (SEPA), the EU, Germany and the UK provided approximately €4.7 million to the reform process of the Electoral Code and provided technical assistance for 2016 to 2017.... In terms of democracy support, the EU, EUMS, Switzerland and Norway allocated funds to state institutions, the civil society sector and media

---

[19] According to the estimates of Hebrew University demographer Sergio DellaPergola's World Jewish Population 2016, Russia is home to 179,500 Jews; Russia's overall population is 144.5 million.

to support good governance, transparency and justice, gender equality and human rights. Through the European Neighbourhood Instrument (ENI), Armenia is to receive between €252 million and €308 million for the period of 2014-2020. A total of 15% is allocated for strengthening institutions and good governance, while the rest was provided to the sectors of economic development and market opportunities (indicatively 35% of the total budget), connectivity, energy efficiency, environment and climate change (indicatively 15% of the total budget) and mobility and people-to-people contacts (indicatively 15% of the total budget). Another 15% was envisaged for complementary support for capacity development, institution building and strategic communication, and 5% for complementary support to civil society development. Support to the electoral process is another sector where EU assistance has played a key role, as exemplified by the basket fund to support the administration of the parliamentary elections in December 2018, in which the EU was swiftly and effectively joined by the United Kingdom, Germany and Sweden.... After the Velvet Revolution, the EU, as well as individual member states re-emphasised the importance of the electoral process and provided further financial assistance aimed at strengthening the capabilities of Armenia's electoral bodies so as to ensure that such critical elections were inclusive and transparent. Financial assistance was provided by the European Union (€1.5 million), Germany (€700,000), UK (£500,000) and Sweden (1.5 million Swedish krona).... A number of civil society organisations have pushed for the implementation of international women's rights conventions.... The "EU4HumanRights" project...has supported Armenian civil society organisations in engaging youth, journalists and human rights advocates in debates on human rights topics such as domestic violence, fair trials, torture, and tolerance. Such support is relevant for fostering wide-spread support for democratic principles and values. The EU has been particularly active in supporting civil society during elections, providing financial support to CSOs for organising election observation missions and increasing citizen participation. A number of CSOs were involved in encouraging participation in the 2018 Parliamentary elections, for instance...The Friedrich Naumann Foundation and the Friedrich-Ebert Foundation, as well as the UK Government...provided to political parties in the form of trainings and study trips.

Further "reforms" regarding market economics and "media diversity" are encouraged by the European Partnership for Democracy, among others, beyond the EU funding that has gone to Factor TV and Media Center. The European Partnership for Democracy (EPD) is, like Chatham House and company, yet another of these neoliberal front organizations. Its members are committed to "democracy," according to their website: "EPD has established itself as a key player on EU democracy support, both vis-à-vis the EU Institutions and the member states, as well as the wider democracy support community (experts, CSOs, donors)." Its members are: Canal France International—Agence française de développement médias (CFI); ARTICLE 19 (London); the Danish Institute for Parties and Democracy; Demo Finland; elbarlament (Berlin); ePaństwo Foundation (Warsaw); European Association for Local Democracy (ALDA); European Exchange; Netherlands Helsinki Committee; the Oslo Center; the Netherlands Institute for Multiparty Democracy; People in Need (Prague); Club de Madrid; the Catholic University of Portugal; and the Westminster Foundation for Democracy (London). The Westminster Foundation for Democracy partners with the World Bank, the UN, the EU, the German Agency for International Cooperation (GIZ), the Norwegian Ministry of Foreign Affairs, and the Organization for Security and Cooperation in Europe (OSCE). It is sponsored by the UK's Foreign and Commonwealth Office.

The European Endowment for Democracy, the NED, the NDI, and the Open Society Foundations, among others, have been central to Armenia's "transformation," which is framed as organic and grassroots but is anything but. One of the major reasons it appears so, beyond the media manipulation and tight control over information, which colors the international and even domestic perception of these color revolutions, is that these groups are primarily focused on supporting NGOs, "alternative" institutions and outlets, and "activists" within the country as proxies; thus, their agitation is at a remove. *RT* ran a report that Armenia, like the Ukraine, was a staging-ground and that the Establishment was going to "export the revolution" to Russia, Kazakhstan, and elsewhere.

A.S. Brychkov and G.A. Nikonorov rightly frame the color revolutions in the context of a logical extension of the Cold War when the End of History didn't occur, as Western proxies are used to undermine national sovereignty along the borders of the Russian sphere of influence to orient these nations in a more "pro-Western" direction; the neoliberal Establishment "create[s] an appearance of grand-scale social transformations that were allegedly in consort with hopes of the peoples" in the interests of "defeating a geopolitical adversary" and gaining another client state which will serve various purposes. The authors provide useful additional context:

The issue of "color revolutions" became much more relevant against the backdrop of global economic crisis, which is still far from being over, and as related to the fight for the limited world's resources, allowing to minimize losses for those countries that will be able to gain control over others' resources. Practically all "color revolutions" follow the same pattern that was tested in the countries of Central and Eastern Europe where they were called "velvet revolutions." "Color revolutions"—in Ukraine (2004, 2014) it was orange as in fruit, in Georgia (2003) it was rose, in Kirgizia (2005) tulip. Our historian N.A. Narochinskaya has observed the repeated pattern of all these "color revolutions," "Their scenarios are almost identical.... Economic and social foundation for these types of processes are characteristic of nations undergoing a transition period." Overthrow of undesirable political regime can be explained by a "cumulative" effect of superimposing internal and external problems that are acted upon by both outside and internal forces engaged within the sovereign state. Social overthrows can be disguised by not only political and economic but also religious demands, depending on the specific region. We can observe, for example, a tendency to stage "color revolutions" in the Central Asian CIS states under the flag of radical Islam.[20]

We will return to the usefulness of Islam later, but suffice it to say for now that it is a useful wedge or vehicle when it needs to be—especially in terms of sowing chaos and discord and "necessitating" the need for ever-increased surveillance. Simply defending borders would be the easiest solution, but evidently this is not possible—unless all of a sudden (à la COVID-19) it is.

In 1998, what in retrospect appears to be a trial run of the color revolutions model took place in a Slovakia that had been receiving significant attention from USAID. EU and US pressure and "anti-fraud" measures were designed to drum the isolationist incumbent Prime Minister Vladimir Mečiar out of office, and an international pressure campaign, extensive domestic propaganda focusing on younger people, and "election observers" essentially ensured Mečiar's defeat as well as Slovakia's eventual accession to the EU and NATO in 2004. The year prior, George Soros and the World Bank were successful in getting the governments of Hungary, Bulgaria, Croatia, the Czech Republic, Macedonia, Serbia and Montenegro, Slovakia, and Romania to endorse the launch of the "Decade of Roma Inclusion."

Speaking of Soros, the day Romanian leader Nicolae Ceausescu and his

---

[20] Brychkov, "Color Revolutions in Russia," 4.

wife Elena were buried (December 30th, 1989) after execution by firing squad on Christmas Day, Romania's first NGO, the Group for Social Dialogue (GDS) formed on the steps of the Bucharest Intercontinental Hotel—less than a week later, George Soros paid the group a visit. Though they did not accept Soros's initial offer for funding, Alin Teodorescu of the GDS remained in contact with George Soros and was instrumental in the establishment of the Soros Foundation in Romania not long after. Its *raison d'être* was, as Jacob Grandstaff describes it on *Medium*:

> ...to develop programs that would provide for the country's lack of civic initiatives and educational alternatives.... The Foundation worked with the Romanian Ministry of Education to introduce textbooks authored by its members into Romanian schools.

In a familiar pattern, USAID and Soros with his "private" foundation Fundaţia pentru o Societate Deschisă (FSD) endeavored to double-team the former communist country into "liberalizing." Their efforts throughout the 1990s laid the groundwork for what was to come; as Grandstaff expands:

> USAID sought to rapidly democratize and liberalize the post-communist country; Soros, meanwhile, understood that before a young, white-collar, liberal elite can guide a country toward the kind of open society he prefers, that young, white-collar, liberal elite must first exist.... "My foundations," brags Soros in his book *The Bubble of American Supremacy* (2004), "contributed to democratic regime change in Slovakia in 1998, Croatia in 1999, and Yugoslavia in 2000." Throughout the 1990s, the Clinton administration worked hand-in-glove with Soros to mold Eastern European policy. "I would say that [Soros's policy] is not identical to the foreign policy of the U.S. government—but it's compatible with it," Deputy Secretary of State Strobe Talbott told the *New Yorker* in 1995. Talbott served as President Bill Clinton's Ambassador-at-Large to Russia and the New Independent States, causing *Business Week* to dub him the "Russian Policy Czar..." In addition to sponsoring Romanian students to study in Western Europe and the U.S., Soros founded Central European University (CEU).... FSD also sponsored hundreds of Romanians to attend conferences on non-profit formation and administration, both at home and abroad. By the turn of the century, FSD's budget had peaked at almost $16 million. The Foundation then transitioned its programs into 12 splinter NGOs that found additional sources of Western funding to supplement their Soros dollars...A new umbrella

organization, Soros Open Network—Romania (SON), formed in 2000.... As Romania moved closer to European Union membership— or democratic maturity in the eyes of Soros's NGOs—the Soros network began engaging in more overt political advocacy.

They were joined in their efforts by "activist/journalist" Stéphanie Roth, operating on a major grant from the San Francisco-based Richard and Rhoda Goldman Fund, which also lavishly funded projects such as the Jewish Community Center of San Francisco, and organizations such as the Charles Stewart Mott Foundation, which funneled donations such as the $426,800 for the Environmental Partnership of Romania through the German Marshall Fund of the United States.

In September 2000, the neoliberal forces converged on Serbia in the so-called "Bulldozer Revolution" to drum incumbent Serbian President Slobodan Milošević out of office the year after round two of a US-directed NATO bombing campaign. As Abel Polese and Donnacha Ó Beacháin write for *Demokratizatsiya*:

> The September 2000 presidential election was also seminal by virtue of the fact that hundreds of thousands of hitherto apathetic young people cast their vote for the first time. This was another result of the work of the anti-regime youth movement OTPOR, which cooperated with political forces and a number of civil society actors to transform youth perceptions about elections... Shortly after Milošević's downfall, it was reported that OTPOR, far from being the spontaneous happy-go-lucky amateurs whose resourcefulness could be attributed to youthful ingenuity and thriftiness, was in fact funded to the tune of millions of dollars by US organizations like the International Republican Institute (IRI), the National Endowment for Democracy (NED), and the United States Agency for International Development (USAID). Indeed, in March 2000, the IRI hosted a secret conference at the Hilton Hotel in Budapest where OTPOR members were trained in nonviolent protest techniques and introduced to Gene Sharp's ideas by veteran activist Bob Helvey.

In 2001, the German Marshall Fund of the United States, the Charles Stewart Mott Foundation, the Ford Foundation, Atlantic Philanthropies, the Rockefeller Brothers Fund, and what is now the Open Society Foundations all banded together to create the CEE Trust, which would be focused on further "liberalizing" Central and Eastern Europe. It ceased operations at the end of 2012 following what Heike Mackerron of the German Marshall Fund believes to have been a resounding success, via *Alliance* magazine: "It wasn't clear that all countries would continue on the path towards democracy and a market economy," but all had achieved EU status and sufficiently liberalized to the grant-makers' satisfaction. It had also incubated a number of other NGOs such as the VIA Foundation in the Czech Republic; the Stefan Batory Foundation in Poland; and the Environmental Partnership Foundations in Bulgaria, the Czech Republic, Hungary, Poland, Romania, and Slovakia.

The impact of Soros's Open Society Foundations and other similar organizations is of course not just limited to Central and Eastern Europe. Soros was involved with the Rose Revolution in Georgia in 2003, an early color revolution. Returning to Grandstaff, this Establishment-backed insurrection in Georgia:

> ...led to the resignation of democratically-elected President Eduard Shevardnadze. Mikheil Saakashvili, who took over after Shevardnadze's resignation, received coaching from U.S. Ambassador Richard Miles, who was also ambassador to Serbia in 2000. Soros's OSI also openly supported Saakashvili and even paid for Georgian student activists to travel to Serbia to learn from veterans the art of non-violently overthrowing a democratically-elected government—a pilgrimage that Saakashvili himself made a year before his succession to power.... After gaining power, Saakashvili awarded Soros's former Open Society Georgia Foundation executive director, Alexander Lomaia, a seat in his Cabinet. The following year, history repeated itself—this time in Ukraine's Orange Revolution.

In the Ukraine, former Obama-appointed US ambassador to Russia Michael McFaul bragged about the neoliberal Establishment's open interference in the Ukraine's election in the *Washington Post*:

> Did Americans meddle in the internal affairs of Ukraine? Yes. The American agents of influence would prefer different language to describe their activities—democratic assistance, democracy promotion, civil society support, etc.—but their work, however labeled, seeks to influence political change in Ukraine. The U.S. Agency for International Development, the National Endowment for Democracy and a few other foundations sponsored certain U.S. organizations, including Freedom House, the International Republican Institute, the National Democratic Institute, the Solidarity Center, the Eurasia Foundation, Internews and several others to provide small grants and technical assistance to Ukrainian

civil society. The European Union, individual European countries and the Soros-funded International Renaissance Foundation did the same...Does this kind of intervention violate international norms? Not anymore. There was a time when championing state sovereignty was a progressive idea, since the advance of statehood helped destroy empires.

That was useful when traditional empires proved to be an impediment to the expansion of global capitalism, but as Kerry Bolton has written in tremendous detail, the destruction of these empires in addition to the vestiges of self-preservation-based regimes such as South African apartheid in order to initiate the next phase of the global garage sale of post-colonialism—and facilitate mass importation of these often disaffected and trained former colonial subjects into Western nations, or to train and return them to foment unrest and/or have allies in key positions—was vital. The corporate and moneyed interests continued plundering of the equatorial world and their hand-in-glove work with dysfunctional and corrupt regimes, to say nothing of the military-industrial complex's enormous financial windfalls from the Third World's seemingly endless civil wars, is producing the Establishment's desired effects—tragic and deadly, but incredibly profitable and useful for weaponized migration.

"Democracy," "pluralism," and "human rights" are all straight out of the doublespeak playbook, directly at odds with the actual reality of the situation, which is that the ruling class is doing everything in its power to pry open "closed" or otherwise traditional and ethnically-homogeneous societies in order to exploit them, make them more amenable to neoliberalism, and enfold them into the globalized system. First, nationalism and post-colonialism were used to destroy the old colonial empires—which were impediments to the opening-up of new markets—and once those had been dismantled, nationalism became the new impediment.

The dismantling of the colonial empires had nothing at all to do with "self-determination," but rather the old empires of Europe had become a barrier to free trade and the opening-up of new markets. When the colonies were granted independence, the white settlers were left exposed and unprotected. While many of these newly-established countries dabbled heavily in Left-wing policy, their decisions were largely based on tribal nepotism, and the financing of their internecine wars and other various projects came from Western capitalists. In fact, it did not matter if the new governments nationalized key industries, so long as they belonged to figures outside the globalist Establishment; if they were insiders, or if the policies began to threaten the outside interests, intervention was necessitated. It is not a coincidence that whether it be Iran in the 1950s or Bolivia more recently, when a key industry such as oil is nationalized, a coup is sure to follow should other forms of subversion and/or pressure fail.

As Kerry Bolton writes in his excellent *Babel, Inc.*, "In 1974 what [was then] called Zaire served notice on 50,000 non-Blacks that their properties and businesses had been nationalized. Conversely, American Big Business was described as 'a financial power in the country.'" It is in the name of "liberal democracy" that South Africa has disintegrated into hellish conditions in just a few short decades. When you see the rainbow Pride flag, perhaps you ought to spare a moment to think on the fate of the Rainbow Nation. This project is about cleaving off states and bringing them into the orbit of neoliberalism and high finance, and then detonating them in the name of greed and malice.

Today national sovereignty is the obstacle to global capitalism in its mutating neo-feudalist form; all particularist regimes which protect the interests of their people, whether Left or Right, from Cuba to Iran to Venezuela to Russia, must be washed away in the awesome septic tide of neoliberalism, which most certainly encompasses neoconservatism.

The aforementioned International Renaissance Foundation is officially a part of the Open Society Foundations; opened in Kiev in 1990, as the Open Society Foundations website reports:

> Ukraine was still part of the rapidly collapsing Soviet Union, placing the new foundation at the forefront of the effort by George Soros, the founder and chair of the Open Society Foundations, to use his fortune to assist the former Communist states of Central and Eastern Europe. After Ukraine became fully independent in 1991, the new foundation gradually expanded its support for Ukraine's often-painful transition to democracy and a market economy. The Open Society Foundations' immediate focus in Ukraine and other former Communist states was modernization and reform of moribund national institutions, and support for emerging civil society groups.... By 1994, the International Renaissance Foundation was the biggest international donor in the country, with an annual budget of roughly $12 million for projects that ranged from retraining tens of thousands of decommissioned soldiers to the creation of a contemporary arts center in Kyiv.

Among the many projects are included:

> The International Renaissance Foundation's support for the modernization of Ukraine's educational system in the early 1990s

[which] included commissioning educators, academics, administrators, and civil society groups to write, edit, and publish hundreds of school and university textbooks, helping to transform the way those subjects were conceived and taught.

...[And] the International Renaissance Foundation has supported the development of independent media outlets in Ukraine, and backed a multi-year campaign to establish an independent public service broadcaster that led to the launch of the National Public Broadcasting Company of Ukraine in 2015.

As regards the neoconservatism element of Ukrainian color revolution precursor Georgia, immediately following the Rose Revolution, Georgia asked to join NATO and then-Secretary of Defense Donald Rumsfeld signed a $15 million contract with the Cubic Corporation to train and arm Georgia's military. As Luiz Alberto Moniz Bandeira reports:

The Rose Revolution...was planned and coordinated from Washington through the ambassador Richard Miles...Richard Miles had played an important role in the toppling of Serbian President Slobodan Milošević when he headed the diplomatic mission of the United States in Belgrade, between 1996 and 1999. Afterwards, he was sent as ambassador to...Belarus, where he set up the coup against President Alexander Lukashenko. He had already operated in Azerbaijan and Bulgaria...With the rise to power of the attorney Mikheil Saakashvili, who had attended Columbia Law School and George Washington University Law School in the 90s, the Bush administration set into motion the Georgia Train and Equip Program (GTEP) between 2002 and 2004, and, after 2005, the Georgia Security and Stability Operations Program (Georgia SSOP), dispatching advisors of the US Special Operation Forces (Green Berets) and the US Marine Corps, among others, for the training of Georgia's military contingents. These contingents participated in operations in Kosovo and, afterwards, in the wars of Afghanistan and Iraq. Later, in the midst of tensions with Abkhazia and South Ossetia, separatist regions that wanted to join Russia, President Mikheil Saakashvili requested that Georgia be allowed to join NATO, encouraged by the United States. Georgia was [also] an ally of the United States in the oil pipeline question.[21]

---

[21] Bandeira, *The Second Cold War,* 48.

This separatism aspect is a common theme as well, such as Crimea in the Ukraine's second color revolution, or the fracture point on Moldova's eastern border with Transnistria—Crimea and Transnistria looking east while the main bodies of the Ukraine and Moldova are being pushed to look west.

As for the Ukraine's first color revolution, Vyacheslav Nikonov outlined the stakes in the 2004 Ukrainian presidential election backdrop of the Orange Revolution; should Viktor Yushchenko—whose wife is a former US State Department official, worked for the White House during the Reagan administration, and has numerous other ties to global finance and foundations—emerge victorious, Ukraine would be likely to gravitate toward NATO and become a member within a few years, but should Viktor Yanukovych prevail, the Ukraine would remain beyond the Establishment's orbit. Yanukovych won the second round of voting in November, but the usual suspects alleged that the Central Election Commission falsified the results; Yushchenko won the December revote under "intense scrutiny" from the "international community." Contrary to the Establishment media's depictions, as always putting the cart before the horse, Poh Phaik Thien writes:

> Freedom House and the Democratic Party's NDI helped fund and organize the "largest civil regional monitoring effort" in Ukraine where they sent in 1,000 trained observers and organized exit polls. It is very important in organizing the exit polls because they seize the initiative in the propaganda battle with the regime and put the onus on the authorities to respond.... Besides foreign influences, the mass media also plays an important role to further stimulate anti-regime forces.

Unsurprisingly, both Shevardnadze in Georgia and Yanukovych were targeted by the Establishment, and mere months after the Orange Revolution, a National Democratic Institute (NDI)-funded NGO in Kyrgyzstan catalyzed the Tulip Revolution, which, as Jacob Grandstaff describes it, "overthrew a democratically-elected president by paralyzing society through mass demonstrations." Askar Akayev of Kyrgyzstan, like Shevardnadze and Yanukovych, was more pro-Russian in orientation. The Open Society Foundations provided funding to the Kyrgyz opposition newspaper *MSN* helmed by Freedom House project director Mike Stone, and offices in Bishkek of the NDI, the International Republican Institute (IRI), the International Foundation for Electoral Systems (IFES), and the Soros Foundation-

Kyrgyzstan[22] all played a role. Intentionally connecting the "regime change" in Iraq to the color revolutions, then-US President George W. Bush used the moniker the "Purple Revolution" to describe the "arrival of democracy" in the country after its 2005 legislative election: "In recent times, we have witnessed landmark events in the history of liberty: A Rose Revolution in Georgia, an Orange Revolution in Ukraine, and now, a Purple Revolution in Iraq."

In a similar move, Lebanon's "Cedar Revolution" in 2005 following the Mossad's probable assassination of former Prime Minister Rafik Hariri was given its name by then-US Under-Secretary of State for Global Affairs Paula Dobriansky (yet another signatory of the Project for the New American Century's Statement of Principles) at a press conference with the intent to link it to the earlier and concurrent "revolutions" as well. It speaks volumes that Freedom House changed Lebanon's rating from "Not Free" in 2005 to "Partly Free" in 2006 following the so-called Cedar Revolution. George W. Bush stated that, "the Cedar Revolution marked one of the most important successes of the freedom agenda,"[23] and credible evidence points to not only NGO involvement, but also according to the *New York Post,* the CIA, the Bundesnachrichtendienst (the German foreign intelligence service), and Direction Générale de la Sécurité Extérieure (the French foreign intelligence service) had been "giving money and logistical support," with the CIA role similar to its support of "pro-democracy movements" in Georgia and the Ukraine. Additionally, the US State Department as part of its larger plan had been pumping money into Syria to fund opposition to President Bashar al-Assad.

Instead of more dominoes falling, however, as Grandstaff states, "Uzbekistan, Kazakhstan, and Tajikistan all avoided Color Revolutions by barring foreign funding for media and politics—Uzbekistan going so far as to outright ban all foreign NGOs like Freedom House" and the Open Society Foundations as well as the BBC. Following the decision, George Soros stated that:

> Uzbekistan is stifling civil society and has a horrendous human rights record. In the use of torture it is worse than Belarus, the only other country to force OSI to close. I commend the decision of the EBRD [European Bank for Reconstruction and Development] to suspend public sector lending and I call on the United States to re-examine its relationship with the Uzbek government.

---

[22] "The foundation helped establish the American University of Central Asia in Bishkek, which opened in 1998 and which is now one of the most highly regarded higher education institutions in the country."
[23] Bandeira, *The Second Cold War,* 53.

Tajikistan also refused to register Freedom House. Hungary has done something similar, Belarus fined and then suspended the Belarusian Helsinki Committee and raided the Open Society office there (as did Kazakhstan) before shutting them down, and though there were plans for a color revolution in Moldova following its 2005 parliamentary elections, it did not materialize. Also in 2005, a mass protest declaring itself to have drawn inspiration from the Tulip Revolution was suppressed in Belarus, and 2006 saw the US and EU impose sanctions on the country for "human rights violations." Uncoincidentally, the attempted "Jeans Revolution" followed the successful re-election of Alexander Lukashenko in March of 2006; the Establishment "contested" the 2020 elections as well, employing an identical strategy. There have been similar attempts in Russia, where NGOs receive foreign funding to de-stabilize the country. In response, Russia has moved to ban "undesirable" organizations such as the National Endowment for Democracy. Others include: Freedom House; the MacArthur, Mott, and Open Society foundations; and the International Republican and National Democratic institutes. Meanwhile, NATO continues to build up in Eastern Europe and the Caucasus.

A few years after the Orange Revolution, the Ukraine applied to begin a NATO Membership Action Plan, but when Viktor Yanukovych prevailed in the 2010 elections, those plans were shelved. The neoliberal cabal's reservations about Yanukovych were well-founded, as he not only declined to align the Ukraine with NATO, but he also did the same with an EU Association Agreement, drawing the country closer to Russia and the Eurasian Economic Union. Upon the decision to suspend the Association Agreement, as if on cue, mass demonstrations were triggered and the familiar chorus of corruption and "human rights violations" echoed through the streets of Kiev, with German NGO Transparency International (which has UNESCO Consultative Status and is a participating organization in the UN's Global Compact) decrying the Yanukovych regime as deeply corrupt, the worst in the world in fact. A second color revolution soon followed with Yanukovych's coerced resignation and the interim government's decision to sign the EU Association Agreement. Joint NATO exercises and military funding came in 2015, 2017 saw the opening of negotiations to join NATO, in 2018 the Ukraine was added to the prospective NATO members list (keeping the company of Bosnia and Georgia), in 2019 the Ukrainian Parliament voted on constitutional amendments that would make EU and NATO accession more seamless, and in June 2020 the Ukraine joined NATO's Enhanced Opportunity Partner interoperability program. Adding additional insight into the kinds of machinations going on behind the scenes to coerce these changes, Viola Gienger of the Atlantic Council writes:

A journalist with experience in development, [Olena] Tregub was working on policy papers and analyzing reforms for the Kyiv Post in 2014 and early 2015, when aides to then-Minister of Economic Development and Trade Aivaras Abromavicius contacted her about joining the agency's efforts. She came on board in February 2015 as an advisor to Abromavicius and became director of the Department of International Assistance Coordination that April…"Olena's idea was 'How do you fight corruption? You make everything transparent,' said Alina Polyakova, the David M. Rubenstein[24] Fellow in foreign policy at the Brookings Institution and a friend of Tregub's. "This became her life's work at the ministry…" The Ukrainian government also had little money for innovation. So Tregub won grants from American philanthropist George Soros's Open Society Foundations and from the United Nations Development Program to hire technical advisors. Another from the European Commission funded the pilot of a new website that would make grant information available for public scrutiny for the first time, Open Aid Ukraine.

As the Establishment continues to both expand and consolidate power, in Europe, the interim step is to continue to consolidate control within the EU and to bring the remaining nations outside the EU under its central control. During the 2014 European Parliamentary (EP) elections, Soros's Open Society Initiative for Europe (OSIFE) donated millions of dollars to organizations to oppose candidates that favored nation-state sovereignty over a more centralized European Union. The Carnegie Endowment for International Peace, as another example, has worked to promote EU association deals with the Ukraine, Georgia, and Moldova, "which have proven to be key drivers of reform in all three countries." Usually the EU will insist that Association Agreements must include commitments to political, economic, trade, and/or human rights reform in a country. We know what that looks like.

Eventually, if Guy Verhofstadt has his way, the EU will become Eurafrica, one giant economic zone with a GDP to rival China's. That all of the unique cultures of not only Europe but also Africa will be homogenized into one bland consumer culture of easily-controlled deracinated individuals is not only not incidental, it is the aim. It is the same aim for the US, Canada, and the Cone Countries to form one giant hemispheric mass of a similar

---

[24] The Jewish David M. Rubenstein is the co-founder and co-Executive Chairman of the Carlyle Group; trustee of the University of Chicago and Johns Hopkins Medicine; and Chairman of the Board of Directors of the Council on Foreign Relations.

nature, and for Australia and New Zealand to be extensions of China and Southeast Asia. Eventually: One World, with perhaps some tidy real estate of the Israelis and the Chinese.

Regarding the central US role in spear-heading this project, A.S. Brychkov and G.A. Nikonorov explain:

> A special office was formed within the US Department of State in charge of staging and managing "democratic revolutions" in any country chosen by the US Government. By enacting this law all nations on the planet deemed "undemocratic" are considered as unable to exercise their governance, thus needing US assistance. Chiefs of missions at US consulates and embassies in sovereign countries are tasked with executing these directives of the State Department. Liberal and pro-Western opposition groups as well as NGOs are forming part of what the US State Department on behalf of so-called "international community" proclaims to be the "true" representatives of their people and uses them to overthrow the undesirable government.[25]

In May 2005, Uzbekistan experienced significant civil unrest and violent clashes between the government and citizens; Uzbekistan was framed as "authoritarian" and roundly condemned for its banning of seditious NGOs like Winrock International, the Eurasia Foundation, and Radio Free Europe in addition to Freedom House and the Open Society Foundations after it became apparent that their rhetoric was designed to incite locals into further unrest and violence. Winrock International was accused by the state of spreading subversive propaganda.

The propaganda function is absolutely crucial. Understanding this, the ruling class has a veritable stranglehold on international media both direct and indirect. As one example, the neoliberal Establishment-backed International Consortium of Investigative Journalists is funded by the likes of the Ford Foundation, the Open Society Foundations, the Swedish Postcode Foundation, the Dutch National Postcode Lottery, the Adessium Foundation, the Norwegian Agency for Development Cooperation (Norad), the Streisand Foundation, and the Omidyar Network, and from their website: "ICIJ is also a participant in the Amazon Services LLC Associates Program, an affiliate advertising program designed to provide a means for us to earn fees by linking to Amazon.com and affiliated sites." Its media partners include ABC (Australia), *The New York Times*, the *Washington Post*, CBC/Radio-Canada,

---

[25] Brychkov, "Color Revolutions in Russia," 5.

BBC Panorama (UK), *Le Monde* (France), *The Guardian* (UK), *Haaretz* (Israel), *SVT* (Sweden), Univisión (United States), the *Toronto Star* (Canada), and many more (for a full list see Appendix C). As these things intersect, the Omidyar Network website announced on July 31st, 2018 in a press release:

> Omidyar Network, the philanthropic investment firm established by eBay founder Pierre Omidyar and his wife Pam, has committed USD 290,000 to Open Society Foundation, a Ukrainian think tank, to launch the Open Access project, a new platform to promote transparency in the management of Ukraine's natural resources and environmental health. The project has been developed and implemented by a group of experts led by the Open Society Foundation, which focuses on projects in the field of public participation and management efficiency, and supported by the Ministry of Ecology and Natural Resources of Ukraine. The Open Access Project will enable interactions among business, civil society, and government related to Ukraine's natural resources and environmental health management.... Olena Boytsun, Investment Director in Central and Eastern Europe at Omidyar Network's Governance & Citizen Engagement initiative noted..."Omidyar Network's Governance & Citizen Engagement initiative has previously committed more than USD 12 million to support similar work by international organizations dedicated to increased transparency around natural resources, such as Natural Resource Governance Institute, Publish What You Pay, and Global Witness. We are glad to support the project and are pleased that it has been made possible due to effective cooperation between civil society and the Ministry of Ecology and Natural Resources of Ukraine..." The project has already received support from a number of donors, such as GIZ, the Department of Natural Resources of Canada (Geomap-200 Project),[26] and the EU Project on the development of the Shared

---

[26] Natural Resources Canada and Geoinform of Ukraine published an explanatory document that reads: "Several joint assessment missions between Canada, the US and several EU countries were conducted between the fall of 2014 and the spring of 2015 to review Ukraine's capacity for collection, management, access and distribution of geological data to support long term development of mineral and energy resources in Ukraine. On September 1, 2016, ESS and Global Affairs Canada (GAC) formalized a development project entitled, 'Building National Geoscience Capacity in Ukraine'.... The goal of the Geomap-200 project is to convert available geological maps of Ukraine into a standardized, modern digital format that will be accessible online to the public and the investment and exploration community. Additionally, active participation from the Geological Surveys from the United States, Poland and Lithuania will provide complementary

Environmental Information System (SEIS) implemented jointly with the European Environment Agency (EEA) and the United Nations Development Programme (UNDP).

Following Brenton Tarrant's mosque shootings in New Zealand in 2019, the Global Forum for Media Development (GFMD) met with Prime Minister Jacinda Ardern about "journalism and news media perspectives on violent and extremist content (CVE) online," which has amounted to using this occurrence as a justification for blanket censorship of anything that runs contrary to the official line on immigration, neoliberalism, et cetera. The GFMD also advises the Department for International Development (DFID) and the UK Foreign and Commonwealth Office (FCO), works with the United Nations, and advises the European Union on various practices discouraging online "disinformation"—meaning, of course, more censorship. Their website features links to information that shrieks "Orwellian" such as, "tackling gender inequality through access to information." Its members include:

o The Media Development Investment Fund (MDIF)
o The World Association of Newspapers and News Publishers (WAN-IFRA): "The global organisation of the world's press. It derives its authority from its global network of 3,000 news publishing companies and technology entrepreneurs, and its legitimacy from its 80 member publisher associations representing 18,000 publications in 120 countries."
o The Syrian Center for Media and Freedom of Expression (SCM): "An independent Syrian civil society organization that works to promote democracy, fundamental rights, and transitional justice in Syria. We strive to reach a Syria that is based on rule of law, rotation of power, freedom of expression and belief, and human rights. We believe that the presence of an active civil society and objective, independent and critical media is indispensable for the development of a democratic, civil State in Syria." Meaning: work to depose Bashar al-Assad.
o BBC Media Action: "An independent, international, development charity. They aim to use the impact that media publications can create to decrease poverty and provide human rights education. In addition to creating their own conversation sparking media, they provide journalists with training and mentoring, and work with legislators to prove the potential impact media can have and the need for policy change."
o Center for Independent Journalism (CIJ) Romania: "Established in 1994,

---

perspectives and case examples concerning the management and dissemination of national geological map data and related information."

offers core courses and specialized training for journalists and students, providing consultants for media organizations, maintaining a journalism library and being a public voice in media freedom matters. It is also involved in advocacy, in curricula development, in media policy formulation and watch-dogging. CIJ is part of the Southeast European Network for Professionalization of Media (SEENPM), a network active in 11 Balkan countries and a member of the Global Media Development Forum."
- The Finnish Foundation for Media and Development (VIKES)
- The German Institute for Communication and Media Training (DIKT)
- The Inter-Africa Network for Women, Media, Gender Equity and Development (FAMEDEV): "A women's media and communication organisation based in Dakar, Senegal. The Organisation was founded in 2001 by women and men engaged in the media, communication, education and information. The founding members are predominantly women and the executive committee is in the majority women journalists, communicators and sociologists. FAMEDEV operates in 22 countries in West and Central Africa and has focal points that coordinate the activities at country level."
- SembraMedia: "A nonprofit dedicated to increasing the diversity of voices…in Spanish."
- Georgian Association of Regional Broadcasters (GARB): "An association of independent broadcasters (20) who support sustainable development of regional broadcasting companies in order to make free speech accessible for the community, to improve the level of their information and civil activity."
- Africa Media Initiative (AMI): "Has been shaped by the most comprehensive research and consultation process ever conducted on the media in Africa. This was done under the auspices of the BBC World Service Trust and the UN Economic Commission for Africa (UNECA) and is included in the 2005 G8 Gleneagles and Commission for Africa recommendations. All relevant regional stakeholders, from the African Union Commission, the African Development Bank and the United Nations Economic Commission for Africa through to every significant African media structure (owners, editors, journalists) have formally endorsed AMI, suggesting a powerful consensus that a healthy media sector is a requirement for improved growth, governance and accountability."
- Canal France International (CFI): "As a subsidiary of France Télévisions Group, CFI receives subsidies from the French Ministry of Foreign Affairs and International Development so as to lead a network of partners from the media sector. On the basis of its previous experience as a television channel,

CFI is able to propose responses adapted to the requirements of media operators from the southern hemisphere, whatever the restrictions and working languages. Their aim is to promote modernization and democratization."
- The Media Diversity Institute (MDI): "Works internationally to encourage and facilitate responsible media coverage of diversity. It aims to prevent the media from intentionally or unintentionally spreading prejudice, intolerance and hatred which can lead to social tensions, disputes and violent conflict. MDI encourages instead, fair, accurate, inclusive and sensitive media coverage in order to promote understanding between different groups and cultures."
- Instituto Prensa y Sociedad (IPYS) Venezuela: "A non-governmental organization active in the promotion, defense and training in free speech, investigative journalism and the right to information. Our team consists of renowned Venezuelan journalists and career oriented professional standards, with national and regional levels. We want the Venezuelan citizens' awareness and exercise their right to freedom of expression and information." This is purely speculation of course, but I struggle to believe that organizations such as this one and other member organizations in the Ukraine, Palestine, and Syria, for example, or really any of these organizations quite frankly, do not serve some subversive function in trying to dislodge regimes opposed to the neoliberal order and/or spreading disinformation regarding the Establishment's activities in these countries and/or serving as propaganda arms of the Establishment under the guise of "plurality." Consider the description of ASML-Syria: "Building the pluralistic foundation for a peaceful and democratic future."
- The Balkan Investigative Reporting Network (BIRN): "A network of non-governmental organisations promoting freedom of speech, human rights and democratic values in Southern and Eastern Europe."

Give me a break.

BIRN's Chairman of the Board is the Jewish Tim Judah, formerly of the BBC before becoming the Balkan correspondent for *The Times* and *The Economist*. Board member Robert Bierman was the General Manager of *Washington Post* Live, the live "journalism" division of *The Washington Post*, and he also founded the Bloomberg Link division of Bloomberg LP. A consideration of some of its partners and donors will prove illustrative; partners include: Al Jazeera English; the Austrian Broadcasting Corporation (ORF); the European Broadcasting Union; *The Guardian*; the ERSTE Foundation NGO Academy; the International Federation of Journalists (IFJ); the Commission for International Justice and Accountability (CIJA); the

Center for Media, Data, and Security, which is part of George Soros's Central European University; the BBC; and Voice of America. Voice of America, like Radio Free Europe/Radio Liberty, is part of the United States Agency for Global Media (USAGM).

BIRN's major donors include several British Embassies, the Charles Stewart Mott Foundation, DANIDA, the European Commission, Freedom House, the National Endowment for Democracy (NED), the OSCE, the Open Society Foundations, Sida, the Rockefeller Brothers Fund, the US Embassies in Skopje and Tirana, the United Nations Interim Administration Mission in Kosovo (UNMIK), UNDP, the Balkan Trust for Democracy,[27] the Delegation of the European Union to Montenegro, the European Union Office in Kosovo, USAID, and Civitates.

Civitates, like BIRN, receives funding from the Charles Stewart Mott Foundation, the Open Society Foundations, Robert Bosch Stiftung, and ERSTE Stiftung, as well as the Stefan Batory Foundation, the Oak Foundation, Fondation de France, Bertelsmann Stiftung, the King Baudouin Foundation, and the European Cultural Foundation, among others. The Orwellian-named European Cultural Foundation states that it supports "the idea of Europe as a shared public space" and provides grants to things like Busy Being Black, "the podcast exploring how we live in the fullness of our queer Black lives," and The Solidarity Space by The Black & African Solidarity Show, "both a creative-based virtual learning platform and arts festival for creatives engaging Black and African communities in Europe." The European Cultural Foundation is partnered with the Open Society Foundations, the King Baudouin Foundation, Robert Bosch Stiftung, the British Council, the Swiss Agency for Development and Cooperation, and two programs of the European Union. Vice Chair of the Supervisory Board is Rien van Gendt, member of the Board of Rockefeller Philanthropy Advisors.

Léonie van Tongeren is the Fund Manager of Civitates. Prior to joining Civitates, she spent five years at the Open Society Foundations, where in addition to managing grants she provided high level programmatic support to the Regional Director for Europe, mostly in relation to managing strategic elements of the Open Society Initiative for Europe. Other grantees in addition to BIRN include:

---

[27] "This award-winning public-private partnership was created in 2003 by the German Marshall Fund of the United States, the United States Agency for International Development (USAID), and the Charles Stewart Mott Foundation."

- The University of Oxford (UK): "The Oxford Internet Institute, a department of the University of Oxford, works on research into the causes, consequences, and policy solutions for misinformation in Europe. Through this project, OII will track misinformation campaigns during the 2019 European Parliamentary elections, research the misinformation campaigns targeting Russian speaking communities who live within Europe and provide regular consultations to European institutions and organizations on the wider ecosystem of misinformation...It will also step up its capacity to track misinformation in the form of fake video content on YouTube and misinformation on encrypted chat platforms like WhatsApp." WhatsApp was founded by the Jewish Jan Koum, who sold it to Facebook. The Ford Foundation and the European Commission fund the OII's Computational Propaganda initiative. Anti-Defamation League (ADL) CEO Jonathan Greenblatt announced that the organization was establishing the Center for Technology and Society (CTS) with a $250,000 seed grant from Omidyar Network plus an additional $1.5 million to support the Center's work, with the ADL's CTS in turning offering fellowships sponsored by the Jewish Robert A. and Renee E. Belfer Family Foundation. One of the inaugural fellows was Samuel Woolley of the OII who is employed by Google's Jigsaw. From the ADL press release: "His fellowship project will work to understand how political bots and algorithms have been leveraged to target the Jewish community and use this understanding to find ways to counter this bias."
- The Center for the Study of Democracy (Bulgaria): "The project will focus on Russian disinformation tactics in several European countries. CSD will coordinate research with the partners in different countries, provide them with a technical tool to track online disinformation narratives and compile the comparative analysis in a guidebook for policy makers to address the issues. The findings of the project will be disseminated to policy makers and key institutions such as NATO to feed into the policy debate."
- Panoptykon Foundation (quite a fitting name, Poland): "Panoptykon Foundation is a non-profit that protects fundamental rights and freedoms in the context of fast-changing technologies and growing surveillance. This project will look into the scale and impact of political micro targeting in Poland and how it is fed in the news and shape the political agenda. It seeks to deliver evidence that will inform European policy makers to the risks that non-transparent, targeted political marketing on platforms represents for public discourse. The activities will cover research (data collection, analysis), awareness-raising, civic engagement and advocacy towards policy makers, using the Polish parliamentary elections (autumn 2019) as main testing ground."

Another GFMD member organization is the Albanian Media Institute, established in 1995 through a grant from Danish International Development Agency (DANIDA) and the Danish School of Journalism. The Albanian Media Institute has partnered with UNICEF in the training of journalists on "children's issues" (read: using children as emotional manipulation to satisfy an agenda); they've also received substantial funding from the Swiss Agency for Development and Cooperation and…George Soros. Remzi Lani, on the European Advisory Board of the Open Society Foundations, is the Executive Director of the Albanian Media Institute. Until 2017, he was the Chairman of the Board of the Open Society Foundation for Albania. The Open Society Foundations also funds GFMD member the Centre for Law and Democracy in Canada. The Centre also receives funding from Global Affairs Canada, CECI, UNESCO, International Media Support, GIZ, and the National Endowment for Democracy.

The Center for International Media Assistance (CIMA) is also a member of the GFMD. It is an initiative established by the National Endowment for Democracy (NED); CIMA collaborated with the Annenberg School for Communication at the University of Pennsylvania on Global Media Law, a networking and information resource. Both CIMA and the NED are funded by the US government directly and by "outside" sources. CIMA receives funding from USAID and the US State Department, as does the NED. CIMA's other funders include: the Open Society Foundations, Bloomberg Philanthropies, DANIDA, the European Commission, the European Endowment for Democracy, the Knight Foundation, Media Democracy Fund, MDIF, the NED, Global Affairs Canada, the Omidyar Network, the French Ministry of Foreign Affairs and International Development, the Government of Norway, the German Federal Ministry for Economic Cooperation and Development (BMZ), the Skoll Foundation, Japan International Cooperation Agency (JICA), the Rockefeller Foundation, the United Nations, the OECD, the David and Lucile Packard Foundation, Google, the John D. and Catherine T. MacArthur Foundation, the German Marshall Fund of the United States, Hivos, the Australian Agency for International Development, Bertelsmann Stiftung, Friedrich Ebert Stiftung, DFID, BBC Media Action, the Ministry of Foreign Affairs of Finland, the Swiss Agency for Development and Cooperation, the Spanish Ministry of Foreign Affairs and Cooperation, the US Agency for Global Media (which includes Voice of America and Radio Free Europe), the Ministry of Foreign Affairs of the Netherlands, the Swedish International Development Cooperation Agency (SIDA), the Belgian Development Cooperation, UNESCO, the Australian Department of Foreign Affairs and Trade (DFAT), the Ministry of Foreign Affairs and Norwegian Foreign Missions, the Bill and Melinda Gates Foundation, and the Ford

Foundation. Adam Schiff is on CIMA's Advisory Council.

Another CIMA donor is the Millennium Challenge Corporation, which provides conditional assistance to impoverished countries contingent upon their "progress" on particular indicators which are in alignment with "opening up" to neoliberalism. It is a US government corporation and has in recent years incorporated "media development" in Moldova and the Ukraine into its conditional disbursement.

In 2008, CIMA and the NED produced their inaugural "Empowering Independent Media" report, written by David E. Kaplan and reviewed by a World Bank consultant and the senior media development advisor with USAID, among others, where the post-9/11 project of accelerating the cooption of the world's media by the neoliberal Establishment was outlined with surprising candor. First, the "state of play":

> In 2006, US donors spent an estimated $142 million on media assistance projects overseas, split almost evenly between government funding and private sources. The amount is believed to be by far the largest from any single country, although at least $100 million more is estimated to come from other nations and international organizations. Most of the U.S. funds go to training and direct assistance to media organizations. Despite dedicated work by staffers at the U.S. Agency for International Development (USAID), the Open Society Institute (OSI), and other donors, funding is widely seen as insufficient...The three major U.S.-based media assistance groups—the International Center for Journalists (ICFJ), International Research & Exchanges Board (IREX), and Internews—spent more than half of their combined budgets, or some $23 million, on training in 2006. Workshops, fellowships, guidebooks, and distance learning are some of the avenues for improving professional skills. Much of the training is carried out by some 81 nonprofit media centers worldwide, which often must struggle to obtain adequate funding.

Internews, by the way, runs a joint project with the World Economic Forum called United for News, with other stakeholders including Vodafone, Bloomberg, Edelman, and the Media Development Investment Fund (MDIF). Internews is yet another NGO with headquarters in Sodom and Gomorrah (California and Washington, DC), London, and Paris. Internews has provided funding to the Regents of the University of California-Berkeley and Freedom House. Internews Europe derives funding from sources such as the European Commission, the UK Department for International Development (DFID), the

Norwegian Agency for Development Cooperation (NORAD), the Ministry for Foreign Affairs of the Netherlands, the Swedish International Development Corporation Agency (SIDA), the UK Foreign and Commonwealth Office, the Oak Foundation, UNESCO, BBC Media Action, the International Planned Parenthood Federation (IPPF), and the European Climate Foundation ("Climate change is the greatest challenge of our time, a global emergency and a real threat. Addressing the climate crisis is also the greatest opportunity for big and bold change to create a fairer and more sustainable society"—its funders include Bloomberg Philanthropies, the IKEA Foundation, the Oak Foundation, and the Rockefeller Brothers Fund). Internews Chairman of the Board Richard Kessler, per his website biography:

> ...has over 40 years of international experience working at senior levels on foreign policy and national security issues.... Kessler's major work achievements included directing State Department authorization legislation, a rewrite of the Foreign Assistance Act of 1961, export control reform, aid to Pakistan, and Iran sanctions. He is one of the few people to have served in both the House and the Senate as a committee staff director. He was also a subcommittee staff director on the Senate Governmental Affairs Committee. Previously he was a professional staff member on the Senate Foreign Relations Committee and on the House International Relations Committee where he was responsible for East Asia, the Pacific, South Asian, and UN peacekeeping policy issues, including re-engagement with Vietnam and Cambodia and independence for East Timor. Kessler wrote the legislation establishing the Fulbright programs in Vietnam and East Timor and worked on human rights and refugee issues including the extension of the Orderly Departure Program for Vietnamese refugees. Prior to working in Congress, Kessler taught international affairs at the School of International Service, The American University; worked as a consultant for various government agencies and private organizations, including the Agency for International Development in Pakistan and Morocco, and as an analyst at various think tanks. He was a Senior Associate at The Carnegie Endowment for International Peace where he worked on ending the Marcos dictatorship in the Philippines, and he co-directed a study on energy and national security at the Center for International and Strategic Studies.

Other US Board members feature individuals such as:

- Pamela Austin: "Pamela Austin leads corporate communications for Facebook, a role she has had since April of 2019. Before settling at Facebook, Austin held the position of Head of Executive Communications for both Samsung and Microsoft. From 2008 to 2011, Austin worked for the Bill and Melinda Gates Foundation, directing their employee communications and engagement."
- Mieke Eoyang: "Vice President for the National Security Program for The Third Way. As the Vice President for Third Way's National Security Program, Mieke is committed to closing the credibility gap between Democrats and Republicans on security issues and crafting a national security strategy that is both tough and smart. She works on every major national security issue—from the details of military personnel policy to the legal framework for going to war—while still making time to mentor the next generation of women in national security. Mieke had a long career on Capitol Hill, most recently serving as Chief of Staff to Representative Anna Eshoo (D-CA). Prior to that, she was the Defense Policy Advisor to Senator Kennedy, the Subcommittee Staff Director on the House Permanent Select Committee on Intelligence, and a Professional Staff Member on the House Armed Services Committee. Mieke began her career as a legislative assistant in the office of Representative Pat Schroeder (D-CO), where she handled the Congresswoman's Armed Services and Foreign Policy work."
- John Montgomery: "Chair of the 4A's Media Leadership Council; has served on the Internet Steering Committee of the World Economic Forum (WEF)."
- Ben Rader: "General Counsel at Goldman Sachs Foundation. He has served as a Vice President of Goldman Sachs since 2005."
- Anna Soellner: "Leads communications for Reddit…Previously, she was VP for corporate communications at the Motion Picture Association of America where she worked on major news events like the Sony hack, gun violence in media and 1st Amendment issues. She also led communications at the Center for American Progress (CAP), the progressive think tank. Anna was among the first employees at CAP, building to an organization of over 250. Anna was as a Luce Scholar in Hong Kong and worked for Martin Lee, a leader of the pro-democracy moment there. In 2016 she co-founded a GOTV effort called My Ride To Vote which funded ride-sharing to the polls for underrepresented communities."
- Cristiana Falcone Sorrell "is a global leader in media, business and social development sectors. She began her career in radio and television, covering foreign affairs including war and humanitarian crises. Over the past 15+

years she has honed her experience as a strategic adviser, investor and philanthropist and acquired vast experience with multinationals, international organizations and the media. As well as working directly for C-suite executives at Sony and Shell, she also held leadership advisory roles with the following companies and international organizations: ILO, IFAD, FAO, UNDCCP, IADB, RAI, Gruppo Espresso, the World Economic Forum and Univision. She presently serves as Senior Adviser to the Executive Chairman and Founder of the World Economic Forum on New Initiatives and Special Projects. Joining the Forum in 2004, she led the Media, Entertainment and Information Industries, building and managing strategic partnerships with industry leaders, policymakers, experts and academics worldwide. In 2006, she pioneered *The Digital Ecosystem* a scenario-based tool aimed at garnering insight into digital disruption and its impact on the future of media. In 2008, in partnership with Yale University, she led the production of an online case study on media opportunities in fast-growing environments, featuring key industry leaders and profiling cutting-edge tech and knowledge. Falcone Sorrell is an early investor and adviser in several young talented hand-picked start-ups. She is a member of the Board of Directors of Viacom and Revlon and holds leadership roles in the following organizations: Internews, The Paley Center for Media, The School of Nutrition and the Feinstein Center for Humanitarian Affairs at Tufts University. As the CEO of the JMCMRJ Sorrell Foundation, she leads transformative initiatives in health, education and poverty alleviation worldwide."

- Robert Bole: "Robert has spent his career in leadership and digital and global strategy for media companies. Most recently, Robert has been General Manager for The Atlantic's CityLab, as well as leading The Atlantic's international growth strategy. Prior he was an advisor to The New York Times, Director of Innovation for the U.S. Agency for Global Media, a federal agency that oversees five regional media networks, and managed digital media strategy for the Corporation for Public Broadcasting."
- Kevin J. Delaney "is a senior editor for *The New York Times*...He is a member of the Council on Foreign Relations."
- Monique Maddy "is the Founder and CEO of EZUZA, a mobile payments company focusing primarily on the un-banked and under-banked in emerging markets. In 1993, Monique founded her first technology services company, African Communications Group (later renamed Adesemi), to finance, build and operate low-cost wireless telecommunications services in emerging markets. Adesemi successfully built the world's first fully integrated wireless 'virtual' phone network...From 1986-1991, Monique

worked for the United Nations Development Program with assignments in New York, Jakarta (Indonesia), Luanda (Angola), and Bangui (Central African Republic)...Monique holds a Bachelor of Science degree in international politics from Georgetown University, a Master's Degree in economics and development studies from the Johns Hopkins University School of Advanced International Studies, and a Master's Degree in Business Administration from the Harvard Business School."
- Kristina Henschen: "Repeatedly recognized as one of the most influential women in the field of development cooperation in Sweden, Kristina Henschen is the Secretary General of the Swedish Public Service Broadcasting Foundation for Development Cooperation; Radio Aid...Henschen also has seven years' prior experience with the Swedish International Development Cooperation Agency (Sida). While working for Sida, Henschen was based in Eastern Europe, Russia, and at its headquarters in Stockholm where she coordinated the Human Rights Programme to Belarus. Kristina also worked with human rights and gender equality for several years for the United Nations Development Programme (UNDP) in Yerevan, Armenia."

Returning to the "Empowering Independent Media" report, we learn how to improve funding and "training" (and as always, some reading between the lines is required):

> Change will happen faster if all the factors—professional development, economic sustainability, legal-enabling environment, and media literacy—are addressed simultaneously.... Independent media development deserves a higher profile within USAID and the State Department, which provide almost half of all current funding. Because media development has an impact across multiple fields, it often receives federal funding as a part of other projects—under civil society and election reform, for example, or AIDS prevention and health care.... USAID, for example, should increase the number of media specialists it employs and continue to improve its projects database so that media programs can be easily searched.... Additional funding models, such as the Media Development Loan Fund (MDLF), should be explored and developed... Funding of issue-specific programs, such as coverage of HIV/AIDS prevention or tax reform, should include components that contribute more generally to support of independent media.... The current integration of USAID programs into the State Department should preserve the locally-based approach used by both agencies.... At media centers

and news outlets, training of journalists should emphasize international standards.... In universities...curricula [should be] reformed.... Improving the legal-enabling environment should be a higher priority.... Additional programs should be targeted at government officials.... IREX's Media Sustainability Index should be expanded worldwide to Asia and Latin America.... There is a need for better coordination among donors as well as implementing groups, and in the field as well as in Washington.... Cell phone messaging, citizen journalism, and blogging are among the innovative tools available.... The International Journalists' Network, already available in five languages, should be expanded into Chinese, Russian, and French. Online resources for media law and investigative reporting should be further developed. The Global Forum for Media Development should grow into an independent, international voice for media assistance, helping unlock needed funding, reforms, and recognition at the highest levels.

That has all happened and more. This network is unbelievably extensive and is absolutely central to the spread of the neoliberal ideology and coordinated propaganda campaigns.

In 1968, IREX (International Research & Exchanges Board) was established by several American universities in conjunction with the Ford Foundation, the US State Department, the American Council of Learned Societies (ACLS), and the Social Science Research Council (SSRC). Current President and CEO Kristin Lord, per her IREX website's biographical description:

> ...was a fellow at the Brookings Institution, where she directed the science and technology initiative of the Project on U.S. Relations with the Islamic World and authored studies on human development in the Arab world and U.S. public diplomacy.... Dr. Lord is a member of the Board of Directors for the U.S. Global Leadership Coalition and the American University in Cairo, and a lifetime member of the Council on Foreign Relations.... Dr. Lord received an International Affairs Fellowship from the Council on Foreign Relations, enabling her to serve as special advisor to the Under Secretary of State for Democracy and Global Affairs from 2005 to 2006.... Prior to joining IREX in 2014, Dr. Lord served as Acting President and Executive Vice President of the United States Institute of Peace, a Congressionally created organization that prevents, mitigates, and resolves violent conflict worldwide. While

at USIP, Lord oversaw the launch of an online education initiative, the creation of the PeaceTech Lab, the expansion of programs on Africa and South/Central Asia, and the development of a five-year strategic plan. From 2009 to 2013, Lord was Executive Vice President and Director of Studies at the Center for a New American Security, where she oversaw the Center's research and served as one of three members of the Center's leadership team. She served as editor-in-chief of 110 CNAS publications during that period and authored significant studies on diplomacy and development, cyber security, U.S. global engagement, and violent extremism.

Executive Vice President for Strategy and Development Aleksander Dardeli:

> ...has held executive and senior management positions with nongovernmental organizations, intergovernmental organizations, and private-sector organizations.... He has cultivated major initiatives and opportunities with the United States Department of State, the United States Agency for International Development, the European Union Commission, the United Nations, and major corporations.... Between 2006 and 2008, Aleksander directed a high-profile project in Kosovo that was embedded in the Office of the Prime Minister of Kosovo and helped prepare the Office of the Prime Minister and six line ministries for Kosovo's transition to independence. His 20 years of experience include serving as Practice Director of DynCorp International/Casals's Global Democracy and Governance Practice, Director of Legal Programs of the East-West Management Institute, and Head of Project Development for the International Development Law Organization, an intergovernmental organization based in Rome, Italy. He has published opinion pieces and commentary on promoting good governance, fighting corruption, strengthening media to produce content that matters, and making foreign aid more effective, and has been interviewed by media outlets including BBC and Voice of America.

IREX's Board of Governors includes people like:

o Niloofar Razi Howe (Chair) "has been an investor, executive, and entrepreneur in the technology industry for the past 25 years, with a focus on cybersecurity for the past ten. Most recently, Ms. Howe served as chief strategy officer and SVP of strategy and operations at RSA, a global cybersecurity company where she led corporate strategy, corporate development and planning, business development, global program management, business operations, security operations, and federal business development. Prior to RSA, Ms. Howe served as the chief strategy officer of Endgame Inc., a leading enterprise software security company, where she was responsible for driving market and product strategy, as well as leading marketing, product management, corporate development, and planning. Prior to her operating roles, Ms. Howe spent twelve years leading deal teams in private equity and venture capital, first as a principal at Zone Ventures, an early stage venture capital firm in Los Angeles, and then as managing director at Paladin Capital Group, a Washington, DC–based private equity fund focused on investing in next-generation security companies. Ms. Howe started her professional career as a lawyer with O'Melveny & Myers and as a consultant with McKinsey & Co...Ms. Howe is a senior operating partner at Energy Impact Partners, a VC fund investing in companies shaping the energy landscape of the future. She is on the board of directors of Morgan Stanley Private Bank, NA, and Morgan Stanley Bank, NA, Recorded Future (Threat Intelligence), on the board of advisors of Dragos (industrial cybersecurity), Enveil, (data security), Picnic Threat (insider threat) and Endgame (endpoint protection & detection). She is a life member at the Council on Foreign Relations and a senior fellow for the Cybersecurity Initiative at New America, a nonprofit, nonpartisan think tank.... Previously she served on the Board of Global Rights, an international human rights organization, as chair, Sibley Memorial Hospital (a member of Johns Hopkins Medicine), as chair of its Investment Committee, and Sibley Memorial Hospital Foundation, as vice chair. Ms. Howe graduated with honors from Columbia College and holds a JD cum laude from Harvard Law School."

o Ambassador David Gross (Vice Chair) "cochairs the Telecom, Media & Technology Practice at Wiley Rein LLP. He is one of the world's foremost experts on international telecommunications and internet policies, having addressed the United Nations General Assembly and led more U.S. delegations to major international telecommunication conferences than anyone else in modern history.... He advises companies and others on international and domestic telecoms, internet, and high-tech strategy focusing on both specific markets and international organizations such as the International Telecommunication Union, the Organization for Economic Cooperation and Development, and the Asia-Pacific Economic Cooperation, as well as many regional organizations. He was appointed by President George W. Bush to serve as the U.S. coordinator for International Communications and Information Policy at the U.S. Department of State from 2001 to 2009."

- Lionel C. Johnson "became president of the Pacific Pension & Investment Institute in July 2014.... He has served as senior vice president of the Initiative for Global Development, as vice president of Turkey, Middle East, and North Africa Affairs at the Chamber of Commerce of the United States, and as senior vice president of Public Affairs at Fleishman-Hillard. Previously, Johnson was vice president and director of International Government Affairs at Citigroup and deputy assistant secretary of the Treasury for International Development, Debt, and Environment Policy in the Clinton Administration. He was also a senior advisor for Resources, Plans, and Policy to Secretary of State Warren Christopher, and a member of the Department of State Policy Planning Staff. He served as deputy director of the Clinton/Gore transition team at the Department of State. As a member of the U.S. Foreign Service, Johnson held assignments in the U.S. Embassies in Haiti, the Philippines, and Kenya. He also served as special assistant to Secretaries of State George P. Shultz and James A. Baker III. Johnson was a senior program officer at the National Democratic Institute for International Affairs...Johnson is a visiting scholar of the Program on International Relations of New York University. He is on the board of the Truman National Security Project, and is a member of the board of trustees of the RAND Corporation in Santa Monica, California. Johnson also serves on the board of directors of Foreign Policy for America, the National Democratic Institute for International Affairs, and the U.S. Global Leadership Coalition."
- Beverly Lindsey "is a senior public relations and communications specialist with extensive experience with for-profit, nonprofit, political, state and federal government organizations.... she worked as the Communications Director at USAID from 2000 to 2001.... Most recently, she was an election monitor with National Democratic Institute for the Bangladesh parliamentary elections in 2009."
- Aleem Walji: "From 2015 to 2020, Aleem was the Chief Executive Officer of the Aga Khan Foundation (AKF) in the United States...Previously, Aleem was Director of the World Bank's Innovation Lab. He oversaw a portfolio of programs related to Open Data, Big Data/Analytics and accountability in public service delivery. Aleem also led initiatives related to financial inclusion, youth engagement and peacebuilding in Muslim societies. Aleem also served as Head of Global Development Initiatives at Google.org.... Aleem also completed a program at MIT on artificial intelligence, blockchain, cloud computing, the internet of things, and cybersecurity."
- Wade Warren "is the Chief Strategy Officer for International Development at Deloitte Consulting. In this role, he leads strategic insight, provides

thought leadership, and brings innovative technology solutions to U.S. foreign assistance and international development clients.... During 27 years with USAID, Warren served in a broad range of senior management positions in the Bureaus for Policy, Planning and Learning, Global Health, and Africa. Additionally, he was the Acting Chief Operating Officer of the State Department's Office of the Director of U.S. Foreign Assistance. Warren also served at USAID's Missions in Zimbabwe and Botswana."

o Aaron Williams: "is a Senior Advisor Emeritus for International Development & Government Relations at RTI.... He served as a senior official at the U.S. Agency for International Development (USAID), where he reached the rank of career minister in the Senior Foreign Service. In 2009 he was appointed by President Barack Obama as Director of the U.S. Peace Corps, serving in that role through 2012. Mr. Williams is a member of the Council on Foreign Relations."

And on IREX's Global Advisory Council are included:

o Peter Ackerman "is the founding chair of International Center on Nonviolent Conflict, which is one of the world's leading authorities on nonviolent conflict...In addition, Dr. Ackerman serves as cochair of the International Advisory Committee of the United States Institute of Peace and on the Executive Committee of the Board of the Atlantic Council. Dr. Ackerman also served on the boards of CARE and the Council of Foreign Relations."

o Paige Alexander "has served in numerous senior positions in the U.S. government, including Assistant Administrator overseeing USAID Regional Bureaus, USAID missions, and development programs in 25 countries, from Europe and Eurasia through North Africa and the Middle East. She draws upon 25 years of experience working in international development, both in the field and in Washington, DC. Paige's other notable positions include executive director of the European Cooperative for Rural Development (EUCORD) in Brussels and Amsterdam, senior vice president at IREX, associate director of Project Liberty at Harvard University's John F. Kennedy School of Government, and consultant to the Rockefeller Brothers Fund, the C.S. Mott Foundation, and the Open Society Institute in Prague."

o Bruce McNamer: "From 2013-2014, he was the Head of Global Philanthropy and Chief Executive Officer of the JPMorgan Chase Foundation.... Before joining TechnoServe in 2004, Bruce was a senior executive/founder in technology start-ups, an investment banker at

Morgan Stanley and a management consultant at McKinsey & Company. Bruce was also a White House Fellow at the National Economic Council.... He has an AB from Harvard and a JD/MBA from Stanford. He is a Member of the Council on Foreign Relations."
o Kristin Carlucci Weed: "Prior to her work with the Carlucci Foundation, Kristin was with the RAND Corporation as a senior national security analyst, headquartered in both their United States and European offices. She has co-authored a number of publications on European regional security issues. She is also a proud military spouse.... [She received a] Master of Arts from Johns Hopkins School of Advanced International Studies."
o Toni Verstandig "serves as Executive Vice President at the S. Daniel Abraham Center for Middle East Peace.... Previously, Ms. Verstandig served as Chair, Aspen Institute's Middle East programs...Ms. Verstandig served as Deputy Assistant Secretary of Near Eastern Affairs at the U.S. Department of State and served as a member of the U.S. negotiation team tasked to reach a comprehensive agreement to end the Arab-Israeli conflict. Ms. Verstandig has provided leadership and experience in healthcare governance as Chair of the Children's National Hospital Foundation Board, as well as the Board of Trustees of the Children's National Medical center. She also serves on the Board of Trustees of the Center for Global Development, the University of Denver's Korbel Graduate School for International Affairs, and the U.S. Institute of Peace International Advisory Council. She is a longstanding member of the Council on Foreign Relations."
o Witney Schneidman "has...experience in the U.S. Department of State [and] the World Bank.... He is also a Non-Resident Fellow at the Africa Growth Initiative at the Brookings Institution."
o Annette Richardson: "Currently a partner at Ambershore Group LLC, Annette is a versatile senior strategic advisor with a unique blend of corporate strategy and public affairs expertise, including extensive experience at the United Nations. Annette served as a Senior Advisor to the UN Office for Partnerships under the leadership of UN Secretary-General Ban Ki-moon and was instrumental in convening some of the most significant high-level dialogues related to public-private partnerships at the UN. Annette designed, curated, and implemented global multi-stakeholder policy, advocacy and outreach programs and campaigns in support of the UN Secretary-General's global development priorities to achieve the Millennium Development Goals (MDGs) and the Sustainable Development Goals (SDGs). She is a former Special Advisor to the Executive Office of the UN Secretary-General for Sustainable Energy and remains a Special Advisor

to the Under Secretary-General and Executive Director of UN Women."
- Paula Dobriansky: "is a senior fellow in the Future of Diplomacy Project at Harvard University's JFK Belfer Center for Science and International Affairs and vice chair of the Atlantic Council's Scowcroft Center for Strategy and Security. From 2010 to 2012, Ambassador Dobriansky was senior vice president and global head of government and regulatory affairs at Thomson Reuters. During this time, she was also appointed the Distinguished National Security Chair at the U.S. Naval Academy. From 2001 to 2009, Ambassador Dobriansky served as Undersecretary of State for Global Affairs. In February 2007, as the President's Envoy to Northern Ireland, she received the Secretary of State's highest honor, the Distinguished Service Medal, for her contribution to the historic devolution of power in Belfast. During her more than 25 years in national security affairs, Ambassador Dobriansky has held many Senate-confirmed and senior level positions in the U.S. Government, including Director of European and Soviet Affairs at the National Security Council and Deputy Assistant Secretary of State for Human Rights and Humanitarian Affairs. From 1997 to 2001, Ambassador Dobriansky served as senior vice president and director of the Washington Office of the Council on Foreign Relations and was the first George F. Kennan Senior Fellow for Russian and Eurasian Studies. During this time, she also served on the presidentially appointed U.S. Advisory Commission on Public Diplomacy. A member of the Council on Foreign Relations and the American Academy of Diplomacy, Ambassador Dobriansky serves on the Defense Policy Board and the Secretary of State's Foreign Affairs Policy Board. She is a trustee of the Trilateral Commission, on the advisory board of Georgetown University's School of Foreign Service, and chair of the Bush Center's Women's Initiative Policy Advisory Council. She received a BSFS summa cum laude in international politics from Georgetown University School of Foreign Service and an MA and a PhD in Soviet political/military affairs from Harvard University."

IREX's major donors include the Gates Foundation, the Ford Foundation, the Open Society Foundations, Facebook, Google, Microsoft, USAID, the World Bank Group, UNICEF, the Carnegie Corporation of New York, Adobe, the Mozilla Foundation, the US State Department, Twitter, WhatsApp, the Millennium Challenge Corporation, McKinsey Social Initiative, Radio Free Asia, and various arms of the governments of Canada, the UK, Switzerland, Sweden, the Netherlands, and many more governmental, extra-, supra-, and non-governmental organizations.

The earlier-mentioned Media Development Investment Fund (MDIF) is:

> ...a fund structure that includes private equity, debt and hybrid funds. With a current portfolio of more than $100 million, all of our funds provide financing to independent media in countries where access to free and independent is under threat.

Reading between the lines, what this means is that they are going to seed money to "independent" media that will toe the legacy media's line on all things neoliberal, providing the illusion of "open dialogue" and "plurality." This is one of the great illusory tricks of the current system: the illusion of choice. Think of all the names we've covered so far and yet they all seem to converge on the same point(s).

The primary focus of the MDIF is to focus on societies that have yet to be "opened up" to the degree that the Establishment would like. One such fund is MMF I, "a $6 million blended-value loan fund providing affordable loans to independent media in OECD-DAC countries. It has invested in companies in countries including Malawi, Serbia, Ukraine and India." It is a partnership between the MDIF and the Swedish International Development Cooperation Agency (SIDA). The MDIF has honed in on Eastern Europe, sub-Saharan Africa, Latin America, and Southeast Asia in particular, though not exclusively.

The MDIF has offices in New York City and Prague, and they also partner with Transform Finance, the European Press Prize, the Global Forum for Media Development (GFMD), and the European Venture Philanthropy Association (EVPA), which itself has overlap with the OECD and was provided financial support from the European Union Programme for Employment and Social Innovation. This is a massive network that is deeply interconnected, and it encompasses international/supra-national governing bodies, individual governments, NGOs and "philanthropies," financial institutions, multi-nationals, service providers, media, academia, technology, and health care.

As these things all intersect, in March and June 2020 the EU, in a press release on their website, announced their:

> ...steps to fight disinformation around the coronavirus pandemic...[and] to resolutely counter disinformation and reinforce resilience of European societies. The coronavirus pandemic has been accompanied by a massive wave of false or misleading information, including attempts by foreign actors to influence EU citizens and debates.

The European External Action Service, together with the Commission, "enhanced strategic communication and public diplomacy in third countries" and "the EEAS East Stratcom Task Force detected and exposed more than 550 disinformation narratives from pro-Kremlin sources on the EUvsDisinfo website."

In what will be particularly disturbing for readers of my book *The Transgender-Industrial Complex*, a March 26th, 2020 joint statement by the members of the European Council declared:

> We will do everything possible to support research, coordinate efforts and seek synergies within the European scientific and research community so as to maximise the full potential of research across the EU. EUR 140 million have already been mobilised for 17 projects, including on vaccines.

These vaccines are highly experimental and have a number of disturbing features, which are discussed in my other writings.

The European Commission further outlines its actions in the June 10th, 2020 press release:

> Building on the work of the newly established European Digital Media Observatory, the EU will further strengthen its support to fact-checkers and researchers...The Action Plan against Disinformation of December 2018 outlined four pillars for the EU's fight against disinformation: 1) improving the capabilities to detect, analyse and expose disinformation; 2) strengthening coordinated and joint responses, i.a. through the Rapid Alert System; 3) mobilising the private sector to tackle disinformation; 4) raising awareness and improving societal resilience. In October 2018, the Code of Practice was signed by Facebook, Google, Twitter and Mozilla as well as trade associations representing online platforms, the advertising industry, and advertisers as a self-regulatory tool to tackle disinformation. Microsoft joined the Code in 2019.... Cooperation has been an important cornerstone of the fight against disinformation with the European Parliament and the Council and between EU institutions and Member States, by using established channels, such as the Rapid Alert System and the EU integrated political crisis response [and] with international partners, including the WHO, the G7 Rapid Response Mechanism, NATO and others.

Thus, when the Commission states that "public harm includes threats to democratic processes," we can understand what that *really* means. Furthermore, as gaslighting is central to the cowardly elites' hold on power, their public releases are actually extremely useful, since we know the opposite of whatever they're saying is pretty much always true.

With one failed color revolution in the books in Belarus, the same tactics were deployed once again in 2020 against President Alexander Lukashenko. Mass protests "spontaneously" erupted after challenger Svetlana Tikhanovskaya was demolished in the election by Lukashenko, protests that were suppressed for obvious reasons, and which of course then prompted the usual string of external condemnations from the "liberal democracies," who claimed the results were fraudulent, and from the press such as *The Guardian*, which in turn colors the perception of the "repressive" regime in the insular Belarus. Svetlana Alexievich said in an interview with Radio Liberty/Radio Free Europe that Tikhanovskaya "was and remains a symbol of change" who "did what she could." Uh huh. Crucially, *there is no evidence of fraud*. It's all speculation and claims made by Tikhanovskaya and her camp (i.e., the neoliberal Establishment), and these speculative claims do not contain a shred of evidence as opposed to the litany connected to the US Presidential Election a few months later.

When Russian President Vladimir Putin stated that he would lend military support to Belarus if a coup was attempted, NATO Secretary-General Jens Stoltenberg said NATO was "watching developments in Belarus closely," and that, "It's absolutely clear from all NATO Allies that the people in Belarus, they have the right to decide their own future without interference from abroad, interference from Russia. And, of course, have the right to have free and fair elections," as reported by *Euronews*. They do, of course, which is why the "liberal democracies" refuse to let them have it. The "best solution would be to replay the match under the control of the OSCE," said the EU's foreign policy chief Josep Borrell. Borrell called on Putin to refrain from intervening in Belarus and to "respect the democratic choices" of the people of Belarus. "If Russia respects the independence and sovereignty of a nation, it must respect the wishes and democratic choices of the Belarusian people," Borrell said. More gaslighting.

According to Jennifer Rankin at *The Guardian*, Polish MEP Robert Biedron, who chairs the European Parliament's delegation to Belarus, stated that, "We must impose sanctions on Belarusian officials responsible for human rights violations." What violations, imprisoning or exiling subversives? Biedron continued, "There must be a price that Lukashenko pays for violations of human rights and fundamental freedoms. Without this price paid by Lukashenko, nothing will change in Belarus. It is our responsibility to support the opposition."

In the same article, support for the opposition also comes in the form of backing Andrei Sannikov, a former presidential candidate now in exile, who says, "Stop all financial aid, start sanctioning everything!" Sannikov also co-founded the NGO Charter 97, which *BBC News* used as a "credible source" regarding "the infringement of basic human rights and liberties by the administration of President Alexander Lukashenko" without any evidence all the way back in 1997. Charter 97, by the way, receives funding from Amnesty International, the German Marshall Fund of the United States, and the Open Society Foundations. Super credible!

Then of course as Steven Kay followed up regarding Montenegro in late August 2020, once again with no evidence of electoral fraud—actually *anticipating* it with no evidence, citing the previously-discussed Establishment front the Organized Crime and Corruption Reporting Project's naming of President Milo Djukanović the Man of the Year in Organized Crime and Corruption in 2015, nominated by Vanja Ćalović, Executive Director of the Network for Affirmation of NGO Sector (MANS), which is a part of the Resource Center on Media Freedom in Europe, supported by the European Commission and run by Osservatorio Balcani e Caucaso Transeuropa (OBCT) as part of the European Center for Press and Media Freedom. OBCT is supported by the European Commission, the European Parliament, and the Open Society Foundations. It is also a part of the Media Freedom Rapid Response network, also funded by the European Commission. The European Center for Press and Media Freedom (ECPMF) is also a part of the Media Freedom Rapid Response network and receives funding from the European Commission, the National Endowment for Democracy (NED), and the Open Society Foundations, among others. Ominously, from *Euronews*:

> The EU, UK government and their allies must therefore be explicit: Djukanovic's position will not be sustainable if he claims a fraudulent election as a mandate. Here, fortunately, the West have more leverage than in Belarus: Montenegro is a member of NATO and a candidate for EU membership. Both must be thrown into jeopardy with external pressure applied once the expected fraud occurs.

So you see how all of this works, this grand shell game of "democracy."

Relying on the power of propaganda and control, we can see a number of potential fault-lines the ruling class can exploit, from class to religion to culture, in order to keep us divided while they continue to consolidate: *ordo ab chao* (order out of chaos). Multiculturalism is a vital aspect of this project;

create a home front riven with tension while destabilizing "un-democratic" regimes abroad through means ranging from and often including propaganda and various forms of subversion, economic sanctions, weaponized migration, assassinations, and/or open warfare. Domestically the color revolution model was applied in the 2020 US Presidential Election after having been tested across the globe for years; however, in this instance the Establishment provided ammunition for *both* sides—both sides in the American context that are completely closed loops.

With the attempted controlled demolition of the United States on the horizon, the Establishment has been laying the propaganda groundwork. As the Jewish Peter Beinart wrote for *The New York Times*:

> The rightful president of Belarus, Svetlana Tikhanovskaya, appeared via video last month before the United Nations Human Rights Council. Her country's August election, she declared, had been "stolen." Despite objections from a representative of the Belarusian government, who said she had no right to address the body, Ms. Tikhanovskaya implored the United Nations to act. "Standing up for democratic principles and human rights is not interfering in internal affairs," she insisted, "it is a universal question of human dignity."[28] No one knows how Donald Trump's Covid-19 diagnosis will affect his presidential campaign, but before falling ill, he repeatedly suggested that he won't accept the results of the election, should he lose. In that case, Joe Biden should follow Ms. Tikhanovskaya's example and appeal to the world for help. For many Americans—raised to see the United States as the natural leader of the "free world"—it may be hard to imagine requesting foreign intervention against tyranny in our own land. But as historians like Gerald Horne and Carol Anderson have detailed, there's a long history of Black Americans doing exactly that... After observing America's 2018 midterm elections, a team from the Organization for Security and Cooperation in Europe cataloged a long list of undemocratic practices...What Mr. Trump is doing this year, the election-monitoring expert Judith Kelley, the dean of the Sanford School of Public Policy at Duke University, recently told The Boston Globe, is the kind of activity that international election observers "would go to countries and write up huge reports about and say, 'Red flag! Red

---

[28] Notice Beinart provides no evidence—nor does Tikhanovskaya—but the claims are taken not just at face value but as evidence simply because they serve a purpose. The statement also ticks all of the rhetorical trope boxes.

flag!'" Democrats should spend the coming weeks working to ensure that this year's O.S.C.E. observer mission—despite being banned from many states, especially in the Deep South—can do exactly that. Then, if Mr. Trump and his allies halt the counting of ballots, or disregard them altogether, Democrats should use the O.S.C.E's report as evidence in an appeal to the same body where Ms. Tikhanovskaya made hers: the U.N. Human Rights Council.

Beinart, by the way, is a fellow at the Foundation for Middle East Peace; its Board of Directors with descriptions from its website includes people like:

o Odeh Aburdene, "a senior advisor to Capital Trust where he focuses on developing strategic relationships with private equity funds such as Blackstone, Quadrangle, Perseus, Centre Partners and the Trident Funds Group. Dr. Aburdene has spoken on the topic of venture capital and economic growth in the Middle East at the Dubai Strategy Forum in 2002, the Jeddah Economic Forum in 2004 and participated in the UCLA conference on Economic Growth in the Middle East in Doha, Qatar in 2006. Dr. Aburdene received his Ph.D. from Fletcher School of Law and Diplomacy, specializing in Oil Economics. His thesis analyzed the impact of Middle East oil on the U.S. balance of payments. Dr. Aburdene also studied the Middle East Oil Industry at The Harvard Center for Middle East Studies. Dr. Aburdene has published several articles on International Monetary issues. He is also a member of New York City Council on Foreign Relations and the International Advisory Board of the Fletcher School of Law and Diplomacy. He served on the Advisory Board of the Rand Center for Middle East Public Policy and the Advisory Board of Search for Common Ground and Seeds of Peace. Dr. Aburdene also serves on the Boards of America-Mideast Educational and Training Services, Inc., the Bethlehem Development Foundation and the Atlantic Council and the Scowcroft Center."
o Edison W. Dick, "served for over 15 years on the Board of Directors of the United Nations Association (UNA/USA) where he was Chair of the Advocacy Committee."
o Joseph Englehardt "is a retired U.S. Army colonel and a former international peacekeeper with over 35 years' experience in the Middle East. He was the U.S. Defense Attaché in Cairo. He also served in Tehran, Ankara, and Beirut. Colonel Englehardt was the Director of Middle East Studies at the U.S. Army War College and Military Adviser to the Assistant Secretary of State for Near Eastern Affairs. Returning to Cairo, he was the Representative of the Director General of the Multinational Force and

Observers, overseeing implementation of the peace treaty between Egypt and Israel from 1998 to 2004."
- Richard W. Murphy "had a 34-year career in the U.S. Foreign Service. After retiring in 1989, he joined the Council on Foreign Relations in New York as the Hasib J. Sabbagh Senior Fellow for the Middle East (1989-2004)."
- Jean Newsom "is former executive director of the Foundation for Middle East Peace. A graduate of the University of California/Berkeley, she has also been editor of the Middle East Journal and publications director at the Center for Strategic and International Studies in Washington, DC."
- Michael Van Dusen "is Senior Advisor to the President for Alumni Relations of the Woodrow Wilson International Center for Scholars. He held the position of Executive Vice President and Chief Operating Officer from 1999-2014. Prior to his time at the Wilson Center, he worked for close to 30 years in the U.S. House of Representatives, serving as staff consultant and then staff director of the Subcommittee on Europe and the Middle East of the Committee of Foreign Affairs, then Chief of Staff of the Committee on Foreign Affairs, and finally as Democratic Chief of Staff of the Committee on International Relations. He holds a doctorate from the Johns Hopkins University School of Advanced International Studies."
- Philip C. Wilcox, Jr. "retired from the U.S. Foreign Service in 1997 after a 31-year career, and was president of the Foundation for Middle East Peace from 2001 to 2014. During his career as a diplomat, he was Consul General in Jerusalem (1988-91), Director for Israeli and Arab-Israeli Affairs, Deputy Assistant Secretary of State for Middle Eastern Affairs, and Principal Deputy Assistant Secretary of State for Intelligence and Research, and Ambassador at Large and Coordinator for Counter-terrorism, from which he retired.... He serves as Chairman of the Board of American Friends of UNRWA, and is a member of the boards of the Rostropovitch-Vishnevskaya Foundation,[29] the International Student House in Washington, DC, and the Washington Institute for Foreign Affairs."
- Molly Williamson "is a retired Foreign Service Officer, having served six presidents, achieving the rank of Career Minister. She is a scholar with the Middle East Institute, a consultant, and frequent guest lecturer at Johns

---

[29] From its website: "RVF (Rostropovich-Vishnevskaya Foundation) is a global development organization that promotes the health and wellbeing of children in need through partnerships that create sustainable, transformational public health programs. RVF creates partnerships to provide all children residing in low- and middle-countries with sustainable access to WHO-recommended vaccines." Its supporters and partners include: the Bill and Melinda Gates Foundation, Pfizer, Merck, GlaxoSmithKline, ViiV Healthcare, Boeing, British Petroleum, the World Bank, USAID, the US Department of Defense, the US Department of Agriculture, the Government of Japan, and the National Institute of Health, Norway.

Hopkins University, Defense Institute of Security Assistance Management (DISAM), and National Joint Staff College. Williamson has been a distinguished scholar in residence with the National Council on US-Arab Relations since 2010. She is also a member of Georgetown University's MSFS oral boards, and a Director on several Boards. Williamson was the Senior Foreign Policy Advisor to the Secretary of Energy with global responsibilities at the nexus of foreign policy and energy policy. When Deputy Assistant Secretary of Commerce, Williamson was responsible for the Middle East, South Asia, Oceania and Africa, advancing trade relations with 86 countries with a trade portfolio valued at over $120 billion/year. Williamson was Principal Deputy, then Acting Assistant Secretary of State, International Organizations Bureau, responsible for the policy and programs affecting UN political and Security Council matters, peacekeeping and humanitarian operations."

If this seems like a lot of names and organizations, that's by design; what is vital for the reader to grasp is the sheer interconnectedness of this project, one where the failed social model is purposely created and proves immensely profitable and advantageous to the ruling class for social control and reengineering purposes. Social fragmentation is (in)valuable for the ruling class—consider what the ruling class truly means when they say they are going to be "investing in diversity." Everything is of a piece, even the reality-inverting jargon and cries of pained victimhood by those doing the most ruthless exploiting. In turn, they have trained legions of indoctrinated shock troops to always cry foul in the interest of splintering the targeted society or societies. This includes both imported and domestic populations, from the rough cohort of imported migrants to the local college kids learning about "systemic oppression" and turning on their own parents, peers, and societies. For added amplifying benefit, the imported populations can learn the same things and be weaponized against the host society. They serve both an economic and an ideological purpose.

Every "closed" society must become "open" to the opposition and the forces of globalism before the new power structure clamps down on any dissent and begins persecuting dissidents. Meanwhile the whole raft of destructive tidings come with the "liberalizers": mass importation of hostile aliens, the celebration of the mutilation of "trans" children and the harvesting of fetuses, the veneration of the dysgenic and defective, the fouling of all that is good. You are likely familiar with all of this, because in the West and increasingly the whole globe, we're living through it.

4

Demographic Warfare

Standing on the sloped shoulders of 2018's Global Compact for Safe, Orderly and Regular Migration, many Western governments have decided to treat this suicide pact as binding and take seriously their commitment to completely replace their populations, as massive in-flows of migrants continue despite the disruptions (but not cessation) brought on by the watershed coronavirus-related events of 2020, as borders become semi-permeable, meaning for citizens they are generally closed but open for the various stripes of migrants ear-marked for importation. This compact, as Czech Prime Minister Andrej Babis states via *AP News*, "in fact, defines migration as a basic human right," a human right reserved only for certain peoples in certain contexts—in short, for the First World to become the Third World, and for the whole world to be naught but a neo-feudalist favela.

Crucially, the United Nations compact makes no distinction between economic migrants and refugees—an enshrinement of what has been the disingenuous rhetorical strategy of the Establishment for years. Any government that supports this compact supports the cessation of its people's very existence. The Global Compact is framed consistent with target 10.7 of the 2030 Agenda for Sustainable Development, also known as the Sustainable Development Goals (SDGs) of the UN, in which Member States commit to "facilitate orderly, safe, regular and responsible migration and mobility of people, including through the implementation of planned and well-managed migration policies, which appears under Goal 10 to reduce inequality within and among countries," according to the Migration Data Portal website. Clearly this globalized form of communistic reduction in inequality is in keeping with the rapid de-industrialization of the West.

Parties and governments intertwined in this globalist network also treat the 2030 SDGs as binding. For example, Canada's Green Party, currently helmed by Annamie Paul (described as "the first Black Canadian and first Jewish woman to be elected leader of a major federal party in Canada"), believes that the SDGs and the "climate emergency must be the lens through which every policy envelope is viewed—the economy, health, education, foreign affairs, immigration, public safety, defence, social welfare, transportation," according to their website. Their actions support their words.

German Chancellor Angela Merkel stated that those who oppose this compact are pursuing "nationalism in its purest form." Well, yes, but it's telling that the Chancellor uses nationalism as an insult, and is very obviously not pursuing governance on behalf of her own nation and people. François Crépeau, director of the McGill Centre for Human Rights and Legal Pluralism and a former UN special rapporteur on the "human rights of migrants" has called the compact the populist swan song. Unsurprisingly, Ahmed Hussen, Minister of Immigration, Refugees, and Citizenship, was very eager for Canada to sign the compact, giving it a strychnine out of ten! The Canadian government's official position is that, "States have a common interest in facilitating safe, orderly and regular migration through the creation of new and expanded regular pathways." Indeed they do—or the ruling class does anyway.

The Canadian Council for Refugees agrees, supporting the UN's mass migration agenda and affirming a few key points that are considered "priority concerns," as their website's statement "UN Global Compact on Refugees and Global Compact for Migration: Our priorities":

o Focus on human rights (with gender-based lens).
o Focus on vulnerable persons (gender-based, minors (especially unaccompanied), LGBTI, people with disabilities, etc.).
o Involve civil society and refugees and migrants themselves meaningfully in the discussions leading to the Compacts.
o Affirm and strengthen the already existing international refugee protection regime; uphold fundamental principles such as *non-refoulement*, right to seek asylum and enjoy meaningful legal status and access to socio-economic integration.
o Underline the importance of permanent status.
o Canada and the international community need to do more to address the problems faced by refugees and migrants. The Compacts offer an important opportunity to challenge ourselves to do more. Canada should do more itself and challenge other countries also to do more.
o Acknowledge and combat xenophobia and racism (including in analysis of causes of forced migration and treatment of migrants – ongoing legacy of colonialism and slavery; in discussions avoid negative or disempowering language to refer to refugees/migrants as this feeds into xenophobia and racism).

Across the Atlantic, the Asylum, Migration, and Integration Fund (AMIF) is the successor to the European Refugee Fund (2008-13, €630 million to "support EU countries' efforts in receiving refugees and displaced persons"), covering the period 2014-20 with a total of €6.6 billion, to:

> Promote the efficient management of migration flows and the implementation, strengthening and development of a common Union approach to asylum and immigration.... Special financial incentives for EU States have been built into the AMIF to support the Union Resettlement Programme, including with focus on common Union priorities. A similar financial mechanism is foreseen for the transfer of beneficiaries of international protection from an EU State with high migratory pressure to another.... This Fund will contribute to the achievement of...specific objectives [such as] Asylum: strengthening and developing the Common European Asylum System...[and] Legal migration and integration: supporting legal migration to EU States in line with the labour market needs and promoting the effective integration of non-EU nationals.... This Fund will also provide financial resources for the activities and future development of the European Migration Network (EMN).

In 2013, the budget available for the EMN was €6 million; the European Commission services coordinate the EMN in cooperation with National Contact Points (EMN NCPs) appointed by EU countries plus Norway, and the EMN NCPs form "national networks with a wide-range of relevant stakeholders." The list of 2014 awarded grants to the European Migration Network National Contact Points (with grant amount):

Member State	EMN NCPs (Beneficiaries)	Grant awarded
Austria	International Organization for Migration (IOM), Office in Vienna	€303,887.29
Belgium	Belgian Immigration Office (DVZ/OE)	€225,798.24
Bulgaria	Chief Directorate Border Police, Ministry of Interior	€54,901.20
Croatia	Ministry of Interior	€29,638.40
Cyprus	Ministry of Interior	€45,391.46
Czech Republic	Department for Asylum and Migration Policy, Ministry of Interior	€76,639.19
Estonia	Estonian Academy of Security Sciences	€158,000.00
Finland	Finnish Immigration Service (Migri)	€380,349.62
France	Ministry of Interior	€262,457.40
Germany	Federal Office for Migration and Refugees	€352,480.96

	(BAMF)	
Greece	Ministry of Interior	€92,986.20
Hungary	Ministry of Interior	€75,999.04
Ireland	Economic and Social Research Institute (ESRI)	€349,249.04
Italy	IDOS Study and Research Centre (01/01/2014–31/03/2014)	€86,000.03
	National Research Council (01/04/2014–31/12/2014)	€221,784.51
Latvia	Office of Citizenship and Migration Affairs (PMLP)	€97,706.00
Lithuania	International Organization for Migration (IOM), Office in Vilnius	€160,000.00
Luxembourg	University of Luxembourg	€458,457.28
Malta	Ministry for Home Affairs and National Security	€55,999.23
Netherlands	Immigration and Naturalization Service Information and Analysis Centre (INDIAC)	€472,847.57
Poland	Ministry of Interior	€95,000.00
Portugal	Immigration and Borders Service (SEF)	€172,219.71
Slovakia	International Organization for Migration (IOM), Office in Bratislava	€184,994.63
Slovenia	Ministry of Interior	€40,000.00
Spain	General Secretariat for Immigration and Emigration, Ministry of Employment and Social Security	€341,993.92
Sweden	Swedish Migration Board	€445,480.83
UK	Home Office Science, Migration and Border Analysis (MBA)	€340,694.85

Funds such as Horizon 2020, the Fund for European Aid to the Most Deprived (FEAD), the European Regional Development Fund (ERDF), and the European Social Fund (ESF) also allocate funds to aiding and incentivizing migration into Europe. EU-sponsored "migration-related spending" eclipsed €14 billion for the time period 2014-20, with allocations continuing to rise.

Despite the ceaseless shrieking for "democracy," Florian Bieber for *Foreign Policy* dismisses "the will of the people" as a "trope," once again showing that democracy only works insofar as it aligns with the agenda of the ruling class. Should a majority—a vast majority in most cases—of the native population of a nation object to the importation of large numbers of aliens in whatever guise—migrant worker, "refugee," immigrant—this is "xenophobic," "racist," et cetera, though of course these kinds of things are never put to vote, they're just done. And where there *is* genuine movement to restrict or God forbid reverse the flow of aliens into a nation, as Chukwu-Emeka Chikezie puts it, "we must disrupt anti-immigration policymaking."

There are a number of mechanisms the ruling class employs in order to get as many migrants into the West as possible. Some of them are fairly straightforward, such as the UNHCR and IOM's "refugee resettlement" racket, and others are more complex, featuring a more "blended" approach, most commonly encompassing "philanthropic capitalism." As an example of the latter, Transform Finance runs a training camp of sorts where attendees are "provide[d] a framework for the intersection of social justice and finance, where financial concepts are learned within the practical context of social justice efforts," according to their website. Co-founder and Chair Morgan Simon is Jewish, as is Board member Aner Ben Ami, a former intelligence officer with the Israeli Defense Forces. Its other co-founder, Andrea Armeni, was a member of the Chai Society at Yale, a members-only Jewish social organization that is also open to select Gentiles "interested in the conversation of Judaism," according to an article in *The Jewish News of Northern California*. Armeni, "now considers himself 'more aligned with Judaism' than with the Catholicism in which he was raised. 'I've kept coming back because it felt right. I've come to share a lot of cultural values with American Jews,' he said." Wilneida Negrón, Project Manager of Capital, Media, and Technology, previously worked with the Ford Foundation, and Emily Sladek, Lead Project Researcher of Capital and Equitable Communities, worked with TRIO.

The Transform Finance Investor Network has committed over $2 billion to this hybrid "philanthropic capitalism." This particular model has been instrumental in mass migration and social engineering; it is one of the ways in which the LGBTQ agenda and its subversive precursors have been enabled to "go global" so quickly and pervasively in such a short period of time. Though mass migration is one particular aspect of the Establishment's efforts to remake the world in its dystopian image—albeit a crucially important one—these things are all inextricably intertwined given the way the system operates.

As with George Soros, Tony Blair is another Establishment archetype. The former UK Prime Minister is a former member of Labour Friends of Israel and has made millions of pounds leveraging his connections as a useful neoliberal accompaniment to the Bush regime's Project for the New American Century's nation-destroying campaigns, including his Windrush Ventures. According to the *Evening Standard*, Windrush is involved in advising Kazakhstan President Nursultan Nazarbayev on "government reforms." Ex-Barclays banker David Lyon is one of the senior-most directors in Windrush.

Windrush is the name of the vessel the *Empire Windrush*, which arrived at Tilbury Docks, Essex in June 1948 carrying hundreds of black Caribbeans, ostensibly to fill a "labor shortage"—fitting given Blair's track record on immigration. The *Empire Windrush* was operated by the New Zealand Shipping Company, which, as Andrew Joyce writes in *The Occidental Observer*:

> Was Jewish owned and operated. The company was for the most part controlled by the Isaacs family, particularly the direct descendants of Henry and George Isaacs…. In May 1948 the ship's Jewish operators were given permission by the British Ministry of Transport to increase their profits by filling to capacity with commercial customers (immigrants rather than contracted troops) at Jamaica before returning to Britain with these new settlers. This momentous decision appears to have been taken very arbitrarily (and certainly un-democratically) since it elicited great shock and confusion among British politicians when it later came to light. They might not have been so shocked had they considered the ethnic origin of the head of the Ministry for Transport who authorized that action. The Minister of Transport in that crucial period was Harry Louis Nathan, formerly a member of the law firm of Herbert Oppenheimer, Nathan and Vandyk, and a distant relative of the owners of the NZ Shipping Company.

The docking of the *Windrush* is commonly cited as the starting-point for multicultural Britain, and indeed Blair continues to do his part with the Tony Blair Institute for Global Change, which endeavors "to help political leaders build open, inclusive and prosperous societies in an increasingly interconnected world." The Institute describes populism as "extremist," which is fitting when we consider that some of its partnering organizations include the Anti-Defamation League (ADL), the Bill and Melinda Gates Foundation, the Overseas Development Institute (ODI), Microsoft Philanthropies, the Blavatnik School of Government at the University of Oxford (founded following a £75 million donation from the Jewish Len Blavatnik), the Center for Strategic and International Studies (the Board of Trustees is Chaired by the Jewish Thomas Pritzker), the Lawrence Ellison Foundation (named after the Jewish Larry Ellison), Nathan Associates London Ltd. (Chaired by the 1999 Distinguished Leadership Award by the Washington Chapter of the American Jewish Committee Edward H. Bersoff), and USAID.

In 2008, Blair was awarded a £2 million salary by JP Morgan Chase to serve as a part-time advisor. Blair, like another former Prime Minister Gordon Brown, is a former member of Labour Friends of Israel and is close with

Michael Levy of the Jewish Leadership Council, another Zionist entity. Levy ran the Labour Leader's Office Fund to finance Blair's 1997 campaign and in 2002 Blair appointed Levy as his personal envoy to the Middle East. In 2003, Sir Thomas Dalyell of the Binns, 11th Baronet came under fire for stating that Blair's foreign policy decisions were unduly influenced by a cabal of Jewish advisers, including Levy, Peter Mandelson, and Jack Straw; we can extend the accusation to the PNAC-driven neoconservatism animating both Blair and Bush at the beginning of the twenty-first century, which was heavily Jewish in membership and staunchly pro-Zionist. Indeed, the conclusion of the 2010s saw a near-perfect symmetrical revival with the part-Jewish Boris Johnson in the UK and the rabidly philo-Semitic Donald Trump in the United States serving as "fascist" bogeymen for the mostly-Leftward media. In practice, they were very, very far from anything resembling fascism, unless a slavish devotion to the hegemony of neoliberal capitalism and the desires of Israel qualify as fascism.

The US State Department's Bureau of Population, Refugees, and Migration (PRM) spends over $3.2 billion annually to help fund mass migration projects—and even in this endeavor, Israel finds a way to get a slice of the pie, as in $7.5 million in fiscal year 2018 for the Humanitarian Migrants to Israel (HMI) Program, which:

> ...provides financial resources for the resettlement of humanitarian migrants from the Former Soviet Union (FSU), Eastern Europe, Africa, the Near East and other countries of distress (read: Jews) in Israel. The grant is implemented by the United Israel Appeal (UIA) through Jewish Agency for Israel (JAFI) who manage a network of absorption centers throughout the country.

Almost $1.6 billion went to the UN High Commissioner for Refugees (UNHCR) and nearly $188.5 million went to the International Organization for Migration (IOM) in FY2018.

The State Department's PRM also disburses funds to several of the major NGO enablers of migrants into Europe, such as the Norwegian Refugee Council (nearly $11.9 million), Caritas Switzerland (nearly $1.5 million), Première Urgence Internationale in France ($4 million), and the Danish Refugee Council (nearly $9.2 million), and other major NGOs facilitating mass migration into the West such as the International Rescue Committee ($40.7 million), Catholic Relief Services ($10.2 million), the Hebrew Immigrant Aid Society (HIAS—over $8.1 million),[30] and the Pan American

---

[30] According to HIAS, "In 1891, Jewish residents of Moscow, St. Petersburg and Kiev were

Development Foundation ($6.65 million).

Another US State Department PRM funding priority is the Refugee Solidarity Network (over $1.6 million in FY2018), per their website: "Since 2014 RSN and sister organization Refugee Rights Turkey have benefitted greatly from PRM support, with the goal of assisting Turkey implement its new migration and asylum framework." Also partnering are Naripokkho and the Center for Legal Aid Bulgaria, whose mission, per their website's description:

> Is to promote the rights of migrants, refugees and asylum seekers on the territory of Bulgaria, through legal aid and advocacy. Since 2009, the CLA has promoted progressive legislative reform and raised awareness on asylum, migration and integration. CLA provides pro bono legal consultations to asylum seekers, refugees and migrants, as well as legal representation in administrative and judicial proceedings on the national and European levels. CLA also engages in research and monitoring, to support their advocacy initiatives, and participate in national, regional and Europe-wide networks.

The Refugee Solidarity Network (RSN) is a member of:

o International Detention Coalition (IDC): "A unique global network. Of over 400 civil society organizations and individuals in more than 90 countries, that advocate for, research and provide direct services to refugees, asylum-seekers and migrants affected by immigration detention."

---

expelled and many came to America. Ellis Island was the place of entry for these new arrivals. The Hebrew Immigrant Aid Society was there to facilitate legal entry, reception and immediate care for them." According to their Wikipedia entry, "Working with the U.S. government, the government of Israel, the United Nations High Commissioner for Refugees, and a host of non-governmental organizations, HIAS assists refugees with U.S. resettlement and follows through with immigrant integration and citizenship programs.... In the United States, HIAS helps resettle refugees from around the world through a national affiliate network of Jewish agencies. It coordinates resettlement services, provides extensive integration and citizenship programs for Russian speaking refugees and immigrants, and gives scholarships to refugees. HIAS also advocates for immigration laws with a network of Jewish, interfaith, and other partners in Washington, DC and nationwide. Additionally, HIAS promotes educational initiatives that encourage Jewish communities to engage in refugee aid and services.... In Latin America, HIAS provides full-service counseling, legal services, and humanitarian assistance for Colombian refugees fleeing to Ecuador and Venezuela. It also facilitates the resettlement and integration of refugees in Argentina and Uruguay. HIAS opened its newest Latin American office in Costa Rica, in February 2017.... In Vienna and Kyiv, HIAS helps Jews and others from 43 countries receive protection and seek asylum or resettlement. In 2016 HIAS opened an office on the Greek island of Lesvos to provide legal services for refugees arriving by sea, predominantly from Syria."

- o International Council of Voluntary Agencies (ICVA): "A platform for increased collaboration and coordination between NGOs and other humanitarian actors, which is crucial to improving the lives of communities affected by humanitarian crisis."
- o The Asia Pacific Refugee Rights Network (APRRN): "An open and growing network consisting of more than 340 civil society organizations and individuals from 28 countries committed to advancing the rights of refugees in the Asia Pacific region. APRRN aims to advance the rights of refugees and other people in need of protection through joint advocacy, capacity strengthening, resource sharing and outreach."

They have also received support from:

- o Google, as "RSN benefits from the support of Google Ad Grants for Nonprofits, which supports RSN's outreach, information dissemination, and fundraising activities"
- o BannerBuzz, which "supports RSN with marketing and communications needs"
- o The Tent Foundation, "The grant provided an opportunity to further develop programming at RSN's sister organization Refugee Rights Turkey, and make connections with advocates working on child protection in neighboring Greece and Bulgaria"
- o The Open Society Foundation Justice Initiative: "Since 2018, OSJI has worked with and supported RSN on efforts to respond to the Rohingya refugee crisis affecting South and Southeast Asia. OSJI and RSN are carrying out research and capacity development with civil society actors in the region."

In Central America, the US government and the World Bank have been very active in subsidizing migration north into America. As Kevin Sieff reports:

> The winding roads into the valley of Nebaj are lined with advertisements for cheap loans. Banks and cooperatives and microfinance operations make their pitches.... here in the Guatemala Highlands, the epicenter of the country's migrant exodus, those loans often fund a different activity, the region's most profitable: smuggling migrants north to the United States.... What enables those payments is a vast system of credit that includes financial institutions set up and supported by the United States and the World Bank, part of the global boom in microfinance over the past two decades. The U.S. government and the World Bank have

each extended tens of millions of dollars in funding and loan guarantees, money that helped create what is now Guatemala's biggest microfinance organization, Fundación Génesis Empresarial, and backed one of its largest banks, Banrural...The International Finance Corporation, an arm of the World Bank, lent the foundation $10 million last year [2018] to "broaden access to finance for micro and small businesses..." Compartamos, a Mexican bank...also received a flurry of USAID grants. It later stirred controversy for imposing interest rates of roughly 100 percent per year.... Throughout the 1980s and 1990s, development organizations devoted growing resources to what advocates called "access to credit" or "financial inclusion." In 2006, the Bangladeshi economist Muhammad Yunus, one of the forefathers of microfinance, won the Nobel Peace Prize for his "efforts to create economic and social development from below."

So this is what "financial inclusion" looks like. Once again we see the ideology of liberalism and the realities of neoliberal economics working hand-in-glove to advance the interests—with interest!—of the ruling class.

It is in the name of neoliberalism, not preposterous notions of "democracy" that the United States ferries its military about the globe toppling "totalitarian" regimes. If you look at the US role in Yugoslavia, Syria, and a slew of other conflicts you will see the notion that we fight these wars for freedom for what it is: a cruel joke. From at least World War I, the root of most global conflagrations has been at heart a struggle between globalists on the one hand and nationalists and/or particularists on the other. Kerry Bolton helpfully provides additional context:

> These protestations of patriotic motivations ring hollow. International banking is precisely what it is called—international, or globalist as such forms of capitalism are now called. Not only have these banking forms and other forms of big business had overlapping directorships and investments for generations, but they are often related through intermarriage. While Max Warburg of the Warburg banking house in Germany advised the Kaiser and while the German Government arranged for funding and safe passage of Lenin and his entourage from Switzerland across Germany to Russia; his brother Paul, a partner of Jacob Schiff's at Wall Street, looked after the family interests in New York. The primary factor that was behind the bankers' support for the Bolsheviks whether from London, New York, Stockholm, or Berlin, was to open up the underdeveloped

resources of Russia to the world market, just as in our own day George Soros, the money speculator, funds the so-called "color revolutions" to bring about "regime change" that facilitates the opening up of resources to global exploitation.[31] Hence there can no longer be any doubt that international capital a plays a major role in fomenting revolutions, because Soros plays the well-known modern-day equivalent of Jacob Schiff.... This aim of international finance, whether centered in Germany, England or the USA, to open up Russia to capitalist exploitation by supporting the Bolsheviks, was widely commented on at the time by a diversity of well-informed sources, including Allied intelligence agencies, and of particular interest by two very different individuals, Henry Wickham Steed, editor of *The London Times*, and Samuel Gompers, head of the American Federation of Labor.

Prior to World War II in the 1930s, in a Germany under NSDAP direction, employers were discouraged from treating women as workplace-widgets and wage-suppressors, and instead the building of families was incentivized by the state with a set percentage of loan forgiveness with the birth of each new child, among other monetary benefits. Under the NSDAP, loans were issued for a set price. Marriage loans up to 1,000 marks were implemented and were repayable in interest-free installments. A quarter of the loan was forgiven at the birth of each child. Unless it could not be produced domestically, imports were banned, with the express goal of making the German economy self-sufficient. This was highly problematic for the proto-neoliberal Establishment, for the dumping of cheap goods into domestic markets is central to their project, which helps create displaced and unemployed workers (think of the effects of NAFTA on both Mexican and American farmers), and the interconnected payment system of war reparations was key in keeping Germany weak and subservient. A prone Germany was also open to large-scale immigration from the East and social subversion.

With the new German economy forming the center of a central European trading bloc largely independent of the globalist system, foreign capital, and—this is key—foreign banking predicated on the centrality of interest, the economic miracle of Germany took place. Adolf Hitler was heavily influenced by the writings of Gottfried Feder, who conceived of an economy free from

---

[31] There is also the not-insignificant and in fact central component to all of this that international finance and the Bolshevik leadership were overwhelmingly Jewish and that the Jewish connection was a primary motivating factor in the meeting of otherwise-strange bedfellows. This aspect remains as vital now, perhaps more than ever, as neoliberalism undergoes its next mutation.

interest, with labor as the most valuable commodity, for only labor, not capital, is productive—an idea that has been present in Western thought dating to classical antiquity.

Capital is a conduit, a medium by which we exchange goods and services, but it is not in and of itself anything beyond the value we place upon it. Feder understood this and deplored the idea of compound interest, which creates nothing but rampant inequality and debt slavery and allows for a parasitic class of financiers to get rich off the work of others. As Feder wrote:

> The idea of interest on loans is the diabolical invention of big loan-capital; it alone makes possible the lazy drone's life of a minority of tycoons at the expense of the productive peoples and their work-potential; it has led to profound, irreconcilable differences, to class-hatred, from which war among citizens and brothers was born. The only cure, the radical means to heal suffering humanity is the abolition of enslavement to interest on money.... It is not to be overlooked that the international collaboration of the great moneypowers represents a completely new phenomenon. We have no parallel for this in history. International obligations of a monetary nature were practically unknown. Only with the rising global economy, with general global commerce, did the idea of international interest-economy establish itself, and here we touch the deepest root, here we have hit upon the innermost source of strength from which the Golden International draws its irresistible power.[32]

In light of Feder's prescient comments on the international collaboration of the great money-powers, the collusion of big capital and the Bolsheviks, and the ultimate smashing of Germany at the hands of the unholy alliance of capitalists and communists in World War II, these historical events and their aftermath in which we are living make much more sense. This unholy alliance persists in the present day, with Antifa and Black Lives Matter fomenters torching cities unmolested, while average people are subject to draconian laws and speech curtailment. Many of the worst excesses of communism are drawn upon to strengthen the Golden International's stranglehold on the population.

As a counter-point to unbridled capitalism, by the mid-1930s, Germany had the strongest economy in Europe. For Sheldon Emry:

> Germany issued debt-free and interest-free money from 1935 and

---

[32] Feder, *The Manifesto*, 7, 13.

on, accounting for its startling rise from the depression to a world power in 5 years. Germany financed its entire government and war operation from 1935 to 1945 without gold and without debt, and it took the whole Capitalist and Communist world to destroy the German power over Europe and bring Europe back under the heel of the Bankers. Such history of money does not even appear in the textbooks of public (government) schools today.

And why would it, as the goal has been to set the default to neoliberalism—and the indoctrinated semi-literate are often the most dangerous Useful Idiots. As George Monbiot writes:

> The zombie doctrine [of neoliberalism] staggers on, and one of the reasons is its anonymity. Or rather, a cluster of anonymities. The invisible doctrine of the invisible hand is promoted by invisible backers...The words used by neoliberalism often conceal more than they elucidate. "The market" sounds like a natural system that might bear upon us equally, like gravity or atmospheric pressure. But it is fraught with power relations. What "the market wants" tends to mean what corporations and their bosses want. "Investment..." means two quite different things. One is the funding of productive and socially useful activities, the other is the purchase of existing assets to milk them for rent, interest, dividends and capital gains. Using the same word for different activities "camouflages the sources of wealth," leading us to confuse wealth extraction with wealth creation.

It is in this environment that corporations are treated as people and people as disposable objects.

From this locus of control, neoliberal capitalism radiates outward, knocking down borders and any impediments to this new "open society." What happened on the heels of "majority rule" is a now-familiar tale; as Kerry Bolton writes:

> Why does a country that had hitherto been so prosperous need to raise capital by selling off its assets? The answer lies in South Africa having been quickly reduced to a basket case, a bottomless economic sinkhole, like every other "decolonized" state on the Dark Continent. The plutocrats who pushed for the destruction of so prosperous a nation apparently had a long-term dialectical plan that seemed, in the short-term, to undermine their profitability. In the

long term, however, the impoverishment of South Africa by the incompetence that invariably results from "majority rule" has obliged South Africa to become an open economy operating an ongoing garage sale (note: read *The State of Africa* by Martin Meredith for the details of how such a practice of strip-mining assets occurred in basically every "post-colonial" sub-Saharan African nation, often enabled by its own so-called "socialist" governments). But so long as South Africa now has universal franchise and has put the redundant Boer in his place, it matters not to most of the useful idiots of the Left who were merely performing their historic role as lickspittles of Money.[33]

This is happening across the West today, while in tandem Cultural Marxists kept the internationalism aspect of their ideology but dropped the workers; it is an inherently bourgeois "movement" that is in lock-step with global capital. Bolton explicates:

[Franklin Delano] Roosevelt wanted the predatory economic system to prevail over the world by the elimination not only of the [German] Reich, but also of all the Allied empires that he equated with the Reich. Today this is called "globalization," and we are having ever more wars—against Serbia, Iraq, Afghanistan, Libya, and so on—to impose this system while the so-called "color revolutions" funded and instigated by the Soros network, the National Endowment for Democracy, USAID, Freedom House, and a myriad of other globalist organizations, subvert and topple regimes that are reticent about opening up to globalization.[34]

So we can see how all of these seemingly variegated aspects of the system all eventually coalesce at the center with the same names and faces as we trace each strand back to the source.

Much like the color revolutions it sponsors abroad, domestically the US Establishment does not need to concern itself with the overthrow and replacement of a non-compliant regime—its designs have moved past that into getting rid of a non-compliant *people*. This is the end-game: through mass unrest and/or paralysis to harden the control and enforce new norm compliance. The anarchy enabled by the Establishment follows straight out of the Bolshevik playbook, from the toppling of statues to the rewriting of the

---

[33] Bolton, *Babel, Inc.,* 92.
[34] Ibid., 57.

history books. Black Lives Matter "activist" Shaun King even called for the destruction of all depictions of a European-appearing Jesus Christ. As former KGB agent and Soviet defector Yuri Bezmenov outlined, the process of subversion of a society's structure occurs through targeting its law and order, social relations, security, internal politics, and foreign policy; to cement control, the subverter follows this step-by-step process: demoralize, destabilize, foment crisis, normalize.

These subversive forces—who are, in fact, the Establishment and its often-unwitting foot soldiers—regard themselves as totally unaccountable and ethnic cleansing and mass genocide as perfectly acceptable in order to further their agenda. What the reader must understand is that the United States government, and any government in the neoliberal axis, is an occupation government that not only does *not* govern on behalf of its people, but actively works against them and does them legitimate harm. These governments and governing bodies do not represent our interests; their priorities are, in fact, antithetical to *all* peoples of the world having healthy homelands to call their own. Democracy this is not—it is a monstrous sham. In proclaiming the desirability of "international law" and "human rights," the US government and all neoliberal-aligned governments besides willingly cede authority further up the pyramid in the form of not just multi-lateral operations but in what will likely form some major part of the One World government's centralized authority at the United Nations.

The United Nations High Commissioner for Refugees (UNHCR)—along with "sister organizations" such as the International Organization for Migration (IOM), the UN Children's Fund (UNICEF), the UN Development Program (UNDP), and the Joint UN Program on HIV/AIDS (UNAIDS)—exists to resettle mostly-Third World peoples into the prone Western world. The UNHCR's annual budget is over $8.5 billion, with 61% of the funding for 2017 coming from just three sources: the governments of the United States and Germany and the European Union. In order to generate increased funding, the UNCHR states the following from the *UNHCR Global Appeal 2019 Update:*

> Bilateral development partners are adapting their programming and development funding to be more inclusive of people of concern. The partnership with the World Bank continues to flourish, offering new financing and funding opportunities to refugee hosting governments. New opportunities related to resource mobilization are also emerging with regional banks, with private sector actors and OECD, as well with the reform of the UN Development System…. In 2019, UNHCR aims to raise $500 million from the private sector:

$355 million from private individuals and $145 million from partners. More than half of the funds ($260 million) will be unearmarked. This will be achieved through: Close collaboration with seven national partners which, collectively, raise more than half of UNHCR's income from the private sector: Argentina con ACNUR, Australia for UNHCR, España con ACNUR (Spain), Japan for UNHCR, Sverige för UNHCR (Sweden), UNO Flüchtlingshilfe (Germany), and United States of America for UNHCR; through dedicated offices in more than twenty national fundraising operations around the world; in partnership with global companies, foundations and philanthropists such as the Bill and Melinda Gates Foundation, Educate A Child, IKEA Foundation, Qatar Charity and UNIQLO.

Other private partners include Sony, Microsoft, UPS, and the Vodafone Foundation.

For the year 2020, the International Organization for Migration (IOM) allocated significant funds for the following initiatives among many others (in the IOM's own description):

o Supporting Labour Migration in Rwanda: To promote safe and orderly migration and labour mobility from Rwanda to Canada by ensuring that migrant workers travel and work under safe and exploitation-free conditions, maximize their newly acquired skills and knowledge and increase remittances. The project intends to support the operationalization of the national labour mobility policy and its guiding framework through facilitating safe labour migration from Rwanda to Canada. It also provides support to ensure that the diaspora participates in economic growth in Rwanda.
o Encouraging Regular Migration in Poland: To promote regular labour migration and encourage the legal and dignified employment of migrant workers in Poland by raising employers' awareness of immigration law and procedures and enhancing their capacities to manage diversity in the workplace.
o Promoting Ethical Recruitment in Slovakia: To support the ethical recruitment of third-country nationals in Slovakia, ensuring the protection of migrant workers and their access to rights, through advice and training for employers on ethical recruitment.
o Community Support Programmes in Australia: To contribute to improved orderly migration and sustainable integration of migrants that will facilitate positive impacts for both migrants and host communities through increased

access to information, visa support, travel services, and post-arrival assistance under the Community Support Programme.
o Safety, Support and Solutions along the Central Mediterranean Route: To contribute to the safety, support and solutions programme along the Central Mediterranean migration route for refugees and migrants in situations of vulnerability through capacity-building for relevant stakeholders, information campaigns and enhancing policy support for governments.
o European Migration Network: To meet the information needs of community institutions, authorities and migration and asylum institutions in Austria, Lithuania and Slovakia by providing up-to-date, objective, reliable and comparable information on migration and asylum, with a view to supporting European Union policymaking in these areas.
o Implementation of the IOM Private Sector Partnership Strategy: To contribute to strengthening organizational capacity in effectively engaging the private sector in IOM operations through enhancing the capacities of IOM staff to identify and engage with private sector donors; increasing partnership with businesses; and the provision of effective support and oversight services for the implementation of the IOM Private Sector Partnership Strategy.

When I say significant funds, I mean significant: the IOM spends over $2 billion annually in the service of its mass migration agenda. It also has a staff of approaching 13,000 people.

The IOM is helmed by Antonio Vitorino, who is or has been on the corporate Boards of several major banks and other major businesses. He is also a member of the Trilateral Commission's European Group, the European Council on Foreign Relations, and the Migration Policy Institute's Transatlantic Council on Migration alongside the earlier-mentioned Michael Chertoff—who oversaw the investigation of the 9/11 terrorist attacks as well as co-authored the PATRIOT Act and spearheaded a national cyber security strategy as Homeland Security Secretary—and Charles Clarke, likewise of the European Council on Foreign Relations.

Remzi Lani is also on the European Council on Foreign Relations, as are Kristalina Georgieva (Managing Director of the IMF), Toomas Hendrik Ilves, Kersti Kaljulaid, George Soros, Alexander Soros, Goran Buldioski (Director, Berlin Office of the Open Society Foundations; Director, Open Society Initiative for Europe), Martina Larkin (Senior Advisor to the Chair and President, World Economic Forum), David Miliband (President and CEO, International Rescue Committee), Heather Grabbe (Director, Open Society European Policy Institute), Gunilla Carlsson (former interim UNAIDS Executive Director and former Swedish Minister for International

Development Cooperation, whose resume also includes Board or Panel membership with the UN Secretary General's High-Level Panel of Eminent Persons on the Post-2015 Development Agenda, the World Bank Group's High Level Advisory Council on Women's Economic Empowerment, GAVI, the Global Fund, and Annexin Pharmaceuticals), and numerous other globalists with connections to, among other organizations: NATO, Edelman, Deloitte, Harvard Kennedy School, the United Nations, the Brookings Institution, Securitas AB (a security services, monitoring, consulting, and investigation group, based in Stockholm, Sweden), Alto Data Analytics ("Alto's international and diverse team combined with artificial intelligence, algorithms and proprietary technologies enable massive real-time analysis of public data"), the World Bank Group, the Aspen Institute, the European Bank for Reconstruction and Development, the Stefan Batory Foundation, Edge Technologies (headquartered in Arlington, Virginia, "Edge provides software products and enterprise services to corporations and government agencies"), Carnegie Europe, the University of Oxford, the Atlantic Council, DatAdat ("a software and data company that specializes in helping a wide variety of political and social organizations, including political parties, NGOs [and] social movements"), the European Central Bank, *The Guardian*, *Le Monde*, the World Trade Organization, En Marche!, Columbia Law School, Langkjær Cyber Defence, EBRAINS ("a platform providing tools and services which can be used to address challenges in brain research and brain-inspired technology development. Its components are designed with, by, and for researchers. The tools assist scientists to collect, analyse, share, and integrate brain data, and to perform modelling and simulation of brain function"), and the CyberPeace Institute.

Let's look a bit more closely at the UN and IOM architecture of "refugee resettlement" and facilitation of mass migration; many Western countries have agreements with the UNHCR to take in pre-selected "refugees" and settle them within their borders. The numbers vary dramatically. Australia, for example, like many Western nations, supports the UNHCR as the international body responsible for initiating the process of "refugee resettlement," which is a massive scam as very few if any of these "refugees" even meet the UN's own definition of a refugee. Like many of its Western cousins, Australia follows the UNHCR's "resettlement needs recommendations," but also has a total resettlement figure often in excess of the UNHCR's recommendations; Australia has an annual total resettlement admission target of close to 15,000 people under programs including the offshore Humanitarian Program of people resettled from "priority regions" in the Middle East, Asia (including South West Asia), and Africa. What does this offshore Humanitarian Program look like? Per the UNHCR's *Resettlement*

Handbook "Australia Country Chapter" from 2018:

> The offshore component of the Humanitarian Program reflects Australia's commitment to the system of international protection. The offshore component goes beyond Australia's international obligations and reflects the desire of Australians to assist those in humanitarian need. The offshore component has two categories. The Refugee category is for people who are subject to persecution in their home country and are in need of resettlement. The majority of applicants who are considered under this category are identified by UNHCR and referred by UNHCR to Australia. The Refugee category contains the following visa subclasses: Refugee, In-country Special Humanitarian, Emergency Rescue and Woman at Risk. The Special Humanitarian Program (SHP) is for people who are outside their home country and subject to substantial discrimination amounting to gross violation of human rights in their home country. A proposer, who is an Australian citizen, permanent resident or eligible New Zealand citizen, or an organisation that is based in Australia, must support applications for entry under the SHP. Whilst SHP applicants are not referred by UNHCR, they may be registered with UNHCR and be a resettlement priority in their own right. The Community Support Program (CSP) is a new way for Australians to help refugees and others in humanitarian need begin a life in Australia. The CSP connects refugees overseas with individuals, businesses and community organisations in Australia who are ready to give them a hand with the practicalities of migration, settlement and employment.

When these "refugees" arrive, they can expect to receive the red carpet treatment, including:

- Airport reception
- On-arrival accommodation and property induction
- Initial food and essential items package
- Assistance to register with Centrelink, Medicare, and a bank
- Help to enroll in relevant education and training and obtain recognition of pre-arrival skills and qualifications
- Assistance with employment services, employment strategies and support services for establishing a business

o Humanitarian entrants are eligible for assistance from employment service programs including jobactive, Transition to Work, and Disability Employment Services

The only receiving countries working with the UNHCR in such a fashion are white countries, with the pseudo-exception of Brazil: Argentina, Australia, Ireland, Iceland, New Zealand, Canada, Romania, Uruguay, Chile, Belgium, Bulgaria, France, Germany, Sweden, Portugal, the UK, Norway, Italy, the Netherlands, Finland, and Denmark. Countries like Turkey, Morocco, the United Arab Emirates, Qatar, Kuwait, and Saudi Arabia provide funding to the UNHCR, but they do not accept any refugees.

In 2019, Sheikh Thani Bin Abdullah Bin Thani Al-Thani of Qatar became the UNHCR's largest individual donor, which is especially salient as huge numbers of Rohingya Muslims and Middle Eastern and African Muslims are permitted and sponsored to flood into the West. In 2017, the Czech Republic smartly withdrew from the UNHCR's "refugee resettlement" scheme.

A 2016 document signed by Mogens Lykketoft, President of the Seventieth session of the United Nations General Assembly, shows a large list of NGOs, universities, and other organizations convened under the auspices of the United Nations for the purposes of a "high level meeting of the plenary of the General Assembly to address large movements of refugees and migrants," September 19th, 2016.

Among the huge number were included: The New School (US); University of Manitoba (Canada); Uganda Network of Young People Living with HIV/AIDS; World Relief (US); Urban Refugees (France); The Slovak Non-Governmental Development Organizations Platform; The Refugee.pl Foundation (Poland); US Committee for Refugees and Immigrants (USCRI); Chatham House (UK); Organization for Aid to Refugees (Czech Republic); RESPECT Network Europe (Netherlands); Open Migration (Italy); NYU School of Medicine (US); National Union of Teachers (UK); National Network for Immigrant and Refugee Rights (US); Nasc Ireland; Migration Council Australia; Kids in Need of Defense (KIND—US); Mikser Association (Serbia); Islamic Relief Humanitare Organization in Deutschland; Johns Hopkins University (US); International Organization of Money Transfer Networks (UK); Human Rights League (Slovakia); Georgetown University (US); Danish Refugee Council; Dalhousie University (Canada); Economic Policy Institute (US); Al-Khair Foundation (UK); Carleton University (Canada); Center for International Migration and Integration (Israel); Caritas Lebanon; and CEAR (Spanish Commission for Refugees).

Some of the UNHCR's major partnering/collaborating NGOs include:

- AMERA International (UK): "Aims to increase access to justice for asylum seekers and refugees; provide legal advice for asylum determination, resettlement, family reunification, and other matters related to the enjoyment of fundamental rights"
- AMES Australia: "Since 1951, AMES Australia has provided a range of comprehensive settlement support programs to migrants, refugees, and asylum seekers settling in metropolitan and regional Victoria"
- Amnesty International
- AsyLex (Switzerland): Free legal counsel and aid to asylum seekers
- Bulgarian Council on Refugees and Migrants: "BCRM is a platform for advocacy, lobbying and fundraising for the protection, reception and integration of refugees and migrants. The BCRM works for further strengthening of the cooperation between the state institutions and the nongovernmental organizations in the field of the national asylum and migration policy and practice"
- Caritas Internationalis
- Chatham House (UK)
- European Lawyers in Lesvos (Greece): "Registered in Germany and Greece...European asylum lawyers provide free, independent legal assistance to asylum seekers...Provided free legal assistance to over 9,000 people on Lesvos."
- European Network on Statelessness (UK)
- Forum Refugies-Cosi (France): "Providing asylum seekers with accommodation and assisting with their integration since 1982...Since 2011, the association has also managed resettlement programmes as part of the agreement with UNHCR."
- Fundacion Migrantes y Refugiados Sin Fronteras (Argentina): "Special attention for the most vulnerable groups" including "ethnic minorities."
- Greek Council for Refugees
- Hebrew Immigrant Aid Society (HIAS)
- International Catholic Migration Commission (ICMC): "Protect and serve uprooted people, including refugees, asylum seekers, internally displaced people, victims of human trafficking and migrants—regardless of faith, race, ethnicity or nationality...Our programs and activities comply with...Catholic social teachings."
- International Detention Coalition (Australia): "Global network of over 400 civil society organisations and individuals in over 90 countries that advocate for research and provide direct services to refugees, asylum-seekers and migrants affected by immigration detention."
- International Rescue Committee (IRC)
- Islamic Relief Worldwide

- Jesuit Refugee Service
- Latter-Day Saint Charities
- Lutheran World Federation
- Macedonian Young Lawyers Association: Provides legal aid and representation to asylum-seekers and migrants and advocates for "human rights" and "anti-discrimination"
- Migrant Offshore Aid Station (Malta): From 2014-17, patrolled the Mediterranean and Aegean, ferrying some 40,000 migrants into Europe; suspended sea-going operations but remains a migrant "advocacy" organization
- Mosaico Azioni (Italy): "Everything concerning the right to asylum...National and regional advocacy through working with European and UN mechanisms (UNHCR, ECRE) as well as regional collaborations of refugee groups around inclusion, influencing migration policy...and creating links among organizations of refugees in Italy."
- Multicultural Youth Advocacy Network (Australia)
- Network for Refugee Voices (Germany)
- New Women Connectors (Netherlands): "New women recognizing the needs for social justice in both the eastern and western worlds, a vision of improving inclusion and social justice for all, here in Europe."
- Norwegian Refugee Council
- Oxfam International
- Portuguese Refugee Council
- Refugee Council of Australia
- Refugee Council of New Zealand
- Refugee Legal (Australia)
- Refugee Solidarity Network (US)
- Refugees International
- Scottish Refugee Council
- Slovenian Red Cross
- UK Lesbian and Gay Immigration Group: "Supports lesbian, gay, bisexual, trans, queer, and intersex people through the asylum system...Carries out strategic litigation and delivers training to government officials, NGOs, and lawyers."
- World Council of Churches

Regarding the resettlement agreements individual countries have with the UN specifically, in Norway, the annual target is 2,120 deferring to UNHCR allocations: 1,000 from sub-Saharan Africa and 1,000 from the MENA region (Middle East and North Africa), plus 120 "other." Norway gives priority to cases referred by UNHCR, but cases referred by the following agents may also be considered: the Ministry of Foreign Affairs; international criminal courts with which Norway has witness resettlement agreements; Norwegian PEN, where the applicant will be part of the Cities of Refuge Network; or Norwegian NGOs "with presence in areas where UNHCR is not represented or does not have a mandate to refer the person for resettlement." A fun chestnut from their UNHCR handbook chapter: "Norway gives priority to men and boys who are vulnerable because of their gender identity, or sexual orientation (LGBTI)." Iceland is also concerned with "medical cases and Lesbian, Gay, Bisexual, Transgender and Intersex (LGBTI) refugees," virtually all of whom hail from the MENA region ("Travel is arranged by IOM in close co-operation with UNHCR. Cost of travel is paid by the Icelandic Government.").

New Zealand's annual resettlement quota was 750 places deferring to "the needs and priorities identified by the UNHCR." In June 2016, the New Zealand government agreed that the annual refugee quota will permanently increase to 1,000 per year from 2018-19. Their cooperation/coordination with the UNHCR "has resulted in the resettlement of a diverse range of nationalities." New Zealand has a special category for "refugees" called Medical/Disabled, which includes up to twenty places for "refugees" with HIV/AIDS.

France's commitment of at least 10,000 "refugee" resettlements for 2018-19 (two years) were to be sourced almost entirely from the Middle East and Africa, with a priority given to Libyans. Booking plane tickets and issuing travel documents is handled by the IOM, with all costs covered by the IOM through European Funding (AMIF) paid by the Asylum Directorate. Additionally, in 2017, France initiated a new private sponsorship program called *corridors humanitaires* with five religious NGOs, with the goal of taking in 500 Syrians or Iraqis from Lebanon. Each "refugee" is eligible to bring in their spouse and children under the age of nineteen, presumably not counting toward the number of "refugees" in the targeted number.

In 2019, Germany was the third-largest donor to the UNHCR after the US and the European Union at $390.5 million. The Federal Foreign Office is responsible for the cooperation with UNHCR, which also provides most of the financial resources, and the Federal Ministry for Economic Cooperation and Development (BMZ) also works with the UNHCR. Germany's 2019 target for UNHCR "refugee submissions" was 5,600, but how many actually arrived through this mechanism is as of press time unknown; what we do know is that the 2018 target was 4,600, and the actual reported number of settled "refugees" was 8,600, all from Africa and the Middle East (including Turkey). We can reasonably assume, then, that the numbers will be much higher than 5,600. According to the UNHCR's country page for Germany:

> The federal states in Germany (Länder) can set up their own humanitarian admission programs, with the consent of the Federal Ministry of the Interior. These programs are implemented and administered by the respective federal state in their own responsibility. Since August 2013 admission programs of fifteen (out of the sixteen) German federal states for Syrians (and Iraqis) with family links in Germany were established. Five of these programs are currently still ongoing. Until today around 23.600 visas were issued in the framework of these programs…. In February 2018 the Federal Ministry of the Interior announced a pilot project for a private sponsorship program on the federal government level for up to 500 refugees…. To continue the implementation of the 1:1, Germany started a humanitarian admission program out of Turkey in January 2017, offering up to 500 places for Syrian refugees on a monthly basis…. The International Organization for Migration (IOM) is entrusted with organizing the transfer to Germany. The Federal Office for Migration and Refugees in Nuernberg/Germany (BAMF) informs IOM who is authorized to depart; IOM then books the flights and provides the BAMF with the travel details. If possible, BAMF staff accompanies the flights.

Over two million predominantly Third World migrants arrived in Germany in the year 2015 alone.

I will here remind the reader that the "refugee resettlement" racket of the IOM and the UNHCR is just one aspect of the huge globalist machine pumping as many non-Westerners into the West as possible, albeit a massive and lavishly-funded aspect. There are a host of other actors and organizations across the board from corporations to governments to "philanthropic organizations" and everything in between—and very often in collaboration. Let's consider a few of the other nations whose governments are collaborating with the UNHCR and, where relevant, other globalist monstrosities such as the EU attempting to replace their own people.

Following the Commission Recommendation on September 27th, 2017, Italy committed to resettle 1,000 "refugees" for the period 2018/2019 hailing from Syria, Palestine, Eritrea, Ethiopia, and Sudan. Nearly 2,000 were resettled over the period 2015-17 from Syria, Eritrea, Iraq, and Palestine. Why would refugees be fleeing Palestine, though, if Israel isn't ethnically-cleansing them? Just one of many cracks in the ridiculous globalist narrative. Italy's Department for Civil Liberties and Immigration of the Ministry of the Interior coordinates the National Resettlement Program, co-funded by the Asylum, Migration and Integration Fund (AMIF); the Department of Public

Security of the Ministry of Interior, the National Asylum Commission, the Ministry of Foreign Affairs, the Ministry of Health, the Protection System for international protection holders and unaccompanied foreign minors (SIPROIMI), the IOM, and the UNHCR collaborate with the Department in the implementation of the National Resettlement Program.

On April 12th, 2016, the Council of Ministers of the Republic of Bulgaria approved the National Resettlement Mechanism Framework, from the *UNHCR's Resettlement Handbook*:

> ...for the purpose of fulfilling Bulgaria's commitments under the Council Conclusions of 20 July 2015, as well as the 1:1 Mechanism under the EU-Turkey Agreement of 18 March 2016, adopted in response to the unprecedented number of refugees and migrants arriving in Europe.[35]

Its "refugees" will be entirely of the Middle Eastern and North African variety (MENA), because apparently centuries of Ottoman occupation weren't enough. Neighboring Romania has conducted several rounds of "refugee resettlement" including forty Iraqis in 2014. In 2017, IOM Romania implemented two projects financed by AMIF where 43 Syrians were resettled from Turkey in accordance with the national resettlement quota; 2019-20 saw the assurance of "the safe transfer of 109 Syrian refugees (from Turkey and Jordan), representing the resettlement quota for Romania for 2018-2019."

Portugal's 2018-19 total resettlement admission target was 1,010, all from MENA; for Ireland, 600 all from MENA; for the Netherlands, 1,750; for Denmark, 1,000; for Finland, 750 "+20%." Further, for Finland, per the *UNHCR's Resettlement Handbook* "Finland Country Chapter" from 2018:

> Finland emphasises the importance of strategic resettlement schemes and programmes and considers it important that resettlement is promoted in the EU. At the moment, Finland participates in the new EU resettlement scheme ("the 50,000 scheme") through the resettlement programme/refugee quota and has pledged in this context 1,670 resettlement places. Finland has also committed resettlement places within the refugee quota to the Evacuation Transit Mechanism (ETM) in response to the situation in Libya. Finland also stresses the need to agree on and implement the EU

---

[35] Further: "Following the Turkey-EU declaration of 18 March, 2016, all EU Member States have been made responsible for a greater commitment to the resettlement of Syrian citizens fleeing the war and already living in Turkey. For every migrant illegally present on the Greek territory returned to Turkey, a Syrian will be resettled from Turkey to the EU."

Resettlement Framework—including the need to get more EU states to participate in the global resettlement work in cooperation with UNHCR.

Belgium's annual resettlement target is 1,150 people, but they are to be "sourced" entirely from the Middle East and Africa. In 2017, this consisted of mostly Syrians (or people posing as Syrian) and the rest Congolese. CGRS, the asylum authority in Belgium, and FEDASIL ("federal agency for the reception of asylum seekers") formulated a proposal based on the UNHCR's projected "global resettlement needs" as well as EU priorities in the Joint European Resettlement Scheme and other EU-driven initiatives. In scanning through the "Belgian country chapter" of the *UNHCR Resettlement Handbook*, I found the following: "The treatment of acute diseases and decompensated chronic diseases that could prevent a refugee from being transferred to Belgium is provided by IOM."

The IOM's partners in the Czech Republic include: The Czech Ministries of the Interior, Labor and Social Affairs, and Foreign Affairs; The US Embassy in the Czech Republic; The British Embassy in the Czech Republic; The European Union; and Open Society Fund-Prague.

Major initiatives proposed for 2020 by regional IOM locations included, in the IOM's words from their *Migration Initiatives 2020*:

o Belgium: "Strengthen labor migration and human development actions by engaging and supporting diaspora communities in Belgium in their respective home countries to promote regular migration opportunities, as well as training initiatives Promote inclusion and social cohesion interventions for migrants, including access to public services and assistance."
o Bulgaria: "Improve social solidarity and acceptance of migrants within the Bulgarian society. Organize capacity-building activities aimed at improving the services offered to persons seeking international protection by strengthening and enhancing the administrative capacity of national institutions and NGOs. IOM will provide training and workshops on different topics, such as administrative capacity."
o Croatia: "IOM aims to organize a nationwide capacity-building and training-of-trainers exercise for first responders, law enforcement and other entities working with migrants. IOM promotes inclusive approaches to health care that are based on multi-country and multicultural collaboration and focus on reduction of health inequalities and enhanced social protection in health."
o Cyprus: "Inclusion and social cohesion, including access to public services.

This will be achieved by raising awareness and campaigning against xenophobia, promoting ethical recruitment of migrant workers and engaging diaspora to contributing in countries of origin through skills transfer."
- Czech Republic: "Strengthen its cooperation with the Ministry of Labor and Social Affairs and Ministry of the Interior to establish foreign workforce schemes."
- Denmark: "IOM seeks to expand its partnerships with governmental counterparts, academia, CSOs and UN agencies to increase awareness on, inter alia, IOM's work in Denmark, migration, IOM's work in relation to the Sustainable Development Goals (SDGs) and the Global Compact for Migration."
- France: "IOM will conduct awareness-raising activities to promote the positive contribution of migrants to host societies through film screenings and community events."
- Germany: "Cooperation with governmental partners, such as GIZ, will be strengthened. Continue to support the Federal Ministry of the Interior, Federal Office for Migration and Refugees and the Federal States of Berlin and Schleswig-Holstein with humanitarian admission and resettlement activities by providing medical check-ups, pre-departure orientation, and transportation services. Continue to implement the Family Assistance Program (FAP) and host the FAP Germany team that counsels refugees in Germany on the possibilities of family reunification. Establish a platform for dialogue and exchange between civil society and the Government for the implementation for the Global Compact for Migration and advocate for a rights-based approach to migration issues with government partners."
- Hungary: "IOM, in close coordination with the regional offices in Bangkok, Brussels and Vienna has reached out to various Hungarian government agencies, such as the Immigration and Asylum Office and the Ministry of Finance to offer a wide range of services related to labor migration to and from Hungary. IOM Hungary will remain involved in IOM's global initiatives intended to protect the rights of migrants through shaping the public perception of migrants and shaping the vocabulary and dialogue surrounding migration. IOM will continue to contribute—among other initiatives—to the 'I am a migrant' campaign and participate in the Global Migration Film Festival."
- Luxembourg: "IOM aims to address labor market shortages by enabling migrants from Nigeria and Senegal to work for a period of one to two years in companies in Belgium, Italy, Luxembourg or the Netherlands."
- Norway: "IOM will continue to participate in seminars on resettlement and integration for civic societies and other stakeholders, in coordination with

- the Directorate of Integration and Diversity. In 2020, it is anticipated that 3,000 refugees from various countries will receive travel and predeparture assistance."
- Poland: "IOM will also continue to engage with the private sector to mainstream migration and migrant integration into their corporate social responsibility policies."
- Portugal: "Provide support for the Government in defining future well-structured labor migration schemes that can swiftly respond to labor market demand. IOM will also remain active in providing comprehensive assistance to the Government in implementing its commitment to resettling refugees to Portugal."
- Romania: "Support the expansion of refugee resettlement programs in partnership with the Government, United Nations High Commissioner for Refugees (UNHCR), and receiving communities. Together with its strategic partners and the Romanian Ministry of Internal Affairs, IOM will continue to provide protection and assistance to refugees and migrants in crisis and in vulnerable situations. In this respect, IOM will facilitate transportation, medical screening, cultural orientation, as well as logistical and movement support to the Emergency Transit Centre (ETC) in Timisoara for refugees selected by UNHCR and the governments of the resettlement countries. Based on the previously successful ETC experiences and resettlement projects, IOM is expected to support the Government in resettling 100 refugees to Romania in 2020. This will further intensify IOM's commitment to resettlement assistance in Romania and contribute to the development of the resettlement program in the country. IOM will continue to provide health assessment and pre-departure health assistance for resettled refugees to the receiving countries, while also providing health assessments for self-payer immigrants bound for Australia, Canada, and New Zealand."
- Slovenia: "Facilitate training opportunities and regional exchanges, IOM will work with municipal authorities and other local actors to increase their capacities for innovative integration measures that will promote diversity and support the inclusion of migrants at the community level. Through comprehensive assistance in family reunification procedures for beneficiaries of international protection, IOM will help refugee families exercise their right to family reunification by helping them navigate the complex administrative procedures and ensure that their family members travel and arrive safely to Slovenia."

The IOM office in Cyprus works closely with the governmental authorities of Cyprus such as the Ministry of Interior and the Ministry of Health, plus UN and EU agencies and in collaboration with "diverse partners within the civil society, local authorities and academia." Various projects include "relocation, resettlement and family reunification, integration, access to services and public awareness to counter the rise in xenophobia and discrimination." IOM facilitates the resettlement and relocation of selected "refugees" to Cyprus in collaboration with the IOM offices in countries of departure. IOM also provides assistance to family members "entitled to reunite with their family in Cyprus by arranging the travel and serving as a contact point for the relatives or sponsors in Cyprus." The relocation program and reception assistance commenced in February 2016 and is funded by the Asylum, Migration and Integration Fund (AMIF) and the governments of Italy and Greece.

Sweden now has an annual resettlement target of 5,000 persons; the main nationalities for the past ten years have been Syrian, Somali, Afghani, Congolese, Sudanese, and Eritrean. In what should certainly put Swedish readers' minds at ease, from the trusty *UNHCR Resettlement Handbook*: "Sweden does not require UNHCR or IOM to carry out a medical examination of refugees selected for resettlement to Sweden." Awesome. Additionally, "Aliens who have lived in Sweden for five years (four years for Convention refugees and those who are stateless) and have proven their identity are entitled to Swedish citizenship." Resettled "refugees" have access to the same public health care services under the same conditions as Swedish citizens, financed by Swedish taxes. But those tax-payers, because Sweden is such a model of democracy, do not have a say in the mass importation of Third World peoples making their formerly-placid country a violent and fractured mess. These "refugees" also:

> ...are entitled to financial assistance if they are unable to support themselves by any other means. Newly arrived persons who partake in the establishment scheme is (sic) eligible for financial allowance. They may also apply for housing grants. Parents receive state allowance also for each child, on equal terms with native Swedish persons.

The International Catholic Migration Commission (ICMC) in Europe provides resettlement personnel through the UNHCR-ICMC Resettlement Deployment Scheme to support UNHCR resettlement activities in field offices. In 2012 alone, the ICMC nominated 36,880 people for resettlement consideration, a good-sized percentage of the total of 74,839 "refugees" submitted by the UNHCR to participating resettlement countries that year. The ICMC Europe office in Brussels works to promote resettlement in Europe and, with its partners the IOM and UNHCR, runs the European Resettlement

Network "to build European resettlement capacity and expertise." They also run the Resettlement Saves Lives Campaign and the SHARE project, building a network of cities, regions, and civil society partners committed to "refugee protection and integration." The ICMC Refugee Support Centre (RSC) in its Turkish and Lebanese offices where it processes "refugees" for resettlement in the United States.

For the UK, their "refugee resettlement" target was 23,000 by 2020 "plus a further 750 per annum." The UK operates four resettlement schemes: Gateway, Mandate, the Vulnerable Persons Resettlement Scheme (VPRS), and the Vulnerable Children's Resettlement Scheme (VCRS). The UK's approach is to—direct quote—"take refugees direct from non-European countries.... The Mandate scheme has no quota, and will resettle refugees from anywhere in the world if they have been referred to the UK by UNHCR." Interesting. Additionally, the government has pledged up to £10 million over five years for "a jointly funded Department of Education and Home Office programme to enable adults resettled through the VPRS and VCRS to access language tuition and integrate into British society."

For Canada, the country's "total resettlement admission target" is 27,000 people annually. In 2017, 17,340 people arrived from the Middle East and 8,490 from Africa with the remaining over 1,000 a global (mostly non-white, obviously, because the ruling class is intensely hostile toward the extant and obstinate white populations it aims to dismantle) smorgasbord just from "refugees" alone. Canada has three resettlement streams: (1) Government-assisted refugees (GARs), typically UNHCR-referred "refugees" that receive income support from the government for their first year in Canada. (2) Privately sponsored refugees (PSRs), "persons in refugee-like situations" identified and supported for their first year in Canada by organizations and individuals. (3) Blended visa office-referred (BVOR) "refugees," referred from the UNHCR and matched with a private sponsor. Income support comes partially from the government and partially from the private sponsor for the "refugee's" first year in Canada.

It should be noted that this is the official description, and huge numbers of these so-called "refugees" remain supported by the government well after the first year; from the 2015 study "Social Assistance Receipt Among Refugee Claimants in Canada":

> Among those who arrived in the early 2000s and whose claim was still active four years later, the rate ranged from 25% to 40%—about half what it had been the year after arrival. During the same period, about 8% of the Canadian population received social assistance income.

Immigration, Refugees and Citizenship Canada and Québec's Ministère de l'Immigration, de la Diversité et de l'Inclusion are responsible for Canada's resettlement policy. "Refugees" destined to Quebec fall under the Canada-Quebec Accord on Immigration.

LIFT Philanthropy Partners (LIFT), with funding from Immigration, Refugees and Citizenship Canada, launched its new *Better Beginnings, Bigger Impact* initiative in 2019 "to help newcomer organizations expand capacity, reach and impact," according to their website. "The Government of Canada is committed to ensuring that high-quality settlement services are provided to all newcomers, including refugees, across Canada," said Ahmed Hussen, Minister of Immigration, Refugees, and Citizenship, as reported on *Newswire*. The ten organizations are, with descriptions in their own words:

- Association for New Canadians, St. John's: "provides wrap-around services, including settlement information and orientation, language learning, skills development and employment counselling to Canadian newcomers."
- Furniture Bank, Toronto: "facilitates the soliciting, transporting, storing and distributing of furniture to people in need; helping to contribute to Canadian newcomers' sense of belonging."
- Global Gathering Place, Saskatoon: "drop-in centre offering English language training, life skills, settlement advice, individual client support, mental health counselling, and a variety of supplemental programs for immigrants and refugees."
- Immigrant and Refugee Community Organization of Manitoba, Winnipeg: "offers safe and secure affordable housing to newcomer families, complemented by holistic, wrap-around settlement service for the whole family, including after-school programs, financial planning and ESL training."
- Immigrant Employment Council of British Columbia, Vancouver: "provides B.C. employers with the solutions, tools and resources they need to attract, hire and retain qualified immigrant talent."
- Immigrants Working Centre, Hamilton: "offers orientation and settlement assistance, English language training, employment services, and community networking and volunteer opportunities."
- Mennonite New Life Centre of Toronto: "provides community employment counselling, language instruction, community mental health counselling and networking opportunities."
- New Brunswick Multicultural Council, Fredericton: "is a bilingual, umbrella organization committed to supporting immigrant-serving agencies, and multicultural and ethno-cultural associations in New Brunswick through advocating and promoting the economic, social and

cultural value in diversity."
- WIL Employment Connections, London: "works directly with employers and job-seekers to provide employment support and career development including assessment, counselling and preparation, assistance with licensure for internationally trained professionals, and volunteer placements."
- Windmill Microlending (formerly known as Immigrant Access Fund), Calgary (head office): "provides microloans of up to $10,000 to internationally trained immigrants so they can obtain the Canadian licensing or training required to work in their field in Canada."

The Canadian Council for Refugees is "a vibrant network of 200 groups and organizations committed to the rights, protection and settlement of refugees and other vulnerable migrants in Canada," and includes for some reason Raphaelswerk e.V. from Germany, as well as other organizations such as: the Jewish Child and Family Service-Settlement Services, Canadian Baptists of Western Canada-Refugee Sponsorship Program, Canadian Lutheran World Relief Refugee Program, Affiliation of Multicultural Societies and Service Agencies of British Columbia, Catholic Social Services-Immigration and Settlement Service, Canadian Muslim Women's Institute, Amnesty International, Jesuit Refugee Service, Canadian Human Rights Commission, Canadian Association of Refugee Lawyers, the Salvation Army, Oxfam Canada, the Presbyterian Church in Canada, International Association for Refugees, Canadian Council of Churches, Tides Canada Initiatives Society-Together Project, and something preposterously called FrancoQueer.

Tides Canada Initiatives Society's Together Project's founding donors were: the Amanda Rosenthal Talent Agency, Frontier, Beverly Bate, Peter Lusztyk, Anna Hill and Jim Creeggan, Diane Hill and Kevin Somerville, Omar Khan, Wayne Perry, Studio Blackwell, Patrick Marshall and Kate Bate, Tendril Studios, and Quidnet Inc. Program partners include the YMCA, the Ritz-Carlton Toronto, Costi Immigrant Services, Koffler, and the Sidra Project. Funding partners and corporate sponsors include: TD Bank; Lyft; the Ontario Ministry of Citizenship and Immigration; the Toronto Foundation; the Lawson Foundation; Immigration, Refugees, and Citizenship Canada; Innoweave; Shopify; Tendril; and #MovetheDial. Tides Canada itself receives significant funding from the Canadian government both federal and local, as well as from sources such as Warner Music Canada, TD Bank Group, Dow Chemical Canada, Diavik Diamond Mine (Rio Tinto owns a 60% stake in and operates the mine), Genus Capital Management, the Amanda Rosenthal Talent Agency, Vanguard Charitable Endowment Program, the United Ways of Toronto and the Northwest Territories, the Sigrid Rausing Trust, the Simons Foundation, the Schwab Charitable Fund, the Oak Foundation, the NoVo Foundation, the RBC Foundation, the New Venture Fund, the Enterprise Rent A Car Canada Foundation, the Clif Bar Family Foundation, the Tides Foundation, and BroadbandTV Corp.

The EU, the UN, the national governments, major corporations and financial institutions, NGOs, and the like are all in lock-step agreement that more Third World immigration into Oceania, South Africa, North America and in some cases South America, and Europe—with these people prioritized above Europeans as their eventual replacements—is always better. For example, the European NGO Platform Asylum and Migration (EPAM), is "the meeting-place of European non-governmental organisations and networks seeking to contribute to the development of asylum and migration policy in the European Union." Its quarterly meetings are co-chaired by the Churches' Commission for Migrants in Europe (CCME) and UNHCR, while quarterly working groups on asylum and migration are chaired respectively by the European Council on Refugees and Exiles (ECRE) and the Migration Policy Group (MPG). EPAM's constituent NGOs are: Amnesty International-European Institutions Office, Caritas Europa, Churches' Commission for Migrants in Europe, Commission of the Bishops' Conferences of the European Community, the European Network Against Racism, European Association for the Defense of Human Rights, Confederation of Family Organizations in the European Union, Protestant Church of Germany-Brussels Office, European Network of Migrant Women, ILGA-Europe, Human Rights Watch, European Council on Refugees and Exiles, European Women's Lobby, International Catholic Migration Commission, International Detention Coalition, the International Rescue Committee, Jesuit Refugee Service Europe, European Federation of National Organizations working with the Homeless, International Rehabilitation Council for Torture Victims, International Human Rights Federation, Social Platform, Médecins du Monde, Commission Justice et Paix, Migration Policy Group, Pax Christi International, Quaker Council for European Affairs, Save the Children-EU Office, Solidar, and the Platform for International Cooperation on Undocumented Migrants (PICUM).

PICUM receives funding from the European Union Program for Integration and Migration, the European Union Program for Employment and Social Innovation, the Sigrid Rausing Trust, the Oak Foundation, the Adessium Foundation, and the Open Society Foundations. PICUM has 158 member organizations in thirty-three countries, mostly in Europe, and its members "uphold the human rights of undocumented migrants by providing essential services, and leading campaigns, actions and advocacy." In 2019, the following eight organizations joined the network: Arbeit und Leben

(Germany), CEPAIM (Spain), MARS (Togo), Red Edition (Austria), SexWorkCall SWC (Romania), Skåne Stadsmission (Sweden), and UTSOPI (Belgium). Some of its other members include: SCOT-PEP: Scottish Prostitutes Education Project, Center for Legal Aid (Bulgaria), Evangelical Lutheran Church of Finland, HIAS Israel, Sex Workers Alliance Ireland, and ICRSE: International Committee on the Rights of Sex Workers in Europe. So apparently "undocumented" prostitutes are a major interest group in the globalist paradigm now. PICUM has annual revenues in excess of $1.2 billion.

The aforementioned ECRE is "an alliance of 106 organisations in 40 countries with its Secretariat in Brussels. The alliance works to promote the rights of refugees, asylum-seekers and other forcibly displaced persons" (see Appendix D for the full list). Since 2016, ECRE has had a Strategic Partnership with UNHCR and receives funding from EU sources such as the European Asylum Support Office (EASO) and AMIF; "philanthropies" such as the Sigrid Rausing Trust, the Oak Foundation, the Adessium Foundation, the Joseph Rowntree Charitable Trust, Stichting Porticus, the Open Society Foundations, the Calouste Gulbenkian Foundation, and EPIM (an initiative of private foundations); and "generous in-kind contributions and pro bono advice" from companies and institutions including: DLA Piper (where US Vice President Kamala Harris' Jewish husband Douglas Emhoff is a partner), Mayer Brown, BPP University, Queen Mary University of London, University of Torino, University of Köln, and the University of Ghent.

The Joseph Rowntree Charitable Trust's funding priorities include things like the Muslim Women's Network UK ("building a network of Islamic feminism allies") and the Scottish Refugee Council. Instead of focusing on legitimate research and education, the University of Glasgow—like Oxford, Manchester, and elsewhere—"brings together researchers, practitioners, NGOs and policy makers working with migrants, refugees and asylum seekers in Scotland by being an internationally recognised research network for Refugees, Asylum and Migration in Scotland." They work with the Scottish Refugee Council and the Scottish Migrants Network, among other organizations.

London South Bank University has also gotten in on the action: with substantial EU funding, from July 2010 to June 2011 before handing off to Learning Unlimited, according to the European Commission website:

> By reaching prospective migrant women in Bangladesh (a significant source of immigration to the UK), the chances of successful integration on their arrival to the UK is greatly increased. "Welcome to the UK" is an innovative three-year project which supports the integration of non-EU migrant women in the UK. The project has

two stages. The first consists of preparing for life in the UK through a sustainable learning programme piloted in Bangladesh by UK volunteers and Bangladeshi teachers. The second stage involves the welcoming of newly arrived non-EU migrant women to the UK, through a learning and support programme. The support and training offered to these non-EU migrant goes beyond simple English language skills. It effectively helps the women to deal with everyday challenges, such as travelling on public transport and accessing public services.

These are the funding priorities of the European Union, apparently.

And there are others. As two more examples among a depressing litany, in 2017, the EU disbursed €94.67 million to the UNHCR for "financing of accommodation for refugees in apartments" in Greece, and in 2015 €5.1 million to the French Ministry of Interior for the "creation of sanitary and humanitarian reception conditions for taking care of irregular migrants present in Calais."

In Europe we see the familiar push to facilitate endless wage-depressors and hyper-consumers' arrival to shovel into the furnace of neoliberal capitalism. LINK-IT is an EU-funded:

> ...innovative project aimed at delivering better integration outcomes for Syrian refugees resettled from Jordan, Lebanon and Turkey to Germany, Portugal, Romania and the United Kingdom.... The tool aims at helping authorities in the receiving countries...support their integration into the labour market at the earliest stage.

Partnering organizations in this endeavor are: International Catholic Migration Commission (ICMC), British Refugee Council (RC), Asociatia Serviciul Iezuitilor Pentru Refugiatii Din Romania (JRS Romania), Caritasverband Fur Die Diozese Hildesheim E.V (Caritas Friedland), and Conselho Portugues Para Os Refugiados (CPR). Another two-year project called Skills2Work, which ran from 2016-2017, was a:

> ...project that provides information for beneficiaries of international protection, representatives of migrant groups, employers, local authorities and service providers in the 9 participating EU member states: Belgium, Hungary, Ireland, Italy, the Netherlands, Slovak Republic, Slovenia, Spain, and the United Kingdom. The Skills2Work project aims to promote labour market integration of

beneficiaries of international protection by promoting the early validation of formal and informal skills and competences.

In a similar vein, the Admin4All project is funded with the support of the Directorate-General for Employment, Social Affairs, and Inclusion of the European Commission managed by the IOM office in Rome and "will target vulnerable third-country new and long-term residents (including refugees) experiencing social and economic disadvantages." The project—active in thirty-five municipalities across seven EU member states: Italy (Bari, Cagliari, Florence, Naples, Milan, Palermo, and Venice), Austria (Bruck an der Leitha, Telfs, Korneuburg, Kufstein, and Schwaz in Tirol), Poland (Gdansk, Krakow, Poznań, Warsaw, and Wroclav), Romania (Bucharest, Cluj, Galati, and Oradea), Greece (Athens, Agios Dimitrios, Nea Philadelphia, Piraeus, Thessaloniki, Kalamaria, Neapoli, and Herakleio), Spain (Madrid and Malaga), and Malta (Birzebbugia, Gzira, Marsa, and Msida)—"aims to enhance the capacity of local governments to develop sustainable strategies and inclusive services for the successful social and economic integration of migrants."

Starting in 2020 and running for three years until 2022, Includ-EU is a project that is being implemented in Slovenia, Greece, Italy, the Netherlands, Romania, and Spain. Includ-EU will be implemented in Slovenia by IOM in close cooperation with local municipalities, with a "commitment to the further inclusion of third-country nationals through labour market integration, health and housing efforts." It is being funded by the EU's Asylum, Migration, and Integration Fund (AMIF). Some of AMIF's principal projects include funding "migrant information centers" in Cyprus, "Improv[ing] reception conditions for asylum seekers and beneficiaries of international protection in Estonia through the support-person service," holding information sessions for "migrants" at "reception centers" in Finland, maintaining "an online service to validate long-stay visas [and] digital management of applications to hire foreign national employees" in France, and "promot[ing] interculturalism, social awareness of issues of acceptance of cultural-racial diversity and the fight against xenophobia and racism" in Greece.

Resistance to the population replacement project must be combated, and the ruling class will obviously employ every means at their disposal. One 2017 policy paper authored by Helen Dempster and Karen Hargrave under the auspices of Chatham House and the Overseas Development Institute (ODI)'s Forum on Refugee and Migration Policy initiative, with support from the German Agency for International Cooperation (GIZ) and the Paul Hamlyn Foundation, views emotional manipulation as a fine tool: "Emotive and value-driven arguments may have more traction than facts and evidence. Successful strategies might highlight the manageability of the situation, while emphasising shared values." Well that sounds awfully familiar, doesn't it? Further:

> Given the several levels on which public attitudes are shaped, it is likely that strategies will be best employed along several different tracks.... Initiatives coming from a liberal point of reference must employ complex and targeted strategies to ensure that efforts go beyond those who are already supportive. The most effective strategies are likely to be those that work on several levels, from politicians and the media to civil society and the private sector.

Indeed. Let's see who else is supporting ODI in addition to the Paul Hamlyn Foundation and GIZ, shall we? Some of the major donors include the EU, USAID, the UN, the World Bank, the IMF, Chatham House, the OECD, PricewaterhouseCoopers, and the Rockefeller Foundation (see Appendix E for a more complete list), a veritable who's who of the Establishment. Both ODI and Chatham House are based in the UK.

One of the largest and most well-funded mass migration organizations is the International Rescue Committee (IRC) and its IRC-UK counterpart; the IRC is run by the Jewish David Miliband. The IRC-UK is funded by: AS Roma; Bernard van Leer Foundation; Edelman; *The Financial Times*; J. Paul Getty, Jr. General Charitable Trust; RELX Group; the Sir James Reckitt Charity; Stavros Niarchos Foundation; the UK Mutual Steam Ship Assurance Association; UBS Optimus Foundation; Vitol Foundation; the Asfari Foundation; the Saïd Foundation; the British Embassy in South Sudan; Danish International Development Agency (DANIDA); Development Cooperation Division of the Department of Foreign Affairs of Ireland (Irish Aid); Dutch Ministry of Foreign Affairs (Dutch MFA); European Commission Directorate General for Development and Cooperation (EuropeAid); European Commission Directorate General Humanitarian Aid and Civil Protection; European Development Fund; French Development Agency (AFD); German Development Bank (KfW); the German Agency for International Cooperation (GIZ); Humanitarian Innovation Fund (HIF); Start Fund; Swedish International Development Cooperation Agency (SIDA); Swiss Agency for Development and Cooperation (SDC); UK Department for International Development (DFID); Action Against Hunger / Children's Investment Fund Foundation; Christian Blind Mission; and the Ethical Tea Partnership, among others.

The Joint Council for the Welfare of Immigrants (JCWI) is another major pro-migration NGO in the UK, which like the ODI also receives funding from the Paul Hamlyn Foundation, as well as: the AB Charitable Trust, the Barrow Cadbury Trust, the British Red Cross, the Esmée Fairbairn Foundation, the Equality & Human Rights Commission, the Hilden Charitable Trust, the Strategic Legal Fund, the Trust for London, and Unbound Philanthropy.

Unbound Philanthropy, "an independent private grantmaking foundation that invests in leaders and organizations in the US and UK working to build a vibrant, welcoming society and just immigration system," is a donor to the Southern Poverty Law Center (SPLC). Unbound claims it is dedicated to "Welcoming newcomers. Strengthening communities." Its mission is to "transform long-standing but solvable barriers to the human rights of migrants and refugees and their integration into host societies...." Grant recipients include the National Immigration Forum, National Immigration Law Center, American Immigration Council, Tennessee Immigrant and Refugee Rights Coalition, Media Matters, Tides Foundation, the radical-left Southern Poverty Law Center, and Hillary Clinton's favorite think tank: the Center for American Progress. Unbound financed the pro-refugee propaganda film *Welcome to Shelbyville*. Since 2008, Unbound has provided at least $2.4 million to the International Rescue Committee (IRC), and its net assets in 2013 were $141 million.

Unbound also partners with the Open Society Foundations, the NoVo Foundation, the Ford Foundation, the WK Kellogg Foundation, and others on the Pop Culture Collaborative, "a multi-year, multi-million dollar hub for high-impact partnerships and grants designed to leverage the reach and power of pop culture in service to social change goals." Pop Culture Collaborative Senior Fellow Ryan Senser:

> ...has consulted and led projects for a range of private, non-profit and advocacy organizations including Consumer Reports, 32BJ-SEIU, Color Of Change, Planned Parenthood Federation, Ford Foundation, Open Society Foundations, IBM, Starbucks, Microsoft, Johnson & Johnson, PepsiCo and the American Heart Association.

Unbound's 2019 grantees in the UK included the Paul Hamlyn Foundation,[36] Joint Council for the Welfare of Immigrants, Immigration Law Practitioners' Association, Refugee Action, Migration Museum Project, and the Runnymede Trust. 2019 grantees in the US included Church World Service, the Migration Policy Institute, Funders' Collaborative on Youth

---

[36] It was named after its founder publishing magnate Paul Hamlyn who "was a migrant, fleeing persecution in Nazi Germany."

Organizing—a project of Bend the Arc: A Jewish Partnership for Justice—and several NEO Philanthropy projects. Per their website:

> Taryn Higashi is the Executive Director of Unbound Philanthropy. Prior to working at Unbound, from 1997 to 2008, Taryn managed the migrant and refugee rights portfolio at the Ford Foundation and served as Deputy Director of the human rights unit from 2001–2008. Previously, Taryn was a Program Officer at The New York Community Trust.... She is a former Chair of the Advisory Board of the International Migration Initiative at the Open Society Foundations and former Co-Chair of the Board of Grantmakers Concerned with Immigrants and Refugees.

Unbound's Board members also have ties to the American Jewish World Service, the Migration Policy Institute,[37] the Rockefeller Foundation, the Central Bank of Ukraine, and PEN International.

The MacArthur Foundation has given several grants to the UN for the Global Forum on Migration and Development as well as sponsoring workshops and seminars on "international migration law" and for the United Nations University's Institute for Environment and Human Security (UNU-EHS), in collaboration with CARE International, to "undertake a special outreach effort for its Guatemala case study on the impact of climate change on migration in the region." It is the US government and the World Bank, however, not climate change, that is facilitating Guatemalans' migration north. CARE received nearly $12 million from the PRM in fiscal year 2018.

CARE International's multilateral funding partners are: European Union through the European Commission Humanitarian Office and Directorate General for Development and Co-operation; Food and Agriculture Organization (FAO); International Labour Organisation (ILO); International Fund for Agricultural Development (IFAD); United Nations Children's Fund (UNICEF); United Nations Development Fund for Women (UNIFEM); United Nations Development Programme (UNDP); United Nations Population Fund (UNFPA); United Nations Human Settlements Programme; United Nations High Commissioner for Refugees (UNHCR); Steering Committee for Humanitarian Response (SCHR); The World Bank; World Health Organization (WHO); and World Food Programme (WFP).

Their bilateral partners are: Australian Agency for International

---

[37] Which has itself received funding from the Open Society Foundations, producing such reports as Judith Kumin's December 2015 "Welcoming Engagement: How Private Sponsorship Can Strengthen Refugee Resettlement in the European Union."

Development (AusAID); Austrian Federal Chancellery; Austrian Federal Ministry of Foreign Affairs; UK Government's Department for International Development (DFID); Agence Francaise de Developpement; Canadian International Development Agency (CIDA); Danish Cooperation for Environment and Development (DANCED); Danish International Development Agency (DANIDA); Dutch Ministry of Development Cooperation; German Ministry of Economical Cooperation and Development (BMZ); Japanese Government; Ministry of Foreign Affairs, ROC; Norwegian Agency for Development Cooperation (Norad); Norwegian Ministry of Foreign Affairs; Republic and canton of Geneva; Swiss Agency for Development and Cooperation (SDC); United States Agency for International Development (USAID); and United States Office of Foreign Disaster Assistance (OFDA).

As one example of a CARE project, the NGO in partnership with the UK Department for International Development (DFID) runs a cash transfer project for women in rural Zimbabwe, where each month, households receive a cash payment into a virtual wallet on their mobile phone. That's it.

CARE's funding sources underscore the inextricability of the Establishment's various entities. What we see here are the various supra- and extra-governmental agencies, the governments themselves, financial institutions, and NGOs all intersecting with each other in order to promote the erosion of borders and facilitate mass migration into the West. There is significant overlap between the funding and/or partnering agencies and organizations across the board. There is almost complete uniformity in the ruling class and their functionaries that mass migration into the West by non-Western peoples in ever-increasing numbers is only ever a good thing and it must be promoted and facilitated at every level and by every mechanism available. Reflecting the inextricability of the various arms of neoliberalism, many of these organizations are also involved in the promotion of the LGBTQ agenda and various other "social justice" causes, with the simple fact that promoting and expanding all of the above is both ideologically and economically beneficial to the ruling class.

The architecture is vast and it is extensive. It is also deeply unpopular with the people whose countries are being invaded, obviously, despite the successful brainwashing campaign of many Westerners who are more concerned with virtue signaling than national sovereignty and having a country that isn't a cratered disaster; nevertheless, according to Bram Frouws, head of the Mixed Migration Center (MMC), Greece's deporting of migrants is "illegal" and emblematic of the "normalisation of the extreme." That opinion, frankly, is completely insane and indicative of where the ruling class has set the frame of acceptable opinion. What's illegal and extreme is flooding entire continents with hostile aliens in order to replace the host population; what is *not* illegal and extreme is a very benign treatment by deporting what is in effect an invading force of mostly fighting-age men. The MMC is part of, and governed by, the Danish Refugee Council through a Steering Committee consisting of DRC HQ and Regional representation. The MMC's work is enabled by funding and/or partnering organizations including: the Swiss Federal Department of Foreign Affairs, the UK Department for International Development (DFID), Denmark Development Cooperation (Danida), the Danish Ministry of Foreign Affairs, the UNHCR, the Intergovernmental Authority on Development (IGAD), the European Union, the Swiss Agency for Development and Cooperation, the United Nations Population Fund (UNFPA), and the Dutch Ministry of Foreign Affairs.

Sadly, as we've already seen evidence of, there are an awful lot of deeply misguided Christian organizations involved in the facilitation of mass migration. A few prime examples to close out this chapter will prove illustrative. The Brussels branch of the Confederation of Christian Trade Unions (CSC) has a "migrants' unit" dedicated to organizing, supporting and advising migrant workers, complete with "political lobbying and media attention-grabbing demonstrations to raise awareness."

MIND (Migration. Interconnectedness. Development.) was a three-year project (October 2017–September 2020), financed by the European Commission (DG DEVCO) with additional financial assistance of the European Union Development Education and Awareness Raising (DEAR) Program. It is led by Caritas Austria with Caritas Europa in the co-lead with ten additional Caritas organizations as partners: Caritas Bavaria (Germany), Caritas Bulgaria, Caritas Czech Republic, Cordaid (Caritas Netherlands), Caritas International Belgium, Caritas Italy, Caritas Portugal, Caritas Slovakia, Caritas Slovenia, and Caritas Sweden. Its objective is "to foster welcoming and inclusive narratives about migration in Europe."

In the spring of 2020, "at the height of the coronavirus emergency, a group of transsexuals, almost all Latin Americans, arrived in the church with amazement and wonder. They asked for help because with the virus they no longer had customers on the street," Don Andrea Conocchia, the parish priest of Torvaianica, not far from Rome, told *Il Fatto Quotidiano*:

> A group of transgender sex workers in Italy is getting help from an unlikely source—the Vatican. About two weeks ago, a trans woman of Torvaianica, a small city located about 23 miles southwest of Rome, went to her local church for help.... She was part of a community of about 20 women, between the ages of 30 and 50, who are struggling financially due to the COVID-19 pandemic.... The 56-

year-old cardinal said that the women, who are most likely undocumented, could find difficulties in getting help from the Italian government.

This is completely out of control, but it is reflective of the Vatican's orientation these days. The reason so many Catholic organizations are committed to facilitating mass migration into the West is the result of the proliferation of Liberation Theology; the philo-Semitic Pope Pius XII, who dedicated an encyclical on "migrants, aliens and refugees of whatever kind who, whether compelled by fear of persecution or by want, is forced to leave his native land" (*Exsul Familia*, 1952); and the subversion of the Church post-Vatican II by Jewish interests and the equally-philo-Semitic Pope John XXIII. It is now the official position of the Vatican that the "right to migrate" (to the West) is a human right. There's a lot more to cover here, but it is beyond the purview of this book.

5

THE HAND THAT FEEDS AND
THE CHURCH OF CLIENTOLOGY

When it comes to immigration, or just about anything for that matter, what the ruling class wants, the ruling class gets. In the United States, the top corporate clients of lobbying firms with the most reports filed since 2003 include Microsoft (429 reports), Oracle (172 reports), and Intel and Qualcomm (140 reports each). Microsoft employs at least 5,000 foreign workers through the H1-B visa program, and companies such as Amazon and Expedia employ thousands more. As Jaeyeon Joo notes:

> Since the incentives for pro-immigration policies are concentrated on powerful economic and political interest groups, their organized and coherent lobbying positively impact the policymakers, leading U.S. immigration policies to accept and legalize more immigrants, continuing the trajectory of the 1965 Immigration and Naturalization Act.

Even major labor unions like the AFL-CIO, the National Association of Home Builders, the National Concrete Masonry Association, and the National Association of Software & Services have been lobbying for more foreign worker visas and more immigration. Until the recent Convergence, unions have been vital in limiting immigration, from the Chinese Exclusion Act of 1882 in the US, as a result of the efforts of the Federation of Organized Trade and Labor Unions, to the Immigration Restriction Act in 1901. The American Federation of Labor (AFL) played a central role in the introduction of the Literacy Test provision in the 1917 Immigration Act, with the explicit intent to "screen and reduce the inflow of unskilled workers in the U.S labor force." Since this is racist or something now, I guess advocating for workers' rights is out the window in favor of mass unskilled ethnic replacements willing to work for pennies on the dollar.

Gearóid Ó Colmáin writes in a 2016 article: "Engels in his book *The*

Condition of the Working Class in England describes how the immigration of brutalised Irish paupers to England sabotaged English working class militancy and was a key component of class divide and rule." This is absolutely key. In 1870, Marx wrote, "Introducing into the local labour market foreign labour lowers wages and alongside that the material, moral and cultural position of the indigenous working class," and described migrants as "obedient mercenaries of capital in its struggle against labour." Also key.

When tailors in Britain unionized in 1865, the capitalist class responded by importing cheap labor from Germany. Gearóid Ó Colmáin also notes that, "If one reads the minutes of the General Council of the First International 1866-1888, one of the problems discussed was the importation by the bosses of Belgian workers into England who were prepared to work for lower rates." Big business in Canada, New Zealand, Australia, and the United States were relentless in trying to import huge numbers of coolies to suppress wages in the late-nineteenth and early twentieth centuries, and it was in no small part the efforts of organized labor to resist the demographic flooding of their nations in the interest of increased profits no matter the social and demographic costs that held the deluge at bay.

Poland, which has resisted European Union "refugee" quotas and large-scale immigration for the most part nevertheless stands poised to continue the same suicidal decision of importing "temporary workers" just as Germany, the US, the UK, and many other Western nations before them have in the name of a "worker shortage" and various other thin justifications for the corporatocracy to pad its bottom line. Indeed, the economists are adamant: old, white Europe and its progeny need infinity immigrants to buoy its economies.

Stefan Hardege, head of labor market and immigration at the Association of German Chambers of Commerce and Industry (DIHK), agrees that the 260,000 annual equatorial imports calculated by Bertelsmann Stiftung's migration report is "realistic." Germany has announced plans to bring in an increase of 25,000 "specialized" workers per year of non-EU origin. Sounds an awful lot like the American H-1B visa, which is a total scam. There is a veritable plethora of various visas in America designed to import as much scab labor as possible (not to mention the "investor" visas, student visas, chain migration, illegal alien migrant labor, et cetera, et cetera). According to Michał Wysocki, an expert on immigration law, Poland's major companies increasingly prefer to hire workers directly because "those employers who invest in importing a foreign worker from so far want to create a bond between them and a company so that they can stay in Poland and bring...their families over." As Marta Kucharska writes for *Equal Times:*

In 2017, Poland granted residency to 683,000 foreigners, according to Eurostat—one-fifth of all such permits issued across all the EU-28 member states and by far the biggest number for a single country. Eighty-seven per cent of those visas were for work. In addition, according to the *OECD International Migration Outlook 2019*, Poland has welcomed a record number of migrants in recent years: in 2017, with 1.1 million registered migrant workers, Poland was the world's top destination for temporary migration, ahead of the United States. Despite receiving record numbers of labour migrants, Poland still needs more workers to power its booming economy—1.5 million more by 2025, according to PricewaterhouseCoopers.

Most of these migrants have traditionally come from other European countries, albeit poorer ones, such as the Ukraine, Moldova, Georgia, and Belarus, but the "pull" factor of higher wages and the easing of visa-free entry to Ukrainians to the EU has found workers pushing west. Consequently, this manufactured "need" has unsurprisingly found a goldmine in the Third World where the population boom is being artificially subsidized by the same globalist entities shrieking that climate change will create millions of displaced refugees who must be imported en masse into the West and select Northeast Asian countries. Kucharska continues:

> The number of Asian workers in Poland is currently still small but this is expected to increase significantly in the coming years. According to data from the Ministry of Labour seen by *Equal Times*, the second highest number of work permits granted to a single country in 2018 went to 22,336 Nepalese workers.... In addition, 10,002 Bangladeshi workers and 9,706 Indian workers were granted work permits in the same year.... There are small numbers of foreign nationals from Africa and even smaller numbers from the Middle East who were granted work permits in 2018...but existing recruitment networks in south-east Asia make the region an ideal source for qualified workers.... The hiring of overseas workers is unlikely to stop anytime soon, especially as business representatives are currently lobbying the government to ease the procedures for hiring migrant workers. The Polish embassy in New Delhi, for example, which covers India, Nepal and Bangladesh, currently has more visa applications than it can process. As a result, many recruitment agencies are now pinning their hopes on workers from the Philippines to fill jobs in the IT sector and workers from Vietnam to fill vacancies in factories and construction. "When we take into

consideration the needs on the market resulting from demographics, the emigration of Poles and the labour shortfall, Poland has no choice but to bring in workers from Asia," says Grzegorz Tokarski, a private sector expert and CEO at Filipino Overseas Workers recruitment company.

Kucharska's article also quotes a "migrant" complaining about "racism" and a dearth of "diversity," as according to imported invoice analyst Latika Bhardwaj, "Poland is not used to brown and black immigrants." Why would it be, and why *should* it be? Despite Poland's avowed resistance to fake refugees being dumped within its borders by the EU, it is being eaten from within by a push to "internationalize" and feed the neoliberal economic machine with cheap, disposable labor and consumers. Continuing with Kucharska:

"Workers from Asia are solid, thorough and accurate, the result of their Asian upbringing," claims a recruiter named 'Jack' from Gdańsk, pitching his services as a recruiter of workers from Nepal, Bangladesh and India on the jobs board of Lento.pl. "They are good at doing repetitive physical jobs, requiring manual skills, stamina and attention." Jack offers companies a 'try before you buy' guarantee—if after a month, a labourer doesn't meet the employer's requirements, the company will get another worker without bearing any costs. *Equal Times* also saw an advert from JDM Poland, a recruitment agency from Warsaw, advertising migrant workers on Gumtree as being "100% available and willing to work more than 200 hours per month." According to the Polish Labour Code, as a rule, working time may not exceed an average of 40 hours in a five-day working week. The agency assures prospective employers that "overtime is at the same rate [of normal pay]." Grzegorz Sikora, communications director for the Trade Unions Forum (FZZ), tells *Equal Times*: "We are dealing with the next stage of the post-colonial world division." While trade unions acknowledge that Poland needs migrant labour, the concern is that "the policy of hiring and the management of these workers does not meet European standards." Social dumping, as well as the driving down of wages and working standards are all dangers that the unions are trying to prevent. "The further east Poland hires its workforce, the graver the problem becomes," says Sikora.

In Romania, despite the "increasing pressure on employers to find skilled workers in order to expand their businesses, recent official data show Romania is far from being considered to be in a 'workforce crisis' situation." This is indicative of the rest of the nations from Japan to Poland, but questioning the narrative is not allowed; besides, as parties like the Republican in the US will tell you, don't you want a "rising tide to lift all boats?" Never mind that the rising tide is drowning the host society in GDP, the true cost is prohibitive, unless of course you happen to be one of these Paul Singer types. For Romania, as Sorin Melenciuc reports for *Business Review:*

> Romania issued work permits during the first two months of this year [2018] for 1,174 foreign employees which came mainly from Vietnam, Turkey, Nepal, China and Serbia, according to General Inspectorate for Immigration data sent to Business Review. Morocco, Bangladesh and Brazil enter for the first time in the top 10 countries of origin in Romanian statistics regarding foreign workers. These figures show a record request for foreign employees in Romania, where businesses struggle with workforce shortages in sectors such as construction, HORECA or logistics...But the real number of foreign workers in Romania is much higher, due to unreported work. "We mention that during the year 2017, the police officers of the General Inspectorate for Immigration carried out 994 actions and controls on the fight against illegal work, at 1,559 companies, which resulted in the detection of 515 foreigners who were engaged in non-legal gainful activities," General Inspectorate for Immigration said to *Business Review.*

In 2019, Hungary issued 75,000 work permits to Chinese, Indian, Vietnamese, and Ukrainian nationals, according to *Asia Times.* And yet, as SNB Romanian trade union head Dumitru Costin states, the employers are abusive toward their scab labor who are "much, much cheaper than the local[s]" and that "it is obvious that they will obey without flinching and work unpaid overtime for fear of being sent back to their country." Hungarian construction worker union head Gyula Pallagi states that employers "exploit the language barriers by faking even their working papers," and Zoltan Laszlo, the head of the Hungarian Metallurgical Trade Union, says that employees are often pushed to work under less-than-ideal conditions under the threat of being "easily replaceable" with Mongolians or Vietnamese.

The rhetoric is all-too-familiar; for Jens Kastner of *Nikkei Asia* (this is a longer quote, but worth excerpting at length):

The Czech Republic and Germany are also trying to attract workers from the Philippines and other Asian countries to fill local positions, as their labor markets face aging populations, a brain drain and lower birthrates. Analysts say that Slovakia, Hungary and Romania will also be forced to open their doors to Asian workers.... some analysts estimate that Poland will face a shortage of four million workers by 2030. As such, the government is particularly keen to attract Filipino workers to its IT, construction and medical sectors, including caregivers for the elderly. "The Deputy Labor Minister [Stanislaw] Szwed has approached us, and in early August we responded with a draft agreement stipulating the protection mechanisms we expect for Filipino workers, which will hopefully be signed during the remainder of this year," said Patricia Ann V. Paez, Philippine ambassador to Poland, in a recent interview with the Nikkei Asian Review...Paez said: "Poland will be an attractive destination for our workers due to its strong labor rights, the shared Catholic faith and strong family values, the only possible drawback being the cold weather..." The Czech Republic has the lowest unemployment rate in the EU of 3.1% and is facing a shortfall of 310,000 workers. To this end, the government loosened immigration rules for Filipino and Mongolian workers in January. It will now take Filipinos just three months from the time of job application to landing in the Czech Republic, half the time it used to take.... From Mongolia, the Czech Republic is hoping to draw in workers in the meat-processing and dairy industries. Both countries signed an agreement in November to train Mongolian workers in those sectors. Vladan Raz, a Czech recruiter with Manila-based EDI Staffbuilders International, said that he is looking to employ Filipinos for local e-commerce platform Alza for a variety of logistics positions. He is also preparing to recruit Filipinos for Czech Airlines Technics and German wholesaler Metro Cash & Carry.... In Germany, the "Triple Win Project" agreed between both countries in 2013 is also coming to fruition, with one of the major hospital operators, Asklepios, welcoming its first six Filipino intensive care and surgery nurses in July, and another 253 to follow in the coming months [2018].... Daniela Zampini, an employment specialist for Central and Eastern Europe at the International Labor Organization, said that acute labor shortages in some industries may push the private sector to challenge some governments' anti-immigration stance. Zampini pointed to Hungary as an example. Construction wages there have been growing at double-digits year-on-year, pushing industry associations to pressure the government to open the door to more Asians to keep costs low.

Even Italy has announced a pathway to legal residency for tens of thousands of "undocumented migrants" through work permit applications in the agricultural sector and for "domestic helpers." Most agricultural production of seasonal fruits and vegetables in the EU Mediterranean region relies on migrant labor. In 2015, just under half of the workforce employed in agriculture was comprised of foreign nationals; 430,000 workers—over half—did not have an official contract.

Migrant labor, especially, has proven extremely useful to the ruling class for a variety of reasons, according to Susan Mannon:

> In the mid-twentieth century, guest-worker programs were popular in both the United States and Western Europe, where labor shortages frustrated seasonal labor recruitment. Such programs came to an end in the 1960s and 1970s as political opposition grew and economic crises deepened on both sides of the Atlantic (Martin, 2003; Castles, 2006). But talk of guest workers resurfaced when the agri-food industry reorganized in the 1980s. By the 1990s, countries like Germany and Spain were reinventing guest-worker programs for twenty-first century economic needs and political realities (Castles, 2006).... The contemporary appeal of guest workers is more or less the same as it was mid-century. Employers can access a steady supply of low wage workers, control workers through the terms of the contract, adjust the size of their work-force with ease, dismiss guest workers as they see fit, mitigate anti-immigrant sentiment in the local community, and avoid some of the social anxieties that surround undocumented migration. The advantages of guest workers are perhaps all the more critical in an era of 'lean' agri-food production, since securing a flexible, low-wage work-force is central to employers' ability to provide quality, low cost products to the market-place (Rogaly, 2008). Guest workers may also prove critical to new immigrant destinations, where the presence of immigrants has become politically and socially contentious.

This strategy of ignoring people's concerns in practice regarding immigration while still serving both the ideological impetus and the Chamber of Commerce interests is central to neoconservatism; in essence, one gets the "deep concern" voiced over immigration, and maybe token resistance on that front, but the numbers still come, and evermore. The neoconservative false binary of "as long as they come here legally" is a totally useless distinction. In a demographic war, and with a totally illegitimate system, who cares if the invading force is arriving via "legal" means if the legality itself is immoral? Remember what Solzhenitsyn said in his *Harvard Address*: "Life organized legalistically has thus shown its inability to defend itself against the corrosion of evil." Exploiting people and pitting them against each other is just part of the divide-and-conquer strategy of the capitalist class endeavoring to usher in the "Great Reset"/The Fourth Industrial Revolution of neo-feudalism and digitized totalitarianism.

An April 2020 report from the *Irish Examiner* revealed that the housing and accommodation of asylum seekers in Ireland has become a billion-euro industry. The largest government-contracted accommodation earner is Mosney Holiday PLC, which had received €139,577,808 as of 2017. East Coast Catering nabbed €130,082,506, and the shares of Bridgestock Ltd, which has "earned" €109,457,663 since 2002, have been held by a British Virgin Islands offshore company since 2011. Aramark has also "won" millions of euros in government contracts to house these "refugees."

These "refugees" are awfully appreciative: March 2020 brought news of hundreds of "refugees" given safe haven in South Africa protesting "xenophobia" and demanding to be relocated. This despite the fact that as Guy Oliver writes, "Asylum seekers can still technically live and work anywhere in the country until their refugee status is determined, and for the most part they are entitled to the same public services as South African citizens." This reminds me of the incident in Italy where a number of "refugees" rioted because the government did not provide a cleaning person for the house they had been given. Speaking of Italy and cleaning people, in April 2020, the Vicenza Financial Police discovered that Moroccan brothers had been running a cooperative that had falsified papers for 160 people from Ghana, Bangladesh, India, and North Africa; they also owed the state hundreds of thousands of euros and were providing fraudulent pay checks. This is just the tip of the iceberg.

When migrants arrive in the West, as is outlined in the September 1996 report entitled *Migration from the developing countries to the European industrialised countries* from the Council of Europe, from Rapporteur Mr. Junghanns, Germany, Group of the European People's Party:

> The importance of ethnic networks for migration patterns is one of the central findings of migration theory. For almost all citizens and ethnic groups from the Third World in almost all western European countries, corresponding communities have emerged that serve as mediation points or bridgeheads for migration. Such communities are

often small, but they can comprise several hundred thousand people. The most significant communities at the present time stem from the "guest worker" migration phase, and this is where the largest immigration figures are to be found at the present time. Many immigrants today try to gain admission by asking for asylum, and there are probably many illegal immigrants in these communities.

In addition to legal immigration and worker visas, other kinds of means for cheap labor can be employed by pressuring the right people *not* to act. A 2011 study by Gordon H. Hanson and Antonio Spilimbergo found that whenever industries like apparel factories, slaughterhouses, and mega-farms, which thrive on employed "undocumented immigrants," experience an uptick in demand for these products, border enforcement relaxes to meet the labor demand and the hours US Border Patrol officers spend in the field have a negative correlation with relative price changes: when industry demand for "undocumented labor" rises, border enforcement falls.

Much of the justification for multiculturalism and mass Third World immigration is couched in platitudes like "compassion" and "tolerance," but in reality it excuses ignorance and fuels the globalist super-state and multi-nationals with cheap labor, hyper-consumers, and anti-white foot soldiers. A secondary "benefit" would seem to be the need for warm bodies to fund the boundless entitlements of the childless West, at least in theory. You can't have indefinite, exponential growth of the welfare state without concurrent population growth, either through birth or immigration, in order to fund the welfare Ponzi scheme. Since the birthrates in the West are so low thanks to the various projects of the ruling class over the past sixty-plus years, we "need" mass immigration. That *not* encouraging brain-altering hormonal contraceptives and artificially suppressing the birth rates might be a better solution is not acceptable to those in power. The Hungarian government's efforts to subsidize a native population increase was universally condemned by the media as "racist," for example.

Beyond the economic factors, the accrual of social "brownie points" for supporting the abolishment of our borders and/or white guilt have successfully weaponized many whites against their own people and civilization; the official narrative is that the facilitation of more non-whites into Western nations is an intrinsic good in and of itself as well as a punishment/means of penance. For Ricardo Duchesne of the Council of European Canadians:

> Organized calls for mass immigration from the Third World were coming primarily from business lobbies looking for cheap labour and

mass consumers.... Soon enough, in the early 2000s, studies started coming out assessing the consequences of diversification. From the beginning, however, these studies tended to be guided by the idea that diversity was a positive goal. No academic was questioning the program itself. Such opposition was deemed to be "bigoted" and "ignorant," not for the educated, beyond the orbit of research proposals. Empirical studies were framed in such a way that negative findings about immigration were categorized as "challenges" to be overcome with further "integration" proposals and calls for policy initiatives to increase opportunities for immigrants. Negative reactions by white members of the host nation were not allowed to enter into the "empirical data" but were summarily disqualified as indications that the community was "xenophobic." Only the criticisms of minorities, or conformists on the left, about "lack of affirmative action," or "lack of integration efforts," was counted as evidence, not against the program, but as further confirmation of the need to expand the program.

It is not my intention here to demoralize the reader, but simply to illustrate how pervasive neoliberalism has become, and how it poses an existential threat to the survival of Occidental Man. It is so dangerous because it is a total system encompassing ideological and economic aspects, much like communism but more insidious because it is less obvious and heretofore (pre-COVID-19) had not called attention to itself as revolutionary, though the beneficiaries remain the same. Neoliberalism works in inversion and "soft power," and whether Left or Right, the interests inevitably converge in the tight grip of the ruling class.

Just in case you had any illusions that the entire ruling class is not aligned against you, three times in twelve years, numerous Fortune 500 companies filed amicus briefs in support of affirmative action for college admissions. As Roger Parloff wrote for *Fortune* in 2015:

> Companies' own affirmative action policies are not directly implicated in the case being argued Wednesday before the Court—which reviews how the University of Texas at Austin selects its freshman class—about 50 prominent businesses have argued in two amicus briefs that they won't be able to get the diverse workforces they need unless colleges, business schools, and engineering institutions can take race into account to achieve diversity goals.

Apple, Facebook, Google, Microsoft, Coca-Cola, Johnson & Johnson, JP Morgan Chase, Goldman Sachs, and Wells Fargo were among the 379 companies to file an amicus brief in support of gay marriage in 2015. In March 2020, over forty major employers including Verizon, Unilever, Uber, Nike, Lyft, Chobani, Amazon, Apple, American Airlines, AT&T, Ben and Jerry's, and Salesforce issued a letter "to oppose bills that target LGBTQ people, and transgender children in particular" as the Human Rights Campaign puts it. The bills in question are from Idaho: the first states that people cannot change the "gender" of their birth certificates, and the second states that, "athletic teams or sports designated for females, women, or girls shall not be open to students of the male sex." The entire ruling class opposes this, and you should know.

As far as what they support, according to the Jewish former Global Head of Active Equities at BlackRock Mark Wiseman, if Canada wants to maintain and grow a "robust economy," it must get to one hundred million people by the year 2100, as reported by *BNN Bloomberg* in 2019. For perspective, Canada now has around 37 million people, and this is after years of large-scale immigration and "refugee" resettlement. To that end, Wiseman and several other peers founded the Century Initiative to get Canada to that point of extreme overpopulation. Yes, it is a massive country, but the vast majority of people live and will presumably continue to live and be settled within 100 miles of the continental US border. 82.2% of the population growth seen in 2018/2019 was due to an influx of immigrants and non-permanent residents.

Wiseman's co-founders included Goldy Hyder (President and CEO of the Business Council of Canada; "Demographics are not going to be relying on just making babies, we're going to need immigration. We have to be able to communicate that from an economic perspective."), Willa Black (Cisco Canada), and Dominic Barton. Barton, Global Managing Partner at McKinsey & Company, is the Chair of the Canadian Minister of Finance's Advisory Council on Economic Growth and the Chair of the Seoul International Business Advisory Council, Canadian Ambassador to China, a Trustee of the Brookings Institution, a member of the Singapore Economic Development Board's International Advisory Council, and a member of the Boards of Memorial Sloan Kettering in New York City and the Asia Pacific Foundation of Canada. He is also the Co-Chair of the Focusing Capital on the Long Term initiative along with Larry Fink (BlackRock), Andrew Liveris (Dow), Cyrus Mistry (Tata,) and Mark Wiseman (BlackRock), which "seeks to develop practical structures, metrics and approaches for longer-term behaviours in the investment and business worlds." The Century Initiative partners with Cisco and the Canadian Imperial Bank of Commerce (CIBC), among others.

The Jewish Ben Bernanke bragged in a 2004 speech that "the Federal

Reserve System has recently expanded its support for international money transfers." Bernanke praised Citizens Bank for creating a remittances program for an immigrant population from the African country of Cape Verde by forming partnerships with two banks from that country, and a number of banks have entered the remittances market through partnerships with existing money transfer organizations. Many banks, such as Bank of America and Citibank, are building remittance services on the existing networks of ATMs. Bank of America charges $10 per transfer. Second Federal Savings in Chicago offers account holders an "amigo card," a second ATM card that can be sent to a family member in Mexico. Wells Fargo initiated a remittances program in 1996 and released Intercuenta Express in 2001 where amounts less than $500 can be sent to Mexico for a flat fee of $10. In the first three years of its program, Wells Fargo made nearly half a million money transfers to Mexico, representing at least $100 million in annual revenue. The World Council of Credit Unions began a remittances project in 1997 and introduced IRNet in July 2000 in partnership with institutions such as Travelex. The types and amount of services have since exploded, in particular as a consequence of the increasing digitization of money and transfer services available via cell/smart phone.

Seizing on the so-called "migrant crisis" of 2015, one of George Soros's planned investments under his very public allocation of $500 million in the 2016 *Wall Street Journal* op-ed titled "Why I'm Investing $500 Million in Migrants" was a joint venture between Soros and Mastercard called Humanity Ventures, which is "intended to be a social enterprise designed to spark economic and social development for vulnerable communities around the world, especially refugees and migrants." This follows, from the year prior, the Mastercard Aid Network; from a 2015 press release, it is described as "an end-to-end, non-financial service designed to streamline aid distribution even in the absence of telecommunications infrastructure. Now, impacted populations can secure basic needs swiftly with the simple dip of a card."

This is reminiscent of Majority, a digital banking service that helps immigrants reach their "American Dream," as the membership-based service "gives immigrants a platform to manage their money, send funds home to their families and carry out long-distance calls at affordable rates. The need for banking services tailored to immigrants inspired the creation of the banking brand," said Magnus Larsson, Majority CEO. Majority is another of what are being called "fintech" startups including Deserve, Nova Credit, and WorldRemit, which rely on these smartphones and tie into the extensive microfinance world as well. With a Majority membership, immigrants/customers receive a prepaid Visa card, an FDIC-insured checking account, fee-free remittance services, unlimited free international calls to twenty-five countries and discounted rates for calls to other countries, and Majority has partnered with Ohio-based Sutton Bank to provide customers with accounts with no overdraft fees or insufficient balance fees, and the card can withdraw cash from over 50,000 in-network ATMs.

According to the IOM's *World Migration Report 2018*, and clearly telegraphing who has a vested interest in the continued mass migration project:

> Recent work by the IMF, McKinsey Global Institute and the OECD, as well as the ongoing work of the World Bank and regional development banks, highlight the importance of ensuring that we remain focused on the successes of migration as well as the challenges.[38]

Further eroding the sovereignty of individual nations and ensuring that the globalist Establishment may operate with impunity so long as the laughable notion of "international human rights law"—*very* selectively applied and most frequently bastardized and twisted to suit the ruling class's agenda—is followed, the IOM and other international organizations are granted immunities and privileges in many countries to support and facilitate their work. Privileges and immunities comprise, inter alia, "immunity from jurisdiction, inviolability of premises and archives, currency and fiscal privileges as well as immunity from taxation on salaries and emoluments paid by the organization."

The IOM is insistent upon "a functioning Common European Asylum System" and "flexible and accessible legal pathways for admission of migrant workers to the EU." This is of course because there is the ubiquitous "labor shortage" across the West, driven by "demographic change," itself a product of the neoliberal system in the instances those pushing the claim that we "need" more labor aren't outright lying, as they usually are. The IOM also states that "the 2030 Agenda for Sustainable Development and the Sustainable Development Goals (SDGs) recognize good migration governance as an enabler of sustainable development." Translation: unending flows of migrants into the West, remittances (to say nothing of social capital, safety, the middle class, et cetera) out. Part of the SDGs is "to reduce inequality within and among countries."

The IOM has a phone application called MigApp which can be downloaded from the Apple App Store or through Google Play on Android phones, which connects these migrants to various resources such as access to

---

[38] McAuliffe, *World Migration Report 2018*, 3.

IOM programs and services, connects the migrants with each other to discuss migration routes and such, and includes a "low cost money transfer" feature. The International Organization of Money Transfer Networks was part of the UN's "high level meeting of the plenary of the General Assembly to address large movements of refugees and migrants," September 19th, 2016 as well, and Western Union, MoneyGram, and Mobile TeleSystems (MTS) are all partners with the IOM in the Ukraine, as one example.

Remittances, money transfers, and microloans are absolutely crucial to this globalized migration system. On the "charitable" side, there exists the Phone Credit for Refugees and Displaced People, which to date has facilitated over one £1 million to tens of thousands of "refugees" to top up their phones, buy SIM cards, and the like. According to *The Economist*, "Phones are now indispensable for refugees," and these kinds of technologies such as money transfer apps "has made migrating to Europe easier." Once again echoing the corruption of a "need" in the same fashion as a "human right," Maria Gabrielsen Jumbert, Rocco Bellanova, and Raphaël Gellert write:

> Photographs of refugees using smartphones have become common in the Western media landscape. Such images were much used to illustrate the arrival of refugees in Europe in 2015 and after. First stirring surprise, being at odds with stereotypes of refugees fleeing war, these images have now become more normalized. Using a phone or a smartphone has eventually become recognized as a matter of need rather than a luxury.

Bristol Refugee Rights in the UK states that phones and credit are a "basic right." In a similar vein, while the British police arrest people for social media posts and the German government sends the police to knock down your door for the same, via *Rueters:*

> Three refugees from Syria, Afghanistan and Cameroon are suing the German state for accessing personal data on their mobile phones, arguing it was an unnecessary invasion of privacy, their lawyer said on Tuesday. German authorities can examine the mobile phones of asylum seekers who do not have valid identity documents under a law passed in 2017 at the height of the migrant crisis in Europe to prevent asylum fraud. But the Berlin-based Society for Civil Rights (GFF), which filed the lawsuits on behalf of the three refugees, argues that this violates their human rights.

Well then. Understanding that the invasion of people's privacy is a huge concern and is ever-increasing in the modern super-surveillance state, the ability of nations to protect themselves is being neutered. As the definition of anarcho-tyranny, people such as you and I are subjected to tracking, data mining, surveillance of all kinds, censorship, and even un-personing, but "refugees" have a right to privacy even if it is a threat to national security. Quite possibly the ability to access this private information is a slippery slope, and I accept that is likely true; however, should these fighting-age men simply be denied entry as part of a sane system, then the problem simply goes away. The "solutions" in the modern context, however, are always designed to require more "solutions." It's like when you see an advertisement for medication to treat some minor condition on television in the US and the side effects virtually guarantee the need for some other medication in a cascade effect. In any case, regarding the high-tech speed train to oblivion, as Morgan Meaker wrote in 2018 for *Wired:*

> Smartphones have helped tens of thousands of migrants travel to Europe. A phone means you can stay in touch with your family—or with people smugglers. On the road, you can check Facebook groups that warn of border closures, policy changes or scams to watch out for. Advice on how to avoid border police spreads via WhatsApp.... Admittedly, some refugees do lie on their asylum applications. Omar—not his real name—certainly did. He travelled to Germany via Greece. Even for Syrians like him there were few legal alternatives into the EU. But his route meant he could face deportation under the EU's Dublin regulation, which dictates that asylum seekers must claim refugee status in the first EU country they arrive in. For Omar, that would mean settling in Greece—hardly an attractive destination considering its high unemployment and stretched social services.... If Omar's phone were searched, he could have become one of them, as his location history would have revealed his route through Europe, including his arrival in Greece. But before his asylum interview, he met Lena—also not her real name. A refugee advocate and businesswoman, Lena had read about Germany's new surveillance laws. She encouraged Omar to throw his phone away and tell immigration officials it had been stolen in the refugee camp where he was staying. "This camp was well-known for crime," says Lena, "so the story seemed believable." His application is still pending.... When sociology professor Marie Gillespie researched phone use among migrants travelling to Europe in 2016, she encountered widespread fear of mobile phone

surveillance. "Mobile phones were facilitators and enablers of their journeys, but they also posed a threat," she says. In response, she saw migrants who kept up to 13 different SIM cards, hiding them in different parts of their bodies as they travelled.... Phones became a constant feature along the route to Northern Europe: young men would line the pavements outside reception centres in Berlin, hunched over their screens. In Calais, groups would crowd around charging points. In 2016, the UN refugee agency reported that phones were so important to migrants moving across Europe, that they were spending up to one third of their income on phone credit.

In 2015, to aid the flow of "refugees" into Europe, Google raised $5.5 million in individual donations then matched it for an $11 million total. Google created the Crisis Info Hub, according to *CNN Business*:

> A site where refugees and migrants can go on their phones to get information on transportation, shelter and services when they arrive in a new country. A collaboration with the International Rescue Committee and Mercy Corps, the open-source project has information for Lesbos, Greece, and is adding more areas soon.

In October 2015, Google added Arabic to its visual translation tool, meaning anyone with the app can point their phone's camera at German or English text and it will be instantly translated to Arabic. Google has also worked closely with the UN to funnel cash payments to "refugees" in Jordan and Lebanon and a group called NetHope "which helps provide internet access in emergencies at locations such as refugee camps."

In Croatia, an engineer named Valent Turkovic endeavored to provide internet access in asylum centers, WiFi evidently being a "human right." Interestingly, the "right to privacy" applies when a government is attempting to authenticate an alien's identity, but there are no objections to the UNHCR using drones to monitor these refugee camps. A team of students from Edinburgh University designed a solar-powered mobile phone charging station for migrants in Greece to keep their phones charged. Refugee Phones is a UK campaign to donate phones, chargers, and SIM cards to "refugees." Crucially, as Maria Ullrich reports for *Spheres*, "The refugees mainly learned about data to satisfy basic needs from other refugees." The information spread along the migratory routes with advice on where to charge phones, what traffickers to trust, and how to avoid the police. Also of vital importance is access to social media, as Ullrich writes:

Social media like Facebook and Twitter for instance are suitable media because information spread through the networks can have a huge range of coverage. Trimikliniotis et al. mention Guantanamo Italia, a protest of Tunisian refugees that were detained in Lampedusa and later sent back to their country of origin. There, they organised a six-months hunger strike to protest against their deportation. Videos and information about their situation were then uploaded on a Facebook page specifically established by a friend. That is how their demand for rights in the end even reached Al Jazeera and France 24 and was consequently spread globally.[39] Social media use also contributed to the visible agency of refugees fleeing through the Balkan region when at the beginning of September the hashtag #marchofhope was spread all over the world. The photos of their collective movement marching with banners from Budapest via the motorways towards Western Europe recall a demonstration, a political act, refugees standing up for mobility. The term "March of Hope" expresses this political character of the migrant collective that had a certain impact on some destination countries. Germany's and Austria's decision to receive refugees was at least influenced by visual impressions of the March of Hope.... Social media provide easy access to various information and can contribute to spreading information to the public, to raise awareness for the situation of refugees and therefore to support or rescue them or to put pressure to politics. The above described case of media usage on the Balkan route presents convincing arguments in favour of considering social media as significantly important for visible collective migrant agency. However, also traditional media, like phones can contribute to refugees' visibility as the case from the Mediterranean Sea and *WatchTheMed-Alarmphone* showed.

In fact, for Ullrich, one tweet may well have set off a chain reaction in the midst of the so-called "migrant crisis" in 2015:

According to the popular German boulevard newspaper *The BILD*, it was a historical tweet of 140 characters from August 2015 that resulted in Germany becoming the primary country to receive Syrian refugees via the Balkan route. The tweet by the German National Office for Migration and Refugees (BAMF) stated that from

---

[39] This use/manipulation of social media is a crucial aspect of astroturfing color revolutions as well, such as in the so-called Arab Spring.

that moment, the Dublin Regulation should not apply to Syrian refugees, meaning they would not be sent back to the country they first entered in the Schengen Area. *The BILD* blamed Merkel for the tweet in their article. There was a widely shared belief that the spread of "welcoming" information through social media was one of the main reasons why many Syrian refugees considered Germany as their preferred country of arrival. The access to social media and the welcoming messages spread using these platforms, were cited as significant pull factors for Syrian refugees to continue walking towards Western Europe from Hungary at the beginning of September 2015.

"European start-ups" that have helped enable "refugees" to flood into the continent over the past several years include, as Bojana Trajkovska of *EU-Startups* lists:

o Moni: "An online payments startup that partnered with the Finnish government to replace the traditional cash disbursements to refugees with a prepaid debit card that avoids the need for a bank account or identity papers."
o Funzi: "Finnish startup created a series of learning packages to assist refugees in Finland, which include information services, employment services and communication and networking skills. Based on 'funzifying' learning content through mobile pedagogy and gamification, Funzi is working with the UN System, NGOs, public organizations, and large private sector enterprises to deliver learning to the world."
o Just Arrived: "A matchmaking platform that connects the newcomers in Sweden to available job opportunities in the Swedish labor market. The app is currently available in English, Swedish, Farsi and Arabic, with more languages to be added in the future."
o Refugee Work: "An Austria-based online jobs platform."
o Mygrants: "An educational online platform for refugees and asylum seekers in Italy, providing information, guidance and legal assistance through all procedural steps of the asylum system, as well as thematic-quiz modules in 3 languages which shape, support and map the skills of immigrants. From departure to disembarkation, Mygrants together with partners and sponsors, is offering immigrants the chance to reach their full potential, free of charge."
o Social Bee: "Founded in 2016 in Munich, Social-Bee is a full-service integration & personnel service, using a temporary employment model to integrate refugees into the labor market and society. Their services include

recruiting, job preparation, training, as well as language education and cultural and corporate integration through targeted programs."
o Refugees Welcome: "Named the first Airbnb for refugees, Refugees Welcome was founded in Germany in 2014 as a digital platform that brings flatshares and refugees together. Besides matching refugees with housing options, they also assist in finding ways to pay for rent, such as microdonations and crowdfunding campaigns."

As we can see, there is a massive infrastructure in place to facilitate the movement of these people into the West in large numbers, essentially taking care of every aspect of the journey. All the "migrants" have to do is show up, and they are obviously being incentivized to do so. Their facilitation and the trial of different strategies and technologies during the "crisis" has been a great opportunity for the tech-driven "New Era of Refugee Investing," as John Kluge and Tim Docking reported in 2019:

> More than three years into the pursuit of the Sustainable Development Goals (SDGs), not one country is on track to achieve them by the 2030 deadline. This conclusion, reached in a recent Brookings Institution report, highlights the enormous human costs associated with not meeting these goals, and implores countries to do more. With heads of state slated to meet at the UN later this year for the first major progress check on the SDGs, it is high time we bring new and innovative approaches to economic growth and investing to bear on the world's social challenges.... Research shows [refugees] are loyal, creditworthy, and investible.... The Refugee Investment Network (RIN) was established in 2018 to...build the "connective tissue" to mobilize investment capital...to mitigate both real and perceived financial risks, some investors are using "blended capital" and other creative financing structures in place of traditional investment approaches. For example, the private sector arm of the World Bank, the International Finance Corporation (IFC), and the Goldman Sachs 10,000 Women program partnered to create the Women Entrepreneurs Opportunity Facility (WEOF), a first-of-its-kind global loan facility for women-owned, small- and medium-sized enterprises. WEOF launched in 2014 with a $100 million investment from the IFC and $43 million from the Goldman Sachs Foundation. This initial capital incentivized other investors to co-invest in a previously unproven market and demonstrate the commercial viability of a new asset class.

Or serf class. Unshackled Ventures does something similar, by "lead[ing] investments and provid[ing] the 'friends and family' capital immigrant teams often don't have. We sponsor visas, provide full immigration support, and a community of resources." In ensuring that the flow of "migrant workers in global supply chains" as the Jewish Aron Cramer, President and CEO of Business for Social Responsibility (BSR) put it in a MacArthur Foundation-funded report, immigration/migration continues to pad the bottom line with consumption, ever-cheaper labor, and shattering social cohesion, benefitting the ruling class enormously. Cramer, part of the Cornerstone Capital discussed at length in John Q. Publius's *The Way Life Should Be?* run by the Jewish lesbian Erika Karp, agrees with Karp, via a 2014 article from the Jewish Funders Network, that this:

> ...creation of new business models that blend profit with a core social mission...is often informed by Jewish values.... As I look around at the corporate social responsibility community it's interesting to see how many of the early leaders and ongoing leaders have come out of the Jewish community."

Cramer refers to this as "catalytic philanthropy," and its purposes are anything but philanthropic. Cramer states that the current model is directly informed by "the Jewish tradition of social activism and *tikkun olam*." It is perhaps best embodied in sentiment by Apax, founded by Alan Patricof, a Jewish pioneer of venture capital and private equity; Apax Partners' name based on a play on Patricof's name: Alan Patricof Associates Cross (x) Border—which today remains one of the largest private equity firms in the world.

Ninety-seven tech companies including Apple, Google, and Twitter filed an amicus brief in February 2017 in opposition to Donald Trump's proposed "travel ban." Naturally a host of literature by pro-mass immigration groups and Jews—often one and the same—formed the basis of their "evidence," including John F. Kennedy's *A Nation of Immigrants*, ghost-written by the Jewish Myer Feldman and published by the Anti-Defamation League of B'nai B'rith.

Jonathan Greenblatt, National Director and CEO of the Anti-Defamation League and former Special Assistant to Barack Obama and Director of the Office of Social Innovation and Civic Participation has a firm grasp on the marketing angle to the "youths" of tomorrow with the marriage of the political and the economic, with the increasingly overt acknowledgement that this is good for the Jews. For Greenblatt from a 2017 *Vox* article:

> Millennials vote with their wallets. And now big firms like BlackRock and Goldman Cap Group and all these other large-scale investment houses are building funds and firms specifically to take advantage of how millennials want to deploy their dollars.

What Greenblatt is discussing is the essence of "philanthropic capitalism": in a nutshell, "equality" and the perception of activism on the part of "social justice" and the global downtrodden being ruthlessly exploited is that it benefits the in-group, who are predominantly Jews along with sycophants/philo-Semites (or intermarried in some fashion, as names like Trump, Clinton, Biden, Harris, and Kennedy evidence), from every conceivable angle in the short- and medium-term. Do you really think the Royal Bank of Canada and Calvert Impact Capital support the Equality Fund, "a dynamic partnership between leading actors in feminist organizing, global philanthropy and impact investing," out of altruism? No, their "vision of gender equality in Canada and around the world" is just using feminism as a means to fracture the family and social cohesion and produce more unattached office drones and consumers, who ideally if white have no children and "necessitate" the importation of a new serf class. Aggrieved imports add to the phalanx of "activists" on the ground in the West, who in turn agitate for more concessions from the middle class and for more importation of aliens to swell their numbers.

This is obviously beneficial to the ruling class, supported by organizations like the IMF, whose official position is that "Advanced economies need immigration to boost labor" and, "Immigrants also support the demographics of advanced economies because their fertility rate is higher than that of natives," meaning so long as the economy keeps humming, you being bred out of existence and totally replaced is a good thing. After all, a France composed of Senegalese and Afghanis wouldn't be appreciably different than a France composed of the French; in much the same way as demographics made the "Paris of the West" Detroit into what it is now, Paris itself is going the way of Detroit, which betrays the fiction. Detroit's collapse/conquest and subsequent "revival" has been a boon to Jewish capitalists like Dan Gilbert in a pattern with centuries of historical precedent. Even if they are not in direct control as is the case especially in the US but most pronounced across the Anglosphere, as Kerry Bolton writes in "Refugee Crisis Serving Globalist Dialectic," by way of example in Moorish Spain, *al-Andalus*:

> Jews came to the top in wealth and power.... The *al-Andalus* civilisation endured for 700 years it did so only through the

strength of its rulers, its fragility caused by its diversity. This Islamic high culture endured despite, not because, of today's heralded dogma of "diversity." The people who gained were the Sephardim, which explains why the most ethnocentric of peoples are so zealous in promoting this "diversity" dogma outside of Israel. Their separatist Zionist agenda can only remain undetected amidst a pluralistic, multicultural regime; among people who have no ethnic self-consciousness.... In the USA the aspect of a PR stunt becomes more obvious with the involvement of the Anti-Defamation League of B'nai B'rith (ADL), which like other Jewish organisations in the USA, has a long record of supporting "civil rights" issues as a battering ram against social, moral and cultural traditions. The ADL has joined with other Jewish organisations to form the Jewish Coalition for Syrian Refugees (JCDR), previously called the Jewish Coalition for Syrian Refugees in Jordan. The ADL does not do anything for anyone unless it serves their ethnocentric purposes.

The ADL "fights tirelessly" for "liberal immigration reforms" and in support of "expansive refugee acceptance policies," denouncing President Trump's proposal to defund sanctuary cities and supporting the granting of legal status to "a large number of illegal immigrants." In 2015, Greenblatt's ADL was "disappointed" by delays in implementing the Affordable Care Act's contraception mandate, and the year following, they filed a legal brief in support of the contraception mandate. The ADL is not just in line with global capital, it is but one of its multitudinous arms, and Greenblatt is a perfect representative: named to the Global Agenda Council of the World Economic Forum, co-founder of Ethos Water (sold to Starbucks), founder of the Impact Economy Initiative at the Aspen Institute to "help policy makers create an enabling environment for the emerging market of social enterprise and impact investing," and former operating partner at Satori Capital—a private equity firm focused on "conscious capitalism."

For the record, the Aspen Institute's Board of Trustees includes Katie Couric, Henry Louis Gates, Michael Eisner, Condoleezza Rice, Laurie M. Tisch, Margot Pritzker, and Laura Lauder. Its major funders include: Steve Ballmer, Mr. and Mrs. Leonard A. Lauder, David M. Rubenstein, Margot and Tom Pritzker, the Laurie M. Tisch Illumination Fund, Jane and Michael Eisner, Steve Tisch, Ann B. and Thomas L. Friedman, Robert E. Rubin, Laura and Gary M. Lauder, Madeleine Albright, Lisa S. Pritzker, John Pritzker, and Renee and Robert A. Belfer. The reader should note the preponderance of wealthy Jewish names here.

Institutional funders include: the Open Society Policy Center, the

Foundation of the Jewish Community Foundation of the East Bay, Amazon, Arizona State University, JP Morgan Chase, WK Kellogg Foundation, Anglo-American Charitable Foundation, Mastercard, AT&T, TIAA-CREF, Walmart, the US State Department, USAID, the Tides Foundation, Starbucks, Stanford University, the University of Oxford, Swisscontact, the Soros Economic Development Fund, the Rockefeller Foundation, Nike, S&P Global, Oxfam, Pfizer, Pepsi, the David and Lucile Packard Foundation, the NoVo Foundation, the Oak Foundation, the Omidyar Network, the Jewish Communal Fund, Mind the Gap, Johnson & Johnson, the Bertelsmann Foundation, Catholic Relief Services, the Chan Zuckerberg Initiative, the Annie E. Casey Foundation, the Charles Koch Foundation, the Branson Center of Entrepreneurship, the British Council, the Susan Thompson Buffett Foundation, the Bezos Family Foundation, Charter Communications, Citi Foundation, GIZ, Comcast, the Clinton Foundation, Disney, the Bill and Melinda Gates Foundation, the John T. Gorman Foundation, GlaxoSmithKline, Global Affairs Canada, the Conrad N. Hilton Foundation, the William and Flora Hewlett Foundation, the Greater Miami Jewish Federation, Blue Haven Initiative (Liesel Pritzker Simmons), Bloomberg Philanthropies, BlackRock, and the Goldman Sachs Foundation.

Goldman Sachs "generously" gave the UNHCR $3 million over the course of just one week at the height of the "refugee crisis" in 2015; longtime Goldman Sachs advisory director and senior investment strategist Abby Joseph Cohen confidently states a position supported by the IMF and others, according to *The Times of Israel:*

> One of the reasons our economy has been stronger and grown faster than the economies in Europe and Japan—and I'm comparing us to the developed economies—is because we have faster population growth. And we have faster population growth in large part because of immigration.

Senior Chairman Lloyd Blankfein was viciously critical of Donald Trump's "tragic" detainment of illegal aliens. Additionally, illegal alien Julissa Arce, a Vice President with Goldman Sachs, has been a major feature of propaganda for years now and doubles as a useful totem. The architects of the power structure understand this well.

Another Goldman Sachs-connected central figure committed to the population replacement of native Europeans is Peter Sutherland, about whom Kerry Bolton writes in the same article:

Peter Sutherland is in the forefront of open border advocacy for Europe. An "Irish Catholic" with a distinctly Ashkenazic countenance, Sutherland has been Attorney General of Eire, director general of GATT and the World Trade Organisation, and is honorary European chairman of the Trilateral Commission, member of the Bilderberg Group steering committee, on the advisory board of the Council on Foreign Relations, and is a chairman of Goldman Sachs, a major player in globalisation. Sutherland is also United Nations Special Representative of the Secretary General for International Migration. Goldman Sachs is the primary corporate contributor in funding the Afro-Levantine demographic shift to Europe. Sutherland explains the plutocratic-globalist agenda for the use of the Afro-Levantine migrants into Europe as being to break down the national-cultural consciousness of Europe such as it exists: "This will demand, first and foremost, that EU leaders overcome the forces that have so far impeded action. One obstacle is anti-migrant populism, which has intensified owing to the serious economic challenges that Europeans have faced. With far-right political parties nipping at their heels, most mainstream politicians avoid taking a stance on migration that might make them seem "soft."

George Soros has drafted a plan that would see at least one million Third Worlders come into the EU annually "for the foreseeable future," presumably because of the economy and in keeping with "Europe's values." Soros has long been linked to the Council on Foreign Relations, though on the condition that he remain anonymous. Still, with the CFR he co-sponsored a conference on NATO at his Central European University in November 1993 and delivered a paper he had written. For its part, the ADL tries to deflect any criticism of Soros as—what else?—"anti-Semitism."

Indeed, in the lead-up to the 2020 US Presidential Election, Greenblatt was joined by such figures as Toomas Henrik Ilves, Shoshana Zuboff (the University of Chicago, Harvard), Laurence Tribe (Harvard Law School), and Yael Eisenstat (ex-CIA officer, former head of election integrity operations for political ads at Facebook, Johns Hopkins, Council on Foreign Relations, the Digital Life Initiative at Cornell Tech) at the behest of Carole Cadwalladr to form the Real Facebook Oversight Board as, in Greenblatt's words, via *The New Yorker,* Facebook "actively and knowingly has facilitated the flow of poison into the population, and enabled waves of anti-Semitism and racism, Holocaust denialism and Islamophobic conspiracies, disinformation and extremism."

While with the Obama administration, via the same previous 2017 *Vox* article, Greenblatt brags, "I helped launch the first social impact bonds in the government, launched all the kinds of new programs to create novel financial instruments that used the capital markets more effectively." Greenblatt is married to Marjan Keypour Greenblatt, "an Iranian Jewish political refugee who is the founder and director of The Alliance for Rights of All Minorities (ARAM)." In 2019, the Brookings Institution hosted the ADL's Task Force on Middle East Minorities Inaugural Event with both Greenblatts present; the theme of this symposium was basically "Iran bad." I don't know if John Bolton was there, but it definitely sounds like something he would be interested in!

Like Greenblatt and the ADL, the Coalition for the American Dream is very supportive of their pet "undocumenteds." The Coalition organized 140 trade associations and businesses in late 2019 in filing an amicus brief in support of the Deferred Action for Childhood Arrivals (DACA) program; they also authored four letters to Congress between 2017-2019 stating that "eliminating DACA would inflict serious harm on US companies, workers, and the economy," via *CNBC*. They also took out ads in *The New York Times, POLITICO*, and the *Wall Street Journal*. Members of this Coalition include Marriott, Doordash, Hilton, Microsoft (which in 2018 spent more than 20% of its immigration-related lobbying expenses on DACA), Google, IKEA, Spotify, Apple, Johnson & Johnson, Tumblr, Facebook, Lyft, PayPal, Uber, Amazon, Chobani, and Western Union.

As a major facilitator and beneficiary of remittances, Western Union sponsors many of these pro-mass migration NGOs, ranging from the Migrant Action Trust in New Zealand to the Migration Policy Institute. The Migrant Action Trust in New Zealand's other partners include the United Way, the Department of Internal Affairs, the Lottery Grants Board, ASB Community Trust, the Auckland Council, the Ministry for Culture & Heritage, the Ministry of Social Development, the New Zealand Community Trust, the New Zealand Post, the Puketapapa Local Board, SkyCity Community Trust, Southpark Corporation, Telecom, the Tertiary Education Commission, the Southern Trust, and the Working Together More Fund.

Just as the entire Establishment supports the Aspen Institute, so too does the Migration Policy Institute enjoy their pretty much unanimous support. The Migration Policy Institute's major donors, in addition to Western Union, include the IOM, Walmart, the US Chamber of Commerce, the Rockefeller Foundation, the Ford Foundation, the German Marshall Fund of the United States, the MacArthur Foundation, the UNHCR, the European Commission, the World Bank, and the Open Society Foundations (for a more complete list, see Appendix F).

Two other illustrative figures who sit at the intersection of these vectors of control to consider are Dorrit Moussaieff and Sophie Wilmès. In a prime example of how the raft of policies under the umbrella of neoliberalism are all connected and how the disproportionately-Jewish and Jewish-influenced ruling class benefits, in an Iceland with 250 Jews tops, Israeli-born Dorrit Moussaieff is married to former longtime President Ólafur Ragnar Grímsson; Moussaieff has been listed by *Harper's Magazine* on the List of the Most Connected People in Britain. She has also been implicated in the significant offshoring of wealth from *The Guardian:*

> Part of a leak from HSBC's private bank in Geneva show Moussaieff had links to offshore companies and to trusts registered outside the UK. Leaked bank files show Iceland's first lady listed as one of three Moussaieff family members who jointly owned a company in the British Virgin Islands called Jaywick Properties Inc. She was also a beneficiary of the Moussaieff Sharon Trust, according to the files. In addition, the HSBC files suggest Moussaieff, who is non-domiciled for UK tax purposes, was in line to inherit further portions of her family's offshore wealth when her 86-year-old mother, Alisa, dies. The Moussiaeff family are best known for running a jewellery shop on New Bond Street, Mayfair, catering to London's super-rich. Building up the business over generations, they are now among the world's wealthiest jewellers. According to the Sunday Times' annual rich list Alisa Moussaieff and her family have a fortune worth an estimated £200m.

In the middle of Iceland's financial meltdown in 2009, not long after the installing of lesbian Prime Minister Jóhanna Sigurðardóttir (in 2010, a year into Sigurdardóttir's tenure as prime minister, Iceland passed a "marriage equality" law; Sigurðardóttir had pledged to create a "new Iceland" and bragged of having "'graduated' from the IMF program—so to speak—and with distinction"), Moussaieff told interviewer Rosie Millard of *The Sunday Times* that she had hit on a solution: in effect, "turning it into a cooler version of Dubai." Toward the end of the interview, Millard relates: "At this point the intercom buzzes. It's a minion, delivering a box containing a ring set with a vivid pink 14-carat diamond, the size of a large pebble. 'South African,' [Moussaieff] says. 'From a royal family.'"

The Jewish Belgian Prime Minister Sophie Wilmès was a financial officer at the European Commission and an economic and financial adviser in a major law firm; she was also previously the Minister of the Budget and Civil Services, which is responsible for the Belgian National Lottery. The Belgian National Lottery provides an annual grant of €10 million to the King

Baudouin Foundation, which features Managing Director at the Institute of International Finance, former US Ambassador to the EU, and International Republican Institute Board member Kristen Silverberg on its Board of Directors[40] and finances "philanthropic" projects that focus on "democracy" and "social justice."

Other prominent Western leaders coming from global capital's incubator or else connected to high finance include Emmanuel Macron of France (Rothschild & Cie), John Key of New Zealand (Merrill Lynch), Malcolm Turnbull of Australia (Goldman Sachs), Romano Prodi of Italy (Goldman Sachs), and Mario Monti of Italy (Goldman Sachs). The aforementioned Rahm Emanuel, Larry Summers, and Robert Rubin are also Goldman Sachs alums, as are: Steve Bannon; Mario Draghi, former President of the European Central Bank; Gianni Letta, Secretary to the Council of Ministers of Italy under Silvio Berlusconi; the Jewish Steve Mnuchin, US Secretary of the Treasury; Chris Grigg, CEO of the British Land Company; Rishi Sunak, British Chancellor of the Exchequer; Tito Mboweni, former Governor of the Reserve Bank of South Africa; Ian Macfarlane, former Governor of the Reserve Bank of Australia; and the Jewish Joshua Bolten, former White House Chief of Staff, and whose father worked for the CIA.

The 2020 US Presidential Election showed in stark fashion the predominance of neoliberal capitalism (often as it intersects with and is inextricable from the outsized Jewish role) with Michael Bloomberg (Salomon Brothers), Tom Steyer (Hellman & Friedman), Deval Patrick (Bain Capital), and Pete Buttigieg (McKinsey), plus candidates like Elizabeth Warren, who reportedly pushed the Jewish Green New Deal advocate Joseph Stiglitz to Hillary Clinton in 2014 as a prospective advisor according to *POLITICO*. Jews Larry Fink (BlackRock Chairman) and Sheryl Sandberg (Facebook Chief Operating Officer) were also listed as close Clinton allies.

According to Wikileaks, the 2008 email exchange between John Podesta (the Center for American Progress) and then-Citigroup executive the Jewish Michael Froman was revealing for many reasons, not least of which was who was being pegged to join the "hope and change" Obama administration, including the Jewish Rahm Emanuel (Wasserstein Perella & Co. and the Freddie Mac Board of Directors, a brief tenure that was plagued by scandal); the Jewish Peter Orszag (Citigroup, Lazard, Council on Foreign Relations); and Jews Robert Rubin and Larry Summers (both also of the Council on Foreign Relations), plus Tim Geithner (Warburg Pincus, former President of the Federal Reserve Bank of New York from 2003-2009, and US Secretary of the Treasury, from 2009-2013; his father worked for the Ford Foundation and

---

[40] Other Board members include Mitt Romney and Lindsey Graham.

USAID). And what about BlackRock, the world's largest asset manager with $7.4 trillion in assets? For John Q. Publius:

> BlackRock owns the largest percentage of shares in.... Telefónica [one of the largest telecommunications companies in the world]. BlackRock was co-founded by current Chairman and CEO Larry Fink, who is Jewish. BlackRock was initially a part of the Blackstone Group, whose Chairman and CEO Stephen A. Schwarzman is also Jewish.... BlackRock's other co-founders were: Ralph Schlosstein (Jewish), Robert Kapito (Jewish), Susan Wagner (Jewish), Barbara Novick (Jewish), Ben Golub (Jewish), Hugh Frater (now Fannie Mae's CEO), and Keith Anderson. [The Jewish] Ivan Seidenberg was on BlackRock's Board of Directors and also serves on the Advisory Board of Perella Weinberg Partners LP, a financial services advisory firm founded by Joe Perella and the Jewish Peter Weinberg, formerly of Morgan Stanley and Goldman Sachs, where he was a partner and CEO of Goldman Sachs International from 1999 to 2005. Weinberg's cousin is a partner and co-head of the Investment Banking Division at Goldman Sachs. Notable Senior Advisors include the Jewish Walter Isaacson—former Chairman and CEO of CNN, President and CEO of the Aspen Institute (a George Soros-funded project; ADL CEO Jonathan Greenblatt is also an alum), and current professor at Tulane University (43% Jewish)[41]—and Louis Susman, former advisor to Ronald Reagan, Barack Obama's ambassador to the UK from 2009 to 2013, and Managing Director and Vice Chairman of Citigroup Corporate and Investment Banking and Vice Chairman of Citigroup Global Markets. Murry Gerber is on both BlackRock's Board of Directors and Halliburton's Board of Directors.... Marco Antonio Slim Domit, Carlos [Slim's] son, is on BlackRock's Board of Directors. BlackRock's Board also includes Council on Foreign Relations member Jessica Einhorn, whose resumé includes stints with the World Bank, the IMF, and the US Treasury and State Department. [42]

The biography of Michael Froman is also illustrative. He was Chief of Staff of the US Treasury Department under Robert Rubin in the late 1990s, after which point he followed Rubin to Citigroup, was an official in the Obama

---

[41] Isaacson is also a member of the Council on Foreign Relations, and has been involved with both the US State Department and Department of Defense, as well as the US Agency for Global Media.

[42] Publius, John Q., *Plastic Empire*, 80-81.

administration, a Council on Foreign Relations fellow, and a Resident Fellow at the German Marshall Fund, where he is now on the Transatlantic Task Force of the German Marshall Fund and the Bundeskanzler-Helmut-Schmidt-Stiftung (BKHS). He was in what is now the European Political Strategy Center (EPSC), a department of the European Commission. Froman negotiated the Trans-Pacific Partnership trade agreement in secret, and as Deputy Assistant Secretary for Eurasia and the Middle East, his work was related to economic policy towards the former USSR and its satellites, in addition to constructing the economic components of the Dayton Accords. Froman also served as liaison of the American Bar Association's Central and East European Law Initiative (CEELI) legal assistance program in Albania; the CEELI was the precursor to what would become the American Bar Association Rule of Law Initiative (ABA ROLI)'s bilateral programs in the region. The Balkans Regional Rule of Law Network (BRRLN) Program functioned in a complementary role from 2013-16 with support from USAID. Additionally, per the ABA's website:

> In the early 2000s, the Balkan Law School Linkage Initiative was a legal education exchange program supported by the U.S. Department of State's Bureau of Education and Cultural Affairs designed to support the rule of law and development of market economy in the Balkans by supporting legal reforms. The program goals were supported by pairing each participating Balkan school with a "sister law school" in the U.S., to share expertise and provide ongoing support to Balkan faculties.

This is a similar strategy to that employed by the Soros network and that of other US State Department and government initiatives.

Another figure prominently involved in the US's Balkan project is Nick Dowling, per his Wikipedia entry:

> He was Director for European Affairs at the National Security Council (NSC) where he coordinated Bosnia and Kosovo policy to help bring an end to the Balkan wars. Prior to that, he was a defense fellow in the Office of the Secretary of Defense, a senior fellow at the National Defense University and a policy advisor for two presidential campaigns and a U.S. Senate campaign. Dowling is the acting president of IDS International, a "smart power" national security firm that trains the US Army and Marines in sophisticated operations. He leads an IDS team with a vast array of stability operations, interagency, reconstruction and regional expertise. After

founding IDS International in 2001, Dowling helped the company become a provider in training on interagency coordination in conflict zones that included Iraq and Afghanistan. He is also a lifetime member of the Council on Foreign Relations.

Based in Arlington, Virginia, IDS International, according to its website:

> Believes in resolving conflict, building innovative approaches to do so...IDS tailors solutions for a diverse range of government, military, nonprofit, and public-sector clients.... IDS has been the U.S. military's leading training partner in interagency and whole-of-government approaches to disaster response, humanitarian assistance, stability operations, and reconstruction. Our curriculum is informed by the collective experience of our seasoned trainers—professionals with recent State Department, USAID, CIA, U.S. military, UN, non-governmental, or other experience in conflict or disaster zones.... Complex missions ranging from operations and maintenance of geographically separated installations for the Afghan National Defense and Security Forces, to performing needs assessments, monitoring, and reporting for the World Food Program, IDS has built a reputation of integrity, excellence, and innovation.

Shock of shocks, Paula Dobriansky is an IDS International Advisory Board member! Additional members are included, with biographies sourced from the IDS International website:

o Joseph Brendler: "Prior to starting his consulting company, MG Brendler was Chief of Staff for the United States Cyber Command. In that role, he directed, integrated, and synchronized the activities of the USCYBERCOM headquarters and led and mentored all staff officers, including the nine executive-level (flag) staff principals.... Previously, as Director of Strategic Planning, Policy, and Partnerships, MG Brendler was responsible for the development of strategy and plans for the evolutionary growth of USCYBERCOM and the execution of its missions to defend the nation against the threat of significant cyber attack. He participated in the development of US military cyber doctrine and of DoD and national cyber policy. Earlier, MG Brendler served as US Army Director of Architecture, Operations, Networks and Space (AONS), where he had oversight of Army network operations and led Army network architecture and strategic planning. Prior to that, he was responsible for policy and operational oversight of all communications and information systems employed by

NATO and US forces in Afghanistan as Chief of C5ISR, US Forces J6, and NATO Forces CJ6, ISAF. MG Brendler also served as the Chief of Staff for the Defense Information Systems Agency (DISA) for two years, prior to his last deployment to Afghanistan."
- Edward Cardon: "Cardon has deployed in support of IFOR/SFOR Bosnia-Herzegovina and on four separate occasions in support of OPERATION IRAQI FREEDOM."
- David Handley "is an independent consultant, working with a variety of organizations for whom he provides guidance and strategic planning on today's most pressing global challenges and opportunities, with an emphasis on the Middle East. From 2012 to 2014, Handley served as managing director for Europe for Veracity Worldwide. Prior to that, he was head of Group Strategic Analysis for BAE Systems, the United Kingdom's largest defense and aerospace company. In that role, he tracked international defense politics, monitored the changing military, security, and threat environment, and produced world-class analysis and assessment on the global challenges facing the defense industry. Handley's career began in the British Secret Intelligence Service (MI-6), where he served for nearly three decades with postings in the Middle East, Eastern Europe, and South America. He then held a number of senior management positions in London, including a posting to the UK Security Service (MI5). He served as the director for the Middle East and Africa and main board director responsible for finance, personnel, and technology issues. As a member of IDS International's Advisory Board, Handley contributes his extensive experience advising government and private sector institutions on key matters related to the international security landscape, specifically in regards to Europe, the Middle East, and Latin America."
- James Kunder "is principal at Kunder-Reali Associates, an Alexandria, Virginia-based consulting firm, which specializes in international development, post-conflict reconstruction and civil-military relations. As a member of IDS International's Advisory Board, he leverages his extensive government and private sector experience managing international development, relief, and reconstruction programs in order to support innovative and agile synergies that work to bridge the civilian-military gap. Prior to founding Kunder-Reali Associates, Kunder worked with global impact firm Palladium to lead a major evaluation project for the US Department of State's Bureau of Intelligence and Research. As part of this work, he examined a number of US government programs designed to counter violent extremism abroad to determine whether they were achieving their objectives. For more than two decades, Kunder served in a

variety of roles for the US Agency for International Development (USAID)."

o Peter Warren Singer "is strategist at New America and an editor at Popular Science magazine. He has been named by the Smithsonian as one of the nation's 100 leading innovators, by Defense News as one of the 100 most influential people in defense issues, by Foreign Policy to their Top 100 Global Thinkers List, as an official "Mad Scientist" for the US Army's Training and Doctrine Command, and by Onalytica social media data analysis as one of the ten most influential voices in the world on cybersecurity and twenty-fifth most influential in the field of robotics. As a member of IDS International's Advisory Board, he has aided in discussions that range from global futures to cybersecurity and social media. Singer's award-winning books include Corporate Warriors: The Rise of the Privatized Military Industry, Children at War, Wired for War: The Robotics Revolution and Conflict in the 21st Century; Cybersecurity and Cyberwar: What Everyone Needs to Know, and Ghost Fleet: A Novel of the Next World War, a technothriller crossed with nonfiction research, which has been endorsed by people who range from the chairman of the joint chiefs, the co-inventor of the Internet, and the writer of HBO's Game of Thrones. His latest is LikeWar: The Weaponization of Social Media, out in October 2018. Singer's past work includes serving as coordinator of the Obama-08 campaign's defense policy task force in the Office of the Secretary of Defense, and as the founding director of the Center for 21st Century Security and Intelligence at Brookings.... Before joining New America, Singer was the founding director of the Project on US Policy Towards the Islamic World at the Saban Center at Brookings, where he was a founding organizer of the US-Islamic World Forum, a global leaders conference. He has worked for the Belfer Center for Science and International Affairs at Harvard, the Balkans Task Force in the US Department of Defense and the International Peace Academy. Singer received his PhD in government from Harvard University and a BA from the Wilson School of Public and International Affairs at Princeton University."

Noah Melgar is Vice President of Cyber and Information Warfare at IDS International, where he, per their website:

> Leverages his industry expertise in building cognitive Big Data intelligence tools, writing cutting-edge cyberspace training curricula, and creating realistic replicated internet environments for training purposes. In 2013, he developed a cyberspace training and

exercise support program to help the Department of Defense (DoD) navigate the ever-expanding world of cyber and information warfare operations. This initial work grew into its own Cyber and Information Warfare department in 2015 and into its own company in 2018. The group offers a range of capabilities that bridge the nexus of social media analytics, software development, network engineering, and cyber planning to help the US government understand and mitigate cyber threats. At IDS, Melgar also oversees day-to-day operations and strategic planning for SMEIR™, a scenario-based capability that provides social media inputs and cyber attacks to help training units better understand the virtual human domain and its relevance to planning and operations. The technology is supported by teams of subject matter experts from Special Operations Forces (SOF) to the intelligence community. Through Melgar's work, SMEIR has been used by US Army Special Operation Forces (SOF), Psychological Operations (PSYOP), and Civil Affairs (CA) units, from the team to the battalion level at the Joint Readiness Training Center, National Training Center, and at civilian locations hosting mission readiness exercises. This is one of many capabilities that enable public and private sector clients to understand, engage, and harness the world of offensive cyber, defensive cyber, and information operations. Melgar has embedded and served as an advisor to Special Forces in rural Afghanistan on population stability operations and The Royal Project in Northern Thailand on illicit crop alternatives.

Oron Strauss, Senior Vice President and CFO, is Chairman and co-founder of Babel Health, a "healthcare data management software company." He is also chairman of Pantheon, "a leading provider of online strategy and development services to mission-driven organizations." These types of connections are especially vital when we consider how the narrative for the coming decade is being shaped, and how Swamp Things that never seem to die and war gaming exercises like Dark Winter[43] are being dusted off by the

---

[43] From the website of the Johns Hopkins Bloomberg School of Health: "On June 22-23, 2001, the Center for Strategic and International Studies, the Johns Hopkins Center for Civilian Biodefense Studies, the ANSER Institute for Homeland Security, and the Oklahoma City National Memorial Institute for the Prevention Terrorism, hosted a senior-level war game examining the national security, intergovernmental, and information challenges of a biological attack on the American homeland...John Hamre of the Center for Strategic and International Studies (CSIS) initiated and conceived of an exercise wherein senior former officials would respond to a bioterrorist induced national security crisis. Tara O'Toole and Tom Inglesby of the Johns Hopkins Center for Civilian Biodefense Studies and Randy Larsen and Mark DeMier of Analytic Services, Inc., (ANSER) were

Biden Administration. The only conclusion is that governments like those of the United States are completely detached from and do not regard themselves as accountable to the people, and there is clearly no daylight between the various arms of the Establishment, be they financial, commercial, academic, the military-industrial complex, or the transgender-industrial complex (consisting of essentially the same actors as those pushing the highly experimental COVID-19 "vaccines" and other transhumanist projects). These are all false divisions that hold no meaning. The system is a monolithic Leviathan, cycling its various functionaries through different departments in the same rotten corporation.

In France, the Attali Commission on Economic Growth was chaired by Jewish mass immigration advocate, early discusser of transhumanism, and World Economic Forum Annual Meeting attendee Jacques Attali, who was appointed by the part-Jewish former President Nicolas Sarkozy (continuing to underscore Jewish nepotism, Sarkozy also appointed the Jewish Joseph Stiglitz to head the Commission on the Measurement of Economic Performance and Social Progress, along with Stiglitz's World Bank Chief Economist successor Nicholas Stern, also Jewish). Among Attali's selections to the committee were included Emmanuel Macron,[44] a close associate of Jewish businessman and former Sarkozy advisor Alain Minc, and Mario "The Full" Monti, a founding member of the pro-EU federalization Spinelli Group, featuring Jacques Delors, Guy Verhofstadt, and the Jewish Daniel Cohn-Bendit. Monti is or has also been involved with the Bilderberg Group (he was on a Steering Committee alongside Peter Sutherland, Richard Perle, and Peter Thiel), the Trilateral Commission European Group, the Atlantic Council Business and Economics Advisors Group (at the same time as Paula Dobriansky), and the European Investment Bank.

---

the principal designers, authors, and controllers of *Dark Winter*. Sue Reingold of CSIS managed administrative and logistical arrangements. General Dennis Reimer of the Memorial Institute for the Prevention of Terrorism (MIPT) provided funding for *Dark Winter*."

[44] From Bénilde, "The creation of Emmanuel Macron.": "Macron, a graduate of France's prestigious ENA (National School of Administration), met Jacques Attali (former adviser to President Mitterrand and now board chairman of news site Slate) through millionaire Henry Hermand (funder of thinktanks La République des Idées and Terra Nova, and a major shareholder in Eric Fottorino's magazine *Le 1*). Attali says: 'Emmanuel Macron? I discovered him; I *invented* him'. In 2007 Attali appointed Macron to the commission he headed, tasked with proposals to promote French economic growth. The commission included 17 business bosses, and Macron filled his address book. Pascal Houzelot (founder of the gay channel Pink TV, who later acquired the Numéro 23 channel and joined the board of *Le Monde*) invited him to dinner. Houzelot was an influential member of the Paris media set and in 2010 introduced Macron, then a banker at Rothschild, to the new owners of the Le Monde group: Matthieu Pigasse, an investment banker, Xavier Niel, founder of Internet provider Free, and Pierre Bergé, former head of Yves Saint Laurent."

The Atlantic Council is an Establishment think tank created in 1961; from its *Annual Report 2019/20: Shaping the Global Future Together:*

> The Atlantic Council's most recent strategic review—involving both staff and board members—laid out six major challenges that are at the center of our work for this new epoch. They include: managing a new era of major-power competition; strengthening open market democracies; redefining and reinvigorating the US role in the world; reinvigorating our rules-based global order; harnessing emerging technologies for good; advancing global resilience through climate-change mitigation and adaptation, and by addressing migratory and public-health challenges.

Burisma Holdings of Hunter Biden fame has been a large donor to the Atlantic Council; other major donors include: Facebook, Goldman Sachs, the Rockefeller Foundation, Google, Palantir, the MacArthur Foundation, the US State Department, Raytheon, the JP Morgan Chase Foundation, HSBC, General Atomics, Airbus, Lockheed Martin, the Embassy of the United Arab Emirates, Blackstone Charitable Foundation, Northrop Grumman, the Swedish Ministry for Foreign Affairs, BP, Dell, General Dynamics, African Rainbow Minerals, Los Alamos National Laboratory, Edelman, PricewaterhouseCoopers LLP, Ministry of National Defense of Lithuania, Ministry of Defense of Finland, United States Department of Energy, British Foreign and Commonwealth Office, DLA Piper, Boeing, BAE Systems, EuroChem Group AG, Microsoft, McKinsey, MIT Lincoln Labs, the National Endowment for Democracy, Thomson Reuters, the US Mission to NATO, the Open Society Foundations, NATO StratCom Center of Excellence, the European Bank for Reconstruction and Development, the European Investment Bank, Viacom, US-India Strategic Partnership Forum, NATO Defense College Foundation, Ministry of Defense of the French Republic, Gilead Sciences, Henry Kissinger, Dov Zakheim, and Salesforce.

The Atlantic Council's International Advisory Board features people like Madeleine Albright, James Clapper (former US Director of National Intelligence), Larry Summers, Rupert Murdoch, Stephen Schwarzman (Blackstone), The Rt. Hon. Lord Robertson of Port Ellen (former Secretary General of NATO), Robert Zoellick (former President of the World Bank), and more. Per their *Annual Report 2019/20*:

> In 2019, the Atlantic Council convened two NATO Engages town halls on the sidelines of official NATO meetings. On April 3, around the commemoration of NATO's seventieth anniversary, the Council

hosted "NATO Engages: The Alliance at 70" in partnership with NATO, the German Marshall Fund (GMF), and the Munich Security Conference (MSC). Our stage became the public platform for key officials and rising leaders, including US Vice President Mike Pence and NATO Secretary General Jens Stoltenberg, to celebrate the alliance's history and success and discuss the challenges facing NATO.... On December 3, alongside the London Leaders Meeting, we convened "NATO Engages: Innovating the Alliance," at Central Hall Westminster. Working with MSC, GLOBSEC, Royal United Services Institute (RUSI), and King's College London, we discussed NATO's future and emerging challenges, such as technology and China. With a stage graced by heads of state, pop stars, and tech gurus alike, the event gathered some six hundred participants, about half of whom were under thirty-five and women.

The Atlantic Council also convenes the Global Energy Forum along with its Global Energy Center and the Future Europe Initiative, the latter of which is aimed at "developing a common strategy in great power competition to confront Russian aggression and Chinese assertiveness together" and "building a transatlantic consensus on issues of global consequence, such as energy markets and supplies, international financial flows, climate change, cyber security, and new technologies." Further, the Atlantic Council states that "The Future Europe Initiative's work is conducted with the strong belief that the resilience and strength of the European Union, alongside the unity of NATO, is a critical national interest of the United States." Another key Atlantic Council project is the Cyber Statecraft Initiative run by Trey Herr, a former a postdoctoral fellow with the Belfer Center's Cyber Security Project at the Harvard Kennedy School; Herr also worked with the US Department of Defense to develop a risk assessment methodology for information security threats.

The Atlantic Council's Foresight, Strategy, and Risks Initiative partners with the Zurich Insurance Group and the University of Denver's Frederick S. Pardee Center for International Futures "to develop forecasts and a series of reports assessing three categories of risk affecting governments and businesses worldwide: cyber, demographic and geopolitical." According to the Pardee Center's website, sitting at the intersection of the globalist project and telegraphing its trajectory:

o "Google's Public Data Explorer provides users with a free, easy to use means of accessing, exploring, and visualizing large datasets and public databases. Now, thanks to collaboration between the Pardee Center and Google, you

can use the Google Public Data site to explore a wide range of forecasts from IFs, including: an updated global forecast replicating Hans Rosling's famous cross-sectional plot of fertility and GDP; global energy demand for UNEP GEO 4 scenarios; relative material power for the United States, China, and India; a map displaying the distribution of malnourished children; and the percentage of people by region with household connections to safe water."
- "The Pardee Center has worked with the RAND Frederick S. Pardee Center for Longer Range Global Policy and the Future Human Condition. One project was to incorporate information on World Bank and IMF lending into the financial flow system of IFs. Another was to explore IFs within the RAND Center's Robust Adaptive Policy or Robust Decision Making approach."
- "Under sponsorship of the European Commission's Fifth Framework Programme (1998-2002) RAND Europe led a large consortium of partners in a long-term forecasting project called TERRA. The IFs team was invited to join the European members of that consortium and to provide the integrated, long-term modeling and forecasting foundation for it."
- "Our team has provided support to the United Nations Development Programme (UNDP) in a number of ways. Most recently, we expanded our ability to measure and visualize each country's progress over time in achieving the SDGs, adding two additional specialized displays in IFs that allow users to forecast the path of SDG achievement across targets to 2030. IFs is also featured in the UN Development Group's online SDG Acceleration Toolkit. Previously, our team presented IFs to the organization's analysts, partners and other data-oriented stakeholders in both Nairobi and New York. The UNDP has also solicited research papers using IFs that provided input used in the 2011 and 2013 Human Development Reports (HDR). The research in support of the 2011 HDR focused on environmental constraints to human development. The research in support of the 2013 report modeled the impact of aggressive but reasonable policy interventions across thematic issue areas."
- "The United Nations Environment Programme (UNEP) produces Global Environment Outlook (GEO) reports under its charge from the United Nations Conference on Environment and Development."
- "Pardee Center personnel have contributed forecasting expertise to three of the U.S. National Intelligence Council's quadrennial Global Trends reports, most recently Global Trends 2030."
- "Our partnership with the U.S. Army Future Studies Group (previously the Chief of Staff of the Army's Strategic Studies Group) explores the future operational environment for the US Army using new structured datasets

and our existing modeling tools, including the IFs model. Our database creation efforts focus on measuring military hardware to construct indices of hard capabilities, military capital stocks, and bilateral 'reach.'"

- "In 2015, our team, along with Dr. Randall Kuhn, led a training on IFs for the Thai Ministry of Public Health as part of a World Health Organization sponsored program. The training focused on understanding current health trends in Thailand, forecasting mortality and morbidity across different disease types, and exploring potential policy interventions that could impact health outcomes."
- "As a successor to the Millennium Development Goal of reducing extreme poverty by 50 percent before 2015, the global community is rapidly moving toward setting a goal of eliminating it by 2030 (using 3 percent as a target for effective elimination). That goal appears very likely beyond the reach of fragile and conflict-afflicted states. The Pardee Center has collaborated with the World Bank's Center on Conflict, Security, and Development to forecast probable and possible levels of poverty in those states and to explore interventions that might accelerate reduction."
- "Our center's relationship with the U.S. Agency for International Development (USAID) has expanded significantly in recent years, as we use IFs to inform the organization's five-year Development Cooperation Strategies at both the regional and country level. Most recently, in partnership with our colleagues at the Institute for Security Studies (ISS) in South Africa, we produced trend and scenario analysis reports for USAID missions in Ethiopia and the Southern Africa region. In 2016, a team of our researchers held an IFs training with the USAID mission in Jakarta, Indonesia. We also completed a report on development trends in Uganda in 2015, which directly influenced the country mission's five-year strategy for budgeting, planning, and resource allocation, and led to further ongoing analysis of key development indicators at the subnational level."
- "Following a presentation of our development trends report for USAID in Southern Africa, Irish Aid asked our team, along with our partners at the Institute for Security Studies (ISS), to expand our trend and scenario analysis in Mozambique."
- "The Overseas Development Institute (ODI) is a leading institution in the global Chronic Poverty Advisory Network. The Pardee Center contributed to a publication of ODI in late 2013 on 'The Geography of Poverty, Disasters, and Climate Extremes in 2030.'"
- "The African Futures Project is an ongoing collaboration between the Pardee Center and the Institute for Security Studies (ISS), headquartered in Pretoria, South Africa. The ISS, established in 1991 as the Institute for Defense Policy, is a pan-African think tank focused on issues of human

security. The Pardee Center and the ISS have come together to leverage each other's expertise and to develop a series of scenario-based, quarterly policy briefs on topics such as the potential for a green revolution or for malaria eradication in Africa (each brief also has a supporting video feature). Together, we provide forward-looking, policy-relevant material like the African Futures 2050 report, a comprehensive look at expectations for human development, economic growth, and sociopolitical change in Africa over the next four decades. To date, the African Futures Project has received funding from Frederick S. Pardee; the Hanns Seidel Foundation; the Open Society Foundation; the British High Commission; Foreign Affairs, Trade and Development Canada, and the governments of Denmark, Finland, Germany, the Netherlands, Norway, Spain, Sweden, and Switzerland."

o "In 2014, the U.S. Department of Defense (DOD) awarded a three-year grant to our center and a team of Korbel faculty as part of its Minerva Research Initiative. Researchers on this multi-faceted project, which the DOD recently extended into its fourth year, analyze previous attempts to predict the onset of state failure, evaluate the drivers of state fragility, build tools and data associated with the drivers of domestic conflict, and use IFs to forecast the probability of future state failure. In parallel with the development of a series of quantitative models that might be used to forecast state failure, our researchers produced 50 qualitative case studies that summarized key circumstances leading to past state failure events around the world. This grant also covered research on modeling dyadic conflict and supported ongoing development of our DataGator tool. In addition, this grant supported the continued development of the Major Episodes of Contention (MEC) database led by Korbel Professor Erica Chenoweth."

o "We also collaborated with the United Nations University's Institute for Environment and Human Security on a publication in Climatic Change that uses IFs to explore climate change and disaster risk."

In addition to Mario Monti of the Trilateral Commission's European Group, we see other major European Group figures such as (with all positions as reported on the Trilateral Commission's May 2020 membership roster):

o Carl Bildt, Co-Chair, European Council on Foreign Relations; former Minister of Foreign Affairs of Sweden; former Chairman, Nordic Venture Network, Stockholm; former Member of the Swedish Parliament, Chairman of the Moderate Party and Prime Minister of Sweden; former European Union High Representative in Bosnia-Herzegovina & UN Special

Envoy to the Balkans; European Deputy Chairman, Trilateral Commission
- Manfred Bischoff, Chairman of the Supervisory Board, Daimler AG, Munich; former Member of the Board of Management, Daimler AG; former Chairman, EADS
- Jean-Louis Bruguière, former Judge on anti-terrorism; former EU High Representative to the United States on the Terrorism Finance Tracking Programme (TFTP/SWIFT), Paris
- Yves-Louis Darricarrère, Senior Advisor, Lazard Frères Bank; Senior Lecturer in Energy Geopolitics, Institut d'Etudes Politiques de Paris; former Member of the Executive Committee of Total and former CEO of Total Upstream, Total Exploration and Production and Total Gas and Power, Paris
- Marta Dassù, Senior Director of European Affairs, The Aspen Institute; Editor-in-Chief, Aspenia, Aspen Institute Italia; former Vice Minister for Foreign Affairs, Rome
- Vladimír Dlouhý, President of the Czech Chamber of Commerce; International Advisor, Goldman Sachs; former Czechoslovak Minister of Economy; former Czech Minister of Industry & Trade, Prague
- Admiral Giampaolo Di Paola, former Italian Minister of Defence; former Chairman of the NATO Military Committee, Livorno
- Louise Fresco, President of the Executive Board, Wageningen University & Research; former Member of the Board of Non-executive Directors, Unilever; former Member of the Supervisory Board of Rabobank; former Assistant Director-General, Head of Agriculture Department, Food and Agriculture Organization of the United Nations in Rome
- Staffan de Mistura, former United Nations Special Envoy for Syria, Milan
- Lucas Papademos, Member and former President of the Academy of Athens and holder of the Chair in Economic Sciences; Honorary Governor of the Bank of Greece; Senior Fellow at the Center for Financial Studies, Goethe University, Frankfurt; former Prime Minister of Greece; former Vice President of the European Central Bank, Athens

The Trilateral Commission's Asia Pacific Group also includes a host of the same types of figures. Significant members of the Trilateral Commission's North America Group include:

- Graham Allison, Director, Belfer Center for Science and International Affairs, and Douglas Dillon Professor of Government, John F. Kennedy School of Government, Harvard University, Cambridge; former Dean, John F. Kennedy School of Government; former Special Advisor to the Secretary of Defense and former Assistant Secretary of Defense

- Herminio Blanco Mendoza, Chairman, IQOM, Mexico City; Deputy Chairman, North American Trilateral Commission; former Mexican Secretary of Commerce and Industrial Development and former Chief NAFTA Negotiator
- Michael Bloomberg, Founder and CEO, Bloomberg LP, New York; former Mayor of New York City
- Mark Brzezinski, President & CEO, Brzezinski Strategies LLC, Washington; former US Ambassador to Sweden
- Michael Chertoff, Chairman and Co-Founder, The Chertoff Group; former Secretary of Homeland Security; Former Judge, U.S. Circuit Court of Appeals for the Third Circuit; Former Assistant Attorney General, Criminal Division, Department of Justice, Washington
- Jared Cohen, Founder and President of Jigsaw, New York; former member of Department of State's Policy Planning Staff
- John M. Deutch, Institute Professor emeritus, Massachusetts Institute of Technology, Cambridge; former Director of Central Intelligence; former U.S. Deputy Secretary of Defense and Undersecretary of Energy
- Paula J. Dobriansky, Senior Fellow, Belfer Center for Science and International Affairs, John F. Kennedy School of Government, Harvard University, Cambridge; Vice Chair, National Executive Committee, U.S. Water Partnership; former U.S. Under Secretary of State for Global Affairs
- Kenneth M. Duberstein, Chairman and Chief Executive Officer, The Duberstein Group, Washington; former Chief of Staff to President Ronald Reagan
- Larry Fink, CEO of BlackRock, New York
- Fiona Hill, Senior Fellow, Brookings Institution, Washington; former Senior Director for European and Russian Affairs on the NSC
- Carla A. Hills, Chairman and Chief Executive Officer, Hills & Company, Washington
- David Ignatius, Columnist, The Washington Post, Washington
- Merit E. Janow, Dean of the Faculty and Professor of Practice, International Economic Law and International Affairs, Columbia University's School of International and Public Affairs (SIPA), New York; former Member, Appellate Body from North America, World Trade Organization
- Henry A. Kissinger, Chairman, Kissinger Associates, Inc., New York; former U.S. Secretary of State; former Assistant to the President for National Security Affairs; Lifetime Trustee, Trilateral Commission
- Nicholas Kristof, Columnist, The New York Times, Scarsdale
- Marne Levine, former Chief Operating Officer, Instagram, Menlo Park
- David Lipton, First Deputy Managing Director, International Monetary Fund, Washington

- Joseph S. Nye, Jr., University Distinguished Service Professor and former Dean, John F. Kennedy School of Government, Harvard University, Cambridge; former Chair, National Intelligence Council; former U.S. Assistant Secretary of Defense for International Security Affairs; former North American Chairman, Trilateral Commission
- David Petraeus, Chairman of the KKR Global Institute, Washington; former Director of the CIA and Commander of the International Security Assistance Force in Afghanistan
- David M. Rubenstein, Co-founder and Managing Director, The Carlyle Group, Washington
- Eric Schmidt, Technical Advisor and Board Member, Alphabet Inc., Mountain View
- Olympia Snowe, Former U.S. Senator; Senior Fellow, Bipartisan Policy Center, Portland
- Bret Stephens, Op-Ed Columnist, The New York Times, New York
- Robert Zoellick, Chairman, AllianceBernstein, New York; former President, The World Bank

Friedrich Merz of the Christian Democratic Union of Germany is also a former member of the Trilateral Commission, and has been or is on the Boards of HSBC, Ernst & Young Germany, IVG, AXA, and more. As a member of the Bundestag, he opposed the minimum wage and argued for cutting social benefits and limiting trade union power, which is in line with BlackRock's modus operandi; BlackRock, a major shareholder in Amazon, has resisted any deal with trade unions in Germany. BlackRock's official position is that it wants the EU to be a single market, and in 2016, Merz was appointed Chairman of the German operations of BlackRock. As the presumptive heir apparent to Angela Merkel, it makes sense given her involvement that Merz is a former Chairman of Atlantik-Brücke, a non-profit designed to "promote German-American understanding and Atlanticism," Atlanticism also being a central fixture of the Atlantic Council's *raison d'être*.

Atlantik-Brücke was founded in 1952 by Eric M. Warburg of the dynastic Jewish banking family, Erik Blumenfeld, Marion Gräfin Dönhoff (the "red countess" and editor of *Die Zeit*), Ernst Friedlaender, Hans Karl von Borries, Gotthard baron von Falkenhausen, and John McCloy. It has awards named after Warburg and Vernon A. Walters, former ambassador, Deputy Director of the CIA, and prominent figure in both NATO and the Marshall Plan. In 1961, he proposed an American military intervention in Italy if the Italian Socialist Party were allowed to participate in government. In 2008, Liz Mohn, Vice Chair of the Executive Board of the Bertelsmann Stiftung, was chosen to receive the Vernon A. Walters Award: "She is being recognized by Atlantik-

Brücke e. V. for her firm commitment to strengthening the transatlantic relationship as well as her contribution to German-Israeli relations." The Atlantik-Brücke's Board features or has featured connections to the Trilateral Commission, EY, Facebook, Baker & McKenzie, the Center for American Progress, Bloomberg, the Aspen Institute-Berlin, the American Jewish Committee, Deutsche Bank, the Royal Bank of Scotland, and the Bank of International Settlements (where Mario Draghi was on the Board).

Atlantik-Brücke's sister organization is the American Council on Germany, a Council on Foreign Relations affiliate, also founded in 1952 by Eric Warburg and John McCloy, among others. McCloy was the President of the World Bank from 1947-1949 (successor to the World Bank's first president, the former owner of the *Washington Post* the Jewish Eugene Meyer, McCloy solidified the relationship between the UN and the World Bank), US High Commissioner to Occupied Germany from 1949-1952, CEO of Chase Manhattan from 1953-1960, and prominent figure in the institutionalization and embedding of the American intelligence apparatus. While with Cravath, Henderson & de Gerssdorff in the 1920s, McCloy helped facilitate massive loans for rebuilding Europe along with JP Morgan Bank, and in the 1930s he represented the interests of the Rockefellers and Paul Warburg, in addition to JP Morgan, in Europe. McCloy was also a Chair of the Ford Foundation and a Board member of the Council on Foreign Relations, serving as Chairman from 1953-1970. Carla Hills, a member of the Trilateral Commission, was a co-Chair with Robert Rubin 2007-2017.

In the late 1930s, the Rockefeller Foundation and the Ford Foundation, with assistance from the Carnegie Corporation, began beefing-up the Council on Foreign Relations, which officially came into existence in 1921 but had been unofficially active since at least June 1918. While with the Ford Foundation, McCloy integrated its operations with those of the CIA, using his connections as a facilitator of CIA operations in Occupied Germany. McCloy oversaw Germany's accession to NATO and its "reconstruction," all the more illuminating when we consider the role of the Council on Foreign Relations (with Rockefeller Foundation funding—McCloy was also a trustee of the Rockefeller Foundation) in producing policy briefs during World War II for conduct and post-war aims called the *War and Peace Studies*. From March 1942, the project supplied research secretaries to the State Department's Advisory Committee on Postwar Foreign Policy, formed at the suggestion of the CFR's Norman Davis and Secretary of State Cordell Hull's secretary Leo Pasvolsky, a "Wilsonian internationalist" and described by Karl E. Meyer as "a Russian Jewish immigrant who as a journalist covered the Paris Peace Conference in 1919 and became a Brookings Institution specialist in international law." As Richard Holbrooke writes for the *New York Times*:

The United Nations did not spring full-blown from the minds of Franklin Roosevelt and Winston Churchill...An obscure but determined State Department official named Leo Pasvolsky had been working in secret on a postwar world organization since the end of 1939, under the direct guidance of Secretary of State Cordell Hull.... By 1944 most key elements of the new organization were in place in Pasvolsky's draft, especially an idea that evolved into the United Nations Security Council—a small group of nations that would be empowered to authorize the use of force.... Pasvolsky...was one of those figures peculiar to Washington—a tenacious bureaucrat who, fixed on a single goal, left behind a huge legacy while virtually disappearing from history.

The American Council on Germany runs a major training program for future leaders called the Young Leaders Program: Craig Kennedy, former President of the German Marshall Fund of the United States is an alumnus. The German Marshall Fund of the United States has provided support to the American Council on Germany. Two American Council on Germany Young Leaders alums were also counterparts: US Chief of Staff Joshua Bolten and German Chief of Staff of the Chancellery Thomas de Maizière. The American Council on Germany's underwriters include Deutsche Bank, Alcoa, DHL, and Eli Lilly, and sponsors include AT&T, Deloitte, Facebook, Joseph Cohen, and Allianz. Patrons include Citi, Guido Goldman, PricewaterhouseCoopers, and Lufthansa. Members of its Corporate Membership Program include Siemens, Warburg Pincus, Daimler, BMW, Deutsche Bank, Deutsche Telekom, Lufthansa, Commerzbank AG, Volkswagen, AT&T, Ernst & Young, PricewaterhouseCoopers, DZ Bank, JP Morgan Chase, Goldman Sachs, and Pfizer. While at Rothschild & Cie, Emmanuel Macron led the acquisition by Nestlé of a subsidiary of Pfizer.

The Israel Council on Foreign Relations (ICFR) is patterned after Chatham House and the Council on Foreign Relations, founded in 1989 by David Kimche, an Israeli diplomat, deputy director of the Mossad, and main facilitating contact during the Iran-Contra affair. The ICFR functions under the auspices of the World Jewish Congress (WJC). Ronald Lauder, an heir to the Esteé Lauder fortune and a member of the Estée Lauder Companies' Board of Directors, is the WJC's President, as well as a member of the Board of Directors of the American Jewish Joint Distribution Committee and a member of the Board of Trustees of the Anti-Defamation League Foundation. In 1983, Lauder took a leave from The Estée Lauder Companies to serve as Deputy Assistant Secretary of Defense for European and NATO Affairs. In 1986, he was appointed Ambassador to Austria by President Ronald Reagan.

MAC Cosmetics, with which readers of *The Transgender-Industrial Complex* will be familiar, is owned by The Estée Lauder Companies.

Lynn Forester de Rothschild is another member of The Estée Lauder Companies' Board. She met her third husband Evelyn de Rothschild at the 1998 Bilderberg Group conference in Scotland, having been introduced to him by Henry Kissinger. The couple was invited to spend their honeymoon at the White House by the Clintons. She is a perfect avatar of the Establishment, especially when we consider her second husband Andrew Stein's role in the New York City political machine and the fact that he was indicted and arrested for lying about his involvement in a multi-million-dollar Ponzi scheme with fellow Jew Kenneth Ira Starr (not the same Ken Starr as authored the Starr Report, although incidentally that Starr did marry a Jewess). Lynn Forester de Rothschild is centrally-located at the nexus of much system activity, per the following from her Estée Lauder biography:

> Lady de Rothschild is the Chair of E.L. Rothschild LLC, a private investment company with investments in media, information technology, agriculture, financial services and real estate worldwide, and she was the Chief Executive from 2002 to 2016. Holdings of E.L. Rothschild LLC include The Economist Group (UK). Lady de Rothschild has been a director of The Economist Newspaper Limited since October 2002. From 2004 to 2007, she was also Co-Chair of FieldFresh Foods Pvt. Ltd., a 50-50 joint venture with Bharti Enterprises, established to develop the agricultural sector in India. From 1989 to 2002, she was President and Chief Executive Officer of FirstMark Holdings, Inc., which owned various telecommunications companies worldwide. She serves on the Board and Executive Committee of The Peterson Institute for International Economics. Lady de Rothschild is a trustee of the Eranda Foundation, a board member of the International Advisory Board of Columbia University School of Law and the Alzheimer's Drug Discovery Foundation. She is a member of the Council on Foreign Relations (USA), Chatham House (UK), the International Advisory Council of Asia House (UK), the International Institute of Strategic Studies (UK), and the Foreign Policy Association (USA).

Though Rothschild is no longer a member of some of those organizations, her deep involvement and connectedness are illustrative.

Andrés Rozental is both on the Advisory Council for the International Institute for Strategic Studies (IISS) and is a Senior Policy Advisor at Chatham House, in addition to being a member of the Trilateral Commission and the founder of the Mexican Council on Foreign Relations in 2001. He is formerly of the Board of the Center for International Governance Innovation (CIGI) in Canada and is a former senior non-resident fellow at the Brookings Institution.

The career diplomat is also an advisor with Airbus Mexico and member of the Board and Risk Management and Audit Committees of HSBC Bank Mexico. Rozental was a speaker at the World Economic Forum on Latin America in Riviera Maya, Mexico in 2015 for a briefing on the Pacific Alliance.

Other members of the IISS's Advisory Council include Amos Yadlin (Director of Tel Aviv University's Institute for National Security Studies after more than forty years in the IDF), Lord Robertson of Port Ellen (British Labour Party politician, 10th Secretary General of NATO from 1999–2004, and Defence Secretary for the United Kingdom from 1997–1999 in the Government of Tony Blair), and Thomas Enders (President of the German Council on Foreign Relations, CEO of EADS and Airbus from 2005-2019). The IISS is supported financially by Facebook, the Cohen Group, Airbus, Booz Allen Hamilton, Raytheon, Northrop Grumman, Lockheed Martin, BAE Systems, Taylor & Francis, Boeing, the British Army, Cargill, Chevron, Shell, Qatar Armed Forces Strategic Studies Centre, KPMG, Los Alamos National Laboratory, the US Army Future Studies Group, NATO, UN Women, the Rockefeller Brothers Fund, the MacArthur Foundation, the Carnegie Corporation, the EU Non-Proliferation Consortium, the Embassy of Israel to the UK, the Organization for Security and Cooperation in Europe (OSCE), Global Affairs Canada, and a slew of defense ministries, military academies and research institutions, and embassies and other development ministries, among other funders.

The aforementioned CIGI in Canada includes Board member Elissa Golberg, former holder of several senior Canadian government positions, including assistant deputy minister of Partnerships for Development Innovation (2015–2017); ambassador and permanent representative to the United Nations in Geneva and to the Conference on Disarmament (2011–2015); director-general of the Stabilization and Reconstruction Task Force (2009–2011); and representative of Canada in Kandahar, Afghanistan (2008–2009). She was also named a Young Global Leader by the World Economic Forum in 2010, and served on the WEF's Global Agenda Council on Violence and Fragility, and Global Future Council on Global Governance, Public-Private Partnerships, and Sustainable Development. In addition to core funding from the Government of Canada and other sources, some of CIGI's donors include the MacArthur Foundation, the Carnegie Foundation, the Visa Foundation, Microsoft, Google (Alphabet), and Global Affairs Canada, incorporated as the Department of Foreign Affairs, Trade, and Development and helmed by Jewish Minister of International Development Karina Gould.

Clearly all roads lead to the same destination. Remember, it was Western, predominantly Jewish capitalists who funded the Bolsheviks, giving rise to the USSR and massacres in the millions; similarly, it was the Jewish Sassoons (of the burgeoning opium trade) and Kadoorie families who are commonly credited with "opening up" China, and it was the Jewish Alan Greenspan who funneled enough money into the coffers of the Chinese Communist Party to keep it solvent before super-charging its economy on the back of outsourcing and dismantling US manufacturing capabilities. In a strategy very similar to that employed in Russia and much of the Eastern Bloc after the fall of the USSR in the 1990s, as Ian Johnson wrote in October 1994 for *The Baltimore Sun:*

> In an effort to assess China's shaky reform program, Federal Reserve Chairman Alan Greenspan is in the midst of a five-day tour of Beijing and Shanghai. The head of the U.S. central bank is meeting his Chinese counterparts, as well as senior Communist Party and government leaders. Mr. Greenspan did not make public his impressions of the meetings, but a source in his delegation said the purpose of his trip was twofold: to demonstrate U.S. support for the capitalist-style economic reforms, which some observers feel are in danger of derailing, and to assess the economic prospects of the world's most dynamic—and potentially most chaotic—economy. Mr. Greenspan's interest in China's economic future is more than academic. China has become one of the world's biggest magnets for foreign capital. Besides private investors, who have been flocking to mutual funds and investment deals that aim for a piece of China's double-digit economic growth, China has become the No. 1 recipient of World Bank loans and the prime focus of lending efforts by the U.S. Export-Import Bank. If China's reform program does sputter to a stop while inflation and unemployment soar, instability could put those loans and investments at risk. Although independent of the Clinton administration, Mr. Greenspan is the fourth top Washington official to visit China in the past eight weeks. He follows Commerce Secretary Ronald H. Brown, Defense Secretary William J. Perry and U.S. Export-Import Bank Chairman Kenneth Brody.

Clearly many of the pumped-up antagonisms on the world stage are play-acting—Shakespeare said it best. What this communicates to us is that the "elites" are generally all on the same page or at the very least willing to play ball with each other, as they have much more in common even in competing factions than with the regular people who comprise the nations they either pretend to govern on behalf of or that house their various headquarters where they avoid paying taxes for critical infrastructure and the like, because that's what parasites do.

6

THE ZIONIST-OCCUPIED GOVERNMENT

In the same vein as the manufactured antagonisms with which we closed the last chapter, another that has been so critical to the maintenance of the astroturfed Right the past twenty years has been that of militarized Islam. Yes, there is ample animosity between Christianity and Islam dating back nearly 1,400 years (since the creation of Islam), but in recent years much of this has been the product of the efforts of Israel and Zionist Western governments on its behalf (for its creation and since) and of the Jewish Diaspora globally.

Western governments do not govern on behalf of or for their own constituencies, in most cases going so far as to "elect a new people" and advantage them at the expense of "their" own populations. The same is true for every client state of the Neoliberal Empire, an ersatz empire built on deception, coercion, fractional reserve banking, and inversion of goodness and godliness. As Kerry Bolton writes in "Refugee Crisis Serving Globalist Dialectic," "The Europe that has been wanted by the USA"—and by extension the pro-Zionist axis—"since 1945 is one that has been thoroughly infected by cultural, social and moral pollution." The targeted subversion and dismantling of European power predates even the monumental World War II, but for all intents and purposes that is when the neoliberal regime achieved global hegemony, with the useful foil of the USSR helpfully ensconced as bogeyman, albeit one that needed to be encircled and checked through proxy wars, espionage, and subversion. Continuing For Bolton:

> Hence the USA and Israel backed *jihadists* on the pretext of fighting extreme Muslim regimes, which happen to be the very regimes that are least theocratic. The US strategy is most discernible since the US backing to the *Mujahedeen* to get the Russians out of Afghanistan, a war which itself contributed significantly to the implosion of the Soviet bloc, arguably the last European colonial empire. *Jihadists* and Albanian gangsters were used against Milosevic to detach the vast mineral wealth of Kosovo from Serbia, and as part of the

encirclement of Russia. Tribal and *jihadist* factions were backed in Libya to oust Gaddafi. Both secularised youth and Muslim radicals were used right across North Africa in the so-called 'Arab Spring'. The only two states left to be mopped up by the Zionist-US-*Jihadist* juggernaut are Iran and Syria. The Islamic State arose as if from nowhere, apparently a mystery to the normally pervasive eyes of Mossad and the CIA, rolling across Syria and Iraq in their new Toyota vehicles. Wherever the Islamic State goes, US and Israeli military hardware follow, not to sustain the regimes that are struggling against the Islamic State, and the myriad of other *jihadist* factions, but to support the latter factions against Syria.[45]

Red lines in the sand be damned, I suppose.

British interference in the Middle East beyond its colonial pretensions included not just the Balfour Declaration's ear-marking of Palestine for the Jews, but significant maneuvering to serve their own geopolitical ends. British Mesopotamian officer Harry St. John Philby was sent on a special mission to the Arabian Peninsula from 1917–1918 to continue to "work with" Ibn Saud and his Wahhabi movement furthering British military and political objectives in the Middle East following the signing of the 1915 Treaty of Darin. Saud's Emirate of Nejd and Hasa agreed to declare war on the "sick man of Europe" the Ottoman Empire, which had been tabbed for topple and its modern Syrian, Jordanian, Lebanese, and Iraqi sections to be partitioned between France and Britain with the Sykes-Picot Agreement of 1916. Russia was to also gain further holdings around the Caucasus.

Saudi Arabia has thusly, since well before the official founding of the kingdom in 1932, remained loyal to its benefactors in the neoliberal axis, particularly the United States, and has proven useful not just in the oil and arms trade, but in, as Askar Enazy puts it, "Wahhabi Salafism persists while its pool of expendable foot soldiers is replenished," not least of which would include the 9/11 hijackers, catalyzing the Project for the New American Century's bellicosity and extensive regime-change operations and "military interventions," many of which have proven to Israel's benefit.

Speaking of Israel, it was only at the behest of his Zionist donors that former American President Harry Truman went against the advice of his State Department and officially recognized the state of Israel (and pressured other

---

[45] Additionally: "The USA will continue push for the expansion of *jihadism* to destabilise the major bugbear, Russia, as the USA already has in Chechnya, some of whose militants have now joined militia's in the Ukraine to fight Russia."

countries such as France with the withdrawal of aid if they did not do the same). The Zionist and pro-Israel lobby has enjoyed tremendous influence in the Anglosphere for quite some time, but it is also a major factor in the European Union; much of the influence comes as a result of American intervention and power, as well as the various Jewish organizations and pressure groups in the US, but this influence is by no means limited to the American source.

Jewish influence transcends matters pertaining to the state of Israel, though these examples are indicative of said influence and power, which are inextricable from the neoliberal system itself. Jews are the system's primary drivers and beneficiaries, and no discussion of neoliberalism and the various factors presently imperiling the West is complete without an understanding of the centrality of Jewish interests. As huge swathes of the West are under the dominion of the Zionist-Occupied Government, it should not be surprising that, as Grégory Mauzé reports:

> While the influence of pressure groups aimed at preserving US support for Tel Aviv is a matter of public knowledge, the activities of these networks in Europe is not so well-known. Since the turn of the century, the latter have been busy cementing their friendly relations with the European Union (EU) and its member States. While the good graces of Brussels are not as vital for Tel Aviv as those of Washington, they are nonetheless strategically important. The EU is Israel's main trading partner and has gradually granted it privileged ally status in domains as crucial as scientific research, technical innovation and intelligence gathering. The Israeli lobby first gained a firm foothold in Europe in the aftermath of the second Intifada which broke out in September 2001.... The lobby was able to count on the backing of its "big brother" in the US. Some of its components are direct offshoots, like the Transatlantic Institute, set up the American Jewish Committee, or B'nai B'rith Europe. Other structures, though they have no organic ties with Washington agencies, use identical methods, like the European Friends of Israel (EFI), founded in 2006, or Europe Israel Public Affairs (EIPA), which functions in a way similar to the powerful American Israel Public Affairs Committee (AIPAC).... By studying the tax returns of charitable organisations it has been possible to ascertain that the bulk of their funding comes from philanthropists living on the other side of the Atlantic, whose sympathies lie with the American and Israeli right-wing, among them Sheldon Adelson.... The lobby can [also] rely on the German coordinator for combatting anti-Semitism,

Katharina von Schnurbein. Closely involved as she is with the principal pro-Israel pressure groups, she diligently passes on their press releases.... Of fundamental interest here is the influence exerted on the European Commission, which holds a monopoly on legislative initiatives, implements all EU decisions and handles financial assistance to third-party countries and cooperation programs. Some directorates general (DG) are the object of especially close attention, such as the DG Taxation and Customs Union (Taxud) in charge of the touchy issue of produce from the colonies, as well as the DG of Research and Innovation (RTD) which finances in particular the European programme "Horizon 2020" in which Israel is a participant.

Horizon 2020 also allocates funds to aid and incentivize migration into Europe and helps fund the European Network Against Racism (ENAR)—"a feminist anti-racist organisation that will keep addressing compounded forms of discrimination within and outside the movement, using an intersectional approach."

This intersectional hierarchy—from a group that is avowedly against *certain* hierarchies, as evidenced by the inchoate screeching to "dismantle the patriarchy"—has been enormously beneficial to Muslims in the West, who can cry oppression with the best of them despite astronomical levels of violence and chauvinism. Remember though, this rhetoric and the war on pattern recognition is part of the larger plan to remake the West in the ruling class' ideal. Are they being riddled with shrapnel from a nail bomb detonated outside an Ariana Grande concert? No, they are not. Instead, they are playing chess-master with population groups as a means to an end. For Gearóid Ó Colmáin from a 2016 article, "The current invasion of Europe is a neocolonial project sponsored by the Ziono-Wahhabi imperial alliance. It is a divide and conquer strategy of the global ruling class," with the Wahhabis (and Muslims more broadly), ultimately and perhaps somewhat paradoxically given their violent fanaticism, expected to be easier to control.

Intersecting with the rhetorical effectiveness of victimology and the usefulness of Muslims as demographic and angst-ridden weapons in the West, their role as "politically conscious" consumers is central to the neoliberal Establishment; as Nabeel Azeez brags with no apparent introspection:

> It was important to us to showcase that Muslim women aren't a monolith, and to include our Black Muslim sisters.... I wrote impassioned op-eds about how important the collaboration was to

me in terms of both beauty inclusivity and sociopolitical resistance, in *Elle* and *New York Times' Women in the World.*

This is representative of the rapidly-expanding iteration of intersectional capitalism, the kind that finds basically every major corporation virtue-signaling about Black Lives Matter on their websites and social media accounts.

But it goes further than that, and the agenda is far more explicable when we understand that their "activism" is directly informed not just by the financial windfall or the political/demographic element, but rather the usefulness at the intersection of intersectionality, politics, and politics as war. As Kerry Bolton explains in "Refugee Crisis Serving Globalist Dialectic":

> In Germany, which it has been suggested should take 800,000 emigrants from Syria, the German-Jewish *plebs* are fearful that this will not only bring in anti-Semitic Muslims but perhaps more worryingly galvanise latent German nationalism and a rejection of multiculturalism. However, it is not a fear shared by IsraAid, an Israeli welfare organisation that has been working with uprooted Syrians and others in the Levant for several years. The German-Jewish organisations want the Muslim emigrants indoctrinated in "German values" (sic), which is to say in the post-1945 self-hating neurosis. Certain of the rabbinate and the higher echelons of Zionism, as well as certain US policy-makers believe they can secularise and control uprooted Islamic youth for the purpose of destroying the culture cohesion of the nations of Europe. In this regard it could be contended that it is not Islamisation that is the ultimate problem for Europe but to the contrary, the amalgamation of alienated Muslim youth as part of the great mass of rootless young who feed off Cola, MTV, Hollywood, and the Hip Hop culture that is being promoted by the US State Department. Neocon strategist Ralph Peters wrote of the traditional cultures, rulers and religious leaders being no match for the allure of US-driven global culture distortion. Likewise the US State Department sees uprooted Islamic youth as the means of destroying the persistent "chauvinism" of such nations as, in particular, France. In 2010 Charles Rivkin, US Ambassador to France, invited a delegation from the Pacific Council on International Policy (PCIP) to France to discuss Arab and Islamic relations in the country, with the purpose of outlining a programme to use Muslim youth to destroy the ethnic consciousness of French youth. One of the three "key themes" was to examine the impact of

Hollywood on French culture. Rivkin developed a "confidential" programme, named "Minority Engagement Strategy," run from his embassy, and exposed by Wikileaks. He stated that the US would "press France" by appealing to her liberal—Jacobin—legacy. This would include a massive propaganda campaign with a focus on the young. This includes changing the educational curricula to promote the roles of non-French minorities in France's history. A Youth Outreach Program had been established by the embassy to push US "values and objectives," by manipulating "French values," with the aim being to mould "future French leaders." The cadre for this would be the 1,000 American English-language teachers in French schools. Rivkin referred to a major aim being to undermine support for "xenophobic political parties." In 2011 the *Globe & Mail* reported that "leadership programs" sponsored by the US Embassy focused on "potential leaders in Muslim groups and other minorities," via the US-sponsored International Visitor Leadership Program. A large proportion of the participants since 2010 have been Muslims. Then Secretary of State Hillary Clinton commented that many of the Egyptians in the program had become active in the riots that overthrew the old regime in Egypt, as part of the well-orchestrated "Arab Spring."

Brand *and* political loyalty in the same one-stop-shop package. This "liberal norm diffusion" is central to the color revolutions; Carol Bellamy and Adam Weinberg state that "any successful strategy needs to be delivered by messengers who are perceived to be authentic and by media that move information in multiple directions." US-directed exchanges create "cultural carriers" or "multipliers," which makes these trained "youths" exceptionally valuable. To that end in Iran, Giles Scott-Smith reports for *American Diplomacy:*

> In March 2006…an unclassified State Department cable entitled "Recruiting the Next Generation of Iran Experts: New Opportunities in Washington, Dubai and Europe…" was part of Secretary of State Condoleeza Rice's new strategy, Transformational Diplomacy, the aim of which she outlined in January 2006 as "to build and sustain democratic, well-governed states that will respond to the needs of their people and conduct themselves responsibly in the international system." The cable announced the formation of an Office of Iranian Affairs to coordinate a network of "outreach posts" for political/economic reporting, the most significant being the Regional

Presence Office (RPO) in Dubai, UAE, designed to connect with the Iranian people and "promote freedom and democracy in Iran." Around the same time, $85m in emergency funding was earmarked for the promotion of democracy in Iran, including support for dissidents and exiles groups; 24-hour radio and television broadcasting; increasing internet gateways; and study opportunities for Iranians to go to the U.S.

In 2008, the Bush administration attempted to establish a "US interests section" at the Swiss Embassy in Tehran, and between 2005 and the summer of 2009 featured numerous seminars, exchanges, and training programs under such topics as "civil resistance." In what is highly unlikely to be coincidental, in June 2009, street protests erupted in Tehran against the presidential election results, a dead ringer for a presumptive color revolution. Fortunately it did not happen, but Iran declared that the US government exchange programs were functioning as "Velvet Revolution Tools," which as we have seen is a correct assessment. Later in the summer of 2009, according to WikiLeaks, Iranian authorities concluded that "exchanges" conducted by the US government in Dubai were:

> "Modelled on the Riga [station]" which was set up to engineer the collapse of the Soviet Union.... its goals in Dubai are to attract the Iranian elite and convince them to act against the interests of the Islamic Republic. In a description of the International Visitor Leadership Program (IVLP)...Iranian authorities also seemed to have conflated public diplomacy programs with separate democracy programming in describing US regime overthrow effort.

These efforts have been going on for a long time, with the US determined to regain influence over, or even better fracture, Iran since their puppet the Shah Mohammad Reza Pahlavi was ousted in 1979. With an Israeli-focused Middle Eastern policy tying into the "needs" of Balkanizing the Middle East and North Africa to serve the neoliberal system, we see 1983 as a crucial year for the beginning of a more covert strategy.

Recall that 1983 saw the formation of the NED, the NDI, CIPE, and what is now the International Republican Institute. Additionally, as Giles Scott-Smith writes:

> During April-May 1983, for a period of four weeks, a group of seven academics and civil servants from Jordan, Kuwait, Morocco, and the West Bank undertook a tour of the United States. The grantees were

academics (primarily theologians), legal officers, and civil servants in their home societies.

And they were invited in order to "sell" them on the idea of "religious pluralism," meaning a weakening of a more traditional view of Islam closer to that of "Westernized" secularism predicated on consumerism and flimsy notions of "tolerance" and "democracy"—in short, the same garbage imposed on the West by its oligarchic "elites" before they decided to dispense with the illusion altogether in the Age of Covid, a topic for another book, perhaps.

As the United States Information Agency report stated, "They were able to see that pluralism, after all, is a valid concept" with the exception of one man; as Scott-Smith writes, "The issue of Iran and its revolution was never far away, and this was exemplified by group member Dr. Okla from Jordan supporting the Iranian regime's use of violence on religious grounds." Where "secularization" was not possible, hardline Islam or even millenarian sects such as ISIS could ultimately prove advantageous to Washington as a tool of destruction. Islamic fundamentalism could also prove helpful with a large Muslim population in the Russian Federation as a tool of destabilization or separatism. The US-backed Al-Qaeda and the Taliban provided funding to Chechen fighters and Vladimir Putin alleges the US was behind the funding of Chechen separatists as well. Given US policy in Afghanistan, the Balkans, and elsewhere, this is eminently possible. Via *BBC News*, Putin states that, "Our security services recorded direct contact between North Caucasus fighters and representatives of US intelligence in Azerbaijan." Indeed, as Ieva Bērziņa notes in "Color Revolutions: Democratization, Hidden Influence, or Warfare" from the National Defence Academy of Latvia Center for Security and Strategic Research in 2014, "A critical view of the 'color revolutions' in the West is rooted in the recognition that the US has an extensive history of interference in the internal affairs of other countries,"[46] its ally Israel perhaps even more so.

Certainly the willingness of the Diaspora to conduct espionage on behalf of the small country belies any irrational "anti-Semitism." The same knee-jerk, shut-it-down impulse occurs any time the Zionist regime carries out a deadly attack in its neighborhood; as one shining example, the US cut off aid to Israel in September 1953 after it continued to divert water from the River Jordan in defiance of the UN. Washington and Israel both kept the aid suspension private until shortly thereafter when Ariel Sharon assaulted a Jordanian village, blew up a school, and killed fifty-three civilians, at which point then-President Dwight Eisenhower made the aid suspension public.

---

[46] Bērziņa, *Color Revolutions*, 5.

Instead of looking to the pair of egregious incidents, then-Israeli Prime Minister attributed the decision to then-CIA Director Allen Dulles' supposed "anti-Semitism," rather dubious when you consider that it was Allen Dulles. Keep in mind in these early days of the Israeli state, its existence was much more tenuous than it is now, and the United States had to play a more delicate game in backing the rogue state.

Despite the incessant shrieking about Russian interference in US elections, we know it is the US or its proxies—or vice versa as the case may be, with the US as a Zionist proxy—that are the worst offenders in terms of interference in sovereign nations' elections and affairs, and this includes in those of its presumptive allies. In 2008, James Bullock, head of public affairs at the US Embassy in Paris, said that the US was committed to "getting to know the future movers and shakers of Europe, because these young people are part of the future of Europe," speaking, of course, about Arab Muslims especially but also black Africans, many of whom have gravitated to Islam as an anti-cultural marker, meaning in opposition to the traditional symbols of Europe. As Scott-Smith puts it, for the US government the goal is to use the "attractions of US soft power—its cultural products, its messages, its opportunities." Scott-Smith expands[47]:

> One result of this was various programmes that aimed to bring groups of young European Muslims to the U.S. on informal learning tours. Two pilot projects, the Muslim Youth Workers Exchange and Muslim (Teenager) Youth Exchange, were contracted out by the State Department to private sector partners, and they both ran twice. The Youth Exchange was run as a joint project: in the U.S. there was the Institute for Training and Development in Amherst, a body dedicated to crafting "inter-cultural experiences" and training programmes for a variety of sponsors and partners; in the Netherlands there was the Nederlandse Jeugdinstituut (Dutch Youth Institute), backed by the ministries of Justice and Home Affairs as

---

[47] In addition, Scott-Smith describes the precursor directly following 9/11: "The Shared Values Initiative (SVI), run by Under Secretary of State for Public Diplomacy and Public Affairs Charlotte Beers, launched in October 2002, and costing $15 million to produce. It was an integrated communication campaign involving public speeches abroad by U.S. diplomats and American Muslims, Internet sites and online chat rooms, the magazine Muslim Life in America, and newspaper advertisements. At the center of the campaign were five television commercials depicting American Muslims discussing their life in the United States. The commercials, or 'mini-documentaries' as the State Department called them, depicted religious tolerance in the United States and the positive experience of living there for ordinary citizens who were Muslim."

part of their action programs for social integration and "de-radicalisation." These were followed up by the Muslim Incentive Program (MIP), which ran from 2003 to 2010 and which will continue in 2011 as the Minority Outreach Incentive Program to reflect a broader focus on all minorities, expanded beyond Western Europe to include Eurasian nations. The aim of the Program was to stimulate a 'transatlantic outlook' amongst these communities who, by and large, had no direct first-hand experience of the United States. Up till 2010 the Program ran only in the Netherlands, Belgium, France, Germany, the UK, and the Scandinavian countries. Through the Program, U.S. embassies in these countries could claim extra exchange grants if they could show that they were being offered to local Muslim grantees. Alongside the MIP, other group projects specifically aimed at building bridges between the US and otherwise unconnected communities were developed. In FY 2010 the State Department circulated 25 European Regional Programs for which U.S. embassies could select candidates, with topics ranging from human trafficking and the role of the arts to U.S.-European Foreign Policy Challenges. Several were directly related to topics of concern as regards U.S. relations with Europe: "Managing Diversity in a Multi-Ethnic Society," "Religion and Community Activism in a Democratic Society," and, in particular, "Current U.S. Political, Social and Educational Issues for Young Muslim Leaders," a two-and-a-half week program in the US which was described as follows:

"This project is designed for young, emerging Muslim leaders of minority communities in Europe representing universities, government agencies, political organizations, media, and religious and community groups. The project will expose these young leaders to the pluralistic nature of the United States and the impact of diversity on political, social and educational issues and institutions in this country. The participants will gain insights into U.S. federalism, the American political system, and the foreign policy decision-making process. They will visit schools and universities to speak with student groups, and explore community issues such as ethnic diversity and integration, gender equality, religious tolerance, and the impact of American values and ethics on local groups and institutions."

The incentive behind these programs is understandable. While the initial goal was to contribute towards de-radicalization in European societies (a goal which has been pushed into the background but has never fully disappeared), the overall aim is to be "all-inclusive…" Other public diplomacy initiatives have also gone down this path, such as the Alliance for Youth Movements that seeks to promote "technology-driven grassroots activism campaigns…" The State Department (specifically, then Undersecretary of State for Public Diplomacy and Public Affairs James Glassman) initiated the project by teaming up with corporate partners (Facebook, YouTube, Google, MTV) to encourage the use of social media outlets as a tool against oppression.

Social media usage was central to the diffusion of Arab Spring propaganda, its apparent "authenticity" betrayed by its engineered intent. That said, social media and media in general is tremendously valuable for many reasons but in this context not just for duping the world at large but in trying to engineer catalyzing events out of some event such as an election or a run-in with law enforcement in order to foment unrest and feed these energies into a regime-approved color revolution. Algorithmic tinkering on social media platforms is a more covert version of a traditional media platform's decisions on what to cover and how, and it is not difficult to get a particular topic or event "trending" for those who control and/or influence said platforms.

As anyone who has voiced an "unapproved" opinion on social media can attest, these platforms are rigidly policed, sometimes as in the case of countries like Germany, Sweden, Finland, and the UK quite literally. The best-case scenario is probably that of Olli Sademies, a former Finns Party politician who was "only" expelled from the party over "hate speech" on social media; over 2,500 people in London alone were detained by police for social media posts in the first half of the 2010s. The Communications Act of 2003 defines illegal communication as "using public electronic communications network in order to cause annoyance, inconvenience or needless anxiety" and carries a six-month prison term or a fine of up to £5,000. In 2016, 3,395 people across twenty-nine reporting police forces were arrested under section 127 of the Communications Act 2003, but as *Breitbart* reports, "The true figure is likely to be significantly higher, as thirteen police forces refused to provide the requested information and two did not provide usable data."

The Council of Europe Commission against Racism and Intolerance (ECRI) publishes reports brow-beating member states that have taken "insufficient steps" to combat "hate speech," with protected categories emphasized as "asylum-seekers, Muslims, persons of African descent, LGBT persons, Roma and the Jewish community." The European Union has provided funds to organizations like the RED (Rights, Equality, Diversity) Network to "monitor extremism" and "combat racism and xenophobia." The RED Network comprises over a dozen NGOs, which are also focused on "reporting and documenting racist and hate crime and discrimination situations and incidents, as well as positive initiatives and policy responses." i-Red is the network leader and has committed to projects such as the Action Plan Against Racism and Discrimination and Pro-Diversity in Greek schools, commissioned by the Ministry of Education where i-RED would lead the consortium with the Aristotle University of Thessaloniki and the University of Crete.

German law requires companies like Twitter and Facebook to not only forward "suspected illegal content" to the FBI-equivalent Federal Criminal Police Office (BKA), but they must also provide the poster's personal information, such as their IP address. The BKA claims that 75% of "hate posts" in Germany are made by "right-wing extremists," which is a gross distortion by some metric, whichever way they're framing it—including what constitutes a "right-wing extremist" and/or a "hate post." A dozen middle-aged people had their apartments in Koblenz raided by police in 2019 for running a Facebook group called "Our Germany is patriotic and free" as part of an operation spanning thirteen federal states. Alas, *were* Germany patriotic and free…

In Finland, Helsinki police have a unit dedicated to policing "online hate" in the same way that many UK police departments do. The West Midlands Police in the UK's "apprehensions" increased 877% from 2014–16. In Sweden, in addition to the official police apparatus (which netted eighteen convictions for "hate speech" in 2017 with "Muslims, Jews, refugees and LGBT people" as protected classes), as *Sputnik News* reports:

> Näthatsgruppen or the Net Hate Group was founded in 2017 as a gathering of individuals joining forces to battle hate and crimes against democracy. The network consists of lawyers, former policemen and programmers, who have created a program that peruses through social media, above all Facebook, for "crimes of opinion."

The group admits to essentially walling-off non-Swedish public figures from criticism, such as Ugandan-born former feminist leader Victoria Kawesa and Culture Minister Alice Bah Kuhnke, the daughter of a Gambian-born father. Jagarhar, a Leftist network of tens of thousands of volunteers monitoring social media founded by Iranian-born journalist Mina Dennert in May 2016 does something similar. The organization's aim is to "fight hatred and xenophobia on the web," and carries out investigations and reports "questionable" content to the authorities. On the other side, any criticisms of Islam, particularly in Europe, have been met with ferocious violence (see: the

Charlie Hebdo massacre, the *Jyllands-Posten* Muhammad cartoon "protests," etc.).

Though Europeans are right to feel appalled that this could be happening in their countries, they must realize that it is being *allowed* and *enabled* to happen in their countries (and in the countries of their Western cousins). As regards Jews specifically, both in the West and from propaganda coming from or about Israel, Muslim attacks feed into the whole "anti-jihad" movement, which has been useful for many Jews to misdirect the natural objections to invasion and culture clash from the cause to a symptom, and to marshal support for Israel. Highly questionable characters such as Ezra Levant have made a career out of this. Further, for Kerry Bolton:

> At the higher ends of the power spectrum, so far from Zionists and US ruling cabals being alarmed at the invasion of Europe by Muslims of the most radical type, they are welcomed as cannon fodder in the obliteration of the vestiges of Western culture. It is the Muslim extremists after all whom both Israel and the USA have long been aiding in creating chaos in formerly stable states such as Libya and now Syria; the same "rebels" who are on a *hijrah* to Europe. One would think that the Zionist leadership of Jewry would be fearful of emigrant Muslim militants as the harbingers of anti-Semitism to Europe. However, as has long been pointed out anti-Semitism is the *raison d'être* of Zionism and the relationship is symbiotic.

Jihadist terrorist attacks are just the most ecstatic example of what Guillaume Faye rightly observed to be on the same continuum as daily "juvenile" and "youth" criminality and violence perpetrated against the native population by the imported and weaponized equatorials. While most of these imported Muslims in Europe and the rest of the West function as ideal hyper-consumers who readily suck down the degenerate "hip-hop culture" exported by the United States, there is also the trend of increasing "radicalization" among the descendants of migrants turning to a more aggressive strand of Islam to act out their grievances on their surroundings. In many cases, they are less "fundamental" in their embrace of Islam and more using it in Faye's view as an identity marker to differentiate from their nominally Christian environs and act out their resentment. That they simultaneously embrace "Western" capitalism is clearly lost on them as they seamlessly fulfill their role in the neoliberal system. As an ersatz counter-point, returning to Bolton:

> The pseudo-Right, attempting to take advantage of Islamophobia promoted by the neocon-Zionist nexus, is following the same flawed

path as the "patriots" who bought the entire anti-Soviet line of the globalist system during the Cold War. Then it was twaddle about fighting "communism," of which there remained little in the USSR; now it is "Islamofascism."

"Fascism" being another useful bogeyman—as of course "we are all united" against abstractions such as "extremism," and even for the so-called classical liberals, jihadis and normal white people who want a homeland to call their own are on the same continuum as that which is well beyond the realm of acceptability. Every condemnation of "identity politics" centered on jihadist Islam must inevitably be counter-balanced by a condemnation of "white supremacists"/Nazis/nationalists/what have you.

A favorite of the Dave Rubin set is Maajid Nawaz, the "anti-extremist" who condemns Scottish nationalists as racist, although it is axiomatic that Scotland—a white country as Scots are white—would remain so should it not be flooded with foreigners, in the same way Kenya—a black country as Kenyans are black—would remain black. For Nawaz, "Violent hostility to outsiders and critics is in the DNA of nationalists, whether on the Left and Right." So it must be those dastardly Scottish nationalists yelling "Allahu Akbar!" before decapitating people in broad daylight with machetes, right? Or is that the result of intelligence agencies, governments, and NGOs weaponizing ideologically-motivated foreigners against their own people?

As the classical liberals are offered as an approved alternative in that libertarian kind of milieu, their condemnation of Islamic extremism is itself right on the edge of acceptability. General mainstream discourse will not condemn it, for it will not even name the source of said "extremism," though "racist" bogeymen will be pumped up as an omnipresent evil lurking everywhere from your yoga class to parliament, or as the culprits of the next false flag even *working in tandem with jihadis!*

According to Kerstin Köditz, regional deputy in Saxony, as reported by *Equal Times*:

> We have a racism problem.... For ten years, we heard things like "foreigners are criminals" in parliamentary sessions and in public debate. The NPD lost its seats in the Landtag in 2014, but the AfD was won seats for the first time in the same election.

According to former Social Democratic MP Wolfgang Thierse, "The danger here is huge and the problem has been downplayed for years" referencing "extreme right-wing violence." Are these "right wingers" raping women and girls on an industrial scale with the complicity of the government, or are they simply citing crime statistics, which are probably dramatically underreported given the government's concerted attempts to suppress anything negative pertaining to their favored foreigners?

Nawaz's buddy Tommy Robinson and other would-be nationalists like Katie Hopkins drape themselves in Israeli flags as though they're not the ones that have, since at least the Balfour Declaration, been fomenting unrest and trying to destabilize the Muslim world while contributing to the ethnic cleansings of millennia-old groups in the Middle East. The "only democracy in the Middle East" is actually at the root of the problem, but as Kerry Bolton points out:

> Given the recent enthusiasm for Israel as a defender of "western values" against rampant Islamism by the pseudo-Right, with the bastardous spectacle of those who would normally be called "neo-nazis" carrying the Israeli flag on their rallies, such as the English Defence League, Reclaim Australia, and European parties such as that of Geert Wilders, the support is not reciprocated by Zionists. For example the primary Israeli lobby in Australia condemned the Australian anti-Islamists and reiterated its advocacy of multiculturalism: "The Australia/Israel & Jewish Affairs Council (AIJAC) strongly supports Australian multiculturalism."

Not in Israel, though, right? According to Dan Feferman and Dov Maimon of the Jewish People Policy Institute:

> The 38,000 illegal migrants currently in Israel pose a dilemma between Jewish humanitarian values on the one hand and Israel's *raison d'être* as the nation state of the Jewish people on the other. World Jewish decision makers should consider their first priority to be ensuring Israel's capacity for future Jewish immigration given expected mass migration waves from distressed countries to the West...In principle, Israel does not bear the responsibility to provide a permanent home to illegal employment seekers, nor does it require them for its own small market.... It is extremely important to seek policy solutions based on partnership between Israel and world Jewry, rather than allowing the issue to become a bone of contention, especially with liberal Jewish communities and organizations.... The migration challenge is especially sensitive given its potential to damage Israel's image in the world.... Between 2015 and 2017, Israel deported 5,260 Ukrainian

nationals and 1,788 Georgians, and efforts continue to deport those who overstay their visas.

It will probably not surprise the reader that Michael Steinhardt, co-founder of Birthright Israel along with Charles Bronfman, is on the Board of the Jewish People Policy Institute. Bronfman is the uncle of Clare Bronfman, implicated in the NXIVM "sex cult" scandal, where she had "invested" around $150 million in what prosecutors call a fraudulent, pyramid organization. Sounds like a microcosm of the Jewish-helmed economy. Bronfman and Steinhardt formed the core of the "Mega Group" that was "concerned with Jewish issues" along with Les Wexner, Leonard Abramson, Laurence Tisch, and Edgar Bronfman, Sr., among others.

As reported by the *New York Times* in 2019, recent revelations about Steinhardt's "requests" are not quite Harvey Weinstein-level, but paint a picture of a disgusting, sex-crazed man, and like Weinstein, "Institutions in the Jewish world have long known about his behavior, and they have looked the other way," said one of seven women who have recounted Steinhardt making sexual requests. According to former ADL head Abe Foxman, "Michael is very passionate, and he is passionate in everything. Call it a passion, call it an obsession, call it a perversion. Some may. I don't—I understand it. It's just the way it comes out, which may disturb people."

Steinhardt is known to be deeply concerned with Jewish marriage with non-Jews as well as Jewish demographics, encouraging Jews to marry and reproduce; as with the Feferman and Maimov quote, at face value, this exhibits a rational and straightforward consideration of the issues of migration and demographics confronting the First World at large, but it is in the blatant hypocrisy that I find issue. Any wealthy white benefactor encouraging whites to marry and have kids is going to be vilified by the Jewish-controlled media as a Nazi, and on top of that, the same people are pushing miscegenation and the suppression of white birthrates, not to mention mass immigration into Western nations. Indeed, the Jewish George Soros stated in his 1997 *Atlantic* piece that ideas of "racial purity...contradict the principles of the open society." Regarding migration, Bolton expands:

> The Zionist support for the modern *hijrah* into Europe is provided by the long-established Hebrew Immigrant Aid Society (HIAS), in the "forefront" of a "multifaith" coalition that is advocating the acceptance of 200,000 Syrians into the USA. This "Multifaith Alliance" started as a "Jewish response" to the Syrian *hijrah*, according to Rabbi Eric J. Greenberg, the alliance's director of communications, programs and interfaith relations. According to the

New York Jewish newspaper *Forward,* the alliance began in 2013 from an appeal by HIAS, and is comprised of "40 groups of all faiths, but Jewish organizations still play a prominent role in the coalition…" As one would expect the rabbinate is using the Holocaust canard. In France, "At a Holocaust memorial event in Paris, French Chief Rabbi Haim Korsia urged Europe's leaders to match the actions of non-Jews who saved Jews from the Nazis by welcoming Syrian refugees." Ron van der Wieken, chairman of the Central Jewish Organization of the Netherlands, despite the "negative feelings" by "some Middle Eastern refugees," "urged Holland to devise a 'charitable' refugee policy." A similar attitude was expressed by Zoltan Radnoti, chairman of the rabbinical board of the Mazsihisz umbrella group of Hungarian Jewish communities. The organisation has set up depots to assist the Syrians et al. The Jewish community in Milan accommodated Middle Eastern and African migrant in the Holocaust Museum. In Brussels, Menachen Margolin, a Chabad rabbi and director of the European Jewish Association, led a delegation of rabbis to deliver goods to the migrants. Since when has Chabad Judaism been well disposed towards anyone other than Jews? The answer to this question is indicated by Julia Kaldori, editor of *Wina*, a monthly publication of the Jewish Community in Vienna. Kaldori is aware that "statistically, Middle Eastern immigrants are responsible for most of the violence driving French Jews to leave in record numbers—nearly 7,000 in 2014 alone. Kaldori hopes that having been helped by Jews, refugees with anti-Jewish views may reconsider." If not, a resurgence in hostility towards Jews would prompt a new influx of Jewish migrants from Europe to Israel and the USA, while Europe can continue falling apart.

According to the World Jewish Congress' Deputy CEO for Diplomacy Maram Stern, "Our answer can't be to close the doors. Not only would it not work, it would be immoral." The obligatory Holocaust reference soon follows. For Amanda Paulson, Martin Kuz, and Noble Ingram from October 2018, "When thousands of Afghan immigrants were resettled in California's Sacramento County over the past decade, volunteers from Congregation B'nai Israel were among those in the county providing aid."

From the same article: "We have Holocaust survivors in our congregation, and so many of us are just a generation or two removed from relatives who went through that experience or were forced to leave their country," says Maryann Rabovsky, chairwoman of the synagogue's immigration and refugee assistance committee. In maddening hypocrisy, Rabbi Sid Schwarz proclaims, "If we take our own experience and have the ethos to care for the stranger stop at the borders of our own community and tribe, then we've learned nothing from history." He continues, "HIAS as an organization has pivoted from an organization that primarily was committed to helping Jewish refugees to, today, an organization that helps refugees because we're Jews." Again, just not in Israel or any of the areas wealthy and influential Jews live.

Case in point, on September 5th, 2019, the YIVO Institute for Jewish Research in partnership with the Consulate General of the Republic of Lithuania in New York and the Lithuanian Culture Institute Panel Discussion under the auspices of Litvak Days NYC featured a presentation by Professor Tomas Venclova (Yale University, Emeritus) entitled, "Lithuanians and Jews: What's Changed and What Hasn't over the last Forty Years?" Professor Venclova was then joined by Jonathan Brent (Executive Director of YIVO), Mindaugas Kvietkauskas (Minister of Culture of Lithuania), Professor Saulius Sužiedelis (Millersville University, Emeritus), and Rabbi Andrew Baker (American Jewish Committee, Director of International Jewish Affairs) for a discussion about "the challenges of rebuilding a multicultural society in contemporary Lithuania." The only time Lithuania was ever "multicultural" was when the Soviet Union tried wholesale population replacement, which seems awfully apropos.

The old adage "follow the money" rings as true here as ever: as reported by the Jewish *Forward*, in July 2014 the Department of Homeland Security allocated to Jewish institutions $12 million, or 94 percent of its annual budget for securing nonprofits. The *Forward* states that of the $151 million disbursed since the program started in 2005 to mid-2014, the vast majority went to Jewish institutions. Jews are, for the record, a paltry 1.5 percent of the US population. During the 2018–19 federal government shutdown over the funding of a US-Mexico border wall, Elizabeth Warren pledged that she would donate her salary to the Hebrew Immigrant Aid Society because HIAS "helps refugees and makes our country stronger in the process." Objecting to this sentiment is, for Human Rights Watch as it describes European populist parties, "extremist."

It is worth noting that Human Rights Watch was co-founded by Jews Robert L. Bernstein, Jeri Laber, and Aryeh Neier, the latter of whom left HRW in 1993 to become president of what became the Open Society Foundations. Neier was succeeded at HRW by the Jewish Kenneth Roth, who was still Executive Director as of press time. Naturally, HRW is tied in to the globalist apparatus, with partners including the Ford Foundation, the Oak Foundation, and the Dutch Postcode Lottery. In 2010, George Soros announced a $100 million grant to Human Rights Watch through the Open Society Foundations. It might seem surprising to read that what is effectively a Jewish organization has come under such attack as "anti-Semitic" for its general support of Palestinians and often antagonistic stance toward Israel. NGO Monitor in particular has been highly critical of HRW, and when we look at who's bankrolling that particular project it becomes superficially even stranger; NGO Monitor receives significant funding from Research + Evaluation = Promoting Organizational Responsibility and Transparency (REPORT) (Formerly AFNGOM), which provided a grant of $1 million in 2016. REPORT is in turn funded by Jewish vulture capitalists such as Paul Singer and Seth Klarman, the former a staunch Republican and the latter formerly the GOP's largest donor in New England.

But this apparent opposition such as AIPAC "versus" J Street is actually an internecine struggle of sorts between Jewish factions for control, and I say apparent opposition because they both support the present policies that are destroying us. It is telling that the most central issue of American foreign policy for decades has been that of the Israeli-Palestinian conflict; though ostensibly concerning the security of our "greatest ally," this fault line is indicative of who is actually in control. When the centrality of an "ally" who's basically never committed any real resources to any of our endeavors but rather leeches off billions of dollars annually—to say nothing of firing on American naval vessels, spying on Americans, stealing military technology, withholding vital intelligence, and their potentially-significant role in 9/11—is the political litmus test of running for office in America, it should be painfully obvious that the United States is, in fact, an occupied country.

In any case, Human Rights Watch is also quick to deploy the "anti-Semitism" rhetorical weapon, stating that in Europe—as always, apparently, because it always seems to be "on the rise"—"anti-Semitism remained a concern in EU member states." It could be the millions of Muslims they've been supporting in their entry into the continent, or it could be a total fabrication, more likely a combination with a heavy dose of the latter. A few "anti-Semitic" incidents against Jews who are not in a power position are very useful to exploit for propaganda purposes, certainly.

Despite the vociferous support of millions of Muslims and other Third World peoples moving into the West because it is "enriching" and we owe a moral debt and all the rest of it, from the mid-2000s to 2017, only six Eritreans and one Sudanese were granted asylum in Israel, but NGOs such as IsraAID have been more than happy to lend a hand facilitating migrants' journeys into Europe and the rest of the West. Many African "migrants" who reach Israel are given stipends to return to Africa, which then form the basis of travel expenses to get to points of departure in North Africa and then on into

Europe. The Hebrew Immigrant Aid Society has dispatched personnel and resources to places like Lesbos in Greece to "help" these migrants, all with the eye of eventually pushing them northward. Then of course there was the near-miss of Israel using the United Nations to resettle 16,000–18,000 of these "migrants" in Canada, Italy, and elsewhere.

HIAS has worked extensively to ensure that not just essentially any and all comers can arrive in the West with minimal friction, but that those of "alternate sexuality" or "identity" may in particular, according to a 2021 article on their website:

> In 2011 Yiftach Millo went out in search of the invisible. In his field research over the next year, Millo found many LGBTQ refugees in Ecuador, Ghana, Israel, and Kenya...Millo, who is himself a gay man and today serves as HIAS Aruba's country director, wrote up his findings in a report for HIAS...HIAS actually assigned Millo his project because, even a decade ago, HIAS was out in the field working with LGBTQ refugees in Nairobi, Kenya. "HIAS was already, at that time, leading the issue," Millo said, noting that Kenya's work was groundbreaking. In other countries some HIAS staff were activists in gay communities. After the release of the report, which was sent to the U.S. State Department's Bureau of Population, Refugees, and Migration, Millo said there was a new understanding...In the United States, a number of HIAS affiliates provide many of the same services as well as resettlement help to LGBTQ refugees and asylum seekers.

On behalf of the US government, HIAS operates a resettlement support center in Vienna, they have a team on the Greek island of Lesbos, and in 2003, HIAS established an office in Kiev "to provide legal protection services to refugees who have fled to Ukraine from more than 30 nations." HIAS and Islamic Relief USA have partnered to provide legal services to refugees in Greece, and HIAS Greece has also formed a key relationship with Lesvos LGBTIQ+ Refugee Solidarity organization.

In 2018, HIAS Greece successfully brought a case before the District Court of Mytilene concerning a "transgender refugee's request to change her identification documentation to match her gender identity." HIAS says that "this legal change will help her find work and ease her integration. It was a win that set a very important precedent for transgender refugees." In 2018, the European Citizens' Initiative (ECI) introduced the "We are a Welcoming Europe" campaign. HIAS Greece joined 129 other civil society organizations to "promote solidarity and respect for refugees across the continent, standing

proudly with peer agencies and the displaced people we serve."
Per HIAS's *Annual Report 2018:*

> Thanks to the quick strategic investment of generous funders who were motivated by their Jewish values to address the plight of children and families at the border, the HIAS Border Fellows Project launched in fall of 2018. This new initiative places attorneys in local partner organizations in Texas and California, serving asylum seekers who would otherwise be left to represent themselves in court.[48]

HIAS also has offices all over Central and South America to help facilitate the movement of migrants north into the US. If this infuriates you, perhaps you'd like to know who funds and partners with HIAS to achieve their objective of demographically replacing ethnic Europeans and European-settled and founded nations.

Their corporate partners include Starbucks, 3M, Airbnb, Chevron, Sodexo, Wix, Rosetta Stone, JW Marriott, and Skill Lab. Major funders include: Islamic Relief USA, the Bill and Melinda Gates Foundation, the Jay Pritzker Foundation, the Church of Jesus Christ of Latter-Day Saints, UJA-Federation of New York, the American Jewish Joint Distribution Committee, the Harry and Jeanette Weinberg Foundation Inc., the American Jewish Committee, the Jewish Federations of North America, the Tikkun Olam Foundation, the Jacob and Hilda Blaustein Foundation Inc., StockX (founded by Dan Gilbert, Josh Luber, Greg Schwartz, and Chris Kaufman), the Conrad N. Hilton Foundation, Elisha Wiesel (Elie's son), the Johnson Family Foundation, the Bellwether Fund of the Tides Foundation, the New York Community Trust, the Lisa and John Pritzker Family Fund, the Pritzker Foundation, DC Capital Advisors, Jim Cramer, the Foundation to Promote Open Society, the Genesis Prize Foundation (the inaugural winner was Michael Bloomberg), and the "indie rock" band Yo La Tengo.

HIAS's partnerships in the US include: the Jewish Family Service of San Diego, Jewish Family & Community Services East Bay, Jewish Family Services of Silicon Valley, Jewish Family Services of Delaware, the Gulf Coast Jewish Family and Community Services, Jewish Family Service of Metrowest, the Jewish Family Service of Western Massachusetts, Jewish Family Services of Washtenaw County, the Jewish Family Service of Buffalo and Erie County, Carolina Refugee Resettlement Agency, US Together Inc., Jewish Family and Community Services Pittsburgh, Jewish Family Service of Greater Seattle, and Jewish Social Services of Madison, plus the Corporation for National &

---

[48] Hetfield, *Annual Report 2018,* 14.

Community Service (CNCS), the Network of Jewish Human Service Agencies (NJHSA), Refugee Council USA (RCUSA), The Church of Jesus Christ of Latter-Day Saints (LDS), UJA-Federation of New York, US Citizenship and Immigration Services (USCIS), US Department of State Bureau of Population, Refugees, and Migration (PRM), US Department of Health and Human Services Office of Refugee Resettlement (ORR), the International Organization for Migration (IOM), and the United Nations High Commissioner for Refugees (UNHCR).

Though not explicitly Jewish in nature like HIAS, another representative organization adjacent to both HIAS and organizations like Chatham House is the European Endowment for Democracy (EED), which focuses on "opening up" Europe's frontier with "democratic initiatives," including "empowering women" and a raft of LGBTQ programs; the EED was established in 2013 and is based in Brussels. In its *Annual Report 2019*, its goal is described as "to provide flexible support to democracy activists, complementing other EU and member state democracy-support programmes." It collaborates with organizations like the Aspen Institute and the German Marshall Fund of the United States, which was founded by the Jewish Guido Goldman; funding partners include the European Union, and the governments of Austria, Germany, the Czech Republic, Lithuania, Romania, Sweden, Belgium, Denmark, Hungary, Luxembourg, Slovakia, the Netherlands, the UK, Slovenia, Norway, Ireland, Estonia, Bulgaria, Cyprus, Finland, Latvia, Poland, and Spain. The government of Canada provides additional funding to "support grassroots democracy in Ukraine."

As Greg Afinogenov writes in his essay "The Jewish Case for Open Borders" for *Jewish Currents*, for Jews:

> As the charge of hypocrisy against Stephen Miller would suggest, it is not hard to dismantle right-wing immigration arguments by appealing to a Jewish conscience rooted in communal memory.... The way out of the nationalist trap in which Jews have been caught since World War II goes through Jewish cosmopolitanism.

In other words, Jewish interests and open borders are synonymous, non-whites' potential inability to distinguish between whites and Jews as the genocidal rhetoric hits a fever pitch evidently notwithstanding. Therein lies the possible pathology, of a desire to harm whites becoming self-destructive. Of course any belief that one can shape humanity like clay is indicative of profound hubris, and as David Cole has cautioned, Jewish lore includes the cautionary tale of the golem, the anthropomorphic clay beast that eventually turns on its master. In pursuing this globalist project, the disproportionately-

Jewish Inner Party very well might have a golem-like situation on its hands, and this is before considering what the white reaction to their targeted destruction may be.

This is all rather uncomfortable to write if we take liberalism as our default, for it actually seems quite "far out there" if we are united in purpose as humans to pursue equality and all of that nonsense. At what point does it become a mission of malice rather than in-group favoritism, understanding that Jews, unique among ethnicities, function better in "open" societies: the multiculturalism, the looser mores, et cetera. At worst they have found success as intermediaries between a subjugated population and its conquerors, such as in the Ottoman Empire and Muslim Spain, but global capital and industrialization, and the eventual rise of mass media and "connective" technologies, has enabled particular Jewish, group strengths to be put to use in crafting an internationalism that disproportionately benefits them. It is also, molded in the Jewish image as it is, subject to Jewish pathology and hysteria, a probable consequence of significant and sustained in-breeding among Ashkenazim especially.

Afinogenov does not believe open borders will come to harm Jews, as he states that even large-scale, center-left immigration rests "on the same foundation as those made by the right." That foundation, for Afinogenov, relies on valuative judgments, which are by necessity exclusionary, which inevitably leads to the Holocaust: "Jewish communities in the Soviet Union, the United States, and Israel all internalized these narratives as a foundational trauma, and invested in territorial nationalism as the only way to prevent a repeat of the Holocaust." Tellingly, most of Theodor Herzl's contemporaries in the nineteenth century rejected his vision of Zionism in order to continue pursuing their particular aims within European societies, including that of the Anglosphere and South Africa. To this day, still less than half of global Jewry resides in its own ethnostate, though Zionist policies influence much of the modern geopolitical scene.

Jewish groups and pro-Israel lobbies are also able to exert significant pressure campaigns both within the West and outside of it, such as when the Zionist Organization of America's president Mort Klein was able to convince Qatar to shelve *Al-Jazeera*'s "viciously anti-Semitic" documentary series *The Lobby*, which is focused on the power of Zionist lobbies in Washington. Qatari officials reportedly met with a number of pro-Israel "activists" and not only promised not to air the series but actively condemned Hamas and pledged to continue to "rehabilitate" relations with Israel.

As the twentieth century wore on, while the West's "democracies" were busy pressuring South Africa to dismantle Apartheid ostensibly for "humanitarian" reasons, but in actuality for reasons ideological and economic as part of the globalized push for "open societies," along with Jews within South Africa, the Apartheid state of Israel was busy interfering in its affairs as far back as the early 1960s. Early in his "career," Nelson Mandela was actually given paramilitary training by the Mossad in Ethiopia, and according to an *AP News* report in late 2013 regarding unsealed documents from Israel's archives:

> Israel maintained a strong interest in Mandela's well-being after his arrest and throughout the Rivonia Trial, where he was convicted of sabotage in 1964 and sentenced to life in prison. According to the archives, Israel also had an interest in the case because about one third of the defendants were Jewish, and Israel feared the case could spread anti-Semitism in South Africa. One letter, dated April 21, 1964 and written by Azriel Harel, an Israeli diplomat in South Africa at the time, called for rallying international opinion to prevent the Rivonia defendants from receiving death sentences. He also suggested that an economic boycott of South Africa be considered. A Foreign Ministry document dated May 18, 1964, discusses efforts to recruit Jewish philosopher Martin Buber and Israeli author Haim Hazaz to sign a declaration in support of the Rivonia defendants.... Alon Liel, who served as Israel's ambassador to South Africa in the early 1990s after Mandela's release from prison, said Israel's courtship of African leaders in the 1960s is well known.

One of the most "celebrated" stories attacking Apartheid, a sort of *Uncle Tom's Cabin* in short story form entitled "Once Upon a Time," was written by the Jewish Nadine Gordimer. In it, concerned by growing unrest and race riots, a family fortifies their home and builds a wall topped with barbed wire, only to have their young child eventually become tangled in the barbed wire and die, the implications obvious.

Now, with those troublesome whites on the ropes, Africa can be further exploited by Israeli/Jewish interests and in exceedingly unethical ways; this includes the lucrative diamond trade in Africa, where as Ezra Nahmad reports:

> Israel has often used questionable methods to lay hands on African mineral resources, methods solidly linked to its diplomatic and military offensives. Both the recent arrest by the Israeli police of Benny Steinmetz accused of money laundering and bribing persons close to the Guinean government, and the US proceedings against Dan Gertler, another Israeli player in the diamond trade, show that

Israel is active in the Kimberley process (an international agreement on the certification of uncut diamonds meant to prevent their sale and purchase for military purposes), but the more of its diamond czars remain abusive, to say the least. In 2010, Gertler was accused of financing the purchase of arms for the Kabila clan in exchange for a monopoly in the diamond trade. The Africa Progress Panel accused him in 2013 of having defrauded the Democratic Republic of the Congo (DRC) of 1.4 billion dollars in mining licenses. And as for Lev Leviev, known as "the diamond king," he built his fortune on his partnership with Angolan President Jose Eduardo Dos Santos and his clan for the control of the diamond industry.

Today, even with an explicitly-Jewish state, the majority of global Jewry chooses to live abroad, the vast majority of them in European and European-settled societies. Most have fled the South Africa they helped dismantle (the 1963 sweep of Rivonia counted six Jews among the thirteen ANC members, and post-apartheid, many Jews were beneficiaries of this existing relationship while the whites were mostly sacrificed to "diversity" and "democracy"). The few remaining are dramatically overrepresented among the country's millionaires, but even from abroad weaponized blacks are treated as pawns by certain power brokers such as the Swazi-Jewish billionaire Nathan Kirsh who has allegedly funneled money to the viciously anti-white Economic Freedom Fighters (EFF).

In their Western environs, approximately 80 percent of Jews hew Leftward and of the remaining 20 percent, most seem to fall into the Sheldon Adelson camp, i.e. "conservatism" as supportive of mass immigration, free trade, amnesty, and the like. Where does this leave the Europeans whose homelands are being detonated by Jewish interest groups, ideological and economic, public and private, religious and secular, when they all seem to horseshoe eventually? The only difference is the question of Israel—the rest seems to be settled.

It is especially telling that in the same January 2020 speech in which he implied Christians are not "people of faith" and condemned "nativists," Michael Bloomberg vowed that as president, he would "always have Israel's back" and would "never impose conditions on our military aid, including missile defense—no matter who is prime minister, as reported by *CBS News*. And I will never walk away from our commitment to guarantee Israel's security." Not quite at the level of Chuck Schumer stating that he was on a mission from his god to defend Israel, but still pretty nakedly open about the Jewish view of both Israel and America's purpose in their "alliance." Israel enjoys blanket bipartisan support and it clearly goes beyond politics for these figures. Granted a great many Jews are sympathetic to the plight of the Palestinians, but why is this the dominant political issue of our time in the West when we are being treated the same way by our own governments?

As much as there are the odd "anti-Semitic" attacks committed against the relatively few non-wealthy Jews by Muslims, these form the back-bone of the globalist dialectic in Europe, as Kerry Bolton describes. The attacks can be either minimized and/or swept under the rug depending on the needs of the ruling class, or used as justification for the faux-Right "alliance" with Jews under siege in the Middle East and now the West. They can also, as we have seen, be used as a pretext for increasing surveillance exponentially.

On the other side, Robert Bowers's Pittsburgh synagogue shooting has been pumped up relentlessly as evidence of the "rising tide of anti-Semitism," a tide that, for the Jewish establishment, is perpetually rising and serves the victim narrative extending back to the Year Zero of the Holocaust. With "white supremacy" as a constant bogeyman, Jews can in turn use the fake victim card to align themselves with Muslims as "allies."

One example is the Sisterhood of Salaam Shalom in the US and Canada, favorably covered by *HuffPost*, where according to Executive Director Sheryl Olitzky, they are "natural allies," and "they've also been grieving the rise of white nationalist violence and planning how they will respond to both anti-Semitism and Islamophobia." The Sisterhood of Salaam Shalom's website leads off with a quote from Maya Angelou in eye-rolling predictability; their 2018 annual conference featured speakers such as Joseph Levin, co-founder of the Southern Poverty Law Center. According to Outreach Director at the SPLC Lecia Brooks in a late 2018 interview with Linda A. Thompson of *Equal Times*:

> Ultimately, white supremacists can't win because they don't have the numbers in terms of the population. They know that the shift is happening; this is their last gap of hope. But the rise of populism isn't just that. It also a response to the culture wars around marriage quality, and equality and acceptance of transgender individuals. Because that's something these movements use too, they try to appeal to people who don't want to be sensitive to or think about these issues. They want to go back to a time when it was simple—just "men" and "women," "husband" and "wife." And especially in countries in the EU that were strongly Christian or Catholic, it's harder to let go.

There's a lot to "unpack" there, from the haughty dismissal of whites' demographic concerns as fringe to the conflation of populism—which by definition relies on majoritarianism and at least some elements of democracy—with "white supremacy," which in the modern parlance means one who would like to keep, say, Croatia Croatian or Hungary Hungarian. The haughty dismissal also belies a deep discomfort with the constant refrain of the neoliberal project's "inevitability," like the Unsinkable Ship of yore. For Brooks, Christians evidently should just "let go" of their countries, their beliefs, and the scientific reality of human beings' sexual dimorphism because it's the current year. Evidently "trans" and mass immigration are also inseparable, and while this is patently absurd, it is real insofar as the ruling class has made them inextricable in their progression of "progress," which is ever-changing but is also an all-or-nothing proposition. Break from the official line on one issue and watch what happens. Brooks is also telegraphing that nothing you love or value will survive this revolution of oligarchs and weaponized equatorials and various disgruntled and/or indoctrinated whites against nature, order, and decency.

For Jordi Vaquer, regional director for Europe with the Open Society Foundations and a co-director of the Open Society Initiative for Europe, there exists a "justice gap" for the deified migrants that "should be seen against the backdrop of a wider assault on the founding values of the European Union currently taking place in various countries across the continent," as reported by *Equal Times*. One of the major precursors to the EU was the European Economic Community, so this is half-true, but with the EU's mutation to where its motto is now the Orwellian United in Diversity, he's closer, with the economic impetus melding together with the importation of a new serf class while the Europeans they'd replace are forced to live in a dystopian hell of women with penises and "hate speech" and constant tracking and surveillance.

Vaquer characterizes push-back against Soros as featuring "classic antisemitic imagery," with the primary example cited being "you are helping migrants arrive and this is because George Soros pays you." Factually accurate, and nothing to do with Soros's Jewish identity, though Sigmund Freud might have something to say about that. Nevertheless, the ancestral homelands of Europeans remaining European is a big issue for Vaquer. When asked in his *Equal Times* interview, "How do you think the new Commission will respond to the rise in hate crimes against religious, ethnic and sexual minorities?" Vaquer responded:

> Poland and Hungary are obvious examples, but Estonia's government also includes a very problematic party [*editor's note: the far-right EKRE party*] and so did Italy until very recently. Today we have governments that are either led or conditioned by forces that

are questioning issues of equality that were previously agreed in principle, forces that are undermining the basic values of the European Union, including anti-discrimination, and not just ethnic and racial discrimination but also gender and LGBT discrimination.

A proposition Union, just like that of the United States, as formulated by the Jewish Ben Wattenberg and a "melting pot," as it were, formulated by the Jewish Israel Zangwill. Isn't that something?

Further underscoring the marriage of "anti-racism" and the capitalist oligarchy, the European Network Against Racism (ENAR) runs something called Equal@work in partnership with Coca-Cola, Sodexo, Inditex, and the Adecco Group, which deals with the usual diversity stuff like self-congratulatory/flagellating seminars and the "Equal@work toolkit on women of colour in the workplace, which looks at how to address racism and sexism against women of colour at work and gives employers tools for an intersectional approach to gender equality and diversity management," according to their website. No word on whether the hitmen from the Colombian death squads hired to take out at least ten trade union leaders by Coca-Cola were present.

They also busy themselves with combating "antigypsyism" and "Afrophobia" and work closely with the EU Coordinator on Antisemitism, which apparently exists, but with the European Parliament's Anti-Racism and Diversity Intergroup also in existence, why not? The ENAR receives funding from—wait for it!—the Open Society Foundations; the European Commission's Rights, Equality and Citizenship Program; the European Union's Horizon 2020 Research and Innovation Program; the Sigrid Rausing Trust; and the Joseph Rowntree Charitable Trust.

When the Jewish European Islamic Summit met in the Italian city of Matera in 2019, the chief concerns were—what else?—anti-Semitism, Islamophobia, and right-wing populists. In 2016, the Muslim Jewish Leadership Council (MJLC) was founded and convened at the King Abdullah bin Abdulaziz International Center for Interreligious and Intercultural Dialogue (KAICIID) in Vienna, which is funded by Saudi Arabia. For the imam Tarafa Baghajati, "Who better to sound the alarm than Jews or Muslims? Together, we want to show that a liberal Europe, one of openness and with respect for human rights, is the right way forward." As if making my point for me, one article I read on DW.com featured the following top two links under Read More: "Germany's Muslims demand better protection amid increased threats" and "German Jews call for anti-Semitism classes for Muslim immigrants," the same immigrants they are working to import en masse into Europe and the rest of the West.

According to the official Government Offices of Sweden:

- A range of measures to combat antisemitism and increase security have been implemented and are ongoing. The measures are carried out both by the Government and by government agencies on behalf of the Government.
- The Swedish Police Authority has raised its ambitions with respect to hate crime. A national contact point for hate crime issues is now in place, as are democracy and anti-hate crime groups in Stockholm, Gothenburg and Malmö. When deemed necessary, the Swedish Police Authority increases its surveillance efforts and takes other security measures to protect Jewish interests.
- The Living History Forum carries out major education initiatives on different forms of racism—historical and present-day—including antisemitism. Within this framework, the Forum produces materials about different forms of racism and provides training for school staff in cooperation with the National Agency for Education. So far, target groups have included school staff and other public sector employees at, for example, the Swedish Police Authority, the Swedish Public Employment Service, the Swedish Social Insurance Agency and social services.
- The Swedish Media Council works to empower children and young people as knowledgeable and informed media users through media and information literacy. The Council is also running a campaign to combat racism on the internet—the No Hate Speech Movement—targeting children and young people.
- The Government has appointed a parliamentary committee to consider the introduction of specific criminal liability for participation in a racist organisation and a ban on racist organisations.
- The Government consults regularly with Jewish organisations on issues that concern them, for example within the context of Sweden's national minorities policy.
- In October 2020, Sweden will host an international forum on Holocaust remembrance and combating antisemitism. The forum will focus on Holocaust remembrance and education, and address the issue of antisemitism on social media. Heads of state and government from around 50 countries, experts, researchers and civil society representatives have been invited to the forum, which will be held in Malmö… In connection with the forum, the Government intends to implement a national initiative that will include schools.

- The Government has appointed an inquiry to propose how a museum to preserve and perpetuate the memory of the Holocaust can be established in Sweden. The Inquiry will present its report in March 2020.
- The Government has allocated funds to support remembrance trips to Holocaust memorial sites in 2018–2022.
- Sweden is an active member of the International Holocaust Remembrance Alliance (IHRA). The Living History Forum represents Sweden in the IHRA along with the Ambassador for human rights, democracy and the rule of law.
- The Government has appointed a special envoy for intercultural and interfaith dialogue, including antisemitism and Islamophobia at international level, based at the Ministry for Foreign Affairs. The special envoy works towards enhancing coordination of intergovernmental efforts and strengthening Sweden's cooperation with key international stakeholders.

In the UK, as in most of the West these days, politics are largely confined within what is colloquially called the "kosher sandwich": in the US it is AIPAC more or less on one side and J Street on the other, whereas in the UK the Labour Friends of Israel[49] is the other slice of bread in the kosher sandwich opposite the Conservative Friends of Israel. CFI has taken over 250 Conservative parliamentarians and activists to Israel on delegations since 2010 and has hosted a number of events for parliamentarians, including a

---

[49] Labour MP Rebecca Long-Bailey was sacked from her position as Shadow Secretary of State for Education in 2020 amidst accusations of "anti-Semitism" for sharing an interview which included the fact that many members of American law enforcement are in fact trained in certain techniques, including restraints, in or by Israel. According to Amnesty International: "When the U.S. Department of Justice published a report…that documented 'widespread constitutional violations, discriminatory enforcement, and culture of retaliation' within the Baltimore Police Department (BPD), there was rightly a general reaction of outrage. But what hasn't received as much attention is where Baltimore police received training on crowd control, use of force and surveillance: Israel's national police, military and intelligence services… Many of these trips are taxpayer funded while others are privately funded. Since 2002, the Anti-Defamation League, the American Jewish Committee's Project Interchange and the Jewish Institute for National Security Affairs have paid for police chiefs, assistant chiefs and captains to train in Israel and the Occupied Palestinian Territories (OPT)." The ADL even brags about the fact that it not only sponsors these trainings, but trains law enforcement itself! It has been conducting its National Counter-Terrorism Seminar in Israel since 2004. From the ADL's official website, they crowed about the following in 2018: "1,280 law enforcement officials in New York and New Jersey were trained in recognizing and preventing extremism in 2018. 1,593 officials from law enforcement agencies across New York and New Jersey were trained in managing implicit bias, Holocaust education and recognizing hate crimes." Furthermore, as recently as 2012, at least one hundred Minnesota police officers attended a conference hosted by the Israeli consulate in Chicago.

briefing for Conservative MPs in Parliament with former IDF head of combat intelligence Miri Eisin and a group of senior leaders from the Anti-Defamation League (ADL) for a range of meetings in Parliament discussing "rising levels of antisemitism and extremism in the UK and worldwide."

In 2017, the Conservative Friends of Israel (CFI) led its first-ever delegation of Welsh Conservatives to Israel and the West Bank, with six Assembly Members. In Tel Aviv, the group met with representatives of the Israel-Britain Chamber of Commerce to discuss opportunities for further trade cooperation between Israel and Wales. Israeli exports to the UK have grown by 286% since 2010, with bilateral trade between the countries exceeding $10 billion.

In 2018, then-Prime Minister Theresa May stated, "We are proud of our pioneering role in the creation of the State of Israel. And today, our relationship is stronger than ever," according to Christians United for Israel. That this was "helped along" by Jewish terrorist assassinations of figures such as Lord Moyne in 1944 or the King David Hotel bombing in 1946, which killed ninety-one people, was not mentioned. The centenary of the Balfour Declaration featured celebrations over the entire year, culminating in a dinner co-hosted by the current Lord Balfour and Lord Rothschild. Addressing guests at the dinner, May hailed the Balfour Declaration as "one of the most significant letters in history. A letter which gave birth to a most extraordinary country." To mark the Balfour Declaration, Israel's Prime Minister Benjamin Netanyahu joined Prime Minister Theresa May in London at the Government's invitation, where the two leaders marked the occasion "with pride." In 2019, then-Home Secretary Sajid Javid visited Jerusalem's Western Wall to pledge fealty as all leaders and senior officials in occupied countries must eventually do, and self-declared "passionate Zionist" Boris Johnson became Britain's new Prime Minister, pledging to support Israel and the Jewish community. The Jewish Dominic Raab was promptly made Foreign Secretary and Javid made Chancellor of the Exchequer. It is worth noting that Johnson himself has Jewish ancestry. Again we see the priorities of governments, and they do not align with their own people's best interests, to put it about as mildly as possible.

In showing how all of this fits together in the neoliberal oligarchy's new world order, Gearóid Ó Colmáin reported a 2016 article titled "Rothschild's 'Slaughter Ships'":

> Many of the refugees/migrants arriving in Europe are being provided with false Syrian passports. Until the violence in Syria in 2011, Syrian passports were printed by French government printers. This fact strongly suggests French government involvement in the

distribution of false Syrian passports.... K-TV revealed that private multi-national project management companies such as ORS Services have been making millions of Euros from the plight of refugees. In 2014 ORS Services received 21 million Euros from the German government and has seen profits doubling since the refugee crisis. The Austrian newspaper *Heute* reported that ORS made 21 million euro this year alone from the migrant crisis. Shareholder finance of ORS Services is managed by the private equity firm Equistone Partners Europe, an affiliate of the Rothschild-owned Barclays Bank, which is considered to be the most influential financial institutions in the world. German economist Wolfang Freisleben has described Barclays Bank as "Rothschilds slaughtership." Barclays is the most important shareholder in both NM Rothschild bank and Lazard Brothers. Former director of Barclays Marcus Agius is married to a daughter of Edmond de Rothschild. Agius was also director of the British Broadcasting Corporation's executive board and served in the Steering Committee of the secretive Bilderberg Group. As in the case of the Arab Spring, some anarchists are once again unwitting tools and fools of imperialist subversion. The Berliner anarchist collective "Peng!" is helping to smuggle immigrants into Europe illegally. This is part of the groups "international solidarity." The organisation is funded by the...Ayn Rand Institute, whose director is Israeli and Zionist ideologue Yaron Brook. Ayn Rand was a Jewish philosopher who promoted the concept of objectivism; the idea that self-interest is the goal in every individual's life and that *laissez-faire* capitalism is the only system compatible with the individual's super-egotism. Here again we see capitalism's reliance on youthful rebellion of a politically correct "leftist" variety in order to further entrench its grip on humanity. A key "weapon" used in 2011 by imperialism to destroy the institutions of the nation-state was the smartphone. Thousands of smartphones were provided to US-funded "activists" during Zionism's "Arab Spring." It is unsurprising, therefore, to see that smartphones are being supplied to thousands of migrants by NGOs once they arrive in Europe. This could become a nightmare for any nation-state refusing to cooperate with imperialism's migration agenda. Researchers in Germany found that migrants were being supplied with smartphones by Austria's A-1 mobile phone company. The A-1 mobile company is controlled by Mexican Billionaire Carlos Slim.... Billionaire George Soros has advised the European Union to increase funding to NGOs and the private sector dealing with the refugee crisis. It looks like Brussels is following his advice with the fund put aside to deal with the crisis now doubling to 9.5 billion euro. Good news for Equistone Partners Europe, the Rothschild banking mafia!... Jewish "humanitarian" agencies such as the Multi-Faith Alliance for Syrian Refugees and the Jewish Coalition for Syrian Refugees in Jordan, who have no interest in the plight of millions of Palestinian refugees of Zionism, are actively offering Syrians in Jordanian camps "resettlement" in Europe and America. What Syrians manipulated by Israeli agencies fail to realise is that these same agencies are responsible not only for the destruction of their country but they could soon be joined in Jordan by Palestinians deported by Israel. Meanwhile, IsraAid, the Zionist entity's international "aid" agency, is active in the Balkans helping migrants get to central Europe…. The German government recently held a conference in Berlin called "Dialogs and Vision for Germany in 2050." The conference predicted that many sociological terms used today will be soon be obsolete…. "Everyone will be so 'mixed' and everyone will have a migration background." This means that the notion of belonging to a country, of being able to retrace one's ancestry through the centuries in the country of one's birth, this notion will be obsolete. In other words, no one will have any identity, other than that of a consumer. Commodity fetishism will constitute the identity of the "Germans" of the future.[50]

Chilling, but this is the neoliberal ideal, the Generic Man of No-Place. Deracinated and wholly reliant on the state and mega-corporations, he (it?) will not offer any meaningful resistance as the neoliberal model gives way in the next decade to medical tyranny and the transhumanists' Panopticon.

---

[50] He also states: "The astronomical number of migrants could never hope to arrive in Germany without being secretly helped by the BND, Germany's secret service."

7

THE NEW NORMAL

With all of the connections outlined so far in this book in mind, as with Dark Winter and Event 201, we see a similar telegraphing of the future script with the Johns Hopkins Bloomberg School of Public Health's Center for Health Security, with funding from the Open Philanthropy Project (primarily funded by the Jewish Dustin Moskovitz and his wife), running the Boosting NATO Resilience to Biological Threats, via their "Current Projects" page on their website:

> These resilience requirements would range from traditionally public health-oriented goals such as having systems of surveillance, detection and rapid response to infectious disease threats, to more defense-related goals such as having attribution capabilities in the event of a biological attack.

Now being prepared for a biological attack and having the requisite expertise, infrastructure, and materials is one thing—and a good thing at that. However, we see in this fusion of the medical-industrial and the military-industrial complexes in this particular exercise and other/additional key intersections (and increasingly fusions) in others such as Event 201 that the globalist Establishment is increasingly relying on the bogeyman of an "Invisible Enemy" to justify its consolidation and centralization of power. All one needs to do is scratch the surface a little bit to see that things are not as they seem. With the initial wave of the pandemic cresting, as *Bloomberg* reports:

> The Bank of Canada tapped BlackRock in March [2020] as an adviser for its purchases of commercial paper, the short-term debt that companies use to fund day-to-day expenses such as payroll. Last month [April 2020] the European Union hired the money manager to advise it on how to incorporate environmental, social, and governance practices into the way EU banks manage risk.

According to the latest data released by the US Federal Reserve, a whopping 48 percent of the ETFs it has bought are managed by BlackRock. It has over $7 trillion in assets under management. "There has never been a company like BlackRock before," says Heike Buchter, via a 2018 article from *DW.* "No one else has comparable access to companies, governments, regulators and central banks than BlackRock."

Jewish BlackRock co-founder and President and CEO of Evercore Partners Ralph Schlosstein calls BlackRock "the most influential financial institution in the world." To put into perspective just how massively influential BlackRock is, they invest in Amazon, Facebook, and Google, donate to Chatham House, and oversaw the merger of Bayer and Monsanto as a major shareholder in both companies. BlackRock owns shares in all thirty DAX companies (DAX is a blue chip stock market index consisting of the thirty major German companies trading on the Frankfurt Stock Exchange). Their influence cannot be understated as this "fourth branch of government" in the US as William Birdthistle calls it, can and does marshal its finances and power to advance whatever causes will most benefit their bottom lines, which we should extend to the companies they have a vested interest in such as the aforementioned. It is not coincidental that big business and high finance/vulture capitalism are totally in sync with things like immigration, "diversity," and LGBTQ "advocacy," and are part of the vast matrix of institutionalized globalization that defines the neoliberal axis. This matrix is the power structure of the Fourth Industrial Revolution, or what is being framed as the Great Reset. The Great Reset is not, however, a reset so much as it is a culmination of the globalist efforts of the last century-plus.

BlackRock, along with Vanguard Group Inc. and State Street, are called the Big Three because they hold roughly 80 percent of all indexed money. Returning to *Bloomberg,* Graham Steele, formerly of the Federal Reserve Bank of San Francisco, says, "They are so intertwined in the market and government that it's a really interesting tangle of conflicts. In the advocacy community there's an opinion that asset managers, and this one in particular, need greater oversight." Indeed, their 2020 contract with the Federal Reserve acknowledges that senior executives "may sit atop of the information barrier" and "have access to confidential information on one side of a wall while carrying out duties on the other side." Over a dozen former Obama officials populate the senior ranks of BlackRock, not least of which is Brian Deese, head of sustainable investing, a key adviser on the Paris Climate Agreement, and head of environmental initiatives for the Obama White House. Deese was also a senior policy analyst for economic policy at the Center for American Progress. Deese's Sustainable Investing Team "is focused on identifying drivers of long-term return associated with environmental, social and governance issues," in keeping with the hard push by the ruling class to use "climate change" as a useful plank for de-industrializing and crippling the West, and as a justification for "refugees" with automation increasingly making the "immigrants doing the jobs we won't do" argument obsolete.

Climate change is likewise a very useful vehicle for resource consolidation and speculation, but it also creates new forms of money-from-nothing trading like carbon trading, creates new industries to profit off, helps guilt environmentally-conscious whites into having fewer children and channeling productive energies into a cause linked with "refugees" and such, and also primes the population for a shift in expectations regarding product availability while also maintaining a consumer economy. BlackRock states that "climate change" is a pillar of its corporate strategy and mission and has joined Climate Action 100+; more than 450 investors with over $40 trillion in assets under management have signed on to the initiative. Climate Action 100+ also includes the PRI, "a UN-supported network of investors, works to promote the incorporation of environmental, social and governance (ESG) factors in investment."

The Investor Group on Climate Change (IGCC) is "a collaboration of Australian and New Zealand investors focusing on the impact that climate change has on the financial value of investments," and the Institutional Investors Group on Climate Change (IIGCC) is the European membership body for investor collaboration on "climate change" with more than 170 members, mainly pension funds and asset managers, across thirteen countries, with over €23 trillion in assets under management—"IIGCC's mission is to mobilise capital for the low carbon transition by working with business, policymakers and fellow investors."

BlackRock CEO Larry Fink stated in a 2019 letter that corporate governance was a major BlackRock priority, showing a keen awareness of that delightful catch-all "human rights." Kindred spirit Vanguard has launched a growing number of "human rights-aware funds" in the spirit of the burgeoning hybrid "philanthropic capitalism" model, and State Street has become a signatory to the UN Global Compact, according to their website: "State Street Corporation supports fundamental principles of human rights, such as those adopted in the United Nations Universal Declaration of Human Rights." State Street is responsible for the notorious *Fearless Girl*, the statue of the little girl "bravely" facing down the Wall Street *Charging Bull*. Far be it from standing up to Wall Street, it *is* Wall Street. In a classic move of conflating female empowerment with consumer capitalism and support for neoliberalism, the statue is actually an advertisement for a "gender diverse companies" index fund and the reveal was set for the day before International Women's Day. In a perfect metaphor for neoliberal occupation (sort of like those obelisks in Washington, DC, London, and the Vatican), duplicates of the statue have been unveiled outside the Grand Hotel in Oslo facing the Stortinget (Norway's Parliament); at Federation Square in Melbourne, Australia; and in Paternoster Square in close proximity to the London Stock Exchange. According to an article on *AdAge*:

> The team at McCann working with State Street wanted the statue to be a girl rather than a woman because she is supposed to "represent a sense of optimism, hope, innocence and determination," said McCann North American Chief Creative Officer Eric Silver.... McCann wanted Fearless Girl to be Latina so she could feel "universal" and "be an inspiration for everybody—fathers who have little girls and husbands who have wives [people who are] white, black, Indian—it should speak to the broadest audience," said Devika Bulchandani, president of McCann XBC and managing director of McCann New York.... McCann Worldgroup Chairman and CEO Harris Diamond created a personal Twitter handle to show his support for Fearless Girl because he said it's "one of those issues that needs people to speak on behalf of" and it's "something that transcends how we think about a piece of work and how it can break into culture and become part of society and create some controversy and conversation."

The conversation is, however, a monologue.

BlackRock has been slowly strangling Europe to death for the better part of two decades; as Owen Walker wrote in a 2018 *Financial Times* article:

> Deals for Merrill Lynch Investment Managers in 2006 and Barclays Global Investors, including the iShares ETF range, in 2009 helped establish BlackRock in Britain. Its influence has since spread across Europe and into the Middle East and Africa. "BlackRock is fast establishing a very dominant presence in markets across Europe," says Mauro Baratta, vice-president of global distribution at Broadridge, a consultancy.... London remains the group's Emea [Europe, Middle East, and Africa] headquarters and the UK accounts for 43 per cent of its assets in the region, but continental Europe is becoming more important. Between 2012 and 2017, mainland Europe's contribution to regional revenue rose from 51 to 58 per cent.... The opening of an innovation and technology centre in Budapest...will have up to 500 staff. The recruitment of 400 staff in the Hungarian capital has nearly doubled BlackRock's continental

workforce in just over a year…The first mainland European market BlackRock focused on for expansion, aside from its already big presence in the Netherlands, was Italy…. If BlackRock is to continue its growth it will have to break into the tightly controlled area of bank and insurance-controlled distribution. The Italian market is heavily skewed towards domestic players.

Well what do you know, in 2019, Italian banks backed an $806 million "rescue plan" for Carige to hand control of the Genoa-based bank to BlackRock, giving it operational control and a waiver from regulatory obligation, after Carige had been placed under special administration by the European Central Bank. BlackRock eventually withdrew from consideration, but this is an important development, particularly as we have seen the importance of BlackRock for the maintenance and expansion of the status quo through the figure of Friedrich Merz in Germany as one example. Additionally, for Walker:

> Michael Gruener, BlackRock's head of retail for Emea, lives in Germany and commutes to London. On the retail side, the efforts have been paying off. BlackRock is the sixth-biggest player in the $1.1tn German wealth market, with a 3 per cent share….ETFs are becoming more popular among German retail investors, says Peter Scharl, head of BlackRock's iShares ETF business in the country…. Despite the strength of local players in Germany, BlackRock has risen from third to second in Broadridge's ranking of top brands as voted by third-party fund selectors…. [In Switzerland,] BlackRock's efforts to grow are paying off. It is the second-biggest player in the crowded $1tn wealth market…. Five years ago, BlackRock bought Credit Suisse's ETF business, which brought $17.6bn assets with it. The deal made BlackRock the biggest ETF provider in Switzerland and the combined business at the time controlled nearly three-quarters of all the assets in physically backed ETFs in Europe. A year previously it had bought Swiss Re's private equity fund of funds business, bringing the volume of its assets in the strategy to $15bn. It doubled down on the Swiss wealth market two years ago by opening a bigger office in Geneva.

Following a meeting between Emmanuel Macron and Larry Fink in 2018, BlackRock selected Paris as the location for its European alternative investment hub; in December 2019, sweeping pension reforms in the country came under massive fire from hundreds of thousands of protestors, via a 2020 article in *Financial Times:*

> Critics of BlackRock recently circulated a photo of Mr Fink sitting alongside the French president at a green finance summit in Paris last year to illustrate the US group's perceived proximity to the government.... Its ties with politicians and its powerful lobbying capability are undeniable. The group counts several former politicians among its ranks: the chairman of its supervisory board in Germany previously served as deputy parliamentary leader of Angela Merkel's CDU between 2002 and 2004, while it also employs former UK chancellor George Osborne as an adviser.

Further, from the "2019–20 French pension reform strike" Wikipedia entry:

> Jean-Paul Delevoye, the High Commissioner for Pension Reforms, was revealed to be funded by the French Federation of Insurances, which has a direct interest in the pension reform. Moreover, being funded by a private company while being a member of the government is illegal according to the French constitution. Articles have also pointed out the proximity between Emmanuel Macron and BlackRock, one of the world's largest asset management funds, which is interested in having the billions of euros of the French pension fund enter the financial market. Multiple meetings between the French government and the firm's representatives have been reported. The promotion of the head of BlackRock's French branch, Jean-Francois Cirelli, to rank of officer of the Légion d'honneur also contributed to highlight this proximity.

BlackRock is a massive investor in weapon manufacturers through iShares US Aerospace and Defense ETF, with the fund's top holdings including the massively-US government subsidized Boeing, plus Raytheon, Northrop Grumman, General Dynamics, and Lockheed Martin, which runs the F-35 fighter plane program in conjunction with the US armed forces as well as the UK, Italy, Netherlands, Australia, Norway, Denmark, and Canada, and five other countries purchase and use the F-35: Israel, Japan, South Korea, Poland, and Belgium. Many of those countries were part of George W. Bush's Coalition of the Willing for invading Iraq, including Poland, Australia, and the UK, who contributed troops. Israel has both purchased and been given surplus F-16s by the US.

Lockheed Martin has also been contracted by the Turkish government for numerous "defense capabilities and other government projects" such as the joint venture with Turkish Aircraft Industries (TAI) on the F-16 fighter plane, originally developed by General Dynamics for the United States Air Force. Turkey, a NATO member, like Israel (Israel's former Defense Minister Avigdor Lieberman has stated, "Keeping Assad in power is not in our security interests," via the Wikipedia entry for "Israel's role in the Syrian civil war.") has been actively involved in the destabilization of Syria for years, and also functions as a stop-over point for huge numbers of "refugees" to be periodically released into Europe.

NATO Secretary General Jens Stoltenberg stressed that "NATO stands in strong solidarity with Turkey and will continue to support Turkey with a range of measures, including augmenting its air defenses." Syria, which has become the battleground of the emerging multi-polar world, shows in stark detail where and how these various interests intersect, although not always, as Turkish clashes with US-backed Kurds show. Turkey, like China, is pursuing its own expansionary interests; however, the majority of its actions, also like China, perversely do serve the ultimate aims of the Establishment. With an ascendant China, Broadridge Financial Solutions published a report that UBS Asset Management, JP Morgan Asset Management, and BlackRock are the top three foreign fund managers set for success in China, with Invesco, DWS, Allianz Global Investors, Schroders, AXA Investment Managers, Credit Suisse, and HSBC rounding out the top ten. BlackRock CEO Larry Fink has stated his intention to a major presence in China. Interestingly, Friedrich Merz has ties to AXA, HSBC, *and* BlackRock.

As the Russian agenda under Putin is generally divergent from these interests, it must not only be countered, but actively undermined. For A.S. Brychov and G.A. Nikonorov in "Color Revolutions in Russia":

> From the time of imposing sanctions against Russia, the US and most of EU member-states openly state that the end goal of sanctions is to undermine the socioeconomic situation in the country to provoke social upheaval and overthrow Putin's regime. As we can see, US-based financial institutions provide funding to public and commercial NGOs created in countries of interest. According to RF Ministry of Justice, just in 2014, there were 4,108 such NGOs registered on Russian soil and all of them received funding from abroad—52 of them were deemed foreign agents. Their activities are coordinated by US and EU consulates and embassies in Russia. The principal coordinator of financial activities in the US is USAID. We can only guess about the amounts of money thrown at the non-violent regime change, but keeping in mind that since 1961 USAID has been receiving 1% of US budget. In 2014, NGOs in Russia

received over 70 billion rubles. Intermediaries between USAID and recipients of moneys, i.e. "protectors" of Russian civil society, are smaller funds, such as IRI, NDI, and NED. These and similar organizations have representatives in 68 countries. Their activities are aligned with US policies and steered by chiefs of diplomatic mission in the respective country, usually the ambassador.[51]

Zbigniew Brzezinski can be considered an illustrative figure regarding the US/NATO/EU axis' stance on and actions against Russia, as a strong, cohesive Russia is antithetical to the client state model; carving up its sphere of influence, for Brzezinski, was vital, and in providing more clarity to the Establishment's obsession over the Ukraine, he famously wrote: "Without Ukraine, Russia ceases to be a Eurasian empire." He advocated for NATO expansion and the Clinton administration's involvement in Yugoslavia including NATO's bombing campaign against Serbia in 1999. Brzezinski served as Bill Clinton's emissary to Azerbaijan in order to promote the Baku-Tbilisi-Ceyhan (Turkey) pipeline and was a member of Honorary Council of Advisors of the US-Azerbaijan Chamber of Commerce (USACC). He also Chaired the American Committee for Peace in Chechnya/the Caucasus, an NGO housed at, naturally, Freedom House. A quick perusal of the list of its members speaks volumes, with Project for the New American Century (see Appendix G) alums abounding and a heavy representation of Jewish neoconservatives such as: Elliott Abrams, Bill Kristol, Robert Kagan, Norman Podhoretz, and Richard Perle.

Morton Abramowtiz (National Endowment for Democracy, Carnegie Endowment for International Peace) is also there. His wife, Sheppie Abramowitz, was a "refugee" advocate for the International Rescue Committee and KIND (Kids in Need of Defense), and their son, Michael, is the President of Freedom House. In yet another non-coincidence, in 2019 Elliott Abrams was appointed Special Representative for a Venezuela that has been squarely in the neocon crosshairs for years, both as a geo-strategic "gem" and for its natural resources, very similar to the Ukraine. Plus, destabilizing the country would provide millions more brown people to flood America with.

From brown to black, here's where it starts to get really fun, with BlackRock and black gold. In "Black gold under the Golan" from *The Economist* in 2015:

---

[51] Brychkov, "Color Revolutions in Russia," 4-5.

A rig carrying out exploratory drilling is hardly a rare sight in the Middle East; but this is no ordinary place. Israeli flags fly on it, though no other country in the world recognises Israel's sovereignty over the area. A few miles to the east, jihadist rebel groups are fighting a bloody war. And few people ever expected that significant amounts of oil might lie there at all, under a dormant volcanic field. Welcome to the Golan Heights [Syria]. Israeli and American oilmen believe they have discovered a bonanza in this most inconvenient of sites. After three test-drillings, Yuval Bartov, the chief geologist of Genie Oil & Gas, a subsidiary of American-based Genie Energy, says his company thinks it has found an oil reservoir "with the potential of billions of barrels."

Halliburton's "sweetheart" contracts from the Iraqi invasion and connection to Project for the New American Century signatory and former US Vice President under George W. Bush Dick Cheney is generally well-known, but less so is that of Genie Energy. In 2015, its Strategic Advisory Board members included Dick Cheney, Larry Summers, Rupert Murdoch, Michael Steinhardt, Mary Landrieu, former CIA Director Jim Woolsey, and Jacob Rothschild. In 2010 it was announced that Murdoch and Rothschild each acquired minority stakes in Genie Oil and Gas, and that Rothschild would partner with Genie Energy to raise capital for the eventual commercialization of its oil shale projects.

Mary's brother Mitch, as Mayor of New Orleans, was responsible for taking down the "offensive" Confederate statues in 2017; in 2010, he had tabbed Goldman Sachs to provide a $20 million investment loan. While Senator, in September 2013, Mary Landrieu introduced the United States-Israel Energy Cooperation Enhancement Bill, which was passed later that year. This legislation was the latest aimed at deepening the "special relationship" and further entrenched the official collaboration begun on February 1st, 1996, when the US Department of Energy and the Israeli Ministry of Energy and Infrastructure (now the Ministry of National Infrastructure—MONI) signed an agreement to establish a framework for energy cooperation. The energy cooperation has gone hand-in-hand with "defense" cooperation, at least for the United States. Israel was not a member of the Coalition of the Willing and has never contributed troops to American efforts on its behalf, despite benefiting enormously, and despite comprising 1.5 percent of the US population, Jews are a scant 0.3 percent of its armed forces, mostly non-combat roles at that. Israel did, however, withhold vital intelligence regarding the Beirut embassy bombing in 1983, knowingly fired on the *USS Liberty* in 1967, and there are legitimate questions surrounding at minimum their foreknowledge of the 9/11 attacks, questions that extend to the lessees of the Twin Towers:

> Silverstein Properties, founded by the Jewish Larry Silverstein, secured the lease just five months before the terrorist attacks of 9/11 and promptly increased the coverage; Silverstein ended up receiving a massive insurance payout of $4.6 billion, although he filed for $7.1 billion since, as he claims, each tower was destroyed and entitled him to a full policy payout of $3.55 billion per tower. New York Court of Appeals Judge Albert Rosenblatt, Jewish, oversaw the negotiations. Silverstein secured the lease through his connection to Lewis Eisenberg, also Jewish, head of the New York Port Authority. Eisenberg and Silverstein had both held positions with the United Jewish Appeal (UJA).[52]

Israel still finds itself as a "major strategic partner" as enshrined by pieces of legislation such as the 2014 United States-Israel Strategic Partnership Act (and by the US's actions on behalf of Israel and the Diaspora for quite some time), sponsored in the House by Ileana Ros-Lehtinen, a Board member of the National Endowment for Democracy (NED). Textual highlights include:

- o Amends the United States-Israel Enhanced Security Cooperation Act of 2012 to change language regarding certain actions to assist in the defense of Israel and to protect U.S. interests from a "sense of Congress" to actions the "President should take."
- o Amends the Department of Defense Appropriations Act, 2005 to extend authority to transfer certain obsolete or surplus Department of Defense (DOD) items to Israel.
- o Authorizes the President to carry out cooperative activities with Israel and to provide assistance to Israel that promotes cooperation in the fields of energy, water, agriculture, alternative fuel technologies, and civil space.
- o Authorizes the Secretary of Homeland Security (DHS), through the Director of the Homeland Security Advanced Research Projects Agency and with the concurrence of the Secretary of State, to enter into cooperative research pilot programs with Israel for: (1) border, maritime, and aviation security; (2) explosives detection; and (3) emergency services.

---

[52] Publius, *Plastic Empire*, 70-71.

- Requires the President to report to Congress regarding the status of Israel's qualitative military edge every two years.
- Directs the Secretary of State to report to Congress regarding the range of cyber and asymmetric threats posed to Israel by state and non-state actors, and joint U.S.-Israel efforts to address such threats.
- Expresses a sense of Congress that the United States and Israel should take steps to increase cyber-security cooperation.
- Expresses the sense of Congress that: (1) the United States and Israel should continue collaborative efforts to enhance Israel's military capabilities, (2) the United States and Israel should conclude an updated Memorandum of Understanding regarding U.S. security assistance to help Israel meet its security requirements and uphold its qualitative military edge, (3) the United States should ensure that Israel has timely access to important military equipment, and (4) the United States should continue to support Israel's right of self-defense.
- Expresses the sense of Congress that the Department of State should continue its coordination on monitoring and combating anti-Semitism with the government of Israel.

Another essential plank outlined is that the Act:

> Amends the Energy Independence and Security Act of 2007, with respect to United States-Israel energy cooperation, to authorize the Secretary of Energy (DOE) to make grants to eligible applicants, including projects involving joint ventures of the U.S. and Israeli governments, to promote...natural gas energy, including natural gas projects conducted by or in conjunction with the United States-Israel Binational Science Foundation, the United States-Israel Binational Industrial Research and Development Foundation; and the United States-Israel Science and Technology Foundation.

Comparing this with the text of the original agreement between the US and Israel reveals some interesting connections to how things have played out since, not least of which was USAID's involvement. Further, from the November 2005 EPACT Section 986 Report on the US-Israel Agreement Concerning Energy Cooperation:

> In the area of renewables, DOE [Department of Energy] has been working with Israel on solar technology. This is a trilateral effort

among DOE, the Egyptian New and Renewable Energy Authority (NREA), and the Weizmann Institute of Science in Israel to demonstrate a 10-Megawatt Integrated Solar Combined Cycle Power Plant, named "Noor Al Salaam," or "Light of Peace," at Zaafarana, Egypt. This project would combine U.S. central receiver technologies (heliostats, tower reflectors, control systems, etc.) developed primarily by McDonnell Douglas Corporation (now a wholly owned subsidiary of the Boeing Company) and Israel's solar beam down receiver technology with natural gas to power high efficiency combined cycle gas turbines. This system could have many applications in a region with ample resources of natural gas and solar energy. This activity is supported by DOE, the U.S.-Israel Science and Technology Foundation (USISTF), the Egyptian NREA, Israel's Ormat Industries, Ltd., Rotem Industries, Ltd., and Weizmann Institute of Science, with the University of Alabama in Huntsville as the prime contractor. A pilot program involving this technology, partially carried out as part of the $5.5M 50/50 cost-shared USISTF program, was completed in 2000. Thus far, the partners have received $2.7 million in support from the U.S.-Israel Science and Technology Foundation. Of these funds, $1.4 million was contributed to support development of the project in Israel and an additional $1.3 million was provided to McDonnell Douglas (now Boeing). The companies involved (McDonnell Douglas/Boeing, Ormat, and Rotem) have more than matched these funds.

Ormat is now Ormat Technologies, and has a number of "green" projects across the globe. CEO Doron Blachar has ties to the pharmaceutical industry. The United States-Israel Binational Science Foundation's Board of Governors features individuals such as (with descriptions from their website):

o Peter J. Hotez, M.D., Ph.D. "is Dean of the National School of Tropical Medicine and Professor of Pediatrics and Molecular Virology & Microbiology at Baylor College of Medicine where he is also the Director of the Texas Children's Center for Vaccine Development (CVD) and Texas Children's Hospital Endowed Chair of Tropical Pediatrics. He is also University Professor at Baylor University, and Fellow in Disease and Poverty at the James A Baker III Institute for Public Policy. Dr. Hotez is an internationally-recognized physician-scientist in neglected tropical diseases and vaccine development. As head of the Texas Children's CVD, he leads the only product development partnership for developing new vaccines for hookworm infection, schistosomiasis, and Chagas disease, and

SARS/MERS, diseases affecting hundreds of millions of children and adults worldwide. In 2006 at the Clinton Global Initiative he co-founded the Global Network for Neglected Tropical Diseases to provide access to essential medicines for hundreds of millions of people…. Dr. Hotez has authored…Blue Marble Health: An Innovative Plan to Fight Diseases of the Poor amid Wealth (Johns Hopkins University Press).… He is an elected member of the National Academy of Medicine, and in 2011 he was awarded the Abraham Horwitz Award for Excellence in Leadership in Inter-American Health by the Pan American Health Organization of the WHO. In 2014–16 he served in the Obama Administration as US Envoy, focusing on vaccine diplomacy initiatives between the US Government and countries in the Middle East and North Africa. In 2018 he was appointed by the US State Department to serve on the Board of Governors for the US Israel Binational Science Foundation, and he received the Sackler Award in Sustained Leadership from ResearchAmerica!"
- Professor Abraham (Avi) Israeli "is the Chief Scientist of the Ministry of Health…He received his Master's Degree from the Sloan School of Management at MIT."
- Dr. Gordon "received his MD/PhD degree at the University of California, San Francisco and completed his Psychiatry residency and research fellowship at Columbia University. He joined the Columbia faculty in 2004 as an Assistant Professor in the Department of Psychiatry where he conducted research, taught residents, and maintained a general psychiatry practice. In September of 2016, he became the Director of the National Institute of Mental Health."
- Cathy Campbell "was the U.S. State Department's program officer for Soviet/Russia science and technology affairs from 1989–1994. Before joining the State Department, Cathy held research positions at the Library of Congress, Rand Corporation and Presearch, Incorporated."
- Dr. Iris Eisenberg "received her PhD in Human Genetics from the Hebrew University of Jerusalem in 2003. Subsequently, she joined Harvard University, Children's Hospital Boston, as an HHMI post-doctoral research associate. Dr. Eisenberg's PhD research focused on investigating the biology of neuromuscular disorders, leading to the identification of the gene (GNE-Myopathy) causing Hereditary Inclusion Body Myopathy. Her fellowship research in Duchenne Muscular Dystrophy piloted the understanding of the role of small non-coding RNAs in the pathology of the disease."
- Reece Smyth, "representing the US Department of State, was a National Security Affairs Fellow for the academic year 2019–20 at the Hoover Institution. A career member of the Senior Foreign Service, Reese served as Charge d'Affaires ad interim at the US Embassy in Dublin from January

2017 to July 2019, where he advanced US bilateral relations with Ireland on trade, investment, and cyber security. Previous assignments include as the political counselor at the US Embassy in Beirut and the deputy director of the State Department's Office of UN Political Affairs. He also served at the US Mission to NATO as the action officer in the NATO-Russia Council, as senior economic officer in the State Department's Office of Arabian Peninsula Affairs, and as a watch officer in the Operations Center. Other overseas tours include Skopje, Sarajevo, and Islamabad. Prior to joining the Foreign Service, Mr. Symth worked in the private sector as a senior trade consultant in Houston, London, and New York. He is a graduate of Baylor University."

As regards from the US-Israel Science and Technology Foundation, according to its report entitled *U.S.-Israel Joint Economic Development Group R&D Mapping Project:*

> During the June 2014 Joint Economic Development Group (JEDG) meeting both governments decided to initiate a review of existing industry-supporting R&D programs offered by each government that have the potential to support additional international cooperation. The U.S. Department of State and Israel's Ministry of Economy directed the US-Israel Science and Technology Foundation (USISTF) to survey a representative group of R&D program offices in each country to gather information, and present non-binding findings on strategies to promote collaboration within the existing programmatic and funding environment in both countries. The survey was intended to create a useful tool for government program managers and the private sector who desire a closer relationship between the two countries in priority technical fields.... A steering committee was established, comprising representatives from the Israeli Ministry of Economy and U.S. Department of State. The Steering Committee elected to survey programs in three sectors: neurotechnology, energy and cyber-security.... Both the NIH Brain Initiative and the Department of Homeland Security Cyber Security Division (CSD) are developing joint programs with other countries and have expressed a willingness to explore greater collaboration with Israel. A similar approach was used successfully on a multi-department and agency basis during the 2013 Bioenergy Challenge. In that project, U.S. government departments and agencies identified research topics of interest, and then OCS and the FCI competitively selected Israeli researchers to visit the U.S.... Both the biomedical

and cyber security fields represent a significant investment of the OCS, though young Israeli companies have limited access to infrastructure. Current OCS program managers were interested seeing further use of financial support to enable small Israeli firms to license U.S. NIH intellectual property and expand participation in clinical trials in the U.S.[53]

Israeli companies expanding clinical trials in the US—surely the reader understands the significance of this.

The United States-Israel Binational Industrial Research and Development Foundation (BIRD) states in its *Annual Report 2019:*

> The U.S.-Israel Binational Industrial Research and Development (BIRD) Foundation works to encourage cooperation between U.S. and Israeli companies in a wide range of technology sectors by providing funding and assistance in facilitating strategic partnerships for developing joint products or technologies.... BIRD's scope extends to Advanced Manufacturing, Agrotechnology, Cleantech and Environment, Communications, Construction Tech, Electronics, FinTech, Gas, Homeland Security and Cyber Security, Life Sciences, Nanotechnology, Semiconductors, Software, and other areas of innovative technology with commercial potential.... The Foundation manages the BIRD Energy Program focused on promoting and supporting U.S.-Israel joint development projects relating to clean energy technologies. This program is the implementation of a cooperation agreement between the U.S. Department of Energy, the Israel Ministry of Energy jointly with the Israel Innovation Authority.... The BIRD Foundation also manages the binational program, "BIRD Homeland Security" a joint U.S.-Israel program to foster and support the development of advanced technologies for First Responders, technologies and methods to secure critical infrastructure and public facilities, safe and secure cities, border protection, including maritime security, technologies in the use of unmanned aerial systems and law enforcement supporting technologies to combat cyber-crime. This program was established by the U.S. Department of Homeland Security (DHS) and the Israel Ministry of Public Security (MOPS) as part of the agreement between the Government of the United States of America and the Government of the State of Israel on Cooperation in Science

---

[53] USISTF, *U.S.-Israel Joint,* 1-2, 4.

and Technology for Homeland Security Matters.... BIRD is pursuing new initiatives, including enhanced U.S.-Israel collaboration in Artificial Intelligence, a sector identified as critical for both the U.S. and Israel.[54]

Indeed, as Johnny Vedmore writes in "Darktrace and Cybereason: The Intelligence Front Companies Seeking to Subjugate the World with the A.I. Singularity":

We are about to experience a monumental change in technology, starting with "next-generation" cybersecurity that will then move quickly into the unknown. Unsupervised A.I., now running on critical networks throughout the world as a "cybersecurity" product, is evolving its own algorithm without the need for humans to be involved. Meanwhile, the wealthy patrons funding this cutting edge future tech are out in force, working to propel our societies into this new, unexplored and dystopian technological frontier...Each of these companies have been built by teams of former intelligence operatives, some of who have sat in the highest echelons of the intelligence apparati of their respective countries. MI5 and C.I.A. both carry considerable weight in these sinister sounding enterprises, but it is Israel's Unit 8200 that are the main group capitalising on this advance into the world-altering realm of unsupervised Artificial Intelligence algorithms...The members of Darktrace are open about their aims. They talk about publicly held data as though they already have the rights to sell it to anyone around the world. Data is the fuel of the Fourth Industrial Revolution and Darktrace has made almost $2 billion in the data business during its relatively short history, reaching Unicorn status with great ease. When Darktrace first launched its website in 2013, its description of the company's vision was entitled, "The New Normal: Learn Human and Machine Behavior to Reduce Cyber Security Risks." Back then we were less familiar with the term "the new normal," but now it surrounds us. Darktrace is already active within the NHS, the U.K. power grid, and many other major parts of Britain's critical infrastructure and they are rapidly expanding around the globe.... In a TechCrunch talk in 2016, the freshly installed co-CEO of Darktrace, Poppy Gustafsson, is caught misleading the audience about the company's origins. She uses the

---

[54] BIRD Foundation, *Annual Report 2019*, 7.

TechCrunch stage to claim that the "spark" for the creation of Darktrace originally came from the mathematicians at Cambridge and downplayed the involvement of intelligence agencies like MI5, GCHQ, and the C.I.A.... Gustafsson, who was initially CFO and COO for the fledgling Darktrace, runs the company alongside the other co-CEO Nicole Eagen, an alumnus of Oracle, a major tech company that also has its origins in intelligence.... Darktrace is officially a completely private enterprise with big investors including KKR, Summit Partners, Vitruvian Partners, Samsung Ventures, TenEleven Ventures, Hoxton Ventures, Talis Capital, Invoke Capital and Insight Venture Partners.... The former Home Secretary under Prime Minister Theresa May, Amber Rudd, became part of Darktrace after her time in government ended in 2019. She is also on the advisory team of Teneo, a consulting firm co-founded and led by Doug Band, the former advisor to Bill Clinton and close friend of the infamous Jeffrey Epstein.... The C.I.A. stalwart, Alan Wade, is one of the most interesting members of the Darktrace advisory team.... Wade co-founded Chiliad alongside Ghislaine Maxwell's sister, Christine Maxwell.... Christine Maxwell was personally involved in leading the operations of the front company used by Robert Maxwell to market the PROMIS software, which had a backdoor for Israeli intelligence, to both the U.S.' public and private sectors.... When it was still active as a company, Chiliad described itself as "the leader in data analysis across clouds, agencies, departments and other stovepipes" and it ran on the computers and databases of nearly every major national security system in the U.S. government.

Israel is the largest cumulative recipient of US foreign aid since World War II, in excess of $140 billion and rising. In 2016, the US and Israeli governments signed a new, ten-year Memorandum of Understanding (MOU) on military aid, covering FY2019 to FY2028, where the US pledges to provide $38 billion in military aid to Israel. Israel has purchased at least fifty of Lockheed's F-35s in three separate contracts, and has made repeated rounds of F-16 acquisitions. These planes are used by Israel to bomb targets in Syria, among other uses.

Boeing and Lockheed Martin are two of the major holdings in BlackRock's iShares US Aerospace and Defense ETF. Like Vanguard, DZ Privatbank S.A. (a subsidiary of DZ Bank from the American Council on Germany's Corporate Membership Program along with Deutsche Bank, Citi, Commerzbank, JP Morgan Chase, and Goldman Sachs, among others) and

Michael Steinhardt, BlackRock also owns shares in Genie Energy, which was given approval to drill for oil through one of its subsidiaries Genie Oil and Gas in the occupied Golan Heights of Syria. Here is yet another intersection of Jewish ethno-religious interests and that of economic and ideological considerations thrown into starkest relief. Meredith Lerner for Citizens for Responsibility and Ethics in Washington reports that Ira Greenstein was, while the US was actively bombing Syria under the pretenses of false-flag chemical attacks by the Assad regime, part of:

> Jared Kushner's team under White House aides Chris Liddell and Reed Cordish. Kushner, Liddell, and Cordish worked in the White House Office of American Innovation on issues related to technology and the private sector. If Greenstein worked on similar issues, his interests in several technology and other companies may have posed conflict concerns. For example, Greenstein held between $100,001 and $250,000 in Apple stock, between $50,001 and $100,000 in Microsoft stock, between $50,001 and $100,00 in Ohr Pharmaceutical stock, and between $50,001 and $100,000 in Bank of America stock while working for the government. Greenstein also maintained at least $250,001–$500,000 in Genie Energy stock throughout his government service. Though Greenstein represented that he left his role as Genie Energy's president before he joined the Trump administration, he did not sign a separation agreement with the company until May 2017, roughly three months after Greenstein started working at the White House. This fact raises concerns about Greenstein's potential involvement with and interest in the company while he was working in government.

The pseudonymous Zanting wrote in a February 2018 piece published on Medium entitled "Ira Greenstein: Jared Kushner's Criminal Deal with Israel Behind US Involvement in Syria for Genie Energy's Control of the Golan Heights":

> Greenstein's boss, the founder of Genie Energy and top Netanyahu donor Howard Jonas [and major NorPAC donor]…made billions through a telecommunications deal made possible under the watch of both the Federal Communications Commission (FCC) and Kushner-directed White House Office of American Innovation (OAI)—for which to benefit said parties for their actions.… Greenstein was also a past President of IDT Corporation, which funneled significant amounts of funds totaling millions of dollars to the Central Fund of

Israel (CFI) through the IDT Charitable Foundation, an organization which has supported individuals that advocate for the killing of non-Jewish (Gentile) children on the basis of race.... Greenstein has been consistently employed in the White House, having attended the Zionist Organization of America (ZOA) Gala hosted by Morton Klein, where "Kushner confidant" Greenstein was present alongside former White House personnel such as Sebastian Gorka and Steve Bannon.

Bannon and former White House Director of Communications Anthony Scaramucci are both Goldman Sachs alums, as is the Jewish US Secretary of the Treasury Steve Mnuchin. Gorka was a Partnership for Peace International research fellow at the NATO Defense College and while in university was part of a British Territorial Army Russian-focused Intelligence Company with a NATO role. There is also the *Breitbart*-Gorka-Bannon-Robert Mercer-Renaissance Technologies connection, with Renaissance being another major Genie Energy shareholder, and *The Wall Street Journal* noted the close friendship of Jared Kushner and Ivanka Trump with Rupert Murdoch's former wife, Wendi Deng Murdoch. Returning to Zanting:

Ira Greenstein held around 100,000 shares in Genie Energy while assuming his position in the administration.... Jason Greenblatt, another senior White House staffer who was Donald Trump's lawyer at the Trump Organization as Chief Legal Officer, also has investments in Genie Energy. Greenblatt is Trump's adviser on Israel.... Another point of inherent subjugation within the Trump administration is IDT Corporation's Michael Glassner, Chief Strategist, including for reelection (2020).... Glassner also joined AIPAC in 2014.... From 1998 to 2001...Glassner moved to New Jersey to work under Lewis Eisenberg, chair of the Port Authority of New York and New Jersey. Glassner was Eisenberg's chief of staff. In 2001, near the end of Glassner's time at the Port Authority, he was involved in the deal that privatized the lease of the World Trade Center to the Silverstein Group. In July 2001, Glassner left the staff of the Port Authority to work for IDT Corporation, a global telecommunications company. According to ABC News, "At IDT, Glassner was chief of staff to the company's CEO, handling external communications as well as government and investor relations..." Genie Energy's Vice Chairman, Geoffrey Rochwarger, heads an organization called Yatar CTU, which works with the Israeli government to enforce both the "Old City" of Jerusalem and territories bordering occupied settlements. Rochwarger, like Ira

Greenstein and Jason Greenblatt—holds a number of shares in Genie Energy. As with its founder, Howard Jonas, Rochwarger also attended Yeshiva University.... Greenstein is or was also Counsel to Global Rish Advisors (GRA), founded by former U.S. diplomat Kevin Chalker, it is a multi-tiered corporation which had gone to Doha, the capital of Qatar, to register a branch last year. GRA Quantum is involved in cyber-security and has on its Advisory Board members such as Matthew Waxman—Columbia Law School alumni like Greenstein—who is also a member of the Council On Foreign Relations (CFR).

Genie is not just Halliburton 2.0 in the same way that the invasion of Iraq following 9/11 was not just about oil, although that is certainly a factor.

Now of course with all of this nation-wrecking in the Middle East and North Africa, *The Economist* has been very consistent in supporting mass migration into Europe as a reflection of its "values." In the UK, the Rothschilds through EL Rothschild own a 21 percent stake in The Economist Group, the media group responsible for *The Economist.* Lady Lynn Forester de Rothschild sits on its Board (as well as that of Estee Lauder; she is the Chair of EL Rothschild investments) and Eric Schmidt, former CEO of Google, is a former Board member of The Economist Group. Former Chairman of Guardian Media Group (publisher of *The Guardian*) Paul Myners has ties to RIT Capital Partners PLC, formerly Chaired by Jacob Rothschild. It has a net value of approximately £3 billion, and Jacob Rothschild is today Honorary President with his family remaining the largest shareholders at around 21 percent. Jacob Rothschild's eldest daughter, Hannah Mary Rothschild, has done a lot of work with the BBC (a much more "diversified" BBC from the one that in 2001 then-Director General Greg Dyke said was "hideously white") and is also a Non-Executive Director of RIT Capital.

The destabilization project of the US as a battering ram for Israel has also hewed very closely to the Yinon Plan, derived from a February 1982 article in *Kivunim* ("Directions") entitled "A Strategy for Israel in the 1980s." Whether it is being used as an actual blueprint or not is unknown, but its general outline does suggest the geo-strategic aims of Israel in the region. The author Oded Yinon essentially concludes that it is in Israel's interest to fracture the surrounding states into warring factions; Yinon is far from alone in this conclusion, as Israel Shahak states in his Foreword to the piece:

> The idea that *all* the Arab states should be broken down, by Israel, into small units, occurs again and again in Israeli strategic thinking. For example, Ze'ev Schiff, the military correspondent

of *Ha'aretz*...writes about the 'best' that can happen for Israeli interests in Iraq: 'The dissolution of Iraq into a Shi'ite state, a Sunni state and the separation of the Kurdish part' (*Ha'aretz* 6/2/1982).

Using the USSR as a bogeyman, the aim is to deceive the Americans. This has been necessary for its population, but not for the neoconservatives, who themselves are heavily Jewish. Yinon astutely observes:

> The essential concepts of human society, especially those of the West, are undergoing a change due to political, military and economic transformations. Thus, the nuclear and conventional might of the USSR has transformed the epoch that has just ended into the last respite before the great saga that will demolish a large part of our world in a multi-dimensional global war.

Such as the one playing itself out before us now. The Yinon Plan is akin to the Kalergi Plan in that it is eminently possible if not probable that it is in some way providing a framework; if it is not, then in spirit we may see the crises today reflected in their blueprints: aggressive Zionism and Israeli expansion in the former and the attempted breeding of Europeans out of existence through a supranational EU-esque Leviathan in the latter—the centrality if not supremacy of Jews in both.

One declassified CIA document dated September 14th, 1983 entitled "Bringing Real Muscle to Bear Against Syria" includes reference to the Golan Heights and considers efforts on the part of Iraq, Turkey, and Israel to knock Syria to pieces, as Syria "continues to maintain a hammerlock on two key US interests in the Middle East," which were focused on Lebanon and a key oil pipeline in Iraq. The document does, however, note that "Israeli involvement is not appealing to Iraq," at the time probably because Operation Opera—a surprise Israeli air strike from 1981 that destroyed an Iraqi nuclear reactor under construction, and probably also the last time Iraq had anything approximating WMDs—was still fresh. Another, from July 1986 entitled "Syria: Scenarios of Dramatic Political Change" concludes that reminiscent of Zaire in the 1970s from earlier, "business-oriented moderates" should be installed. The plan does not appear to have changed much, though Iraq has obviously been kicked to pieces in the interim, along with most of the other countries in the region. Returning once again to Zanting and Genie Energy, the hits just keep on coming:

> Kushner's wife, Ivanka [Yael] Trump, reportedly had "convinced" her father to order the attack on Syria along with former Deputy National

Security Adviser Dina Powell. Powell, like former National Economic Council Director Gary Cohn, is a heavy hitter from Goldman Sachs—one of the primary instigators of the financial crisis of 2007–2008. Greenstein's son, Jonathan Greenstein, is also a lawyer for Goldman Sachs.... The CEO as well as Chairman of one of Genie Energy's largest shareholders, BlackRock, visited the White House just a few days after the airstrikes (April 11th). Laurence Fink and the monolithic firm that he represents—as well as proximal involvement by Goldman Sachs—stand to gain from both lobbying and utilizing the U.S. military for their own self-interest(s). Subsequently, BlackRock's former [pre-1995] parent company Blackstone and its CEO Stephen Schwarzman also met on the same day. Schwarzman was also an adviser to then President-elect Donald Trump. BlackRock is also one of the largest shareholders of Raytheon, the defense contractor that manufactures Tomahawk cruise missiles. The U.S. Navy has requested Raytheon to replace these under a modified contract. [Ira] Greenstein also owns shares in Axalta Coating Systems, which paints components and vehicles for Raytheon. Like the Kushner's $250,000,000 credit line for Cadre through Soros Fund Management, they have also received funds from Blackstone, for real estate. Lord Jacob Rothschild sits on the International Advisory Board of Blackstone.

Schwarzman and Fink are on the Executive Committee for the Partnership for New York City (see Appendix H) together, along with David Solomon (Goldman Sachs) and Leon Black (Apollo Management). Making the connection more explicit, Zanting reports:

> U.S. Senator Joe Manchin (D-WV) previously met with Genie Energy's chief scientist, Harold Vinegar, on behalf of the American Israel Educational Foundation—referred to as the "charitable arm of AIPAC." *Jewish Insider*: "Meeting with Dr. Harold Vinegar, chief scientist of Israeli Energy Initiatives at Genie Energy, and Binyamin Zomer of Noble Energy, to discuss the importance of energy to the economies of Israel, the United States, and West Virginia..." Genie Energy's founder, Howard Jonas, donated to U.S. Senator Bob Menendez (D-NJ) just a few days before attacking Syria—as well as only a few days after tightening sanctions on Iran. Founder of Apollo Global Management Leon Black donated within 24 hours of the airstrikes. Menendez would later approve of the strikes having been conducted. This pattern continued with both Manchin and

Menendez in turn also voting in favor of U.S. Ambassador to Israel David Friedman. Friedman has a number of underlying interests in Israel.

Genie Energy has also expanded into the "alternative" energy sector by acquiring a controlling interest in the Finnish "renewable electricity" provider Lumo Energia.

The having a "finger in every pie" strategy works for a multitude of reasons. Sure, it's sound business practice to diversify, but that's not what is at issue here: what we are discussing is the masquerade of righteous "justice" by some of the most reprehensible people on earth today, or of any era for that matter. These "alternative energies" are merely a way to transition to other environment-destroying technologies and continue to pad profits. For example, though it is a generally-accepted belief, an article of faith as the term "denier" presupposes, that "climate change" is driven by carbon emissions, what do we make of the fact that the University of Texas Energy Institute found in 2017 that storing solar energy in batteries for nighttime use actually increases both energy consumption and carbon dioxide emissions? We're not meant to make anything of it, because the current orthodoxy does not involve thinking from the compliant masses, at least as the so-called "elites" would have it, and it certainly does not involve honesty on their part. Progress apparently looks like bombing innocent people to pieces, releasing toxic chemicals into the environment, and chemically-castrating children because their sex and "gender" do not "correspond." They not only want to dismantle, discard, and replace the obstinate groups that get in the way of their psychopathic project, they want them *erased*. Show me virtue and justice in this system, and I'll show you a lie.

8

THE DARK UNDERBELLY

With criticism through the official channels largely walled-off through various means of censorship and non-white identities indulged and catered to within the confines of Europe in the short- and medium-term, the EU apparatus has continued strengthening its outer reaches to absorb more of these protected classes, but in schizophrenic fashion, millions of euros ostensibly going to *combatting* migration in Libya have instead found themselves in the hands of jihadist militias, with EU- and UN-funded "detention centers" also becoming literal open-air slave auction sites. In a December 31st, 2019 report published by *Al Jazeera:*

> The EU has sent more than 327.9 million euros to Libya, with an additional 41 million approved in early December, largely funnelled through UN agencies. The AP found that in a country without a functioning government, huge sums of European money have been diverted to intertwined networks of militiamen, traffickers and coast guard members who exploit migrants. In some cases, UN officials knew militia networks were getting the money, according to internal emails.

A UNHCR report from late 2018 also noted these allegations, and the head of the militia, Mohammed Kachlaf, is under UN sanctions for human trafficking. Evidently, many migrants were cut, shot, and whipped with electrified hoses, and recounted instances of forced labor and prostitution, the same *Al Jazeera* article reports.

In response, Charlie Yaxley, a UNHCR spokesman, addressed the concerns by stating, "UNHCR does not choose its counterparts. Some presumably also have allegiances with local militias." Considering the United Nations has situated itself as a moral authority, this speaks volumes about their actual attitudes and agenda. Their vague "values"-based terms are highly flexible and are deployed selectively, totally dependent on the context and the agenda. Furthermore, EU leadership needs to appear accountable to its constituencies, and so "getting tough" on migration in response to public demands meets the need to appear to address these concerns and maintain its "legitimacy" against large-scale insurrection, when nothing will change at the top level, and in any case there are multitudinous ways to continue to flood the continent with alien peoples.

The trafficking aspect permitted along the frontiers is becoming increasingly pervasive across the globe, a consequence of the creation of networks both official and unofficial by the ruling class. Probably the most disturbing aspect of globalization is the extensive underground human trafficking network that has been allowed to flourish, but the trafficking takes many forms, from sex to organ to drug trafficking, and like the various "-isms" and projects pushed by the ruling class, there is often significant overlap between the major players and, as you might guess, a central Jewish role.

Many Israelis and Diaspora Jews operate where, as Susanne Lundin puts it, "regular shadow economies—with reference to Nordstrom's discussion of global shadow zones—govern existence and where goods, weapons, money, people and bodies, etc. constitute components of the international market." As Assaf Gur wrote in 2019's "A Field Guide to Israeli Organized Crime" for *Tablet*:

> Israel, which loves calling itself the Start-up Nation because of its impressive accomplishments in high tech, is also an exporter of highly organized and deadly crime. In 2016, the Israeli news site Mako estimated that organized crime in Israel generated as much as NIS 50 billion, or US$14 billion, each year. Israel's crime families now have branches in Europe, America, Africa, Australia, and Asia.... Wikileaks has exposed a diplomatic cable sent in May of 2009 by the U.S. Embassy in Tel Aviv to the Department of State and the FBI. In the cable, then-Ambassador James Cunningham expressed his concern about the rise of organized crime in Israel. In the cable, which Cunningham titled "Israel: The Promised Land of Organized Crime?" he wrote that "five or six families have traditionally controlled organized crime in Israel. The Abergil, Aboutboul, Alperon, and Rosenstein families are among the best-known, but recent arrests and assassinations have created a vacuum at the top, and I believe that newcomers like Mulner, Shirazi, Cohen, and Domrani are closing the gap."

In November 2004, Ze'ev Rosenstein, described as "a dominant force on the world Ecstasy market," was arrested in Israel on an international arrest warrant on charges that he had imported over 700,000 tablets to New York. In 2010, he was indicted on murder and two counts of manslaughter. In accordance with the extradition treaty between Israel and the US, he was returned to Israel to serve his sentence in an Israeli prison. As part of his plea agreement, he had confessed to having hired assassins to kill rival mafia leaders in Israel, which netted him an extra five years on top of the twelve he was sentenced for drug trafficking. In 2017, Rosenstein refused to testify against underworld rival Yitzhak Abergil (who stated that the works of Ayn Rand had profoundly shaped his worldview) despite the fact that Abergil allegedly tried to have Rosenstein killed multiple times. The Abergils are notorious for their role as one of the prominent crime families of the Israeli underworld, with operations spanning the globe. In July 2015, the Abergils and eighteen other associates were indicted and arraigned by the Tel Aviv District Court; the indictment specifically highlighted the syndicate's operations from 2002 to 2006, when it imported and exported ecstasy, cocaine, hashish, and other drugs around the globe, from North America to New Zealand, Japan, Europe, and South America. Numerous murders were committed over this time span.

When Oded Tuito died in June 2004, his legacy was as perhaps the most influential individual in opening the American market up to ecstasy, smuggling literally millions of tablets into the country using young ultra-Orthodox Jews who he would recruit through the yeshivas and, later on, elderly Orthodox Jews, believing correctly that these groups would not be profiled as smugglers. The Israeli share of the American ecstasy market is generally pegged at around 75 percent, according to a 2005 article in *Haaretz*, and it comes not just through drug mules but, as the US State Department's 2003 report states, "Israeli drug-trafficking organizations are the main source of distribution of the drug to groups in the U.S, using express mail services, commercial airlines, and recently also using air cargo services." Continuing from the article:

> How did Israel become a central player in this dubious game? The explanation is apparently historical in character. A report of the U.S. Drug Enforcement Administration (DEA) explains, in understated language, that, "Israeli drug traffickers, perhaps thanks to their long-standing ties in Antwerp, continue to be the major elements in the transfer of large shipments of Ecstasy from Belgium [to the United States]." Underlying this cautious formulation is the assumption that Israeli mobsters have been operating for years in Belgium.... Israel is at the center of international trafficking in Ecstasy and Israeli crime

organizations, some of them linked to similar organizations from Russia, achieved a dominant status in the Ecstasy market in Europe.

Generally, the media misnomer "the Russian mafia" refers to Jewish mobsters and their interconnected criminal enterprises, not those of ethnic Russians. One of the most notorious "Russian" mafiosos, Semion Mogilevitch, trafficker of weapons and pimp to hundreds of Russian and Ukrainian girls in Prague and Budapest, was apprehended in early 2008, but not only did this go largely unremarked-upon, in the few places it was deemed newsworthy, Mogilevitch's "Jewishness" was evidently not fit to print. Speaking of sex trafficking, as many as 8,000 Russian women are smuggled into New York City and the metropolitan area alone every year to work in strip clubs, massage parlors, or as domestic servants. The women's passports are confiscated to restrict their movement, and those who try to leave or refuse to "work off" their $5,000 smuggling fee are threatened with violence.

There is a strong Jewish presence in the drug trade in Europe, particularly cocaine and ecstasy, and it has involved some seemingly unlikely figures such as the Vice President of the Central Council of Jews in Germany, Michel Friedman, whose law firm and apartment were raided on suspicion of Friedman's violating the Narcotics Act. In the summer of 2016, three ultra-Orthodox Israeli men were charged with attempting to smuggle thousands of ecstasy pills from Germany to Israel. One suspect was arrested upon landing at Ben Gurion Airport in possession of six kilograms—13,000 pills—of ecstasy in his suitcase and another kilo of "raw drug material of great worth." The Tel Aviv-to-Antwerp-to-Amsterdam-to-New York City (or Miami) route "is a classic smuggler's path," said a Belgian police officer.[55]

According to FBI documents, the Jewish Ludwig Fainberg was the middleman for an international drugs and weapons smuggling ring between Colombian cartels and the "Russian Mafia" in Miami in the 1990s. Fainberg

---

[55] From Camiel, "Ultra Orthodox Jews Running Drug Empire": "Ultra-Orthodox Jews served as couriers for a major international drugs ring that operated in the Netherlands, Belgium, France, Israel and the United States, Israeli police said Tuesday. The syndicate, led by two Israelis living in Europe, was one of the world's largest producers of the synthetic drug ecstasy, police said. Updating arrest figures announced by Dutch police Monday after dawn raids on the ring's drug laboratories in the Netherlands, Israeli police said at a news conference that 41 suspects had been detained overseas and another eight in Israel.... About one million ecstasy tablets were seized by police in Israel and abroad, the spokesman said.... Two Israelis, one residing in the Netherlands and the other in Belgium, were the masterminds behind the operation, and an ultra-Orthodox man recruited young religious Jews to smuggle the drugs. All three are in custody, Israeli police said. Dutch police said Monday's raids on 35 addresses in the Netherlands and the Belgium city of Antwerp marked the culmination of a three-year investigation. Along with laboratory equipment used in making synthetic drugs, five kilograms (11 lbs) of Semtex high explosive as well as weapons, cars and money were also recovered, a Dutch police spokeswoman said."

was eventually arrested and charged, then deported to Israel. Soon, though, as Victor Malarek describes in *The Natashas: Inside the New Global Sex Trade:*

> He turned up in Canada with dreams of making it rich in the flesh trade. Not long after his arrival he married a Canadian and moved into a comfortable apartment along the Ottawa River with his new bride and his ten-year-old daughter from a previous marriage.

His immigration status was approved by the Jewish then-Minister of Citizenship and Immigration Elinor Caplan. Several prominent Canadian rabbis were arrested in the 1990s for selling narcotics, such as Rabbi Meyer Krentzman, former director of the Canadian Zionist Federation, former director of the Jewish National Fund of Montreal, and former director of the Jewish Educational Council. In 1996, a Canadian embassy official in Tel Aviv, Douglas Wardle, was using diplomatic mail to smuggle Colombian cocaine.

On the Israeli front, in April 2004, former energy minister Gonen Segev (along with two other men) was remanded in custody at the Tel Aviv Magistrate's Court on suspicion of attempting to smuggle 25,000 ecstasy pills into Israel from the Netherlands in addition to the use of a forged diplomatic passport. Segev claimed that his friend, "an Israeli lawyer," gave him the package weighing over ten pounds and told him it was M&Ms. In the US, New York and Miami, with significant Jewish populations, proved to be major transit points for not just ecstasy but other narcotics, explosives, organs, and even people, but their notoriety by the late 1990s caused prominent Jewish traffickers to begin looking further west in the US, especially Los Angeles and Las Vegas, also with large Jewish populations. This in turn provided more options even further west: in September 2000, for example, Japanese police arrested Israeli David Biton on a charge of smuggling 25,000 ecstasy tablets into Japan.

Las Vegas became a key piece in what the media dubbed the Jerusalem Network's trafficking operations; the Network controlled most of the city's ecstasy trade. In November 2004, Gabriel Ben-Harosh, head of the Jerusalem Network, was extradited from Canada to the US; Ben-Harosh, along with four other Israelis, stood accused of extortion and money laundering. As the web became clearer, the Jerusalem Network's Las Vegas operations were but one piece of a vast international operation and was in fact connected to the Abergil family and its extensive reach. Over a decade later and with the network still going strong, Montreal "businessman" Samy Bitton, whose connection to the Abergils dated to at least 2003, was sentenced to eighteen months in prison in Israel for importing 800 kilograms of cocaine in January

2016. Bitton, promoter of a luxury condo project at Montreal's Old Port called 5e Quai, was arrested in Israel and pleaded guilty to charges of money laundering, tax evasion, and the importation of drugs. Bitton had laundered $10 million Canadian dollars that helped finance various assassination attempts and a bombing in Tel Aviv. In the judgment, it was revealed that as but one of the many trafficking pipelines, almost a ton of cocaine had been transported from Peru to Montreal stashed in an industrial machine. In Israel, the cocaine was stored in a building owned by Bitton's company, Sanielle Finance.

From a 2013 article in *The Times of Israel*:

> Months after the UN's World Drug Report for 2013 indicated that Israel was located at the crossroads between several drug trafficking routes, Israel has reported become a "major hub" in the international cocaine trade—with abuse of the substance increasingly on the rise, especially among white-collar Israelis…. The World Drug Report noted that in 2011, Israel registered an increase in the amount of cocaine seized in the country, possibly en route from Africa to the Balkans and Eastern Europe through West Africa and the Levant, particularly Israel, Lebanon, and Syria. "A link between this emerging route and the Near and Middle East cannot be excluded," concluded the report. In 2012, the US State Department's International Narcotics Control Strategy Report (INCSR) listed Israel as having "a significant domestic demand for illegal drugs." The report also noted an increase in money laundering in Israel and a connection between drug money and "terror financing and human trafficking"…. In January 2013, three Bolivian citizens were arrested at Ben Gurion International Airport as they tried to smuggle seven kilograms of liquid cocaine into the country.

In 2012, according to an article in *The Times of Israel* from that year, a Tel Aviv sushi restaurant was exposed for having taken coded orders from clients and then delivering cocaine to their homes.

The International Narcotics Control Board (INCB), which implements UN drug treaties and conventions, named Brazil and Israel among "countries that are major manufacturers, exporters, importers and users of narcotic drugs" in 2012. On June 26th, 2012, a *Haaretz* article declared: "IDF soldiers suspected of drug trafficking along Israel's border with Egypt." Twelve soldiers and junior officers were named. In June 2013, *Haaretz* reported that Israeli/Colombian Isaac Perez Guberek Ravinovicz and eleven Colombian enterprises were named by the UN as major contributors to drug trafficking:

"Ten Panamanian companies, 11 Colombian companies and one based in Rosh Ha'ayin allegedly built (a) network that laundered hundreds of millions of dollars of drug money." Further reported was a Department of Treasury announcement which read:

> Isaac Perez Guberek Ravinovicz, a Colombian national, and his son, Henry Guberek Grimberg, a dual Colombian and Israeli national, lead a money laundering network based in Bogota, Colombia that launders narcotics proceeds on behalf of numerous drug trafficking organizations, including organizations based in Colombia.... [They] primarily rely upon the use of ostensibly legitimate textile companies within Colombia to engage in trade-based money laundering.

Colombia has actually been very central to this extensive global Jewish crime network, and we will continue to see it crop up.

In August 2008, prosecutors alleged Yitzhak Abergil and his brother Meir were using Hispanic gang the Vineland Boyz to supply ecstasy throughout the Los Angeles area and were also contracted to kill Sami Atias after he tried to steal a 165-pound ecstasy shipment from Belgium, worth an estimated $7 million on the street. Cocaine and hashish were also being trafficked in addition to ecstasy with the Jerusalem Network, and there were embezzlement, money laundering, and loan sharking operations concurrent.

Moshe Matsri, also known as "Moshe the Religious," is, according to the FBI, "a well-known crime figure in the San Fernando Valley [with] significant ties to the Abergil organized crime family, which is based in Israel and also operates internationally." Matsri was found guilty in October 2014 of conspiracy to commit money laundering, conspiracy to distribute at least five kilograms of cocaine, eight counts of money laundering, attempted distribution of at least five kilograms of cocaine, attempted possession with intent to distribute at least five kilograms of cocaine, and conspiracy to commit extortion. Matsri and his subordinate Shay Paniry were apprehended in July 2013 following a joint FBI, DEA, and LAPD investigation. In addition to Matsri and Paniry, the indictment named several co-defendants: Youval Geringer-Ganor, sixty-two, of Los Angeles; Yaron Cohen, forty-five, of Amsterdam; Ibrahim Oter, sixty-four, of Brussels; Nisim Sabag, thirty-eight, of Los Angeles; and Hector Miguel Gomez-Navarro, twenty-five, of Cudahay. Matsri and his co-defendants "conducted complex, layered transactions to wire money through shell accounts in locations as far-flung as the Marshall Islands, Cyprus, and Gibraltar," according to the sentencing memo that also outlines that they "used a network of trusted individuals to bypass the financial system entirely, using 'hawala' transactions to move cash instantaneously from New York to Los Angeles, and from Vancouver to Los Angeles." Two other major pipelines appear to have been shipping cocaine from Panama to Israel and Colombia to the US.

One of the most central roles Jews play in the drug trade is money laundering for the cartels. In the late-1980s and early-1990s, Jewish Manhattan diamond traders[56] and goldsmiths were heavily involved. Avraham Sharir, who owned a gold shop on 47th Street, confessed to laundering $200 million for the Cali cartel. Religious figures such as Rabbi Yosef Crozer were also heavily involved; Crozer was arrested in February 1990 and gave the names of thirty Orthodox Jews in the community implicated in the operations to police. As the 1990s became the 2000s, New York still played a prominent role, as Robert Gearty and Greg B. Smith reported in November 2002:

> An international money-laundering ring run by New York Hasidim washed millions of dollars in cocaine proceeds for the Colombian cartels, prosecutors disclosed yesterday [November 1st, 2002].... The group laundered at least $1.7 million for the druglords, holding secret meetings with the Colombians in Miami and midtown Manhattan, according to papers filed by Manhattan U.S. Attorney James Comey. The suspects were brazen—up to $500,000 would be laundered at a time. One of the suspects, Avraham Zaltzman, allegedly bragged that he "could pick up money anywhere and wire it anywhere," according to FBI affidavits accompanying the arrests. Zaltzman was so brazen that he allegedly picked up drug money himself in Madrid in April and flew to London, where he was detained by British Customs. They found $460,000 concealed in his vest. Yesterday, FBI and Customs agents arrested Zaltzman and Aaron Bornstein, both of Borough Park, Brooklyn. Bornstein runs an interior design business there, and Zaltzman is a part-time printer who spends most of his time in Israel, officials said. A third man who was believed to be the ringleader, Akiva Apter, remained a fugitive. Three others were named as unindicted co-conspirators.

A November 2002 article in *The Guardian* highlights the role Hassidic Jews in New York played in "cleaning" profits from Colombian cocaine cartels, and

---

[56] In Australia, Orthodox Jew Nachum Goldberg, member of an international ring that included diamond merchants in Israel, Belgium, and Sydney, Goldberg laundered an estimated $90 million "dirty money" to Israel over thirteen years through a bank account set up for a fake charity called United Charity.

in May 2002 Samuel M. Katz wrote an extensive and informative article entitled "Israeli Drug Smugglers' Global Monopoly on Ecstasy":

> Authorities say Israeli crime groups have for several years had a virtual monopoly on global distribution of Ecstasy.... On May 3, 10 Israelis, including haredim, were arrested as members of a four-nation smuggling ring that allegedly sent hundreds of thousands of Ecstasy pills from the Netherlands to the United States, through Israel and Canada. Then a few weeks later, police in Spain announced they had captured Israeli Oded Tuito, described as a major international Ecstasy smuggler. Tuito was wanted in the United States for allegedly heading an organization that channeled hundreds of thousands of Ecstasy pills into the country from northern Europe.... At the end of May, Sammy the Bull (Salvatore Gravano), the one-time underboss of the Gambino family and allegedly the head of La Cosa Nostra in the southwest, pleaded guilty to running a multi-million-dollar Ecstasy ring in Arizona. According to the *New York Times*, the ring purchased Ecstasy pills "from a man named Ilan Zarger, a drug supplier based in Brooklyn who has ties to the Israeli mob." The links between Israeli narcotics importers and Lebanese brokers were strengthened after the 1982 Israeli invasion of Lebanon.... The poppy fields of the Beka'a Valley supplied manufacturers in Sicily and Marseilles with the raw product needed to produce heroin, and a considerable part of the Lebanese economy is based on the export of poppy products from the ports of Tyre, Beirut, and Tripoli. According to a Jordanian intelligence officer who works counter-narcotics, "Israeli soldiers marched into Lebanon like liberating heroes-and smuggling arrangements and routes were established" soon afterward. Drug smuggling along Israel's border with Egypt is also robust.... On April 5, 2000, U.S. federal agents intercepted two 40-pound FedEx packages of Ecstasy, that, according to the Boston Globe, had been shipped to hotel rooms in Boston and Brookline, Mass. The recipients, Yaniv Yona and Ereza Abutbul, were Israelis. A few months later, U.S. Customs officials in Los Angeles seized Ecstasy shipments of 650,000 and 2.1 million tablets, respectively, on flights from Paris; agents in upstate New York seized 100,000 pills that had been transported across the St. Lawrence River from Canada. In 2000, DEA and Customs agents seized 11.1 million doses of the drug (up from a few hundred thousand in 1995).... DEA agents and detectives say Israelis have been involved in almost all the major busts. They have included Sean Erez, currently awaiting

extradition from the Netherlands; Shimon Levita, a New York yeshiva student who was sentenced to 30 months in a federal boot camp for participating in the ring allegedly run by Erez; and Jacob Orgad, identified as an Israeli national with operations in Texas, New York, Florida, California, and Paris. A man identified by Customs as head of one of the biggest "drug importation rings," Israeli Tamer Adel Ibrahim, remains at large.

In 2001, it came to light that Sean Erez, "a Canadian-Israeli with US residence," had been running a massive ecstasy smuggling operation using young Hassidic recruits who thought they were smuggling diamonds, which apparently makes it okay. Erez's network mostly centered on an Amsterdam to and from New York pipeline. Neither the ecstasy trade nor the "cleaning" operation were novel phenomena, even then. In 1993, the FBI and DEA exposed a massive Sephardic money laundering operation that was centered on the triangle of Colombia, the United States, and Israel, but encompassed numerous other countries. As Edmund Mahony writes, this Sephardic group "provided a service which enabled the cocaine cartel based in the Colombian city of Cali to reinvest profits in production and distribution." The FBI first penetrated the network in 1991, and quickly learned how extensive its operations were. Mahony reports:

> The launderers also discussed using the undercover agent to expand into Italy and Canada.... As the agent's relationship with the laundering network grew, investigators were able to identify its members and methods of operations. The network was dominated by a closely knit group of Sephardic Jews. Sephardim are a minority among Jews and are descendants of those who settled around the Mediterranean Sea after being expelled from Spain in 1492.... The network was run by Szion Jacob Abenhaim, 43, a Moroccan with dual Israeli-Colombian citizenship who lived in Cali, according to the indictment. FBI and Drug Enforcement Administration agents describe Abenhaim as a veteran of the Cali cartel who worked his way up the organization ranks to a position near the top. He had subordinates in Israel and New York and is personally responsible for laundering hundreds of millions of dollars in drug profits, the agents said.... The two indictments promise to be only the beginning of a long legal process leading to a trial. Abenhaim is in jail in Paris and must be extradited to the United States. French authorities late last year captured him during a five-day Hanukkha shopping spree. Ever wary, he bribed the manager of a top Paris hotel to give him a

room without registering. Another defendant, Raymond Chochana, 38, is also jailed in France and fighting extradition. He has homes in Jerusalem and New York and was arrested in Paris while flying from Israel to Morrocco.

In March 1988 in Seattle, four men, including a rabbi, were arrested in an international money-laundering conspiracy that sent millions of dollars to Panama and Colombia. The four were among thirteen people, including a group of Israeli nationals, named in a federal complaint filed in New Jersey charging them with violating federal currency laws that require large transactions to be reported. Federal prosecutors in New Jersey said as much as $25 million in cashier's checks and money orders may have been sent to Colombia and Panama, as well as to banks in London, Germany, and Israel. Most of the checks were sent to the Colombian Medellín cartel or General Manuel Antonio Noriega in Panama, who was instrumental in the export of cocaine to the US and had worked as an intermediary and provided safe haven for the Medellín Cartel, which for some time before he became an informant utilized the "talents" of Jewish smuggler Max Mermelstein.

According to Victor Ostrovsky, formerly of the Mossad, in his *By Way of Deception*, the Mossad was using the Thai heroin trade as a way to raise funds for top secret operations the 1970s and 1980s:

> The Mossad had made its first contact with the opium growers in Thailand [in the late 1970s]. The Americans were trying to force farmers to stop producing opium and grow coffee instead. The Mossad's idea was to get in there, help them grow coffee, but at the same time help them to export opium as a means of raising money for Mossad operations.

As the 1980s wore on, Jewish figures and the Mossad began strengthening ties in Latin America, particularly in Colombia and Panama, and entering into the cocaine trade and the ancillary arms trade in force.

One key figure was Israeli Colonel Yair Klein, who helped arm and train the Medellín cartel's para-military forces. Klein taught these men to make bombs—one of which was detonated on a commercial flight, killing 117 people—and to conduct political assassinations, such as that of presidential hopeful Luis Carlos Galan in 1989. After a major battle with one of Pablo Escobar's lieutenants in Colombia, authorities discovered almost two hundred Israeli Galil assault rifles; these weapons and other munitions were believed to have been approved for sale by Israeli Defense Minister, former Prime Minister, and later Nobel Peace Prize winner Yitzhak Rabin.

The Mossad had been providing weapons and training to Noriega's Unidad Especial Anti-Terror (*UESAT*). Michael Harari, a Mossad agent working as an advisor for Noriega, in 1982 became the point-man for what was known as the Harari Network in order to arm the CIA-backed Nicaraguan Contras and to funnel cocaine from Colombia north into the US; this joint project was instigated at the behest of both the Reagan administration and the Israeli government. Klein and Harari were in close contact. Prior to his assignment in Panama, Harari had carried out assassinations of major Palestinian figures and had mistakenly assassinated a Moroccan man in Norway believed to have been Ali Salameh. He was reassigned to Mexico City before arriving in Panama and ingratiating himself to Noriega's predecessor, Omar Torrijos. Harari re-vamped the Panamanian forces and oversaw the transfer of Noriega's drug profits into secure Swiss bank accounts.

The Mossad was also active in Guatemala and Costa Rica, where, as Peter Dale Scott and Jonathan Marshall write in *Cocaine Politics: Drugs, Armies, and the CIA in Central America*, "pro-Contra drug enterprise Frigorificos de Puntarenas made unexplained payments to an account in Israel of the Israel Discount Bank."[57] In Honduras, the Arms Supermarket was another operation established by the CIA and the Mossad. Arms dealer Gerard Latchinian contracted the Israeli security firm International Security and Defense Systems (ISDS) to train bodyguards for Army Chief of Staff General Gustavo Alvarez Martinez and Emil Saada of ISDS was also involved in supplying arms to the Contras. Saada had business ties with the Jewish ex-Vice President of Honduras Jaime Rosenthal, in 2015 along with his son Yani Rosenthal and nephew Yankel Rosenthal labeled a "specially designated narcotics trafficker" under the Foreign Narcotics Kingpin Designation Act, his Banco Continental liquidated for money laundering. The Rosenthals' family holdings had made them a top five conglomerate in Honduras.

ISDS International is still active today, and there is an ISDS Brazil branch as well. Clients include a number of sporting events and leagues, as well as Santander, Coca-Cola, Nestlé, Banco de Mexico, and ASIS International, among many others. ASIS International is headquartered in Alexandria, Virginia, and is a "professional organization for security professionals." ISDS has several focus areas, but of particular relevance to this book are critical infrastructure and cyber security. As you could probably guess with an organization that states that it has strong relationships with the US federal government, ISDS client ASIS International partners with the Security Industry Association on the COVID-19 Response Partnership; critical

---

[57] Scott, *Cocaine Politics*, 78.

relationships as described on the ASIS International website are included the FBI, ATF, DHS, US Chamber of Commerce, the Overseas Security Advisory Council, the Office of the Director of National Intelligence, and more. Past Presidents have included individuals such as Thomas Langer of BAE Systems and Richard Chase of General Atomics. ASIS Europe's 2019 seminar featured "the latest drone and counter-UAV systems, integrated access control and surveillance technology, to smart crowdsourced cyber security testing, crisis, risk management and intelligence platforms and mass communications applications."

Far from being a great asset or partner for the US, Israel and its intelligence arms have long parasitized Americans. Documents obtained by *The Guardian* in 2013 revealed that the US-Israeli intelligence relationship "arguably tilted heavily in favor of Israeli security concerns. 9/11 came, and went, with NSA's only true Third Party [counter-terrorism] relationship being driven almost totally by the needs of the partner." In 2009, the NSA agreed to provide raw intelligence data to Israel and the agreement placed *no legally binding limits on the use of the data by the Israelis*. The NSA routinely sends ISNU (the Israeli Sigint National Unit) raw data, and that same year, *The New York Times* reported on "the agency's attempt to wiretap a member of Congress, without court approval, on an overseas trip." Israeli intelligence is apparently allowed "to disseminate foreign intelligence information concerning US persons derived from raw Sigint by NSA." As Whitney Webb wrote in August 2020 for *Unlimited Hangout:*

> Anonymous "volunteers" from an opaque group founded by a former commander of Israel's Unit 8200 have been granted access to some of the most critical private and public networks in the US' healthcare and pharmaceutical sectors, with the help of a US federal agency now run by a former Microsoft executive.... An odd group of "cyber threat intelligence" analysts with ties to the US government, Israeli intelligence and tech giant Microsoft have "volunteered" to protect US healthcare institutions for free and have even directly partnered with US federal agencies to do so. They have also recently expanded to offer their services to governments and social media platforms to target, analyze and "neutralize" alleged "disinformation campaigns" related to the Coronavirus crisis.... Calling themselves the cyber version of "Justice League," the Covid-19 Cyber Threat Intelligence (CTI) League was created earlier this year in March and has described itself as "the first Global Volunteer Emergency Response Community, defending and neutralizing cybersecurity threats and vulnerabilities to the life-saving sectors related to the current Covid-

19 pandemic..." The CTI League has offered its services "pro bono" to a variety of groups in the private and public sector, which has allowed the League's members access to the critical systems of each. For instance, they work closely with the Health Information Sharing and Analysis Center (H-ISAC), whose members include Johnson & Johnson, Pfizer, Merck, Amgen, Blue Cross Blue Shield and Athenahealth, among others. H-ISAC's president, Denise Anderson, works closely with the National Cybersecurity and Communications Integration Center, part of the Department of Homeland Security (DHS). According to H-ISAC's Chief Security Officer (CSO), Errol Weiss, the organization has been partnered with the CTI League since "very early on" in the Coronavirus crisis. The CTI League also works with unspecified law enforcement partners in the US and works particularly closely with the US Cybersecurity and Infrastructure Security Agency (CISA), an independent federal agency overseen by DHS. The current CISA director, Christopher Krebs—who was previously the Director of Cybersecurity for Microsoft, told CSO Online in April that "CISA is working around the clock with our public and private sector partners to combat this threat. This includes longstanding partnerships, as well as new ones that have formed as a direct result of Covid-19, including the Covid-19 Cyber Threat Intelligence (CTI) League."

Probably nothing to see here, though, right? They're just doing this to protect us, you see. It has nothing at all to do with the fact that data is the fossil fuel of the World Economic Forum-driven Fourth Industrial Revolution, and is completely unconnected to the exploding surveillance state, the aggressive implementation of all sorts of genetic and data mining operations, the rapid development of artificial intelligence, or the mRNA "vaccines" rushed to market which, according to Moderna, are "faster, cheaper, and more potent than regular vaccines."

In late 1987, an Israeli arms dealer named Zvi Gafni was arrested in Hong Kong on suspicion of attempting to broker a deal with the Chinese communists, something Israel had been doing for some time, and to handsome profits. At approximately the same time—and the connections here are a little convoluted—it appeared that several Mossad agents, possibly having gone rogue, were supplying arms to the IRA and selling mass quantities of cannabis in Great Britain from Lebanon; two other Israelis with possible government connections were apprehended in March 1987 for attempting to smuggle cocaine from Colombia into Britain. In each of 1985, 1986, 1987, and 1988, massive drug smuggling rings in the Northeastern

United States were uncovered with Israelis at the center.

The role of the Israeli government in these illicit operations often remains somewhat unclear, but we do know that International Credit Bank of Geneva founder Tibor Pinchas Rosenbaum had a close relationship with the Israeli government; in the 1970s, the Defense Ministry held an account at the bank to buy arms in Western Europe, and other accounts were held by the Histadrut (the Israeli labor federation), Solel Boneh (the Histadrut-owned supply and construction company), Zim Integrated Shipping Services Ltd., and Israel Corporation. Once, when then-Director General in the Defense Ministry Shimon Peres called Rosenbaum and told him that Israel needed $7 million within twenty-four hours for national security, Rosenbaum found the money overnight and received a commission of $500,000. Rosenbaum was Treasurer and member of the Governing Council of the World Jewish Congress and a member of the presidium of the Orthodox World Mizrachi Movement. In April 1975, via *The New York Times:*

> An indictment was handed up in Israel...charging the country's most prominent financial official, Michael Tzur, with fraud, bribery and a breach of trust.... The complaint against Mr. Tzur, accusing him of having illegally transferred more than $20-million out of Israel, centers on his relations with Rosenbaum...[Tzur] became general manager of Israel Corporation, a Government-supported development company, and it was from this post that he signed the chits for transfers of money to Mr. Rosenbaum's bank in Geneva. Israel Corporation and some other depositors in the International Credit Bank discovered that monies on account had been transferred to personal trusts of Mr. Rosenbaum registered in Liechtenstein. This is the second banking scandal involving Israel. Joshua Benson, former manager of the Israel British Bank, which was put into liquidation in Tel Aviv in October after rescue efforts fell through, has just been sentenced to 12 years by a Tel Aviv court for having stolen $47-million from the bank. That bank's London subsidiary with $125-million of deposits and links with London insurance and real estate companies, has also collapsed. Geneva's Finabank, owned by the Italian financier Michele Sindona, under indictment in Milan, is the latest of a number of Swiss banks to have closed in recent months. Founder of the bank 16 years ago, Mr. Rosenbaum is still its president and major stockholder. An ordained but nonpracticing rabbi who was close to many in the Israeli Establishment, Mr. Rosenbaum built his bank into an institution with intimate relations with Israel. I.C.B. handled some Israeli international business, such

as European arms purchases, and helped channel funds from the international Jewish community into Israel...Their arc parallels in the Israel-British Bank scandal and J.C.B. Like Mr. Rosenbaum, the Israel-British chairman, Harry Landy, the brother-in-law of Joshua Bension, who was jailed for stealing the money, was well-connected in the international Jewish community. Until last year Mr. Landy was vice president of the senior Jewish laymen's organization in Britain the Board of Deputies of British Jews...In both cases large sums of money were transferred Liechtenstein-registered companies. Both banks, Israeli sources said, were encouraged by the former Finance Minister, Mr. Sapir.... To raise additional capital, Israel Corporation made special efforts to woo South African, Iranian and German investors. The investigators said that funds from these investors were diverted into the Liechtenstein trusts starting in 1972. According to a source who knows the Rosenbaum operation, Mr. Rosenbaum was introduced to Scopitone by Alvin Ira Malnik and Sylvain Ferdman, who both played roles in other I.C.B. activities. Mr. Malnik, Scopitone's promoter, is a Miami Beach lawyer identified by the Federal Bureau of Investigation as having represented underworld figures and has been indicted on tax charges in the United States. Earlier, he founded the Bank of World Commerce in Nassau, which until it was struck off the commercial register on July 2, 1965, reputedly served as a conduit for moving gambling funds into Switzerland. Mr. Ferdman, an economic adviser to I.C.B., has opened accounts at the Geneva bank for Mr. Malnik and for such figures as John Pullman, who served a prison sentence for violating United States liquor laws and who now lives in Lausanne. Mr. Pullman has been named by the Justice Department as the financial adviser of the mobster Meyer Lansky. I.C.B. was cited by Life Magazine in 1967 as one of the Swiss banks that received funds that mobsters skimmed from casinos in the United States and the Bahamas, then recycled into mob-controlled investments in legitimate American businesses.

Jews have been a fixture of organized crime in North America since at least the 1920s, and even prominent Jewish families like the Bronfmans made their fortune bootlegging liquor. The Jewish Arnold Rothstein basically ran the New York underworld in the 1920s, creating the largest gambling empire the US had ever seen. He also made a fortune in bootlegging. The Jewish Abner Zwillman was a major criminal figure in New Jersey and with the Jewish Joseph Reinfeld, the pair imported an astonishing 40 percent of the alcohol that entered the US during Prohibition. The major Jewish gangster Meyer Lansky smuggled weapons out of New York to Palestine to the IDF precursor Haganah (Israel did not officially exist yet). According to Robert Rockaway, many other Jews from the criminal underworld donated tens of thousands of dollars to the Haganah. Lansky also played a key role in supervising heroin smuggling operations from Corsica.

Prior to World War II, many major Eastern European cities such as Warsaw and Odessa were under the control of Jewish gangsters. Historian Dr. Mordechai Zalkin, senior lecturer in the Department of the History of the Jewish People at Ben-Gurion University of the Negev in Be'er Sheva says:

> When I work in an archive in Eastern Europe, and it doesn't matter whether it's in St. Petersburg or Moscow, one of the things that interests me is the collection of police files. What used to be classified intelligence files are now open. The police collected information as part of their work, and when I open the files, from 150 years ago, I find detailed reports about Jewish criminals. The archives have enough material for 100 historians and for 100 years, and even then they won't finish.[58]

As Coby Ben-Simhon wrote in *Haaretz*:

> One of the major episodes in which a Jewish criminal organization was involved occurred in Vilna in February 1923. It received unusual coverage in the local Yiddish paper. For four consecutive days the paper's lead stories dealt with the events. A Jewish gang that called itself the "Gold Flag" kidnapped a boy from a wealthy family for ransom. According to the police, the man behind the kidnapping, Berl Kravitz, had belonged to the Capone gang in the United States a few years earlier. A report dated February 1905 from the Hebrew paper *Hazman* ("The Time"), which was published in Vilna, sheds light on one of the sophisticated methods of operation of the Jewish criminals. They seem to have had no shame…Vilna was not an exceptional hothouse of crime. Organizations like Gold Flag and the Brothers Society operated also in Warsaw, Odessa, Bialystok and Lvov.... Jews could be found at almost all levels of underworld activity, from the individual thief to gangs that numbered more than 100 members. The large organizations operated in the cities, which they divided into sectors among themselves.

---

[58] Quoted in Finkelstein, *The Holocaust Industry*, 5.

Each organization had a charter, a clear hierarchy and internal courts, and its work was divided according to different areas, such as theft, protection money, prostitution, pickpocketing and murder.... One of the most famous roadmen, Dan Barzilai, a Jew by all accounts, who ran a well-known gang of thieves in the Warsaw area, was captured in 1874. His gang had 27 members, 14 of them Jews. They descended upon estates around Warsaw and attacked merchants' coaches on the roads, making off with furs, jewelry and horses...Jewish underworld figures roamed the streets without fear. Everyone knew them, they even entered Jewish literature. In his work, "In the Vale of Tears," Mendele Mocher Sforim (penname of Shalom Jacob Abramovitsch, 1835-1917) provides an exceptional description of one type of Jewish criminal organization, cruel and dark. In the novel Jewish mobsters use underhanded methods to kidnap Jewish girls from poor, remote towns and then force them to work as prostitutes. This was a fairly common phenomenon. The Jewish society described here by Mendele is perverted and rotten. Sixteen-year-old Biela, from the town of Kavtsiel, falls victim to this well-oiled scheme. She was promised work in a household and one of the prostitutes explains what she must do: "The virgins of Kavtsiel are in demand here, and if they are clever and know why they are in demand, they end up getting rich and everyone is happy." The innocent Biela doesn't have a clue about what is meant, but afterward learns from the older prostitutes and the pimps how to be seductive and how to perform.

In the 1860s, Jews were in control of the white slavery market in Odessa, which specialized in trafficking Russian girls to Turkey; the brothels in what is now-Istanbul were also largely controlled by Jews. In Constantinople, prostitutes contributed money to "have their pimps called to Torah on holidays." As Edward Bristow shows in *Prostitution and Prejudice*, by 1889 an official census of prostitution recorded that Jewesses ran 203 of the 289 licensed houses, or 70 percent of the total number of brothels throughout the Pale of Settlement. According to Bristow, in Rio de Janeiro, Brazil, Jewish immigrants from Russia, Poland, Hungary, and Romania were so strongly identified with prostitution in the late 1800s that "the kaftan, a Jew's traditional long gown, became synonymous with pimp." Of 199 licensed whorehouses in Buenos Aires, Argentina, in 1909, 102 were run by Jews.

In 1912, at least 271 of 402 prostitution traffickers on a Hamburg, Germany police list were Jewish. The "golden era" of white slavery and sex trafficking by the Jews was only briefly interrupted by World War II, and not much has changed since. In 1994, the *US News and World Report* published the observations of a Frankfurt policeman patrolling the red-light district: "It's all owned by Jews. Practically everything in this area is owned by German Jews. There is a single cabaret here owned by a German, but the rest belongs to the Jews." That could have just as easily been a report from 1924 during the Weimar Era.

In 1998, Israeli commentator Jonathan Rosenblum, noting that a CNN documentary had revealed that Israel had the highest rate of prostitution in the world, said that, "once again anti-Semites portray us as sexual libertines and perverts to undermine our moral authority. Today we cheerfully admit the charges." Well there you go. According to official estimates, the number of trafficked women reached 3,000 in the late 1990s and early 2000s. The trafficking victims came from the post-Soviet states, particularly Russia, Ukraine, Moldova, Belarus, and Uzbekistan; they ended up in one of 300–400 brothels, where they worked seven days a week, serving up to thirty clients each day.

The so-called Russian Mafia, often obscuring the Jewish identity of many of these criminals operating in the former USSR, has invested over $4 billion in real estate and businesses serving as fronts in Israel for their sex trafficking. To contextualize the extent of this operation, the International Organization of Migration estimates that more than 160,000 people have been trafficked from the Ukraine alone since the fall of the Soviet Union. With the authorities, while the traffickers themselves enjoyed a "forgiving attitude," the trafficked women were considered offenders. They were classified as illegal aliens or even criminals for having entered Israel illegally. The police concentrated on apprehending the women and deporting them as soon as possible, seeing the matter as one of migration. That said, the deported women were probably very fortunate.

The US State Department reported via their *2017 Trafficking in Persons Report – Israel* that:

> Women from Eastern Europe, Uzbekistan, China, and Ghana, as well as Eritrean men and women, are subjected to sex trafficking in Israel; some women arrive on tourist visas to work willingly in prostitution, but are subsequently exploited by sex traffickers.

Many Israeli-Palestinian and Israeli-Druze women in prostitution are not included in the formal statistics. From Novi Levenkron and Yossi Dahan's report *Women as Commodities: Trafficking in Women in Israel 2003* we learn:

> In Israel, the struggle to eradicate trafficking has barely begun, and most authorities do not live up to their declared principles. Sometimes their operations amount to no more than a sham—a case of lip service only.... Efforts to combat trafficking in women in Israel are still not proportionate to the extent of the phenomenon and the gravity of the offense.[59]

Of the interviewees for the report, 48 percent were from Moldova, 28 percent from the Ukraine, and 14 percent from Russia.

Contrary to the official Israeli claim that migrant workers are the main source of the massive demand for prostitution, the interviews of Levenkron and Dahan show that the overwhelming majority of the clients are Israelis. Many "clients" of the brothels include policemen. Forty-four percent (!) of the women interviewed testified that policemen were clients of the brothels, 13 percent referred to friendly relationships between policemen and pimps, and three women reported seeing money change hands between pimps and police.

> These visits have a devastating effect on the victims' faith in the police. They corroborate the pimps' claims to having connections in the police force, and the women conclude that there is no point in running away. As one woman commented cynically: "I can meet my clients at the brothel, there's no need for me to go to the police to see them."[60]

The interviews also reveal that the clientele include minors. In one case the visit to a brothel was given as a bar mitzvah present to a thirteen-year-old "man." Another interviewee stated:

> The woman pimp sent me to a group of five minors aged 14-16. They were waiting for me in a [bomb] shelter, put a mattress on the floor and raped me. The other minors standing in line watched and laughed. I didn't think that I could feel so humiliated. Even now I don't believe that it happened and I just want to cry. The next day I hurt all over and I couldn't get up. I told the woman pimp that I couldn't work and she said she didn't care. I had to bring her money and not just be there. She treated her dog better.[61]

---

[59] Levenkron, *Women as Commodities*, 6.
[60] Ibid., 43.
[61] Ibid., 32-33.

Tal Zohar was arrested in 2003 for running the Escort Plus Web site, where young Eastern European women were "hired" and housed in Israel where they would be sold to the highest bidder. According to the prosecution, Zohar even cheated his victims concerning their wages, but as Ofri Ilani wrote in a July 2007 article for *Haaretz*:

> Zohar's case is unusual, mainly because the Israeli law enforcement system seldom tries and convicts pimps who operate virtual brothels. This, despite the existence of several dozen such sites. The Tapuz portal, for example, has 38 sites listed in its "Escort Agencies" category.

A September 28th, 2004 article from *Haaretz* noted that in Israel:

> Police...arrested 40 suspected members of a Russian-Israeli prostitute smuggling ring in the last few days. The gang is believed to have brought hundreds of women into Israel in the past decade. The suspects allegedly took advantage of a lack of coordination between government offices and brought the women in under the Law of Return, establishing bogus family ties and claiming grants from the Absorption Ministry.

A May 2007 article from *Haaretz* reported that Noam Reizin, owner of a Haifa brothel, was sentenced to five years in jail for human trafficking. In August 2007, *Haaretz* reported that, "Two years ago, S., 47, came from Ukraine to work as a domestic in the home of an Israeli businessman. The employment company abroad that contracted her told her she had 'nothing to worry about,' with respect to her new boss." According to S., however, her employer—a resident of a wealthy Tel Aviv suburb, who works at a foreign consulate in Israel—"withheld most of her salary, took her passport, did not let her leave the house unless he was with her, and raped her. In many cases, S. says, her employer's friends who came to dinner or parties sexually molested her, and one of them also raped her."

Dr. Martin Brass determined in 2002 that many of the clients are "ultra-Orthodox Jews...whose sex lives are determined by Halachah (religious law), which tells them when they can or cannot have sex with their wives":

> So, on Thursday (boys' night out in Israel) busloads of Orthodox Jews travel from Jerusalem, Haifa, and points beyond to Tel Aviv for a few brief moments of passion in a massage parlor, behind a sand dune, or in an alley. Other customers are accountants, lawyers, policemen,

and politicians. "The entire spectrum of Israeli society is keeping the hookers in business," Detective Shachar, veteran on the Tel Aviv vice detail said. "Many of the prostitutes in Israel, especially those of Arab descent, are abused by Jews expressing their 'racial-nationalist fervor.'" The girls… "find that their Jewish customers only come to them after a Palestinian terrorist act to get their own brand of sexual revenge laced with racial-nationalistic fervor…and they do it with hate and anger."

On October 29th, 2019, *Haaretz* published a story relaying the news that fifteen people had been arrested in the Tel Aviv area with the suspects allegedly operating a complex network, bringing women from Russia and Ukraine to Israel to be pimped out. Their leader had previously been convicted of similar crimes, though only served a ten-month sentence. This is not an isolated incident; an Israeli parliamentary committee found that human trafficking is a $1 billion annual market in the country, and yet, in 2006 for example, there were only seventeen trafficking convictions. The Parliamentary Inquiry Committee headed by Knesset member Zehava Galon of the Yahad party found that between 3,000 to 5,000 women are smuggled into Israel annually to be sold into prostitution, though that number is almost surely higher. The primary sources are from the former USSR, particularly Russia, the Ukraine, and Moldova, though the Central Asian republics, Georgia, and Belarus are also part of this vast international network based in Israel. The targeting of mostly white women was also reflected in the trafficking operation of Jeffrey Epstein and Ghislaine Maxwell.

Until 2013, when Israel finished construction of a 150-mile fence along its border with Egypt, often these women would be smuggled across the border by Bedouins who also brought in illegal weapons and narcotics. In March 2009, *Haaretz* ran a story stating that police had cracked what they believed to have been Israel's largest human-trafficking ring, allegedly responsible for smuggling thousands of women from the former USSR, Cyprus, Belgium, and England into Israel to be forced into prostitution. Twelve Israelis and twenty others were arrested, with the suspected leader Rami Saban, who was previously under investigation for alleged involvement in hiring contract killers from Belarus to assassinate "leading Israeli underworld figure Nissim Alperon."

In addition to sex trafficking, the former USSR, Cyprus, and the general northerly area above Israel in addition to the United States have proven fruitful for organ harvesting. In Israel—one of the largest organ-buying countries—organ donation rarely occurs because of the Jewish idea that having a deceased relative whose body is incomplete prior to burial or cremation is associated with misfortune. It's apparently fine if the misfortune befalls on the poor gentiles selling the organs, however. The targeting of the vulnerable—financially, cognitively,[62] age-wise, et cetera—is common practice in the lucrative international organ trade, dominated by Israelis and Diaspora Jews with some outside assistance. According to a *Bloomberg Markets* magazine report from November 2011 describing:

> A network of organ-trafficking organizations whose reach extends from former Soviet Republics such as Azerbaijan, Belarus and Moldova to Brazil, the Philippines, South Africa and beyond.... Many of the black-market kidneys harvested by these gangs are destined for people who live in Israel.... The dearth of available organs in Israel has spawned a new class of criminals.... Traffickers prey on the most-vulnerable people. Moldova, the poorest country in Europe, is one of their prime hunting grounds. Dorin Razlog, a shepherd with an eighth-grade education who lives in Ghincauti, says recruiters for a trafficking ring told him cash for a kidney would lift him out of poverty.... The Ukrainian Interior Ministry broke up the ring that bought Razlog's kidney and arrested its leader—a Ukrainian-born Israeli national—in 2007...[Another ring used the] ABU Clinic in Baku, Azerbaijan, where doctors performed at least 13 of the transplants...mostly for Israelis.

In 2019, police in Cyprus arrested an Israeli man named Moshe Harel described as the ringleader of a world-wide organ trafficking network that operated out of Kosovo for years, securing donors from Eastern Europe and Turkey to come to Kosovo with the promise of a €12,000 payday for a kidney, which would then be sold to other Israelis. Harel's gang worked closely with Yuri Katzman, a Belarussian-born Israeli and "recruiter" and his gang who were behind the AB Clinic in Azerbaijan. Israeli police had arrested Harel in 2012 in a "related investigation," but he was never extradited to Kosovo; one prosecutor said the donors were treated like garbage.

That same year, Kazakhstan held a doctor for performing illegal transplants to sell organs from destitute people from the Ukraine, Kyrgyzstan, and Tajikistan to wealthy Israelis. *The New York Times* ran a piece in 2014 reporting that "brokers" from Israeli were directing "desperate" people to Costa Rica for transplants; the year before, the "tip of the iceberg" of the organ

---

[62] In February 2019, Israeli police arrested five people, including an American rabbi who heads a yeshiva, for allegedly running an international baby trafficking ring that targeted mentally disabled mothers. One alleged accomplice is Rivkah Segal, a rabbi's wife, suspected of abusing her legal guardianship over an expectant mother with mental health problems.

trafficking network was revealed, with Dr. Francisco Mora Palma, head of nephrology at the large Calderon Guardia Hospital, and an employee at Costa Rica's Public Security Ministry were in touch with Israeli doctors and were "testing the suitability of the local residents" whose organs were to be harvested in Israel, according to the Attorney General's Office. As researcher Nancy Scheper-Hughes wrote in a 2014 piece for the *New Internationalist*:

> Israeli brokers, for example, recently confided that they either have to pay to gain access to deceased donor pools in Russia or Latin America (Colombia, Peru and Panama in particular), or they have to set up new temporary sites and locations (Cyprus, Azerbaijan and Costa Rica) for facilitating illicit transplants quickly and for a short period of time, already anticipating police, government and/or international interventions. They are always prepared to move quickly to new locations where they have established links to clandestine transplant units, some of them no more sophisticated than a walk-in medical clinic or a rented ward in a public hospital.

In April 2007, police in Turkey arrested Zaki Shapira in the course of a gun battle between police and armed robbers at a hospital on suspicion of involvement in an illegal organ transplant ring that performed operations at a private hospital in Istanbul, which should have been shut down by court order a month earlier for illegal transplants. In 1996, Shapira had been prohibited from performing transplants in Israel after an investigation by the health ministry suspected him of being involved in organ trafficking. Shapira was one of seven Israelis charged in 2015 for organizing and/or performing transplants in Azerbaijan, Sri Lanka, Turkey, and Kosovo, using paid local donors for Israeli recipients. Boris Wolfman was a kidney trafficker who had worked for Shapira and was arrested in Turkey in 2015. Wolfman recruited Syrian and Palestinian kidney sellers in various detention centers.

A December 2007 *Haaretz* piece reported that two Haifa men had been sentenced to jail for trafficking in humans for the purpose of harvesting their organs, having persuaded Arabs from Galilee and central Israel who were mentally ill or mentally challenged to agree to have a kidney removed for payment, using ads in the newspaper to offer money for organ donation and then not paying the donors. In October 2016, *Haaretz* reported that three Israelis, one of whom was a surgeon, were arrested in Turkey on suspicion of organ trafficking.

In 2003, a South African transplant surgeon working at a public hospital wrote an open letter warning his fellow surgeons about "Israeli transplantations" in regard to a trafficking operation about which the Israeli government was little help in aiding investigators. This operation turned out to be a sprawling network that included Brazil, South Africa, and numerous other points. *The Economist* reported that the operation especially flourished in South Africa between 2001 and 2003. Alison Weir reports that:

> Donors were recruited in Brazil, Israel and Romania with offers of $5,000–20,000 to visit Durban and forfeit a kidney. The 109 recipients, mainly Israelis, each paid up to $120,000 for a "transplant holiday." They pretended they were relatives of the donors and that no cash changed hands.

In 2004, a legislative commission in Brazil reported, "At least 30 Brazilians have sold their kidneys to an international human organ trafficking ring for transplants performed in South Africa, with Israel providing most of the funding." From the *Bloomberg Markets* magazine report from December 2011:

> In November 2010 in Durban, Netcare Ltd. (NTC)—South Africa's largest hospital company—pleaded guilty to violating the Human Tissue Act, which prohibits buying and selling organs. Netcare paid 7.8 million rand ($848,464) in fines and penalties. It admitted to allowing 92 transplants in which donors from Brazil, Israel and Romania sold kidneys to Israeli patients. Four doctors are awaiting trial on trafficking charges.... Aliaksei Yafimau shudders at the memory of the burly thug who threatened to kill his relatives. Yafimau, who installs satellite television systems in Babrujsk, Belarus, answered an advertisement in 2010 offering easy money to anyone willing to sell a kidney. He saw it as a step toward getting out of poverty. Instead, Yafimau, 30, was thrust into a dark journey around the globe that had him, at one point, locked in a hotel room for a month in Quito, Ecuador, waiting for surgeons to cut out an organ.... The man holding Yafimau against his will was Roini Shimshilashvili, a former kickboxer who was an enforcer for an international organ-trafficking ring.... Doctors removed Yafimau's left kidney in July 2010 and transplanted it into an Israeli woman.... The Israeli-eastern European organ-trafficking rings have also extended their reach to the U.S.

Scheper-Hughes says she remembers over the course of her research an Israeli surgeon telling her that Palestinian laborers were "very generous" with their kidneys, and often donated to strangers in exchange for "a small honorarium" (right), and a heart surgeon admitted that in some cases, organs were harvested from brain-dead donors who were "not quite as dead as we might like them to be."

In 1990, a *Washington Report for Middle East Affairs* article by Mary Barrett reported that among Palestinians, "widespread anxiety over organ thefts...has gripped Gaza and the West Bank since the intifada began in December of 1987." In 2009, Swedish journalist Donald Boström was accused of "anti-Semitism" and "blood libel" for his reporting on the involuntary "donating" of organs by Palestinians slain by the IDF; as Boström wrote on his website:

> When the Swedish daily newspaper *Aftonbladet* on August 17, 2009 published an article where a number of Palestinian families accused Israel of stealing organs from their sons after they were killed, the reaction was immediate. The global explosion of my article caused a political crisis between the Swedish and Israeli governments and almost cost my life. However, the Israeli government, fully aware of the activities at the institute, chose to not, for an inexplicable reason take the opportunity and stop it all. Instead, they started a campaign with the message "claiming that organs are stolen in Israel is a medieval anti-Semitic blood libel". "Something like that has never happened". Prime Minister Netanyahu's government demanded the Swedish government to condemn the article, and the newspaper to retract it, and me to apologize.

The thing is, Israel knows this is going on and, as Alison Weir writes:

> The Israeli government has enabled the practice. For many years the Israeli health system subsidized its citizens' "transplant holidays," reimbursing Israelis $80,000 for medical operations abroad. Much of the remaining costs could often be obtained from government-subsidized Israeli insurance plans. In addition, Israel's Ministry of Defense was directly involved.

In 2001, a district judge found Israel's state morgue, the L. Greenberg Institute of Forensic Medicine, had performed hundreds of autopsies and had removed body parts without the families' permission—and sometimes in direct opposition to their expressed wishes under the supervision of Dr. Yehuda Hiss, Israel's chief pathologist and the Director of the Institute. Israel's very first successful heart transplant actually used a stolen heart.

In 2009, self-described "matchmaker" Levy Izhak Rosenbaum, an

Israeli living in Brooklyn, was apprehended by the FBI for brokering the sale of black-market kidneys buying them for $10,000 and up-selling them for as much as $160,000. The Justice Department charged Rosenbaum with conspiracy to commit human organ trafficking. Rosenbaum worked with Sammy Shem-Tov in Jerusalem to lure young men and women to sell their kidneys. Throughout the 1990s, Rosenbaum was the man to go to among Israeli "transplant tourists" looking for a safer though pricier option than India or Romania, "more familiar than Istanbul, and less distant than Durban, South Africa," among the dozens of destinations offered by Israeli brokers arranging the transplants abroad. According to the Associated Press in 2009:

> Nancy Scheper-Hughes, an anthropology professor at the University of California at Berkeley and the author of an upcoming book on human organ trafficking, said that she has been tracking the Brooklyn-connected ring for 10 years and that her contacts in Israel have called Rosenbaum "the top man" in the United States. Scheper-Hughes said she was told Rosenbaum carried a gun, and when a potential organ seller would get cold feet, Rosenbaum would use his finger to simulate firing a gun at the person's head. Rosenbaum was arrested in a sweeping federal case that began as an investigation into money laundering and trafficking in kidneys and fake designer bags. It mushroomed into a political corruption probe, culminating in the arrests this week of 44 people, including three New Jersey mayors, various other officials, and five rabbis.

As Benyamin Cohen of *Slate* would have you believe, rabbis trafficking in black market organs "uncovers more complicated issues," which is the parlance of any Establishment hack trying to obscure something morally reprehensible and/or deeply contradicting of the narrative, especially when, like Cohen, it involves that of his co-ethno-religionists. It is telling that Hollywood closed ranks and offered up a few token hides like Harvey Weinstein during the #MeToo scandals, but otherwise protected its own. Similarly, the Jeffrey Epstein/Ghislaine Maxwell underage trafficking was also kept under wraps, mostly with closed lips and disavowals, but also with a very suspicious death.

We know prominent figures such as former Israeli Prime Minister Ehud Barak held a multi-million-dollar business partnership with Jeffrey Epstein until at least 2015, and in 2004, Epstein gave Barak $2.3 million for "research." Former Reddit CEO and "diversity consulting non profit" head Ellen Pao said that "we knew about her [Maxwell] supplying underage girls for sex" from at least 2011. Epstein was very close with the billionaire Les Wexner—handled his finances in fact—and in 2003, Wexner told *Vanity Fair* that Epstein had "excellent judgment and unusually high standards." Epstein's charity donated to the New York Jewish Federation and in 2008, Epstein made a gargantuan $46 million donation to one of Wexner's charities. Alan Dershowitz is another prominent Jew to be connected to Epstein. This is all trying to be kept as quiet as possible.

As disturbing as all of this is, it is just the tip of the iceberg. Whether it be the immense profits accrued from selling opium to the Chinese market by the Jewish Sassoon family, the black market during Soviet communism or in trafficking banned imported items under Catherine the Great, the Jewish role in the Trans-Atlantic Slave Trade, organ trafficking, or baby trafficking and child pornography, we see an outsized Jewish role—more often than not Jewish centrality—in these global operations.

Epstein and Maxwell are far from alone in sex trafficking as we've seen, and that already odious endeavor is compounded when we add children and minors. In the summer of 2018, Colombia issued an international arrest warrant for Israeli citizen Assi Ben-Mosh, who local police told *El Heraldo* "ran an international human trafficking, drug dealing and sex tourism network" through a hotel he owned. By December, the number stood at fourteen Israelis suspected by Colombian authorities to include child sex trafficking in their network, which marketed tour packages from Israel to Colombia. Ben-Mosh's network allegedly extended to Ecuador, Brazil, and Mexico. According to a December 10th report from *The Times of Israel*:

> Colombian authorities said Israeli tourists would stay at hotels and take yacht trips and go to drug and alcohol-fueled private parties where women and minors were offered as "sex slaves." The children and teens were paid $63-126 for each "meeting" with Israeli tourists, and were forced to join a WhatsApp group called "Purim," presumably named for the drunken celebrations that take place around the Jewish holiday, the Ynet news site reported. Members of the network established tourism sites and hotels throughout the country, giving the operation an outward veneer of respectability. However, at the same time, they targeted boys and girls who came from troubled homes or had a background of financial difficulties, and forced them into sex work. Proceeds from the trafficking ring were then reinvested into property and companies.... According to a report by Hadashot, one of the Israelis is also being held on suspicion of murder and others are also suspected of money laundering.

In the year 2000, an Israeli diplomat by the name of Arie Scher and another Jewish man named George Schteinberg were found to have been running a child prostitution ring in Rio de Janeiro for Jewish tourists from Israel. Schteinberg, a teacher of Hebrew and social studies, had been recruiting poor children to pimp out to their clients, as well as photographing these children for nine different Hebrew-language child pornography websites. Schteinberg was nabbed by the police, but Scher took refuge in the Israeli embassy before being shuttled off to Israel.

This is a long-running and pervasive problem that is not just limited to child pornography but includes other kinds of sex trafficking, drug trafficking, organ trafficking, and money laundering, with Israel as the hub and many members of the Jewish Diaspora part of this intricate global network. This is without question a consequence of globalism, a process that has in no small part been driven by Jews and the advancement of Jewish interests at the expense of pretty much everyone else outside of their useful gentile functionaries. As an example of the grisly intersection of regime-change wars and organ trafficking, Carla del Ponte, chief prosecutor at The Hague tribunal for Balkan war crimes, wrote in her 2008 book *The Hunt: Me and War Criminals* that under the aegis of the NATO- and US-backed scum in the Kosovo Liberation Army, hundreds of young Serbian prisoners were taken from Kosovo to Albania to have their organs removed and sold on the black market.

Later in the year 2000, in Italy, three journalists exposed a Jewish-run child pornography ring that was doing business in Italy, Sweden, and the United States. Instead of running their documentary, their Jewish boss, Gad Lerner, fired them, accusing them of "blood libel," in what seems like a knee-jerk response. The journalists had discovered that the ring was tied to a massive child pornography syndicate in Murmansk, Russia, which was also run by Jews. Law enforcement apprehended some of their sellers in Milan, Italy, and some of their buyers in Stockholm, Sweden, in September 2000. The FBI arrested the Jewish Seth Bekenstein (brother of Bain Capital's Josh Bekenstein) in December 2000 on charges of possession of child pornography with intent to distribute. The Russian syndicate bosses in Russia were arrested but released after orchestrating some kind of deal with the authorities. Seth Bekenstein was sentenced to just eighteen months in prison, however several years later and having relocated to Mexico, Bekenstein was arrested when he visited Portland, Oregon in February 2011 for sexual exploitation of minors and transporting child pornography. The contents of the pornography in Bekenstein's possession upon his first arrest is stomach-turning:

Some of the child pornography was extreme, even for child pornography. Its highest-priced wares were videos in which children were tortured to death on camera, after they were raped. There were scenes of little boys or girls, sick with fear, begging for their lives, before their bodies were cut open and their organs were removed, one by one.

Conclusion

The system does not and cannot exist to satisfy human needs. Instead, it is human behavior that has to be modified to fit the needs of the system...Man in the future will no longer be a creation of nature, or of chance, or of God...but a manufactured product.

–Ted Kaczynski

Without question, the long shadow cast over the earth today is one of evil. Of this there can be no doubt. Deception being the central method by which the ruling class operates, the hall of mirrors created through media, academia, and sham political "discourse" is rife with enough wild distortions to drive anyone into confusion and, perhaps, madness. With technology as a force multiplier, and with a likely assist from artificial intelligence if not now then certainly imminent, the ability to coordinate from behind the scenes and obfuscate "on stage" is made that much more potent. Illusion and delusion rule while the self-styled "masters of mankind" proceed to shape the globe in their hideous image.

I cannot stress enough the all-encompassing nature of this project. As we have seen the connections abound in this book, it should give the reader no comfort to see where this is headed and how the next mutation of this system—what the World Economic Forum founder Klaus Schwab calls the Fourth Industrial Revolution, one based on digitization and transhumanism—essentially has now use for them beyond their temporary utility. Eventually humanity itself will be outsourced, just as so much of the production capacities of the West have been.

Schwab—who has been an associate of the Jewish Henry Kissinger's (also a Davos participant) since his time at Harvard in the mid-1960s—and his WEF was in its first iteration the European Management Forum, with the first European Management Symposium held in 1971 and attended by numerous Harvard academics and other individuals such as IBM President Jacques Maisonrouge, the Jewish Herman Kahn (co-founder of the Hudson Institute, military strategist and systems theorist for the RAND Corporation, a prominent futurist, and considered one of the fathers of scenario planning), and Otto von Habsburg, the last crown prince of the Austro-Hungarian Empire and Vice President then President of the International Paneuropean Union, which published Count Richard von Coudenhove-Kalergi's manifesto *Paneuropa* in 1923.

Kalergi—heavily influenced by his marriage to the Jewish actress Ida Roland and a strange worship of Jews—is most known for what is commonly called the Kalergi Plan derived from his 1925 book *Practical Idealism*, where "Eurasian-Negroids" would replace "the diversity of peoples" with a "diversity of individuals." An associate of both Winston Churchill and Charles de Gaulle as well, Kalergi had a massive influence on the shaping of Europe's (mis)direction in the twentieth and now twenty-first centuries. The European Society Coudenhove-Kalergi awards a prize every two years to major figures who have proven themselves to be committed to Kalergi's vision, including Angela Merkel, Jean-Claude Juncker, and Ronald Reagan. Kalergi was a major supporter of aspects of the visions of American President Woodrow Wilson and the gay Jewish communist Kurt Hiller. In 1921, he joined a Viennese Masonic lodge and the year following, with Otto von Habsburg, founded the International Paneuropean Union. Next, via Wikipedia:

> According to his autobiography, at the beginning of 1924 his friend Baron Louis de Rothschild introduced him to Max Warburg who offered to finance his movement for the next three years by giving him 60,000 gold marks. Warburg remained sincerely interested in the movement for the remainder of his life and served as an intermediate for Coudenhove-Kalergi with influential Americans such as banker Paul Warburg and financier Bernard Baruch.

Baruch, the Warburgs, and the Rothschilds are all Jewish.

Schwab's second Forum meeting in Davos featured former Nazi and NASA rocket scientist Wernher von Braun and the Jewish "industrial democracy" thinker and activist Charles Levinson, who joined DuPont in 1978. Levinson's inclusion is especially notable for it marks the beginning of what we might think of as "corporate activism." The third European Management Symposium in 1973 featured a speech by Italian industrialist Aurelio Peccei summarizing *The Limits to Growth*, a book echoing the concerns of Thomas Malthus and Peccei's contemporaries such as Paul Ehrlich that had been commissioned by the Club of Rome, which he co-founded and served as its first president. The Club was founded at David Rockefeller's estate in Bellaggio, Italy in 1968. This is the same *David Rockefeller* who founded the Trilateral Commission with Zbigniew

Brzezinski (Board member of the Council on Foreign Relations from 1972-1977) in 1973; Rockefeller was also Chairman of the Board of the Council on Foreign Relations from 1970–1985.

Along with the Ford Foundation, the Rockefeller Foundation began pumping significant funding into the Council in the late 1930s; additionally, Paul Warburg was a member of the Board from its establishment until 1932. The Warburg's and other major Jewish Wall Street financiers—as well as other major Jewish bankers such as Olof Aschberg—were the primary bankrollers of the Bolsheviks in Russia. Other former Council on Foreign Relations Board members from the past include: George H.W. Bush, Henry Kissinger, Walter Lippmann, Paul Volcker, Allen Dulles, Alan Greenspan, Cyrus Vance, Richard B. "Dick" Cheney, William S. Cohen, Richard C. Holbrooke, Donna Shalala, Robert Zoellick, Madeleine Albright, Tom Brokaw, Colin Powell, Penny Pritzker, and George Soros. Some active members include Lorene Powell Jobs, Larry Fink, and Janet Napolitano. Notable Club of Rome members have included Mikhail Gorbachev, Joe Stiglitz, and Pierre Trudeau.

We cannot reduce things into false binaries such as communism versus capitalism, as I have plainly illustrated. Neoliberalism and neoconservatism—two sides of the same coin—are at present paving the way for the Fourth Industrial Revolution, which will combine all of the worst aspects (and most beneficial to the ruling class) of the system that have come before. But it is not even about systems in the sense that debating ideology and systems is reserved for those without power to become blinded by that which would ultimately subjugate humanity anyway. The will-to-power is something the ruling class has in spades, and the will to continue to consolidate that power is even stronger. They're not going to honor some silly election result they set up to keep us all distracted while they continue to choke out the possibilities of independent existence for any of us. They will use whatever means they have or can invent to hold power and expand it. They do not worry if the social credit model instituted by the Chinese Communist Party which is surely coming is consistent with (fill in the blank: "our values," "the free market," etc.). What matters is that as a means of social control *it works*.

And no, this is not some fantastical conspiracy theory: in December 2020 four researchers from the International Monetary Fund (IMF) posited that a user's internet search history using "machine learning" should form a vital component of said user's credit score, all the more vital as we transition to fully digital currency. Publicly, "cancel culture" does a pretty effective job of wiping out Wrongthink, but this invasive measure goes much further. Eventually, Klaus Schwab has written that augmented individuals will be able to live "Yelp" anyone's social credit score they see.

The so-called "open society" is one that will by design eventually descend into chaos, for eventually the New World Order will use this to their advantage: *ordo ab chao* ("order out of chaos"). Every wedge is used to break apart solid structures from social cohesion to the family—consider "diversity," "radical individualism," transgenderism, et cetera. These are all designed to create a singular entity, both individualistic in all the wrong ways and collectivist in the same (or right ways from their perspective), totally reliant on the state/mega-corporation(s) to be molded however the "elites" see fit. They want wet clay for their golems, and that is what they are getting. They "open up" to eventually lock down. They want total control, and they are playing for keeps.

It is my sincere hope that this book has allowed the reader to see behind the veil and witness the true nature of the globalist One World project sold as something quite different than its grisly reality.

All is not lost, however. These are, in fact, only the opening salvos in the coming struggle for humanity, and armed with this information and a greater awareness of the true threats and of the true enemy, the way I see it, we've only just begun to take back our sovereignty and our souls. In closing I ask you: Will you struggle to be truly free, or will you resign yourself to ignominious slavery?

Appendix A: World Bank and IMF Meeting

Major organizations represented at the World Bank and IMF's annual meeting in 2019:

The Open Society Foundations
American Jewish World Service
International Renaissance Foundation
Ministry for Foreign Affairs of Finland
Citibank
US Department of Commerce
The United Nations
International Organization for Migration (IOM)
Oxfam International / Oxfam America / Oxfam GB
Islamic Relief USA
Strength in Diversity Centre, Nigeria
US-India Strategic Partnership Forum
The Union of Arab Banks
Bretton Woods Project
Norwegian Refugee Council USA
World Economic Forum
Council on Foreign Relations
International Rescue Committee
Bill and Melinda Gates Foundation
Policy Lab
The Brookings Institution
African Forum and Network on Debt and Development
Chamber of Digital Commerce
World Bank / The World Bank Group
Cross Border Benefits Alliance, Europe
Center for International Private Enterprise
ActionAid UK
Pew Research Center
Friedrich-Ebert-Stiftung
YMCA USA
US-Angola Chamber of Commerce
Ministry of Finance and Development Planning, Venezuela
Catholic Relief Services
Tanenbaum Center for Interreligious Understanding
Human Rights Watch
Open Society Institute Assistance Foundation, Tajikistan
World Savings and Retail Banking Institute
European Association of Cooperative Banks (EACB)
Heinrich Boell Stiftung North America
Somalia NGO Consortium
Uganda Debt Network
Soros Foundation, Kazakhstan
Jesuit Refugee Service
Data2X, UN Foundation
Freedom House
Atlantic Council
American University
Open Society Foundations International Migration Initiative
The Rockefeller Foundation
InterAction
Thomson Reuters Foundation
McKinsey & Co.
New York University
EDFI: European Development Finance Institutions
Treasury of Latvia
Central Bank of Somalia
Embassy of Malaysia
Abu Dhabi Commercial Bank
Bank of South Sudan
Bank of Portugal
Central Bank of Nigeria
Qatar Central Bank
Sharjah Islamic Bank

Central Bank of Argentina
Kuwait Fund for Arab Economic Development
Central Bank of Libya
Embassy of Iraq in DC
Government of Belize
Ministry of Commerce and Investment, Saudi Arabia
Embassy of Mexico
Israel Innovation Authority
Government of North Macedonia
Ministry of Foreign Affairs, Greece
Ministry of Finance, Japan
Ministry of Finance and Embassy of Israel
Ministry for Foreign Affairs, Sweden
Embassy of Germany
Ukrgasbank-Ukraine
Reserve Bank of New Zealand
Ministry of Economy of the Republic of Belarus
Embassy of Switzerland
SENELEC (Senegal National Company of Electricity)
Inter-American Development Bank
Embassy of the Kingdom of the Netherlands
Bank of Slovenia
Norwegian Ministry of Foreign Affairs
UK Department for International Development (DFID)
Ministry of Finance, China
Central Bank of the Republic of Turkey
Development Bank of Southern Africa
Embassy of the People's Republic of China in the USA
South African Reserve Bank
Treasury of Kosovo
Swedish International Development Agency (SIDA)
Permanent Mission of Ireland to the UN
The Central Bank of Bangladesh
Binational Agriculture Research and Development, Israel
Government Debt Management Agency, Hungary
Ministry of Finance, Estonia
Ministry of Finance and Treasury of Bosnia and Herzegovina
Central Bank of West African States
Export-Import Bank of the United States
Deutsche Bundesbank
West African Monetary Agency
Ministry of Development & Investments, Greece
National Commission for Privatization, Sierra Leone
US Environmental Protection Agency (EPA)
Deloitte
Google
Lloyds Banking Group
Federal Ministry for Economic Cooperation and Development, Germany
TD Bank
Visa
Mastercard
Morgan Stanley
Goldman Sachs
JP Morgan Chase
Israel Discount Bank of New York
Vodafone
Moonshot Global
Eurasian Development Bank
Pepsi
Credit Suisse
PayPal
Rothschild & Co.
The Rohatyn Group
The Omidyar Network
University of Pennsylvania
Yale University
Frankfurt School
German Agency for International Cooperation (GIZ)
Bloomberg LP
Banco Safra SA, Brazil
University of Chicago
Stanford University

Harvard University / Harvard Kennedy
   School of Government / Harvard
   Graduate School of Education
The Cohen Group
Pfizer
Columbia University
Cornell University
Johns Hopkins University
USAID

Appendix B: Chatham House Funders

The following is a comprehensive list of Chatham House funders for 2018/19. The reader will note the length here, and it is vital the reader understand just how uniform and wide-ranging support for these seismic and destructive projects is:

£500,000 - £999,999
Department for International Development, UK
Foreign & Commonwealth Office, UK
Robert Bosch Stiftung

£250,000 - £499,999
Chevron Ltd
Children's Investment Fund Foundation
John D. and Catherine T. MacArthur Foundation
Open Society Foundations
Public Health England
Royal Dutch Shell

£100,000 - £249,999
AIG
Asfari Foundation
Bill and Melinda Gates Foundation
BP plc
Cabinet Office, UK
Carnegie Corporation of New York
Chatham House Foundation
CLP Holdings Ltd
European Commission
ExxonMobil Corporation
ExxonMobil Foundation
EY
Garvin Brown IV
Glencore
Global Affairs Canada
Global Challenges Research Fund, UKRI
International Federation of Pharmaceutical Manufacturers & Associations
Janus Friis
Koç Holding
Korea Foundation
MAVA Foundation
Ministry of Foreign Affairs, the Netherlands
Richard Hayden
Stavros Niarchos Foundation
Zoetis

£50,000 - £99,999
Aga Khan Foundation
Barclays
British Red Cross
Deutsche Gesellschaft für Internationale Zusammenarbeit (GmbH)
Equinor
HSBC Holdings
Humanity United
IKEA Foundation
Internet Society
Konrad Adenauer Stiftung
Lockheed Martin UK
Marcos Bulgheroni

McKinsey & Company
Ministry of Defence, UK
Ministry of Foreign Affairs, Japan
Ministry of Foreign Affairs, Norway
Mo Ibrahim Foundation
Nomura Foundation

Norwegian Agency for Development
    Cooperation
Reliance Industries Limited
S&P Global
Sandia National Laboratories
Santander

£25,000 - £49,000
Al Sharq Forum Foundation
Anglo American plc
Baha Bassatne
BHP
British Army
Chris Rokos
Clifford Chance LLP
Corporacion Andina de Fomento
Credit Suisse
Crescent Petroleum
Daiwa Institute of Research
Danish International Development
    Agency
DeepMind Ethics & Society
Eni S.p.A.
European Bank for Reconstruction and
    Development
Federal Department of Foreign Affairs,
    Switzerland
Forum of Strategic Dialogue
Gavin Boyle
Herbert Smith Freehills LLP
Huawei Technologies
Institut Montaigne
Institute of National Security Strategy
Intesa Sanpaolo S.p.A.
Japan Bank for International
    Cooperation
JETRO London
JLL
JP Morgan Securities Plc
KPMG LLP

Leonardo S.p.A.
Linklaters Business Services
Ministry of Defence, Finland
Ministry of Defence, Norway
Ministry of Finance, Japan
Mitsubishi Corporation
Mitsui & Co. Europe plc
Mohamed Mansour
National Endowment for Democracy
Orsted UK
Refinitiv
Richard Sharp
Rio Tinto Ltd
Rockefeller Foundation
Rolls-Royce plc
Schlumberger Limited
Simon Patterson
Sir Simon Robertson
Sir Trevor Chinn CVO
Skoll Global Threats Fund
Standard Chartered Bank
Swedish International Development
    Cooperation Agency
SystemIQ
Taipei Representative Office in the
    United Kingdom
Tim Bunting
Tim Jones
Total S.A.
UPS Europe
World Health Organisation

£10,000 - £24,999
Accenture
Aiteo
Amit Bhatia

Anadarko Petroleum Corporation
Atkin Foundation
B & S Europe

Appendix B: Chatham House Funders

BAE Systems plc
Baillie Gifford & Co
Bank of America Merrill Lynch (BAML)
Bayer AG
BBC
BlackRock Investment Management (UK) Ltd
BNP Paribas
Boeing Deutschland GmbH
Brown Advisory
BT Group plc
Castlereagh Associates
CDC Group Plc
Celeres Investments
China International Capital Corporation
Citi
City of London
Control Risks
Dame Clara Furse DBE
David and Lucile Packard Foundation
De Beers Group Services UK Ltf
Deloitte
Delonex Energy
Department for International Trade, UK
Department of Foreign Affairs and Trade, Australia
Dr Allen Sangines-Krause
Dr Annalisa Jenkins
DTCC (The Depository Trust & Clearing Corporation)
Eaton Vance Management
EI Advisory Ltd
Embassy of the People's Republic of China
Embassy of the Republic of Angola
Embassy of the Republic of Korea
Eurofighter Jagdflugzeug GmbH
EuroJet Turbo GmbH
European Climate Foundation
European Scientific Working Group on Influenza
Freshfields Bruckhaus Deringer LLP
FTI Consulting LLP
GardaWorld
Gerson Lehrman Group Ltd.
GlaxoSmithKline Services Unlimited
GMF Black Sea Trust
Great Britain Sasakawa Foundation
Henry Luce Foundation
Hiroshima Prefectural Government
Honeywell International
Huw Jenkins
International Committee of the Red Cross
International Crisis Group
International Development Research Centre, Canada
International Maritime Organization
Investec Asset Management
Japan Economic Foundation
Jersey Finance Limited
Kuwait Petroleum Corporation
LetterOne
Lloyds Bank
Lloyd's Register Group
Lutheran World Relief
Marc & Isabelle Hotimsky
Martin Fraenkel
MetLife
Microsoft Limited
Ministry of Foreign Affairs and Trade, the Republic of Ireland
Moody's Invetors Service Limited
Morgan Stanley
NATO Defense College
Nomura International plc
Norinchukin Bank
North Atlantic Treaty Organization
OHB SE
Olayan Europe Limited
Oliver Wyman
Organisation for the Prohibition of Chemical Weapons
Paul Rivlin
Petrofac Services Limited
Pew Charitable Trusts
Prince Mahidol Award Foundation

Prudential plc
Richard Lounsberry Foundation
Rolls-Royce plc
Rolls-Royce Power Systems AG
Royal Bank of Scotland
S.P. Lohia
Saudi Petroleum Overseas Ltd
Scottish Power
Sir Evelyn de Rothschild and Lady Lynn Forester de Rothschild
Sir Joseph Hotung
Smith Richardson Foundation
Société Générale
S-RM Intelligence and Risk Consulting
Staatsolie Maatschappij Suriname N.V.
Stephen Brenninkmeijer
Stiftung Mercator

Sumitomo Mitsui Banking Corporation Europe Limited
The Economist
The Future of Russia Foundation
The Kamini and Vindi Banga Family Trust
Tony Gumbiner
Toshiba Corporation
Tullow Oil plc
UK Labour Party
US Department of State
Vanguard Asset Services, Ltd
Vodafone
Volkswagen AG
Waterloo Foundation
Willis Towers Watson
Wood Mackenzie Power and Renewables

£3,000 - £9,999

Actis
Aegila Capital Management
AETS France
Agility Global Logistics FZE
Air Liquide
Airbus
Akbank
Alaco Ltd
Albany Associates (International) Ltd
Alexander Soros
Alfred Herrhausen Gesellschaft
Alison Myners
Allen & Overy
Amnesty International
Andrew Farran
ANZ Bank
APCO Worldwide
Apple
Arawak Energy Limited
ArcelorMittal
Argentem Creek Partners LP
Argus Media Ltd
Asahi Shimbun (Europe)
Associated British Ports

Aviva
Baker & McKenzie LLP
Banca d'Italia
Bank of England
Bank of Japan
BD Global Health
BDO
Bloomberg
BMO Global Asset Management
BPL Global
Breakthrough Media
Brenthurst Foundation
British Council
British Library
Brown Brothers Harriman
Bruno Deschamps
Cadwalader
Casey Family Programs
Caspar Romer
Catherine Petitgas
Catherine Zennström
Catia von Huetz & Rattan Chadha
Cayman Islands Islands Government, Policy Coordination Unit

CBS News
CCC Group Companies
Centre for Army Leadership
Cleary Gottlieb Steen & Hamilton
Clyde & Co
CNOOC International
Coface
Coffey
Covington & Burling LLP
CRU International Ltd
Cultural Entrepreneurship Institute Berlin
Curtis, Mallet-Prevost, Colt & Mosle LLP
Darktrace Limited
David Archer
David Pearl
David Pollock
DBJ Europe Limited
DBRS Ratings Ltd
Debevoise & Plimpton LLP
Department of Health, UK
Deutsche Börse Group
Diageo
Elena & Oleg Koshikov
Embassy of Algeria
Embassy of Austria
Embassy of Belgium
Embassy of Brazil
Embassy of Chile
Embassy of Finland
Embassy of France
Embassy of Germany
Embassy of Greece
Embassy of Hungary
Embassy of Ireland
Embassy of Israel
Embassy of Italy
Embassy of Japan
Embassy of Romania
Embassy of Sweden
Embassy of Switzerland
Embassy of the Arab Republic of Egypt
Embassy of the Argentine Republic
Embassy of The Czech Republic
Embassy of the Kingdom of Bahrain
Embassy of the Kingdom of the Netherlands
Embassy of the Republic of Indonesia
Embassy of the Republic of Iraq
Embassy of the Republic of Poland
Embassy of the Republic of the Sudan
Embassy of The Republic of Turkey
Embassy of the Royal Kingdom of Saudi Arabia
Embassy of the State of Qatar
European Investment Bank
Fitch Ratings
Flint Global
Fr Lürssen Werft GmbH & Co. KG
Frogmore
G4S Risk Consulting Ltd
Gemcorp Capital
Glenn Earle
Global CCS
Globeleq Africa Ltd
Google
Gordon Lawson
Hendrik Du Toit
High Commission for the Islamic Republic of Pakistan
High Commission for the Republic of South Africa
High Commission of Australia
High Commission of Canada
High Commission of India
High Commission of New Zealand
HM Treasury, UK
Hogan Lovells International LLP
Hong Kong Economic & Trade Office
House of Commons Library
House of Lords Library
Humane Society International
Independent Television News
Indian Professionals Forum
INPEX
Institute for Global Change
Interessengemeischaft Deutsche Lutwafte e.V.
International Association of Oil and Gas Producers

International Institute for Environment and Development
Investcorp International Ltd
ITOCHU Corporation
Jamie Reuben
Japan Oil Gas and Metals National Corporation
Japan Petroleum Exploration Co Ltd
Jim Daley
John Swire & Sons Ltd
K&L Gates
K2 Intelligence
King's College London - Department of Political Economy
Kosmos Energy LLC
Krull Corp
Kyodo News
Lara Fares
Legal and General
Liz Mirza
Lucien Farrell
Makuria Investment Management
Marubeni Europe plc
Matheson & Co Ltd
McBain Family Foundation
Michelin
Ministry of Foreign Affairs and Trade, New Zealand
Mishcon de Reya
Mitsubishi Heavy Industries Europe Ltd
Mizuho Bank
Mondi Group
MUFG Bank
NHK Japan Broadcasting Corporation
Nikkei Inc
Noble Energy Inc
Novamont
Oxfam
Oxy
Permira Advisers LLP
Ploughshares Fund
Point 72 UK Ltd
Portland
Power of Nutrition
Qatar Foundation

QBE European Operations
Rabobank International
Reed Smith
Regent's University London - International Relations Department
Rheinmetall MAN Military Vehicles GmbH
Roger Wolf
Ron Sandler CBE
Royal Embassy of Denmark
Royal Embassy of Norway
Saberr
Saipem
Sanofi
Save the Children
Scottish Government
Seven Investment Management
Shearman & Sterling LLP
Shumeet Banerji
Steppe Capital
Sullivan & Cromwell
Susan Burns
SustainAbility
Symantec Security (UK) Ltd
Tangy Morgan
Tata Ltd
Taylor & Francis Group
Telegraph Media Group
Thales
The Guardian
The Yomiuri Shimbun
Tikad
TIU Canada Ukraine Holdco Ltd
Trafigura
Travers Smith LLP
Trina Rackwitz
UBS
UK Defence Solutions Centre
UNICEF
Uniting to Combat NTDs
University of Sussex
Vitol
Wellcome Trust
William Blair
XL Catlin

Zadig Asset Management
Zentrum für Internationale

Friedenseinsätze
Zhong Lun Law Firm

£0 - £2,999

Ana Paula Salinas
Anglia Ruskin University, Department of Humanities and Social Sciences
Asia Foundation
Brunei Darussalam High Commission
Brunel University, Department of Politics & History
Centre for European and International Studies Research
Climate and Land Use Alliance
Climate Focus North America Inc.
Commonwealth Parliamentary Association Secretariat
Cyd Harris
Delya Allakhverdova
Doughty Street Chambers
Ellen Comberg
Embassy of Armenia
Embassy of Bangladesh
Embassy of Costa Rica
Embassy of El Salvador
Embassy of Georgia
Embassy of Iceland
Embassy of Kuwait
Embassy of Lebanon
Embassy of Luxembourg
Embassy of Mexico
Embassy of Monaco
Embassy of Mongolia
Embassy of Philippines
Embassy of Portugal
Embassy of Spain
Embassy of the Dominican Republic
Embassy of the Hashemite Kingdom of Jordan
Embassy of the Republic of Azerbaijan
Embassy of the Republic of Belarus
Embassy of the Republic of Bulgaria
Embassy of the Republic of Croatia
Embassy of the Republic of Estonia
Embassy of the Republic of Kazakhstan
Embassy of the Republic of Latvia
Embassy of the Republic of Lithuania
Embassy of the Republic of Macedonia
Embassy of the Republic of Moldova
Embassy of the Republic of Serbia
Embassy of the Republic of Slovenia
Embassy of the Republic of Uzbekistan
Embassy of the Republic of Yemen
Embassy of the Slovak Republic
Embassy of Ukraine
Energy Intelligence Group
ERSTE Stiftung
European Endowment for Democracy
European Fund for the Balkans
Frances Reynolds
General Secretariat of the Council of the European Union
Goodenough College
Government of Gibraltar
High Commission for the Republic of Mozambique
High Commission for the Republic of Rwanda
High Commission for the Republic of Singapore
High Commission of Cyprus
High Commission of the Republic of Seychelles
High Commission of the United Republic of Tanzania
HP Inc UK limited
Ida Levine
Janine Freiha
Kathryn Raphael
King's College London, Department of War Studies
Kurdistan Regional Government
Kuwait Investment Office
League of Arab States
London School of Economics, Department of International Relations

Loughborough University London, Institute of Diplomacy and International Governance
Maria Sukkar
Maya Rasamny
Nanyang Technological University, S. Rajaratnam School of International Studies
National Institute for African Studies
NEPAD Secretariat
Overseas Development Institute
Petra Horvat
Porticus Foundation
Quebec Government Office
Rotary International
Royal College of Defence Studies
RTI International
Saferworld
Saori Sugeno
School of Oriental and African Studies (CISD)
Sightsavers
Susan Walton
The Elders Foundation
United Nations Economic and Social Commission for Western Asia
United Nations High Commissioner for Refugees
United Nations University, MERIT
University College London, Department of Political Science (School of Public Policy)
University College London, School of Slavonic and East European Studies
University of Bath, Department of Politics, Languages and International Studies
University of Birmingham, School of Politics and Society
University of East Anglia, School of Politics, Philosophy, Language and Communication Studies
University of Kent, Department of Politics & International Relations
University of Newcastle, Department of Politics
University of Notre Dame, London Global Gateway
War Child UK
Webster University Geneva, Department of International Relations
World Animal Protection
World Food Programme
Yvonne Winkler

Appendix C: ICIJ Media Partners

The full list of the International Consortium of Investigative Journalists' media partners:

15min.lt (Lithuania)
24Chasa (Bulgaria)
ABC (Australia)
ABC Color (Paraguay)
Aftenposten (Norway)
Al Nahar TV (Egypt)
Alalam Aljadeed (Iraq)
L'Alternative (Togo)
amaBhungane Centre for Investigative Journalism (South Africa)
ANCIR (South Africa)
ARIJ (Jordan)
Aristegui (Mexico)
Armando.info (Venezuela)
BBC Panorama (United Kingdom)
Búsqueda (Uruguay)
El Trece (Argentina)
CBC/Radio-Canada (Canada)
Center for Investigative Reporting in Pakistan (Pakistan)
Centro de Periodismo Investigativo (Puerto Rico)
Charlotte Observer (United States)
Ciper (Chile)
Columbia University (United States)
CommonWealth (Taiwan)
Confidencial (Nicaragua)
Connectas (Colombia / Panama)
Consejo de Redacción (Colombia)
Convoca (Peru)
Daily Monitor (Uganda)
Daily Nation (Kenya)
DataBaseAR (Costa Rica)
De Tijd (Belgium)
Delo (Slovenia)
Dépêches du Mali (Mali)
Direkt36 (Hungary)
DR (Denmark)
L'Economiste du Faso (Burkina Faso)
Efecto Cocuyo (Venezuela)
El Comercio (Ecuador)
El Confidencial (Spain)
El Faro (El Salvador)
El Universo (Ecuador)
L'Evenement (Niger)
Expresso (Portugal)
Falter (Austria)
Fusion (USA)
Gazeta Wyborcza (Poland)
Guardian (United Kingdom)
Haaretz (Israel)
Het Financiiele Dagblad (Netherlands)
ICIJ (United States)
IDL Reporteros (Peru)
Indian Express (India)
Inkyfada (Tunisia)
Knack (Belgium)
Korea Center for Investigative Journalism/Newstapa (South Korea)
KRIK (Serbia)
Kyiv Post (Ukraine)
Kyodo News (Japan)
L'Espresso (Italy)
lexpress.mu (Mauritius)
La Nación (Argentina)
La Prensa (Panama)
La Sexta (Spain)
Le Desk (Morocco)
Le Matin Dimanche (Switzerland)
Le Monde (France)
Le Soir (Belgium)
Malaysiakini (Malaysia)

Mcclatchy (United States)
Ink Centre for Investigative Journalism (Botswana)
MO* (Belgium)
NDR (Germany)
Novaya Gazeta (Russia)
O Estado de S. Paulo (Brazil)
OCCRP (Eastern Europe)
Ojo Público (Peru)
ORF (Austria)
OuestAf (Senegal)
Pagina 12 (Argentina)
El Pitazo (Venezuela)
Poderopedia Venezuela (Venezuela)
Politiken (Denmark)
Premium Times (Nigeria)
Premières Lignes (France)
Proceso (Mexico)
Protagon (Greece, Cyprus)
Radio AmmanNET (Jordan)
Radio NZ (New Zealand)
Rede TV (Brazil)
Reykjavík Media (Iceland)
Rise (Romania)
RMJI (Mali)
Rozana FM (Syria)
Runrun.es (Venezuela)
Semanario Universidad (Costa Rica)
Sonntagszeitung (Switzerland)
SVT (Sweden)
Süddeutsche Zeitung (Germany)
Tempo (Indonesia)
The Asahi Shimbun (Japan)
The Australian Financial Review (Australia)
The Irish Times (Ireland)
The Malta Independent (Malta)
The Miami Herald (United States)
The Namibian (Namibia)
The New York Times (United States)
The Washington Post (United States)
Times of Malta (Malta)
Toronto Star (Canada)
Trinidad Express (Trinidad and Tobago)
Trouw (Netherlands)
TVI24 (Portugal)
TVNZ (New Zealand)
Univisión (United States)
UOL (Brazil)
Vedemosti (Russia)
Verdade (Mozambique)
VOA Zimbabwe (Zimbabwe)
WDR (Germany)
YLE (Finland)
České centrum pro investigativní žurnalistiku (Czech Republic)

Appendix D: ECRE Member List

The European Council on Refugees and Exiles' (ECRE) member list. ECRE also has international partnerships with organizations not based in Europe.

Member	Country
ACCEM	Spain
Active Citizen Europe	Belgium
aditus	Malta
Aitima	Greece
Amnesty International - EU Office	Brussels-International
Amnesty International Sweden	Sweden
Arbeiterwohlfahrt	Germany
ARC Foundation	United Kingdom
Asam	Turkey
ASGI	Italy
Asilo in Europa	Italy
AsyLex	Switzerland
Asylkoordination Österreich	Austria
Asylum Protection Center	Serbia
Belgrade Centre for Human Rights	Serbia
British Red Cross	United Kingdom
British Refugee Council	United Kingdom
Bulgarian Helsinki Committee	Bulgaria
Bulgarian Red Cross	Bulgaria
Caritas Europa	Brussels-International

Member	Country
Caritas Germany	Germany
Caritas Luxembourg	Luxembourg
Caritas Sweden	Sweden
CCME-CEC	Brussels-International
CEAR	Spain
Centre for Peace Studies	Croatia
CEPAIM	Spain
Civil Rights Program Kosovo	Kosovo*
Croatian Law Centre	Croatia
Cyprus Refugee Council	Cyprus
Danish Refugee Council	Denmark
Der Partitätische Gesamtverband	Germany
Diaconia Germany	Germany
Diakonie Refugee Service	Austria
Dutch Council for Refugees	The Netherlands
Entraide Pierre Valdo	France
Estonian Refugee Council	Estonia
Female Fellows	Germany
Finnish Refugee Advice Centre	Finland
Flemish Refugee Action	Belgium
Forum Réfugiés-Cosi	France
France Terre d'Asile	France
French Refugee council	France
German Red Cross	Germany
Globally Connected	Brussels-International

Member	Country
Greek Council for Refugees	Greece
Greek Forum of Refugees - GFR	Greece
Grupa 484	Serbia
Hebrew Immigrant Aid Society	Ukraine
Helsinki Foundation for Human Rights	Poland
Human Rights League - Slovakia	Slovakia
Hungarian Helsinki Committee	Hungary
ICMC	Brussels-International
ICORN	Norway
ILPA	United Kingdom
International Eurasia Press Fund	Azerbaijan
International Rescue Committee	Brussels-International
IRCT	Brussels-International
Irish Refugee Council	Ireland
Island Panorama Centre	Iceland
Italian Council for Refugees	Italy
Jesuit Refugee Service - Europe	Brussels-International
Jesuit Refugee Service Malta	Malta
Latvian Centre for Human Rights	Latvia
Lithuanian Red Cross	Lithuania
Macedonian Young Lawyers' Association	North Macedonia
Memorial Human Rights Centre	Russian Federation
Menedék	Hungary
MOSAICO – Action for Refugees	Italy

Member	Country
MUDEM - Refugee Support Center	Turkey
Mülteci-Der	Turkey
NANSEN	Belgium
NOAS	Norway
Norwegian Refugee Council	Norway
OPU	Czech Republic
Oxfam Italia Intercultura	Italy
Passerell	Luxembourg
PIC - Legal-Informational Centre for NGOs	Slovenia
Plattform Asyl Für Menschenrechte	Austria
Portuguese Refugee Council	Portugal
Pro Asyl	Germany
Psychosocial Innovation Network (PIN)	Serbia
Red Cross EU	Brussels-International
Red Cross Iceland	Iceland
Refugee Action	United Kingdom
Refugee Rights Association	Cyprus
Refugee Rights Turkey	Turkey
Rescate	Spain
Romanian National Council for Refugees	Romania
Scottish Refugee Council	United Kingdom
Slovenská humanitná rada	Slovakia
Solentra	Belgium
Solidarity Now	Greece

Member	Country
SOS Children's Villages	Brussels-International
Soutien Belge OverSeas – SB OverSeas	Belgium
Spanish Red Cross	Spain
STAR (Student Action for Refugees)	United Kingdom
Swedish Red Cross	Sweden
Swedish Refugee Advice Centre	Sweden
Swiss Refugee Council	Switzerland
The Centre for Refugee Support	Belarus
The Swedish Network of Refugee Support Groups	Sweden
UAF	The Netherlands
União de Refugiados Em Portugal – UREP	Portugal
Vaša prava BiH	Bosnia and Herzegovina
Verein Projekt Integrationshaus	Austria

Appendix E: ODI Major Funders

A more complete list of the Overseas Development Institute's (ODI) major funders:

GIZ
Paul Hamlyn Foundation
UK Department for International Development (DFID)
USAID
MasterCard Foundation
United Nations
IKEA Foundation
Irish Aid
European Union
Netherlands Ministry of Foreign Affairs
Department of Foreign Affairs and Trade Australia (DFAT)
Swedish International Development Cooperation Agency (SIDA)
Agence Française de Développement (AFD)
PricewaterhouseCoopers
Swiss Agency for Development and Cooperation (SDC)
Government of Uganda
European Commission
Hivos East Africa
New Venture Fund
OECD
World Bank
Oxfam GB
University of Manchester
Chatham House
Norwegian Refugee Council
Bank of Papua New Guinea
Rockefeller Foundation
Danish International Development Agency (DANIDA)
IMF
Save the Children
Asian Development Bank (ADB)
International Rescue Committee (IRC)
Danish Refugee Council
Heinrich Böll Foundation
New Zealand Agency for International Development (NZAID)
War Child
Adam Smith International
Unilever UKCR Ltd
Norwegian Agency for Development Cooperation (Norad)
Catholic Relief Services
Christian Aid

Appendix F: MPI Major Funders

The list of the Migration Policy Institute's major funders:

Western Union
International Rescue Committee (IRC)
IOM
JM Kaplan Fund
Walmart
US Chamber of Commerce
Inter-American Development Bank
MacArthur Foundation
US Census Bureau
US Department of Homeland Security
Rockefeller Foundation
Bill and Melinda Gates Foundation
OECD
UNHCR
World Health Organization
Ford Foundation
European Commission
SEIU
Manhattan Institute
Unbound Philanthropy
Delegation of the European Union to the United States
UN Office for the Coordination of Humanitarian Affairs
Office of Refugee Resettlement, US Department of Health and Human Services
Carnegie Corporation
Government of Mexico, Ministry of Foreign Affairs and Secretariat of the Interior
Bureau of Population, Refugees, and Migration, US Department of State
Government of Italy, Ministry of Labor and Social Policy
Danish Refugee Council
Booz Allen Hamilton
Government of the Netherlands
Centre on Migration, Policy and Society (COMPAS), Oxford University
King Baudouin Foundation
Foundation for Population, Migration and Environment (BMU), Switzerland
Government of Canada, Citizenship and Immigration
German Marshall Fund of the United States
Catholic Legal Immigration Network, Inc.
Annie E. Casey Foundation
Boston Foundation
Hamburg Institute for International Economics (HWWA)
Atlantic Philanthropies
Government of Germany, Bundesministerium des Innern (BMI)
Evelyn and Walter Haas, Jr. Fund
Government of Taiwan, National Immigration Agency
Government of Finland, Ministry of Foreign Affairs
National Center for Border Security and Immigration (NCBSI), University of Arizona
Global Commission on International Migration
Barrow Cadbury Trust
Zellerbach Family Foundation
Urban Institute
US Conference of Catholic Bishops Migration and Refugee Services
WK Kellogg Foundation
Bertelsmann Stiftung
Grantmakers Concerned with

Immigrants and Refugees
Government of Moldova
Government of Greece, Ministry of Foreign Affairs
World Bank
Government of Sweden, Ministry of Justice and Ministry of Employment
Open Society Foundations
Government of Spain, Ministry of Labor and Immigration
Government of Norway, Ministry of Justice and Ministry of Children, Equality and Social Inclusion
Government of the United Kingdom, Home Office and Department of International Development

Appendix G: New American Century

Project for the New American Century Statement of Principles, June 3rd, 1997

American foreign and defense policy is adrift. Conservatives have criticized the incoherent policies of the Clinton Administration. They have also resisted isolationist impulses from within their own ranks. But conservatives have not confidently advanced a strategic vision of America's role in the world. They have not set forth guiding principles for American foreign policy. They have allowed differences over tactics to obscure potential agreement on strategic objectives. And they have not fought for a defense budget that would maintain American security and advance American interests in the new century.

We aim to change this. We aim to make the case and rally support for American global leadership.

As the twentieth century draws to a close, the United States stands as the world's preeminent power. Having led the West to victory in the Cold War, America faces an opportunity and a challenge: Does the United States have the vision to build upon the achievements of past decades? Does the United States have the resolve to shape a new century favorable to American principles and interests?

We are in danger of squandering the opportunity and failing the challenge. We are living off the capital—both the military investments and the foreign policy achievements—built up by past administrations. Cuts in foreign affairs and defense spending, inattention to the tools of statecraft, and inconstant leadership are making it increasingly difficult to sustain American influence around the world. And the promise of short-term commercial benefits threatens to override strategic considerations. As a consequence, we are jeopardizing the nation's ability to meet present threats and to deal with potentially greater challenges that lie ahead.

We seem to have forgotten the essential elements of the Reagan Administration's success: a military that is strong and ready to meet both present and future challenges; a foreign policy that boldly and purposefully promotes American principles abroad; and national leadership that accepts the United States' global responsibilities.

Of course, the United States must be prudent in how it exercises its power. But we cannot safely avoid the responsibilities of global leadership or the costs that are associated with its exercise. America has a vital role in maintaining peace and security in Europe, Asia, and the Middle East. If we shirk our responsibilities, we invite challenges to our fundamental interests. The history of the twentieth century should have taught us that it is important to shape circumstances before crises emerge, and to meet threats before they become dire. The history of this century should have taught us to embrace the cause of American leadership.

Our aim is to remind Americans of these lessons and to draw their consequences for today. Here are four consequences:

- we need to increase defense spending significantly if we are to carry out our global responsibilities today and modernize our armed forces for the future;
- we need to strengthen our ties to democratic allies and to challenge regimes hostile to our interests and values;
- we need to promote the cause of political and economic freedom abroad;
- we need to accept responsibility for America's unique role in preserving and extending an international order friendly to our security, our prosperity, and our principles.

Such a Reaganite policy of military strength and moral clarity may not be fashionable today. But it is necessary if the United States is to build on the successes of this past century and to ensure our security and our greatness in the next.

Signatories:

Elliott Abrams
Gary Bauer
William J. Bennett
Jeb Bush
Dick Cheney
Eliot A. Cohen
Midge Decter
Paula Dobriansky
Steve Forbes

Aaron Friedberg
Francis Fukuyama
Frank Gaffney
Fred C. Ikle
Donald Kagan
Zalmay Khalilzad
I. Lewis Libby
Norman Podhoretz

Dan Quayle
Peter W. Rodman
Stephen P. Rosen
Henry S. Rowen
Donald Rumsfeld
Vin Weber
George Weigel
Paul Wolfowitz

Appendix H: Partnership for NYC

The Partnership for New York City (2020)

CO-CHAIRS

William E. Ford
Co-Chair, Partnership for NYC
CEO, General Atlantic

Steven R. Swartz
Co-Chair, Partnership for NYC
President & CEO, Hearst

PARTNERSHIP OFFICERS

Catherine Engelbert
Secretary, Partnership for NYC
Commissioner, WNBA

George H. Walker
Treasurer, Partnership for NYC
Chairman & CEO, Neuberger Berman Group LLC

Deanna M. Mulligan
Vice Chair, Partnership for NYC
President & CEO, The Guardian Life Insurance Company of America

Kathryn S. Wylde
President & CEO, Partnership for New York City

Kevin P. Ryan
Vice Chair, Partnership for NYC
CEO & Founder, AlleyCorp

EXECUTIVE COMMITTEE

Lee S. Ainslie, III
Managing Partner
Maverick Capital

Jeff T. Blau
Chief Executive Officer
The Related Companies, L.P.

Ajay Banga
Chief Executive Officer
Mastercard

Albert Bourla
Chairman & CEO
Pfizer Inc.

Leon Black
Chairman & CEO
Apollo Management, L.P.

Michael L. Corbat
Chief Executive Officer
Citigroup

James Dimon
Chairman & CEO
JPMorgan Chase & Co.

Blair W. Effron
Co-Founder
Centerview Partners LLC

Catherine Engelbert
Commissioner
WNBA

Laurence D. Fink
Chairman & CEO
BlackRock, Inc.

William E. Ford
Chief Executive Officer
General Atlantic LLC

Jeff Gennette
Chairman & CEO
Macy's, Inc.

Daniel Glaser
President & CEO
Marsh & McLennan Companies, Inc.

Barry M. Gosin
Chief Executive Officer
Newmark Knight Frank

Kelly Grier
U.S. Chairman & Americas Managing Partner
Ernst & Young LLP

Kenneth M. Jacobs
Chairman & CEO
Lazard Ltd

Brad S. Karp
Chair
Paul, Weiss, Rifkind, Wharton & Garrison LLP

Charles R. Kaye
Chief Executive Officer
Warburg Pincus LLC

Henry R. Kravis
Co-Chairman & Co-CEO
Kohlberg Kravis Roberts & Co.

Rochelle B. Lazarus
Chairman Emeritus
Ogilvy & Mather Worldwide

Kewsong Lee
Co-Chief Executive Officer
The Carlyle Group

Martin Lipton
Senior Partner
Wachtell, Lipton, Rosen & Katz

Peter W. May
President & Founding Partner
Trian Partners

John McAvoy
Chairman, President & CEO
Con Edison, Inc.

Deanna M. Mulligan
Chief Executive Officer
The Guardian Life Insurance Company of America

John Paulson
President
Paulson & Co., Inc.

Debbie Perelman
President & CEO
Revlon, Inc.

Charles E. Phillips, Jr.
Chairman
Infor

Steven L. Rattner
Chairman & CEO
Willett Advisors, LLC

Steven Rubenstein
President
Rubenstein Communications, Inc.

Kevin P. Ryan
CEO & Founder
AlleyCorp

Alan D. Schnitzer
Chairman & CEO
The Travelers Companies, Inc.

Alan D. Schwartz
Executive Chairman
Guggenheim Partners, LLC

Stephen A. Schwarzman
Chairman, CEO & Co-Founder
Blackstone

David M. Solomon
Chairman & CEO
Goldman Sachs & Co.

Rob Speyer
President & CEO
Tishman Speyer

Stephen Squeri
Chairman & CEO
American Express Company

Robert K. Steel
Chairman
Perella Weinberg Partners

Steven R. Swartz
President & CEO
Hearst

James S. Tisch
President & CEO
Loews Corporation

Joseph Ucuzoglu
Chief Executive Officer
Deloitte

George H. Walker
Chairman & CEO
Neuberger Berman Group LLC

BOARD OF DIRECTORS

In Memoriam: David Rockefeller
1915-2017

Ellen Alemany
Chairman & CEO
CIT Group Inc.

Robert Bakish
President & CEO
ViacomCBS Inc.

Neil Barr
Managing Partner
Davis Polk & Wardwell LLP

Candace K. Beinecke
Senior Partner
Huges Hubbard & Reed LLP

Stephen Berger
Chairman
Odyssey Investment Partners, LLC

William H. Berkman
Co-Chairman & CEO
Digital Landscape Group, Inc.

Michael W. Blair
Presiding Partner
Debevoise & Plimpton LLP

Kathy Bloomgarden
Chief Executive Officer
Ruder Finn, Inc.

John Bruckner
President, NY
National Grid

Martin S. Burger
Chief Executive Officer
Silverstein Properties, Inc.

H. Rodgin Cohen
Senior Chairman
Sullivan & Cromwell LLP

Stacey Cunningham
President
NYSE

Anthony J. de Nicola
President
Welsh, Carson, Anderson & Stowe

William R. Dougherty
Chairman, Executive Committee
Simpson Tacher & Bartlett LLP

Lynne Doughtie
U.S. Chairman & CEO
KPMG LLP

Brian Duperreault
Chief Executive Officer
American International Group, Inc.

Douglas Durst
Chairman
Durst Organization Inc.

Joel S. Ehrenkranz
Partner & Co-Founder
Ehrenkranz Partners L.P.

Hafize Gaye Erkan
President & Board Member
First Republic Bank

Joseph R. Ficalora
President & CEO
NY Community Bancorp, Inc.

Winston C. Fisher
Partner
Fisher Brothers

Alan H. Fishman
Chairman
Ladder Capital Finance LLC

Mark T. Gallogly
Co-Founder & Managing Principal
Centerbridge Partners

Dexter Goei
Chief Executive Officer
Altice USA

Timothy Gokey
Chief Executive Officer
Broadridge Financial Solutions, Inc.

James P. Gorman
Chairman & CEO
Morgan Stanley

Alan Gorsky
Chairman & CEO
Johnson & Johnson

Johnathan N. Grayer
Chairman & CEO
Weld North LLC

Robin Hayes
Chief Executive Officer
JetBlue Airways Corporation

Jonathan S. Henes
Partner
Kirkland & Ellis LLP

Paul Horgan
Head of U.S. Commercial Insurance
Zurich Insurance Group Ltd

Michael A. Khalaf
President & CEO
MetLife, Inc.

William P. Lauder
Executive Chairman
The Estée Lauder Companies, Inc.

Richard S. LeFrak
Chairman & CEO
The LeFrak Organization

Joey Levin
Chief Executive Officer
IAC

Allan Levine
Chairman & CEO
Global Atlantic Financial Company

Howard W. Lutnick
Chairman & CEO
Cantor Fitzgerald L.P.

Vikram Malhotra
Senior Partner & Chairman of the Americas
McKinsey & Company, Inc.

Joel S. Marcus
Executive Chairman & Founder
Alexandria Real Estate Equities, Inc.

Theodore Mathas
Chairman & CEO
New York Life Insurance Company

Heidi Messer
Co-Founder & Chairman
Collective[i]

Ken Moelis
Chairman & CEO
Moelis & Company

Greg Mondre
Co-Chief Executive Officer
Silver Lake

Thomas Montag
Chief Operating Officer
Bank of America Corporation

Oscar Munoz
Executive Chairman
United Airlines, Inc.

Jon Oringer
Executive Chairman
Shutterstock, Inc.

Douglas L. Peterson
President & CEO
S&P Global

Michael A. Peterson
Chairman & CEO
Peter G. Peterson Foundation

Deirdre Quinn
Co-Founder & CEO
Lafayette 148 New York

Michael Roberts
President & CEO
HSBC Bank USA

James D. Robinson, III
Co-Founder & General Partner
RRE Ventures

Michael I. Roth
Chairman & CEO
Interpublic Group

Steven Roth
Chairman & CEO
Vornado Realty Trust

William C. Rudin
Co-Chairman & CEO
Rudin Management Company, Inc.

Timothy Ryan
U.S. Chairman & Senior Partner
PricewaterhouseCoopers, LLP

Faiza Saeed
Presiding Partner
Cravath, Swaine & Moore LLP

Scott Salmirs
President & CEO
ABM Industries Inc.

Suzanne Shank
President & CEO
Siebert Williams Shank & Co., LLC

Joshua Silverman
Chief Executive Officer
Etsy, Inc.

Charles Stewart
Chief Executive Officer
Sotheby's

Paul J. Taubman
Chairman & CEO
PJT Partners Inc.

Paul Todd
Chief Executive Officer
GLG

Bridget van Kralingen
Senior VP, Global Markets
IBM Corporation

David Winter
Co-Chief Executive Officer
Standard Industries Inc.

Robert Wolf
Chief Executive Officer
32 Advisors, LLC

David M. Zaslav
President & CEO
Discovery, Inc.

Strauss Zelnick
Partner
ZMC

EX-OFFICIO

Sophia Hudson
Partner, Kirkland & Ellis LLP

Richard Jeanneret
Americas Vice Chair
Ernst & Young LLP

Charles Weinstein
Chief Executive Officer
EisnerAmper LLP

Bibliography

Introduction:

Clinton, Hillary. "Remarks at the New Silk Road Ministerial Meeting," New York: US State Department, September 22, 2011. https://2009-2017.state.gov/secretary/20092013clinton/rm/2011/09/173807.htm

Haass, Richard. 2017. "World Order 2.0: The Case for Sovereign Obligation." *Foreign Affairs,* January/February 2017. https://www.foreignaffairs.com/articles/2016-12-12/world-order-20

Inskeep, Steven. "George Soros Discusses Efforts to Spread Democracy." *NPR Morning Edition.* May 9, 2005. https://www.npr.org/templates/story/story.php?storyId=4635465

1: The Open Society Foundations and the Soros Network

Andreou, Aggelos. "Europe's Far-Right Exploits COVID-19 for Anti-Refugee Propaganda." *Balkan Insight,* June 4, 2020. https://balkaninsight.com/2020/06/04/europes-far-right-exploits-covid-19-for-anti-refugee-propaganda/

Aron, Leon. "Russia's Revolution." *Commentary*, November 2002. https://www.commentary.org/articles/leon-aron/russias-revolution/

Bruck, Connie. "The World According to George Soros," *The New Yorker*, January 15, 1995. newyorker.com/magazine/1995/01/23/the-world-according-to-soros

Buldioski, Goran. "Balkan Conspiracy Theories Come to Capitol Hill." *Foreign Policy*, March 28, 2017. https://foreignpolicy.com/2017/03/28/soros-gop-letter-open-society-macedonia-albania/

Fitton, Tom. "US Gives Soros Groups Millions to Destabilize Macedonia's Conservative Government." *Judicial Watch*, February 28, 2017. https://www.judicialwatch.org/corruption-chronicles/u-s-gives-soros-groups-millions-destabilize-macedonias-conservative-govt/

Gaetan, Victor. "Macedonia to George Soros and USAID: Go Away." *The American Spectator*, March 24, 2017. https://spectator.org/macedonia-to-george-soros-and-usaid-go-away/

Klarin, Mirko. "Never Again: Judgments on a Decade of Bestiality." In Open Society Foundations, *Building Open Society.*

Marusic, Sinisa Jakov. "New 'Stop Soros' Movement Unveiled in Macedonia." *Balkan Insight*, January 18, 2017. https://balkaninsight.com/2017/01/18/macedonia-forms-anti-soros-movement-01-18-2017/

Open Society Foundations. *Building Open Society in the Western Balkans: 1991-*

2011. New York: 2011. https://www.opensocietyfoundations.org/uploads/b52ff050-5ec4-4df7-b078-e02cf5374bd9/open-society-western-balkans-20111004.pdf

Open Society Initiative. *Soros Foundations Network 2002 Report.* New York: 2002. https://www.opensocietyfoundations.org/uploads/569ceb5a-5a08-472e-ac5f-00b0c0595cf2/a_complete_report_0.pdf

Open Society Initiative. *Soros Foundations Network 2006 Report.* New York: 2006. https://www.opensocietyfoundations.org/uploads/cbdbf3ce-5497-4a41-adbc-7160c825817e/a_complete_3.pdf

Open Society Initiative. *Soros Foundations Network 2007 Report.* New York: 2007. https://www.opensocietyfoundations.org/uploads/3d4ebf2b-918b-4621-a226-dc7a886d8faf/a_complete_4.pdf

Palmer, Joanne. "Stronger Than the Storm." *Jewish Standard*, December 20, 2013. https://jewishstandard.timesofisrael.com/stronger-than-the-storm/

Papić, Žarko. The Aid Dilemma: Lessons (Not) Learned in Bosnia and Herzegovina. In Open Society Foundations, *Building Open Society.*

Soros, George. "The Capitalist Threat." *The Atlantic,* February 1997. https://www.theatlantic.com/magazine/archive/1997/02/the-capitalist-threat/376773/

The United States Agency for Global Media. *USAGM 2018 Annual Report.* 2018. https://www.usagm.gov/wp-content/uploads/2019/08/USAGM-AR-2018-final.pdf

2: The American Foreign Policy Battering Ram

Barnett, Thomas P.M. *The Pentagon's New Map: War and Peace in the Twenty-First Century.* New York: G.P. Putnam's Sons, 2004.

Baumer, Lilach, Orr Hirschauge and Tomer Ganon "Psy-Group CEO Touted Company's Ability to 'Change Public Discourse' on a National Level." *Calcalist*, September 10, 2018. https://www.calcalistech.com/ctech/articles/0,7340,L-3747246,00.html

Ben Solomon, Ariel. "Exclusive: Intelligence Entrepreneur Joel Zamel Speaks out for First Time Since Mueller Investigation." *Daily Caller,* July 9, 2019. https://dailycaller.com/2019/07/09/exclusive-intelligence-entrepreneur-joel-zamel-speaks-out-for-first-time-since-mueller-investigation/

Bolton, Kerry. "Are American Interests Behind The "Spontaneous" Revolts in North Africa?" *World Affairs: The Journal of International Issues* 15, no. 3. 2011. 12–35. https://www.jstor.org/stable/48504826.

Bolton, Kerry. "Last Empire: How Europe Lost Africa." Accessed September 13, 2021. https://www.kerrybolton.com/last-empire-how-europe-lost-africa/#_edn1

Brychkov, A.S. and G.A. Nikonorov. "Color Revolutions in Russia: Possibility and Reality." *Vestnik Akademii Voennykh Nauk (Journal of the Academy of Military Sciences).* 3 (60). 2017. https://www.armyupress.army.mil/Portals/7/Hot%20Spots/Documents/Russia/C

olor-Revolutions-Brychkov-Nikonorov.pdf
Council of Europe. "Migration from the developing countries to the European industrialised countries." Doc. 7628. September 5, 1996. https://assembly.coe.int/nw/xml/XRef/X2H-Xref-ViewHTML.asp?FileID=7609&lang=EN
Entous, Adam and Ronan Farrow. "Private Mossad for Hire." *The New Yorker*, February 11, 2019. https://www.newyorker.com/magazine/2019/02/18/private-mossad-for-hire
"Estonia: Embassy's Efforts to Promote Racial Tolerance." From the US Embassy in Tallinn to Secretary of State. *WikiLeaks*. June 16, 2006. https://wikileaks.org/plusd/cables/06TALLINN578_a.html
Goldstein, Matthew, Steve Eder, and David Enrich. "The Billionaire Who Stood by Jeffrey Epstein." *The New York Times,* October 12, 2020. Updated October 13, 2020. https://www.nytimes.com/2020/10/12/business/leon-black-jeffrey-epstein.html
Hentoff, Nat. "Dinner with Gen Chi." *The Washington Post,* January 26, 1997. https://www.washingtonpost.com/archive/opinions/1997/01/26/dinner-with-gen-chi/7f40aced-9fec-4490-9c04-604267ff5ac4/
Ignatius, David. "Innocence Abroad: The New World of Spyless Coups." *The Washington Post*, September 22, 1991. https://www.washingtonpost.com/archive/opinions/1991/09/22/innocence-abroad-the-new-world-of-spyless-coups/92bb989a-de6e-4bb8-99b9-462c76b59a16/
Jennings, Ray Salvatore. "Upgrading U.S. Support for Armenia's Postrevolution Reforms." Carnegie Endowment for International Peace. February 14, 2019. https://carnegieendowment.org/2019/02/14/upgrading-u.s.-support-for-armenia-s-postrevolution-reforms-pub-78353
Landler, Mark. "Worldly at 35, and Shaping Obama's Voice." *The New York Times,* March 15, 2013. https://www.nytimes.com/2013/03/16/world/middleeast/benjamin-rhodes-obamas-voice-helps-shape-policy.html
Lavers, Michael K. "Activists: State Department 'has abandoned full support of LGBTI people.'" *Washington Blade*, June 24, 2019. washingtonblade.com/2019/06/24/activists-state-department-has-abandoned-full-support-of-lgbti-people/
Liebkind, Joe. "The Crucial Role of Powerbrokers in International Affairs." *International Policy Digest,* October 17, 2019. https://intpolicydigest.org/the-crucial-role-of-powerbrokers-in-international-affairs/
Margit, Maya. "John Hopkins CEO: Big data could turn coronavirus pandemic around." *The Jerusalem Post,* July 3, 2020. https://www.jpost.com/health-science/johns-hopkins-ceo-big-data-could-turn-coronavirus-pandemic-around-633713
National Endowment for Democracy. *Strategy Document: January 1992.* Washington, D.C., 1992. https://www.ned.org/docs/strategy/1992_Strategy_Document.pdf

Norton, W.W. *9/11 Commission Report.* Official Government Edition. 2004. p. 499. https://rb.gy/fechco.

Ó Colmáin, Gearóid, "Coercive Engineered Migration. Zionism's War on Europe." *Dissident Voice,* January 16, 2016. https://dissidentvoice.org/2016/01/coercive-engineered-migration-zionisms-war-on-europe/

Ó Colmáin, Gearóid. "The Balkanisation of Europe: Neo-Prometheism and Neo-Ottomanism." *Dissident Voice,* January 27, 2016. https://dissidentvoice.org/2016/01/the-balkanisation-of-europe-neo-prometheism-and-neo-ottomanism/

O'Sullivan, John. "In Defense of Nationalism." *The National Interest,* December 1, 2004. https://nationalinterest.org/article/in-defense-of-nationalism-564

Publius, John Q. *The Way Life Should Be?* Ostara Publications. 2020.

Rivers, Caintlin, et al. *Resetting Our Response: Changes Needed in the US Approach to COVID-19.* Baltimore, MD: Johns Hopkins Center for Health Security, 2020. https://www.centerforhealthsecurity.org/our-work/pubs_archive/pubs-pdfs/2020/200729-resetting-our-response.pdf

Roberts, Sam. "Leslie H. Gelb, 82, Former Diplomat and *New York Times* Journalist, Dies." *The New York Times,* September 1, 2019. https://www.nytimes.com/2019/08/31/us/leslie-gelb-dead.html

Scott-Smith, Giles. "The Heineken Factor? Using Exchanges to Extend the Reach of Soft US Power." *American Diplomacy,* June 2011. https://americandiplomacy.web.unc.edu/2011/06/the-heineken-factor/

Shoup, Laurence. *Wall Street's Think Tank: The Council on Foreign Relations and the Empire of Neoliberal Geopolitics, 1976-2014.* Monthly Review Press. 2015.

"State-to-State Cooperation: New Mexico and Israel." *Jewish Virtual Library,* Accessed September 27, 2021. https://www.jewishvirtuallibrary.org/new-mexico-israel-cooperation

Stoddard, Lothrop. *The Revolt Against Civilization: The Menace of the Under-Man.* New York: Charles Scribner's Sons, 1922.

Ungerleider, Neal. "Why This Company Is Crowdsourcing, Gamifying the World's Most Difficult Problems." *Fast Company,* December 6, 2013. https://www.fastcompany.com/3022299/why-this-company-is-crowdsourcing-gamifying-the-worlds-most-difficult-problems

3: The Color Revolutions

Bandeira, Luiz Alberto Moniz. *The Second Cold War: Geopolitics and the Strategic Dimensions.* Springer, 2017.

Bart, Katharina. "Family Feud at Safra Sarasin?" *Finews,* December 9, 2019. https://www.finews.com/news/english-news/39154-safra-sarasin-jacob-safra-david-safra-rivalry-succession

BBC World Service. "Belarus government accused of human rights abuses." *BBC News,* November 11, 1997. http://news.bbc.co.uk/2/hi/europe/29562.stm

Beinart, Peter. "America May Need International Intervention." *The New York*

Times, October 6, 2020. https://www.nytimes.com/2020/10/06/opinion/us-united-nations-election.html

Bolton, Kerry. *Babel Inc: Multiculturalism, Globalisation, and the New World Order.* Black House Publishing, 2019.

Eichner, Itamar. "Report: 25% of wealthiest Russians are Jewish." *Y Net News,* November 2, 2014. https://www.ynetnews.com/articles/0,7340,L-4587086,00.html

"Empowering Independent Media: US Efforts to Foster Free and Independent News Around the World," National Endowment for Democracy. 2018. https://www.cima.ned.org/wp-content/uploads/2015/02/CIMA-Empowering_Independent_Media.pdf

Euronews, AP, and *AFP.* "Belarus crisis: EU calls on Moscow to refrain from intervening." *Euronews,* Updated August 8, 2020. https://www.euronews.com/2020/08/28/belarus-dozens-arrested-at-protests-as-lukashenko-changes-tactics-to-quell-unrest

Gienger, Viola. "Anti-Corruption Reformer Ready for Round Two." *The Atlantic Council Blog,* December 3, 2018. https://www.atlanticcouncil.org/blogs/ukrainealert/anti-corruption-reformer-ready-for-round-two/

Grandstaff, Jacob. "George Soros's Antidemocratic Influence on Romania." *Medium,* May 12, 2018. https://medium.com/@Jacob_Grandstaff/george-soross-antidemocratic-influence-on-romanian-politics-34cedad51774

Grigoryan, Hasmik and Stepan Grigoryan. "European democracy support in Armenia." European Partnership for Democracy. July 2019. https://epd.eu/wp-content/uploads/2019/07/European-democracy-support-in-Armenia.pdf

Harding, Luke. "Belarus president Lukashenko urged to quit: 'Leave before it's too late.'" *The Guardian,* August 13, 2020. https://www.theguardian.com/world/2020/aug/13/belarus-nobel-prize-winner-tells-lukashenko-leave-before-its-too-late

JTA and Ron Kampeas. "Know Your Oligarch: A Guide to the Jewish Billionaires in the Trump-Russia Probe." *Haaretz,* Updated May 28, 2018. https://www.haaretz.com/us-news/know-your-oligarch-a-guide-to-the-jewish-machers-in-the-russia-probe-1.6113189

Kay, Steven. "Montenegro is heading the same way as Belarus. Not enough is being done to avoid disaster." *Euronews,* Updated September 2, 2020. https://www.euronews.com/2020/08/29/montenegro-is-heading-the-same-way-as-belarus-not-enough-is-being-done-to-avoid-disaster-v

Keay, Justin. "Armenia: Making The Velvet Revolution Work." *Global Finance,* October 10, 2019. https://www.gfmag.com/magazine/october-2019/armenia-making-velvet-revolution-work

Luhn, Alec. "National Endowment for Democracy is first 'undesirable' NGO banned in Russia." *The Guardian,* July 28, 2015. https://www.theguardian.com/world/2015/jul/28/national-endowment-for-democracy-banned-russia

McFaul, Michael. "'Meddling' in Ukraine." *Washington Post,* December 21, 2004.

https://www.washingtonpost.com/archive/opinions/2004/12/21/meddling-in-ukraine/5d366823-55e9-4716-9cf8-8b80a816b4ff/

Milner, Andrew. "The CEE Trust: a job well done?" *Alliance,* December 1, 2012. https://www.alliancemagazine.org/analysis/the-cee-trust-a-job-well-done/

Ó Beacháin, Donnacha and Abel Polese. "The Color Revolution Virus and Authoritarian Antidotes." *Demokratizatsiya: The Journal of Post-Soviet Democratization.* Vol. 19, Issue 2. Spring 2011. http://www.demokratizatsiya.org/issues/spring%202011/polese.html

"President Addresses and Thanks Citizens of Slovakia." The White House. February 4, 2005https://georgewbush-whitehouse.archives.gov/news/releases/2005/02/20050224-1.html

Rankin, Jennifer. "Calls for EU to impose sanctions on Belarus after disputed elections." *The Guardian,* August 10, 2020. https://www.theguardian.com/world/2020/aug/10/calls-for-eu-to-impose-sanctions-on-belarus-following-disputed-elections

"Revolution is the new black: How Western money funds overthrow-your-government classes." *RT,* February 13, 2019. https://www.rt.com/news/451372-camp-yerevan-protests-us-money/

"Russia's Crackdown on NGOs Includes Some Unexpected Targets." *Philanthropy News Digest,* July 14, 2015. https://philanthropynewsdigest.org/news/russia-s-crackdown-on-ngos-includes-some-unexpected-targets

Thien, Poh Phaik, "Explaining the Color Revolutions," *E-International Relations.* July 31, 2009. https://www.e-ir.info/2009/07/31/explaining-the-color-revolutions/

4: Demographic Warefare

Assunção, Muri. "Pope's charity sent money to group of transgender sex workers near Rome, after coronavirus crisis halted their income." *New York Daily News,* May 1, 2020. https://www.nydailynews.com/coronavirus/ny-coronavirus-pope-charity-help-trans-sex-workers-rome-20200501-43cha5sox5as3juhjbdtfsbsme-story.html

Asylum, Migration and Integration Fund (2014-2020). European Commission. Accessed September 29, 2021. https://ec.europa.eu/home-affairs/funding/asylum-migration-and-integration-funds/asylum-migration-and-integration-fund-2014-2020_en

Bieber, Florian. "How Europe's Nationalists Became Internationalists." *Foreign Policy,* November 30, 2019. https://foreignpolicy.com/2019/11/30/how-europes-nationalists-became-internationalists/

Bolton, Kerry. "Wall Street & the November 1917 Bolshevik Revolution." *Counter-Currents,* October 28, 2013. https://counter-currents.com/2013/10/wall-street-and-the-november-1917-bolshevik-revolution/

"Canadian Input to the Office of the Special Representative to the Secretary General on International Migration for the Secretary General's Report on the Global

Compact for Safe, Orderly, Regular Migration." United Nations Refugees and Migrants. https://refugeesmigrants.un.org/sites/default/files/stocktaking_canada.pdf

Chikezie, Chukwu-Emeka. "En route to the Global Compact on Migration, we must disrupt anti-immigration policymaking." *Equal Times*, November 22, 2017. https://www.equaltimes.org/en-route-to-the-global-compact-on?lang=en#.YVSFILhKjIU

Conway, Carrie, Resonance Frontier Market Solutions. "Evaluation of the Humanitarian Migrants to Israel (HMI) Program." U.S. Department of State Bureau of Population, Refugees, and Migration. March 1, 2019. https://www.state.gov/wp-content/uploads/2020/06/FINAL-DOS-PRM-HMI-Evaluation-Report-Resonance-2019.pdf

"Czech Republic to stay out of UN pact on migration." *AP News*, November 14, 2018. https://apnews.com/article/d3cec1e810bf407eab321360f30ee36c

Dempster, Helen and Karen Hargrave. *Understanding public attitudes towards refugees and migrants.* Chatham House. June 2017. https://cdn.odi.org/media/documents/11600.pdf

Dimitrov, Atanas and Angelov, Goran. "Refugee Integration in the EU: Challenges and Economic Impact." *Economic Alternatives*, 4. 2017. 584-600. https://www.unwe.bg/uploads/Alternatives/6_EAlternativi_english_4_2017.pdf

Emry, Sheldon. *Billions for the Bankers, Debts for the People.* Lord's Covenant Church, 1982.

Feder, Gottfried, *The Manifesto for the Abolition of Enslavement to Interest on Money.* Joseph C. Hubers Verlag: Munich. 1919. Translated into English by Hadding Scott, 2012.

Global Compact for Safe, Orderly and Regular Migration. Global Compact for Migration. July 11, 2018. https://refugeesmigrants.un.org/sites/default/files/180711_final_draft_0.pdf

Hutchison, Claire. "Tony Blair's company Windrush ventures sees profits triple." *Evening Standard.* January 8, 2016. https://www.standard.co.uk/business/tony-blair-s-company-windrush-ventures-sees-profits-triple-a3151841.html

J. Correspondent. "The Chai Society—Yale's members-only Jewish club." *The Jewish News of Northern California*, July 20, 2001. https://www.jweekly.com/2001/07/20/the-chai-society-yale-s-members-only-jewish-club/

Joyce, Andrew. "The SS Empire Windrush: The Jewish Origins of Multicultural Britain." *The Occidental Observer,* July 12, 2015. https://www.theoccidentalobserver.net/2015/07/12/jews-the-ss-empire-windrush-and-the-origins-of-multicultural-britain/

Kumin, Judith. *Welcoming Engagement: How Private Sponsorship Can Strengthen Refugee Resettlement in the European Union.* Brussels: Migration Policy Institute Europe, December 2015. https://www.migrationpolicy.org/sites/default/files/publications/Asylum-PrivateSponsorship-Kumin-FINAL.pdf

LIFT Philanthropy Partners. "LIFT Philanthropy Partners Launches Better

Beginnings, Bigger Impact." *Newswire,* May 28, 2018. https://www.newswire.ca/news-releases/lift-philanthropy-partners-launches-better-beginnings-bigger-impact-683855161.html

"List of 2014 Awarded Grants to the European Migration Network National Contact Points." European Commission. https://ec.europa.eu/home-affairs/system/files/2016-12/list_of_2014_awarded_grants_to_the_european_migration_network_national_contact_points.pdf

Lu, Yuqian, Marc Frenette, and Grant Schellenberg. "Social Assistance Receipt Among Refugee Claimants in Canada." *Economic Insights*, No. 51. October 2015. https://publications.gc.ca/site/eng/9.803789/publication.html?wbdisable=true

Lykketoft, Mogens. "Letter to all Permanent Representatives and Permanent Observers to the United Nations." The President of the General Assembly. August 23, 2016. https://paperzz.com/doc/8688319/refugees-and-migrants

Migration Initiatives 2020. International Organization for Migrations. 2019. https://publications.iom.int/system/files/pdf/mi_2020.pdf

Monbiot, George. "Neoliberalism—the ideology at the root of all our problems." *The Guardian,* April 15, 2016. https://www.theguardian.com/books/2016/apr/15/neoliberalism-ideology-problem-george-monbiot

Pius XII. *Exsul Familia Nazarethana.* Papal Encyclical. 1952. https://www.papalencyclicals.net/pius12/p12exsul.htm

Reuters, Thomson. "Angela Merkel defends UN migration pact, rejects 'nationalism in its purest form.'" *CBC News,* November 21, 2018. https://www.cbc.ca/news/world/merkel-bundestag-un-migration-1.4914192

Rudin, James A. "Vatican II: The Beginning of the End of Catholic Anti-Semitism." *The Washington Post,* October 25, 2012. https://www.washingtonpost.com/national/on-faith/vatican-ii-the-beginning-of-the-end-of-catholic-anti-semitism/2012/10/25/f2a2356e-1ee2-11e2-8817-41b9a7aaabc7_story.html

Sieff, Kevin. "The migrant debt cycle." *The Washington Post*, November 4, 2019. https://www.washingtonpost.com/world/2019/11/04/migrant-debt-cycle/

"Unbound Philanthrophy." Influence Watch. Accessed September 30, 2021. https://www.influencewatch.org/non-profit/unbound-philanthropy/

United Nations Higher Commissioner for Refugees (UNHCR). *UNHCR Resettlement Handbook.* Geneva: United Nations, April 2018. https://www.unhcr.org/en-us/protection/resettlement/4a2ccf4c6/unhcr-resettlement-handbook-country-chapters.html

United Nations Higher Commissioner for Refugees (UNHCR). *Global Appeal: 2019 Update.* Geneva: United Nations, 2019. https://reporting.unhcr.org/sites/default/files/ga2019/pdf/Global_Appeal_2019_full_lowres.pdf

Westerby, Rachel and Sophie Ngo-Diep. *Welcome to Europe! A comprehensive guide to resettlement.* International Catholic Migration Commission Europe.

July 2013. https://www.icmc.net/wp-content/uploads/2019/07/130731-icmc-europe-welcome-europe-comprehensive-guide-resettlement.pdf

5: The Hand that Feeds and the Church of Clientology

ANSA. "Busted: Italian cleaning cooperative falsifying documents for migrants." *Info Migrants,* April 14, 2020. https://www.infomigrants.net/en/post/24070/busted-italian-cleaning-cooperative-falsifying-documents-for-migrants

Bénilde, Marie. "The creation of Emmanuel Macron." *Le Monde diplomatique.* May 2017. https://mondediplo.com/2017/05/06Macron

Bernanke, Ben S. "Financial Access for Immigrants: The Case of Remittances." Speech at the Financial Access for Immigrants: Learning from Diverse Perspectives conference, Federal Reserve Bank of Chicago. April 16, 2004. https://www.federalreserve.gov/boarddocs/speeches/2004/200404162/

Bolton, Kerry. "Refugee Crisis Serving Globalist Dialectic." Accessed October 29, 2021. https://www.kerrybolton.com/refugee-crisis-serving-globalist-dialectic/

Bowers, Simon. "Iceland president's wife linked to offshore tax havens in leaked files." *The Guardian,* May 2, 2016. https://www.theguardian.com/news/2016/may/02/iceland-presidents-wife-linked-to-offshore-tax-havens-in-leaked-files

Cavan, Susan J., editor. *Annual Report 2019/20: Shaping the Global Future Together.* Atlantic Council. 2020. https://www.atlanticcouncil.org/wp-content/uploads/2020/07/AC-Annual-Report-20192020.pdf

Ó Colmáin, Gearóid. "President Vladimir Putin: An Enigma." March 15, 2016. https://www.gearoidocolmain.org/president-vladimir-putin-an-enigma/

Duchesne, Ricardo. "Diversity Is Destroying The Cohesion And Social Capital Of Western Nations." Council of European Canadians. November 10, 2017. https://www.eurocanadian.ca/2017/11/diversity-destroying-cohesion-social-capital-whites.html

Edelstein, Shari. "PhilanthroCapitalism: Corporate Trends and Jewish Philanthropy in the 21st Century." Jewish Funders Network. October 6, 2014. https://www.jfunders.org/philanthrocapitalism_corporate_trends_and_jewish_philanthropy_in_the_21st_century

Erenhouse, Ryan. "MasterCard Transforms Aid Distribution." MasterCard. September 24, 2015. https://newsroom.mastercard.com/press-releases/mastercard-transforms-aid-distribution/

Halpern, Sue. "The Ad-Hoc Group of Activists and Academics Convening a 'Real Facebook Oversight Board.'" *The New Yorker.* October 15, 2020. https://www.newyorker.com/tech/annals-of-technology/the-ad-hoc-group-of-activists-and-academics-convening-a-real-facebook-oversight-board

Hanson, Gordon H. and Antonio Spilimbergo. *Illegal Immigration, Border Enforcement, and Relative Wages: Evidence from Apprehensions at the U.S.-Mexico Border.* IDB Working Paper No. 271. September 1996. https://papers.ssrn.com/sol3/papers.cfm?abstract_id=1815958&rec=1&srcabs=41

132&pos=1

Higgins, Tucker. "Scores of companies tell the Supreme Court that allowing the Trump administration to end DACA will hurt the economy." *CNBC.* October 4, 2019. https://www.cnbc.com/2019/10/04/major-companies-tell-supreme-court-ending-daca-will-hurt-the-economy.html

Holbrooke, Richard. "Last Best Hope." *New York Times,* September 28, 2003. https://www.nytimes.com/2003/09/28/books/last-best-hope.html

Johnson, Ian. "Greenspan in China for firsthand look at economic reform." *The Baltimore Sun,* October 26, 1994. https://www.baltimoresun.com/news/bs-xpm-1994-10-26-1994299141-story.html

Joo, Jaeyeon. "The convergence of public opinion and interest group lobbying and the disruption of the Trump administration in United States immigration policy." *Korean Journal of International Studies*, 17, No. 2. August 2019. 189-215. http://dx.doi.org/10.14731/kjis.2019.8.17.2.189

Jumbert, Maria Gabrielsen, Rocco Bellanova, and Raphaël Gellert. "Smart Phones for Refugees: Tools for Survival, or Surveillance?" *PRIO Policy Brief,* 4. 2018. https://www.prio.org/Publications/Publication/?x=11022

Junghanns. *Migration from the developing countries to the European industrialised countries.* Germany: Group of the European People's, September 5, 1996. Partyhttps://assembly.coe.int/nw/xml/XRef/X2H-Xref-ViewHTML.asp?FileID=7609&lang=EN

Kastner, Jens. "Poland cracks door open for Filipino workers." *Nikkei Asia,* August 17, 2018. https://asia.nikkei.com/Economy/Poland-cracks-door-open-for-Filipino-workers

Kelly, Heather. "How Google used $11 million to help refugees." *CNN Business,* October 26, 2015. https://money.cnn.com/2015/10/23/technology/google-org-refugee/

Kluge, John and Tim Docking. "The New Era of Refugee Investing." *Stanford Social Innovation Review,* January 14, 2019. https://ssir.org/articles/entry/the_new_era_of_refugee_investing

Kucharska, Marta. "Despite the anti-immigrant rhetoric, Poland receives more migrant workers than anywhere else in the world." *Equal Times,* October 11, 2019. https://www.equaltimes.org/despite-the-anti-immigrant#.YXmfX57MLIU

"Liz Mohn receives the Vernon A. Walters Award." Bertelsmann Stiftung. March 17, 2008. https://www.bertelsmann-stiftung.de/en/press/press-releases/press-release/pid/liz-mohn-erhaelt-vernon-a-walters-award/

Mannon, Susan E., et al. "Keeping Them in Their Place: Migrant Women Workers in Spain's Strawberry Industry." *International Journal of Sociology of Agriculture & Food,* 19, No. 1, September 2, 2011. 84. https://digitalcommons.usu.edu/cgi/viewcontent.cgi?referer=https://www.google.com/&httpsredir=1&article=1329&context=sswa_facpubs

McAuliffe, Marie and Martin Ruhs, editors. *World Migration Report 2018.* Geneva: International Organization for Migration, 2017. https://www.iom.int/sites/g/files/tmzbdl486/files/country/docs/china/r5_world_migration_report_2018_en.pdf

McNeil, Shane. "Canada needs to get to 100 million people by 2100: BlackRock's Wiseman." *BNN Bloomberg,* October 25, 2019. https://www.bnnbloomberg.ca/canada-needs-to-get-to-100-million-people-by-2100-blackrock-s-mark-wiseman-1.1337065

Meaker, Morgan. "Europe is using smartphone data as a weapon to deport refugees." *Wired,* July 2, 2018. https://www.wired.co.uk/article/europe-immigration-refugees-smartphone-metadata-deportations

Melenciuc, Sorin. "Foreign workers employment at record high in Romania; Vietnam, Nepal, Morocco, Bangladesh and Brazil among top 10 countries of origin." *Business Review,* March 23, 2018. https://business-review.eu/news/almost-1200-foreign-employees-got-work-permits-in-romania-in-2018-vietnam-nepal-morocco-bangladesh-and-brazil-among-top-10-countries-of-origin-162525

Meyer, Karl E. "Weighing Iraq on Morgenthau's Scale." *World Policy Journal,* 20, No. 3. Duke University Press, 2002. 89-92. https://www.jstor.org/stable/40209880

Millard, Rosie. "Dorrit Moussaieff: How to revive Iceland." *The Sunday Times,* February 1, 2009. https://www.thetimes.co.uk/article/dorrit-moussaieff-how-to-revive-iceland-xvsplh59gtj

Moore, Aoife and Paul Hosford. "Special Report: How accommodating asylum seekers turned into a billion-euro industry." *Irish Examiner,* April 27, 2020. https://www.irishexaminer.com/lifestyle/arid-30996215.html

Oliver, Guy. "South Africa's 'Afrophobia' Problem." *American Renaissance,* March 14, 2020. https://www.amren.com/news/2020/03/south-africas-afrophobia-problem/

Parloff, Roger. "Big Business Asks Supreme Court to Save Affirmative Action." *Fortune,* December 9, 2015. https://fortune.com/2015/12/09/supreme-court-affirmative-action/

"Phones are now indispensable for refugees." *The Economist,* February 11, 2017. https://www.economist.com/international/2017/02/11/phones-are-now-indispensable-for-refugees

Publius, John Q. *Plastic Empire.* Ostara Publications, 2020.

Recode Staff. "Full transcript: Anti-Defamation League CEO Jonathan Greenblatt on Recode Decode." *Vox,* November 17, 2017. https://www.vox.com/2017/11/17/16667352/transcript-anti-defamation-league-ceo-jonathan-greenblatt-rights-hate-speech-jew-recode-decode

Rodina, Mihaela and Ionut Iordachesku. "Romania, Hungary fill labor shortage with Asians." *Asia Times,* November 10, 2019. https://asiatimes.com/2019/11/romania-hungary-fill-labor-shortage-with-asians/

Schaps, Karolin. "Refugees take Germany to court over mobile phone data checks." *Reuters,* May 5, 2020. https://www.reuters.com/article/germany-refugees-privacy-idINL8N2CN7BW

Solomon, Shoshanna. "Immigrants are key to economic growth, Goldman guru says." *The Times of Israel,* March 27, 2019. https://www.timesofisrael.com/immigrants-are-key-to-economic-growth-

goldman-guru-says/
Soros, George. "Why I'm Investing $500 Million in Migrants." *Wall Street Journal,* September 20, 2016. https://www.wsj.com/articles/why-im-investing-500-million-in-migrants-1474344001
Trajkovska, Bojana. "10 European startups tackling the refugee crisis." *EU-Startups,* September 6, 2018. https://www.eu-startups.com/2018/09/10-european-startups-tackling-the-refugees-crisis/
Ullrich, Maria. "Media Use During Escape—A Contribution to Refugees' Collective Agency." *Spheres,* June 23, 2017. https://spheres-journal.org/contribution/media-use-during-escape-a-contribution-to-refugees-collective-agency/

6: The Zionist-Occupied Government

Afinogenov, Greg. "The Jewish Case for Open Borders." *Jewish Currents.* July 15, 2019. https://jewishcurrents.org/the-jewish-case-for-open-borders
Azeez, Nabeel. "Marketing to Muslim Consumers is Easier (and Harder) Than You Think." *Dropkick Copy,* January 14, 2018. https://dropkickcopy.com/marketing-muslim-consumers-easier-harder-think/
Bellamy, Carol and Adam Weinberg. "Educational and Cultural Exchanges to Restore America's Image." *The Washington Quarterly,* 31. No 3. July, 2008. https://ur.booksc.eu/book/31876509/8299d0
Bērziņa, Ieva. *Color Revolutions: Democratization, Hidden Influence, or Warfare.* National Defence Academy of Latvia Center for Security and Strategic Research. December 2014. https://www.naa.mil.lv/sites/naa/files/document/1_WP2014%20Color%20revolutions.pdf
CNN Wire. "Elizabeth Warren Says She Will Donate Congressional Salary to Refugee Aid Nonprofit During Shutdown." *KTLA,* January 1, 2019. https://ktla.com/news/nationworld/elizabeth-warren-says-she-will-donate-congressional-salary-to-refugee-aid-nonprofit-during-shutdown/
Ó Colmáin, Gearóid. "Rothschild's 'Slaughter Ships.'" *Dissident Voice,* January 24, 2016. https://dissidentvoice.org/2016/01/rothschilds-slaughter-ships/
Ó Colmáin, Gearóid. "The 'German Quesiton.'" *Dissident Voice,* January 31st, 2016. https://dissidentvoice.org/2016/01/the-return-of-the-german-question/
Enazy, Askar H. "Saudi Wahhabi Islam in the Service of Uncle Sam." Middle East Institute. October 1, 2009. https://www.mei.edu/publications/saudi-wahhabi-islam-service-uncle-sam
European Endowment for Democracy. *Annual Report 2019: Supporting people striving for democracy.* 2020. https://www.democracyendowment.eu/en/resources/annual-report.html
Federman, Josef. "Document: Israeli Mossad trained Mandela." *AP News,* December 23, 2013. https://apnews.com/article/37f88cba81fd4690be621ffee72a5e71
Feferman, Dan and Dov Maimon. "An Integrated Jewish World Response to Israel's

Migrant Challenge." The Jewish People Policy Institute. March 8, 2018. http://jppi.org.il/en/article/english-an-integrated-jewish-world-response-to-israels-migrant-challenge/#.YYAmEJ7MLIU

Hetfield, Mark. *Annual Report 2018*. Hebrew Immigrant Aid Society. 2018. https://www.hias.org/sites/default/files/10.19_-_hias_ar2019_layoutoptions_v35_web.pdf

JTA. "Jewish Groups Get 94% of Homeland Security Grants." *Forward*, July 29, 2014. https://forward.com/news/breaking-news/203059/jewish-groups-get-94-of-homeland-security-grants/

Knaebel, Rachel. "Fighting far-right violence in Germany is 'the challenge of a generation.'" *Equal Times*, September 26, 2018. https://www.equaltimes.org/fighting-far-right-violence-in?lang=en#.YYAlF57MLIU

Kuruvilla, Carol. "American Jews And Muslims Are 'Natural Allies' With Close Bonds, Study Finds." *HuffPost*, May 2, 2019. https://www.huffpost.com/entry/jewish-muslim-allies-ispu_n_5cc9e017e4b0d123954d74ba

Mauzé, Grégory. "Israeli Networks of Influence in Brussels: Behind the Scenes." *Orient XXI*, January 31, 2019. https://orientxxi.info/magazine/israeli-networks-of-influence-in-brussels-behind-the-scenes,2886

Montgomery, Jack. "British Police Arrest At Least 3,395 People for 'Offensive' Online Comments in One Year." *Breitbart*, October 14, 2017. https://www.breitbart.com/europe/2017/10/14/british-police-arrest-at-least-3395-people-for-offensive-online-comments-one-year/

Nahmad, Ezra. "Israel's Triumphant Return to Africa." *Orient XXI*, September 19, 2017. https://orientxxi.info/magazine/israel-s-triumphant-return-to-africa,2006

Otterman, Sharon and Hannah Dreyfus. "Michael Steinhardt, a Leader in Jewish Philanthropy, Is Accused of a Pattern of Sexual Harassment." *The New York Times*, March 21, 2019. https://www.nytimes.com/2019/03/21/nyregion/michael-steinhardt-sexual-harassment.html

Paulson, Amanda, Martin Kuz, and Noble Ingram. "For love of strangers: Behind the Jewish legacy of welcoming refugees." *The Christian Science Monitor*, October 31, 2018. https://www.csmonitor.com/USA/Society/2018/1031/For-love-of-strangers-Behind-the-Jewish-legacy-of-welcoming-refugees

Perry, Tim. "Mike Bloomberg rallies Jewish voters with speech decrying nativism." *CBS News*, January 26, 2020. https://www.cbsnews.com/news/mike-bloomberg-rallies-jewish-voters-with-speech-decrying-nativism/

Rainsford, Sarah. "Russia's Putin: US agents gave direct help to Chechens." *BBC News*, April 27, 2015. https://www.bbc.com/news/world-europe-32487081

Samber, Sharon. "How HIAS Came to Work With LGBTQ Refugees." Hebrew Immigrant Aid Society. June 1, 2021. https://www.hias.org/blog/how-hias-came-work-lgbtq-refugees

Stren, Maram. "OPINION - Closing Europe's borders is not the right answer to the refugee crisis." World Jewish Congress. September 2, 2015.

https://www.worldjewishcongress.org/en/news/maram-stern-closing-europes-borders-is-not-the-solution-to-the-refugee-crisis-showing-solidarity-is-9-3-2015

"Swedish 'Thought Police' Brings Elderly Ladies to Justice for 'Hate Speech.'" *Sputnik News,* March 2, 2018. https://sputniknews.com/20180302/sweden-thought-crime-1062161593.html

"Theresa May: UK-Israel ties are 'stronger than ever.'" Christians United for Israel. December 13, 2018. https://www.cufi.org.uk/news/theresa-may-uk-israel-ties-are-stronger-than-ever/

Thompson, Linda A. "Lecia Brooks of the SPLC: 'We're in this 'growing pains' moment and I think we'll be ok. It's just going to get really ugly first.'" *Equal Times,* October 19, 2018. https://www.equaltimes.org/lecia-brooks-of-the-splc-we-re-in#.YYFrI57MLIU

WikiLeaks. "Cablegate: Iran: Tehran Show Trial Again Cites Usg Exchange Progams [sic] As." *Scoop,* August 25, 2009. https://www.scoop.co.nz/stories/WL0908/S00117.htm?from-mobile=bottom-link-01

7: The New Normal

BIRD Foundation. *Annual Report 2019.* BIRD: Israel-U.S. Binational Industrial Research and Development Foundation. 2020. https://www.birdf.com/wp-content/uploads/2020/05/BIRD-Annual-Report-2019.pdf

"Black gold under the Golan." *The Economist,* November 7, 2015. https://www.economist.com/middle-east-and-africa/2015/11/07/black-gold-under-the-golan

CIA. "Bringing Real Muscle to Bear Against Syria." United States of America Central Intelligence Agency. September 14, 1983. http://www.gospanews.net/en/wp-content/uploads/2019/09/CIA-RDP88B00443R001404090133-0.pdf

CIA. "Syria: Scenarios of Dramatic Political Change." United States of America Central Intelligence Agency. July 30, 1986. https://www.mintpressnews.com/wp-content/uploads/2017/03/CIA-RDP86T01017R000100770001-5.pdf

"EPACT Section 986 Report on the U.S. – Israel Agreement Concerning Energy Cooperation." *Jewish Virtual Library,* November 2005. https://www.jewishvirtuallibrary.org/u-s-israel-agreement-concerning-energy-cooperation-november-2005

Knight, Ben. "Angela Merkel's rival Friedrich Merz and the vast, shadowy power of BlackRock." *DW,* November 29. 2018. https://www.dw.com/en/angela-merkels-rival-friedrich-merz-and-the-vast-shadowy-power-of-blackrock/a-46492601

Lerner, Meredith. "OGE Declines Former Kushner Team Member Ira Greenstein's Financial Disclosure." Citizens for Responsibility and Ethics in Washington. May 15, 2019. https://www.citizensforethics.org/reports-investigations/crew-investigations/oge-declines-kushner-team-ira-greenstein-financial-disclosures/

Massa, Annie and Caleb Melby. "In Fink We Trust: BlackRock Is Now 'Fourth Branch of Government.'" *Bloomberg,* May 21, 2020. https://www.bloomberg.com/news/articles/2020-05-21/how-larry-fink-s-blackrock-is-helping-the-fed-with-bond-buying

Riding, Siobhan. "BlackRock hit by backlash in France." *Financial Times,* January 26, 2020. https://www.ft.com/content/2e2322e6-658d-4b32-848d-e8e0d87cca98

Ros-Lehtinen, Ileana. "H.R.938 - United States-Israel Strategic Partnership Act of 2014." 113th Congress of the United States of America. March 3, 2013. https://www.congress.gov/bill/113th-congress/house-bill/938

Stein, Lindsay. "Eight Things You Didn't Know About 'Fearless Girl.'" *AdAge,* May 3, 2017. https://adage.com/article/agency-news/things-fearless-girl/308863

"The Battle for Ukraine." *Wall Street Journal Opinion,* November 27, 2013. https://www.wsj.com/articles/SB10001424052702303653004579213664244095466

USISTF. *U.S.-Israel Joint Economic Development Group R&D Mapping Project.* US-Israel Science and Technology Foundation. 2018. http://www.usistf.org/wp-content/uploads/2018/03/JEDG-Executive-Summary-PDF.pdf

Vedmore, Johnny. "Darktrace and Cybereason: The Intelligence Front Companies Seeking to Subjugate the World with the A.I. Singularity." *Unlimited Hangout,* November 3, 2020. https://unlimitedhangout.com/2020/11/reports/darktrace-and-cybereason-the-intelligence-front-companies-seeking-to-subjugate-the-world-with-the-a-i-singularity/

Walker, Owen. "BlackRock ready to spread its web across Europe." *Financial Times,* July 22, 2018. https://www.ft.com/content/e19ab3d4-8b67-11e8-bf9e-8771d5404543

Yinon, Oded. "A Strategy for Israel in the Nineteen Eighties." *Kivunim,* 14. February 1982. https://www.voltairenet.org/IMG/pdf/A_strategy_for_Israel_in_the_Nineteen_Eighties.pdf

Zanting. "Ira Greenstein: Jared Kushner's Criminal Deal with Israel Behind US Involvement in Syria for Genie Energy's Control of the Golan Heights." *Medium,* February, 18 2018. https://medium.com/@zanting/ira-greenstein-jared-kushner-s-criminal-deal-with-israel-behind-u-s-873da65223ce

8: The Dark Underbelly

Ambagtsheer, Frederike, et al. *Trafficking in human beings for the purpose of organ removal: a case study report.* HOTT Project. November 2014. http://hottproject.com/userfiles/Reports/3rdReportHOTTProject-TraffickinginHumanBeingsforthePurposeofOrganRemoval-ACaseStudyReport.pdf

Associated Press. "Libya militias rake in millions in European migration funds: AP." *Al Jazeera,* December 31, 2019. https://www.aljazeera.com/news/2019/12/31/libya-militias-rake-in-millions-in-

european-migration-funds-ap
Barrett, Mary. "Autopsies and Executions." *Washington Report for Middle East Affairs,* April 22, 1990. https://www.wrmea.org/1990-april/autopsies-and-executions.html
Ben-Simhon, Coby. "World of our (god)fathers." *Haaretz,* October 21, 2004. https://www.haaretz.com/1.4722855
Brass, Martin. "Sex Slavery in Israel: Half-Billion-Dollar 'Industry' Largely Staffed By Sex Slaves." *Soldier of Fortune,* October 2002. 32. https://aldeilis.net/english/sex-slavery-israel-half-billion-dollar-industry-largely-staffed-sex-slaves/
Bristow, Edward. *Prostitution and Prejudice.* Schocken, 1983.
Camiel, Deborah. "Ultra Orthodox Jews Running Drug Empire." *Reuters,* October 16th, 1999. https://www.islam-radio.net/crime/drugs/orthodrugs.htm
Cohen, Benyamin. "Organ Failure." *Slate,* July 24, 2009. https://slate.com/human-interest/2009/07/the-arrests-of-rabbis-who-trafficked-body-parts-uncover-more-complicated-issues.html
Cohen, Gili. "IDF Soldiers Suspected of Drug Trafficking Along Israel's Border With Egypt." *Haaretz,* June 26, 2012. https://www.haaretz.com/soldiers-suspected-of-drug-trafficking-along-egypt-border-1.5187187
Droney, Pat. "Former Reddit CEO of Ghislaine Maxwell: 'We knew about her supplying underage girls for sex....'" *Law Enforcement Today,* July 8, 2020. https://www.lawenforcementtoday.com/former-reddit-ceo-of-ghislaine-maxwell-we-knew-about-her-supplying-underage-girls-for-sex/
Eyadat, Fadi and Ruth Sinai. "Brothel Owner Sentenced to Five Years in Jail for Human Trafficking." *Haaretz,* May 6, 2007. https://www.haaretz.com/1.4819258
Eyadat, Fadi. "Two Haifa Men Sentenced to Jail for Organ Trafficking." *Haaretz.* December 17, 2007. https://www.haaretz.com/1.4966670
Farnsworth, Clyde H. "A Global Bank Tangle and Its Lost Millions." *The New York Times,* April 9, 1975. https://www.nytimes.com/1975/04/09/archives/a-global-bank-tangle-and-its-lost-millions.html
Feingold, Sivan. "U.S.: Israeli Played Lead Role in International Drug Money Laundering Ring." *Haaretz,* July 11, 2013. https://www.haaretz.com/israel-news/business/.premium-u-s-israeli-involved-in-drug-money-1.5293999
Finkelstein, Norman G. *The Holocaust Industry: Reflections on the Exploitation of Jewish Suffering.* New York: Verso, 2000.
Gearty, Robert and Greg B. Smith. "Bust drug money ring." *New York Daily News,* November 2, 2020. https://www.islam-radio.net/crime/drugs/hasidimdrugs.htm
Goren, Yuval. "Police Arrest 12 in Raid on Israel's Largest Human-trafficking Ring." *Haaretz,* March 9, 2009. https://www.haaretz.com/1.5085272
Greenwald, Glenn, Laura Poitras and Ewen MacAskill. "NSA shares raw intelligence including Americans' data with Israel." *The Guardian,* September 11, 2013. https://www.theguardian.com/world/2013/sep/11/nsa-americans-personal-data-israel-documents
Gur, Assaf. "A Field Guide to Israeli Organized Crime." *Tablet,* February 5, 2019. https://www.tabletmag.com/sections/israel-middle-east/articles/a-field-guide-

to-israeli-organized-crime
Guttman, Nathan. "The Agony of Ecstasy." *Haaretz*, Updated October 28, 2005. https://www.haaretz.com/1.4839043
Haaretz Staff. "Detectives smash massive ring trafficking in women." *Haaretz*, September 28, 2004. http://www.fpp.co.uk/online/04/09/Israeli_sexslaves_2.html
Hunter, Jane. "Cocaine and Cutouts: Israel's Unseen Diplomacy." *The Link*, 22, No. 1. January-March 1989.
Ilani, Ofri. "Virtual Pimps May Pay the Price." *Haaretz*, July 3, 2007. https://www.haaretz.com/israel-news/culture/1.4949087
"Israeli Organized Crime Figure Sentenced to 32 Years in Federal Prison for Drug Trafficking, Money Laundering and Extortion." The United States Attorney's Office Central District of California. July 31, 2015. https://www.justice.gov/usao-cdca/pr/israeli-organized-crime-figure-sentenced-32-years-federal-prison-drug-trafficking-money
Katz, Samuel M. "Israeli Drug Smugglers' Global Monopoly on Ecstasy." *Moment Mag*, May 7, 2002. https://www.islam-radio.net/crime/drugs/israelidrugsmuggler.htm
Lendman, Stephen. "Israel: Major International Cocaine Trafficking Hub." *RINF News*, October 22, 2013. http://rinf.com/alt-news/editorials/israel-major-international-cocaine-trafficking-hub/
Levenkron, Nomi and Yossi Dahan. *Women as Commodities: Trafficking in Women in Israel 2003*. The Hotline for Migrant Workers, Isha L'Isha - Haifa Feminist Center, and Adva Center, 2003. https://adva.org/wp-content/uploads/2014/09/TraffickingReport2003Engfinal.pdf
Lichtblau, Eric and James Risen. "Officials Say US Wiretaps Exceeded Law." *The New York Times*, April 15, 2009. https://www.nytimes.com/2009/04/16/us/16nsa.html
Lundin, Susanne. "Organ economy: organ trafficking in Moldova and Israel." *Public Understanding of Science*, 21 (2). 2012. 226-241. https://citeseerx.ist.psu.edu/viewdoc/download?doi=10.1.1.1004.2102&rep=rep1&type=pdf
Mahony, Edmund. "13 Indicted in Drug Money Laundering Scheme." *The Hartford Courant*, May 26, 1993. https://www.courant.com/news/connecticut/hc-xpm-1993-05-26-0000101623-story.html
Malarek, Victor. *The Natashas: Inside the New Global Sex Trade*. New York: Arcade Publishing, 2004.
Osava, Mario. "BRAZIL: Poor Sell Organs to Trans-Atlantic Trafficking Ring." *Inter Press Service News Agency*, February 23, 2004. http://www.ipsnews.net/2004/02/brazil-poor-sell-organs-to-trans-atlantic-trafficking-ring/
Ostrovsky, Victor. *By Way of Deception: The Making of a Mossad Officer*. Stoddart Publishing, 1990.
Peleg, Bar. "Israel Police Arrest 15 Suspected of Operating Human Trafficking and Prostitution Ring." *Haaretz*, October 29, 2019. https://www.haaretz.com/israel-

news/.premium-israel-police-arrest-15-suspected-of-operating-human-trafficking-prostitution-rin-1.8055376

Porter, David and Carla K. Johnson. "First case of organ trafficking in U.S.?" *NBC News* via the Associated Press, July 24, 2009. https://www.nbcnews.com/id/wbna32132371

Pulwer, Sharon. "Three Israelis Arrested on Suspicion of Organ Trafficking." *Haaretz*, October 29, 2016. https://www.haaretz.com/israel-news/.premium-three-israelis-arrested-on-suspicion-of-organ-trafficking-1.5454478

Sack, Kevin. "Transplant Brokers in Israel Lure Desperate Kidney Patients to Costa Rica." *The New York Times*, August 17, 2014. https://www.nytimes.com/2014/08/17/world/middleeast/transplant-brokers-in-israel-lure-desperate-kidney-patients-to-costa-rica.html

Scheper-Hughes, Nancy. "Human Traffic: Exposing the Brutal Organ Trade." *New Internationalist*, May 1, 2014. https://newint.org/features/2014/05/01/organ-trafficking-keynote

Scott, Peter Dale and Jonathan Marshall. *Cocaine Politics: Drugs, Armies, and the CIA in Central America.* University of California Press, 1991.

Sherman, Gabriel. "The Mogul and the Monster: Inside Jeffrey Epstein's Decades-Long Relationship with his Biggest Client." *Vanity Fair*, June 8, 2021. https://www.vanityfair.com/news/2021/06/inside-jeffrey-epsteins-decades-long-relationship-with-his-biggest-client

Sims, David. "Jews Use Pedophilia for Profit and to Own, Control, and Destroy the Powerful." *National Vanguard*, January 28, 2018. https://nationalvanguard.org/2018/01/jews-use-pedophilia-for-profit-and-to-own-control-and-destroy-the-powerful/

Smith, Michael, Daryna Krasnolutska, and David Glovin. "Organ Gangs Force Poor to Sell Kidneys for Desperate Israelis." *Bloomberg Markets*, November 1, 2011. https://www.bloomberg.com/news/articles/2011-11-01/organ-gangs-force-poor-to-sell-kidneys-for-desperate-israelis

TOI Staff. "Cops pinch sushi-based cocaine ring." *The Times of Israel*, December 27, 2012. https://www.timesofisrael.com/cops-pinch-sushi-based-cocaine-ring/

TOI Staff. "14 Israelis suspected of running child sex trafficking ring in Colombia." *The Times of Israel*, December 10, 2018. https://www.timesofisrael.com/14-israelis-suspected-of-running-child-sex-trafficking-ring-in-colombia/

Traubmann, Tamara. "Ukrainian National Says Employer Raped Her, Confiscated Passport." *Haaretz*, August 13, 2007. https://www.haaretz.com/1.4961538

United States Department of State. *2017 Trafficking in Persons Report – Israel*, June 27, 2017. https://www.refworld.org/docid/5959ecb4a.html

Vulliamy, Ed. "Hassidic link to drugs barons." *The Guardian*, November 9, 2002. https://www.theguardian.com/world/2002/nov/10/drugsandalcohol.uk

Webb, Whitney. "Meet the IDF-Linked Cybersecurity Group 'Protecting' US Hospitals 'Pro Bono.'" *Unlimited Hangout*, August 27, 2020. https://unlimitedhangout.com/2020/08/investigative-reports/meet-the-idf-linked-cybersecurity-group-protecting-us-hospitals-pro-bono/

Weir, Alison. "The gap between supply and demand." *The Economist*, October 9,

2008. https://www.economist.com/international/2008/10/09/the-gap-between-supply-and-demand

Winstanley, Asa. "How Israel armed the drugs cartels – part 1." *Middle East Monitor,* July 11, 2018. https://www.middleeastmonitor.com/20180711-how-israel-armed-the-drugs-cartels-part-1/

Yaakov, Yifa. "As cocaine's popularity rises, Israel's significance in global drug trade grows." *The Times of Israel,* October 19, 2013. https://www.timesofisrael.com/as-cocaines-popularity-rises-israels-significance-in-global-drug-trade-grows/

Conclusion

International Monetary Fund. "Brave New World." *Finance & Development,* 57. No 4. December 2020. https://www.imf.org/external/pubs/ft/fandd/2020/12/pdf/fd1220.pdf

Appendices

A: "Spring Meetings 2019: Participant List." World Bank Group and International Monetary Fund. April 14, 2019. https://www.worldbank.org/content/dam/meetings/external/springmeeting/Participant-List.pdf

B: "Donors to Chatham House." Chatham House. Accessed March 2020. https://www.chathamhouse.org/about-us/our-funding/donors-chatham-house

C: "Media Partners." International Consortium of Investigative Journalists. Accessed November 2021. https://www.icij.org/about/media-partners/

D: "Our Members." European Council on Refugees and Exiles. Accessed November 2021. https://ecre.org/members/

E: "ODI funders for the 2019/20 financial year (over £1,000)." Overseas Development Institute. 2020. https://cdn.odi.org/media/documents/odi_funders_2019-20_A2x2p23.pdf

Annual Report 2009. London: Overseas Development Institute, 2009. https://cdn.odi.org/media/documents/4910.pdf

F: "Funders." Migration Policy Institute. Accessed November 2021. https://www.migrationpolicy.org/about/funders

G: "Statement of Principles." Project for the New American Century. June 3, 1997. http://web.archive.org/web/20070810113753/www.newamericancentury.org/statementofprinciples.htm

H: "Board of Directors." Partnership for New York City. Accessed March 2020. https://pfnyc.org/board-of-directors/